International bestseller

Named a Book of the Year
Observer, Daily Telegraph, ... an

A Book of the Week

Praise for
FORGOTTEN ALLY

"Deserves to be read by anyone interested in China, World War II, and the future of China's relations with the rest of the world . . . Mitter masterfully constructs these interlocking stories of battles, famines, massacres, diplomacy, and intrigue . . . Excellent." — *Washington Post*

"Restor[es] a vital part of the wartime narrative to its rightful place . . . A remarkable story, told with humanity and intelligence; all historians of the Second World War will be in Mitter's debt . . . No one could ask for a better guide." — *Guardian*

"A major contribution to the one aspect of the Second World War of which we know far too little, and should know much more of if we are to understand the new superpower today. It is a model of clarity and good writing." — Antony Beevor, *Times* (UK)

"Superb . . . Mitter offers a lucid and moving account of the conflict's staggering military tragedies. But it is also a first-rate political and social history of China's wartime years . . . Mitter's elegant, rigorous, and balanced account is an ideal guide to traumas that continue to cast a long shadow over the region." — *Daily Telegraph*

"Important and compelling . . . Closely examin[es] Beijing's role in the Allied war effort, the heavy and often thankless price paid by the Chinese in their fight against Japan, and the impact of China's wartime traumas on the country's postwar development . . . Fascinating." — *Wall Street Journal*

"A book that has long cried out to be written . . . An authoritative account of one of the cornerstones of the Second World War."
— *Observer* (UK), "Books of the Year"

"Superb . . . World War II, Mitter points out, started not on the plains of Europe but with an accidental firefight in 1937 at the Marco Polo Bridge, a few miles southwest of Beijing." — *New York Times Book Review*

"A masterly account . . . Blends wide, deep scholarship with an accessible narrative that includes an admirable focus on [the war's] effects on ordinary people . . . Mitter's great achievement is to have encompassed a multi-faceted story in a readable, coherent, and gripping manner that should rescue this horrific conflict from the neglect it has suffered in the West and explain why history lives on in East Asia." — *Times* (UK)

"Illuminating and meticulously researched . . . It is the voice of the Chinese . . . that gives the distinctive tone to Mitter's narrative. From the diaries of Chiang Kai-shek to those of national journalists and middle-class Chinese fleeing the conflict, these first-person observations are woven skillfully into his chronicle of the battles and struggles." — *Economist*

"Powerful . . . Mitter excels . . . in placing China's wartime experience in a robustly international framework . . . General readers curious to learn more about Chinese history should welcome any new book by Mitter." — *Daily Beast*

"An important, timely contribution to shedding light where there is currently much darkness . . . A harrowing story . . . Compelling . . . Demonstrates why to this day the Chinese view Japan with such animosity." — *Financial Times*

"Rana Mitter dissects the complexities of Chinese politics with superb clarity, and his book ought to be required reading for anyone trying to understand that vast and enigmatic country and its place in the world." — *Mail on Sunday*

"The best narrative of that long-ago war, whose effects still linger in China today." — *Spectator*

FORGOTTEN ALLY

China's World War II, 1937–1945

RANA MITTER

Mariner Books
Houghton Mifflin Harcourt
BOSTON   NEW YORK

For Katharine

First Mariner Books edition 2014

Copyright © 2013 by Rana Mitter

www.hmhco.com

First published in Great Britain by Allen Lane, an imprint of Penguin Books, 2013

Library of Congress Cataloging-in-Publication Data
Mitter, Rana, date.
Forgotten ally : China's World War II, 1937–1945 / Rana Mitter.
pages cm
ISBN 978-0-618-89425-3 (hardback)   ISBN 978-0-544-33450-2 (paperback)
1. Sino-Japanese War, 1937–1945. 2. World War, 1939–1945 — China.
3. China — History — 1937–1945. I. Title.
DS777.53.M555 2013
951.04′2 — dc23
2013026746

Book design by Chrissy Kurpeski

Printed in the United States of America
8 2021
4500832759

La muerte
entra y sale
y sale y entra
la muerte
de la taberna.

[Death
goes in and out
out and in
death
from the tavern.]

— FROM FEDERICO GARCÍA LORCA,
  "MALAGUEÑA"
  (1921)

CONTENTS

DRAMATIS PERSONAE

Chen Bijun: Wang Jingwei's wife, and also a significant figure in the "peace movement" that ultimately led to collaboration with Japan.

Chiang Kai-shek: Leader of China's Nationalist Party from 1926 to his death in 1975. Chiang was China's leader during its war against Japan from 1937 to 1945.

Winston S. Churchill: British prime minister, 1940–1945, 1951–1955.

Archibald Clark Kerr: British ambassador in China, 1938–1942.

Dai Li: Chiang Kai-shek's security chief, who used torture and intimidation against enemies of the government, in particular the Communists.

Clarence Gauss: US ambassador in China, 1941–1944.

He Yingqin: Minister of war in the Nationalist government.

Hirota Kôki: Japanese foreign minister, 1937–1938.

Patrick Hurley: US ambassador in China, 1944–1945.

Nelson T. Johnson: US ambassador in China, 1929–1941.

Konoye Fumimaro: Japanese prime minister, 1937–1939, 1940–1941.

Long Yun: Canny Yi (Lolo) militarist who ruled Yunnan province in southwest China for much of the wartime period, and maintained a wary relationship with Chiang Kai-shek.

Mao Zedong: Leader of China's Communist Party, 1943–1976. Mao achieved paramount power during the war years, sidelining and eliminating rivals, and preparing his party for its ultimate victory against Chiang Kai-shek's Nationalists in 1949.

George C. Marshall: Chief of staff of the United States Army, 1939–1945.

Matsui Iwane: Japanese commander who took Nanjing in 1937 and was in overall charge of Japanese troops during the massacre of 1937–1938.

Song Meiling: Chiang Kai-shek's wife and a powerful political figure in her own right in the Nationalist government. She spoke fluent English and was Chiang's channel to the Americans.

Lord Louis Mountbatten: Supreme commander, Southeast Asia Command, 1943–1946, who clashed frequently with General Stilwell.

Franklin D. Roosevelt: President of the United States, 1933–1945.

T. V. Soong (Song Ziwen): Chiang's brother-in-law, foreign minister for a period, and a relatively liberal figure within the Nationalist Party.

Josef V. Stalin: General secretary of the Communist Party of the Soviet Union, 1922–1953.

Joseph W. Stilwell: "Vinegar Joe," the American general sent as Chiang Kai-shek's chief of staff after Pearl Harbor, who quickly fell out with his commander.

Sun Yat-sen: Tireless revolutionary and briefly president of China, 1912, shut out of power after the overthrow of the emperor in 1912 as military leaders undermined the new republic.

Tôjô Hideki: Japanese prime minister, 1941–1944.

Wang Jingwei: Joined the Nationalist revolution early and was a close ally of Sun Yat-sen. Wang achieved high political office but little real power under Chiang, and defected to form a collaborationist government under the Japanese in 1938, based in Nanjing.

Zhou Enlai: Senior figure in the Communist movement who served as Mao's representative in Chongqing for much of the war.

Zhou Fohai: Nationalist government official who would become close to Wang Jingwei and eventually help him to defect to Japan.

PRONUNCIATION GUIDE

Most Chinese names in this book have been rendered into the internationally accepted pinyin system of romanization. While correct pronunciation of pinyin takes some training, the only sounds that are wholly different from standard English pronunciation are "q" (which sounds like a "ch" as in "church") and "x" (which is a "sh" as in "sheet"). For more details the Internet has a wide range of pinyin pronunciation guides. In some cases, better-known alternative romanizations are used, such as Chiang Kai-shek rather than Jiang Jieshi. Also, I have preserved the older Wade-Giles system of romanization where it appears in the original document, but have generally added a pinyin version in brackets afterward.

PROLOGUE: CITY ON FIRE

I N THE SPRING OF 1939 Europe was still, albeit uneasily, at peace. But some seven thousand kilometers to the east, the Second World War was already well under way.

On May 3 the sky was clear above the southwestern Chinese city of Chongqing. The weather was sweltering. Not for nothing is Chongqing known as one of "China's three furnaces," where temperatures regularly rise to 104 degrees Fahrenheit or higher. At noon Zhang Xiluo, a reporter for the *Xinminbao* newspaper, was getting ready for lunch. In the bustling city around him, the locals were going about their usual business. On the docks, stevedores hauled boxes on and off the ships that plied the Yangtze. Passengers descending from the boats would be mobbed by dozens of sedan-chair bearers. Chongqing is famous as a *shancheng,* a "mountain city" — far better to be carried up the steep hills that separate the river from the upper town, if you could afford it.

In the markets, traders and their clients bargained for rice, vegetables, and meat. The number of customers was greater than at any time in the city's history. In October 1937 the Nationalist government of China had announced that it could no longer defend the existing capital at Nanjing to the east against a Japanese invasion that had begun three months earlier. Chongqing therefore became the temporary capital. Millions of refugees had fled westward, and Chongqing's population swelled. A city of fewer than half a million inhabitants in 1937 more than doubled in size within eight years. Aside from the crowded markets, the refugees' presence was clear from the ugly, slapdash buildings, made from mud and metal girders, that had rapidly sprung up across the local landscape. These shanties gave an already slovenly-looking city an even more unkempt air.

Suddenly, as he was sitting down to eat, Zhang heard a sound whose terrifying significance he knew well. "At about noon, we heard a short alarm signal," he recalled. "I didn't even finish my meal, but got ready to go and hide away in the air-raid shelter in the newspaper office in Jintang Street." Half an hour passed. Then an even more urgent siren began howling in short, continuous bursts. The last few people left in the newspaper office grabbed their possessions and ran down into the shelter.

Zhang was lucky. The particular refuge where he found himself was one of the most advanced in the city, built by the government air-raid defense agency. It was outfitted with electric lights, communications equipment, and supplies of food and drink. Many of the city's poorer inhabitants had only makeshift shelters much less able to withstand a powerful blast from the sky. One man later wrote that in his household, "when the air-raid siren sounded, our whole family of more than ten people just hid under our table."[1] The British consulate in the city had placed a large Union Jack on its roof to proclaim neutrality and warn off air-raid pilots, but there were no guarantees of safety, even for the privileged. Not long before, a Japanese bomb attack on a water-treatment plant had also hit the nearby diplomatic building.

At 12:45 p.m. dots appeared in the sky, thirty-six of them. They swiftly grew larger and louder. From airfields in occupied China, the Japanese Navy could dispatch Type 96 Land Attacking aircraft able to fly over one thousand kilometers on a single fueling. The Japanese were almost invulnerable and could bomb the Chinese government in exile into submission.

From inside the shelter Zhang heard the noise of aircraft engines. First he made out the pitifully small number of Chinese air-force fighters sent up to engage the enemy. Not long afterward, he heard the sound of bombs dropping, and then the booming response of Chinese anti-aircraft guns. The raid continued for a full hour before the all-clear finally sounded at 2:35 p.m.

Zhang went out to see the damage. All across the city, from the docks to the residential districts, buildings were gutted, bombed into hollow wrecks. So complete was the destruction that the surviving buildings seemed to him strangest of all: at one junction, a cluster of banks stood undamaged amid the rubble of endless flattened structures. Even hours later, as darkness fell, the city was filled with the sounds of moaning and screams for help. "It was truly unbearable to hear," Zhang recalled. The journalist interviewed the wounded and relatives of the dead before rushing back to the office to write the story for that night's edition.

The next day, May 4, Zhang was in a local park, talking to Fan Changjiang, one of the era's star journalists at the prestigious newspaper *Da gongbao.* They came across a woman weeping. She, her husband, and their children had been unable to reach a shelter, and when the bombers struck, they had been in the park. Her husband was killed outright, and her two children were wounded. "Why didn't the Japanese devils kill all of us?" she cried. "How are we going to live now?" In later years, one man remembered a story from that terrible day: the man's father had been talking to a group of young factory workers when the bombs fell. He heard a violent noise, and before his very eyes the workers were "turned into bloody, fast-flying bits of flesh." This man's mother knew of an even worse tale: in the darkness of one of the larger shelters, people had stampeded in a desperate rush to avoid the raid. In the crush, many who tripped and fell were simply trampled to death.[2]

But the city had not escaped yet. That afternoon, on May 4, the sirens sounded once more. At 5:17 p.m. twenty-seven Japanese aircraft appeared and began to bomb Chongqing again. "It was like being in a tiny boat, constantly shaking," recalled one survivor. "Outside, bomb shrapnel was flying, window glass was shattering and falling to the floor . . . and there were the sounds of the enemy planes buzzing and machine-guns firing." Terrified but also curious, he looked out of the window and saw "the whole sky was lit up by flames, and the surrounding buildings were collapsing one by one. Our beloved homes were being flattened and turned into a sea of fire." When the all-clear signal sounded, just after 7:00 p.m., Zhang Xiluo's newspaper office was still standing, but the buildings all around had been destroyed.[3]

The May 4 bombing had used fewer planes than the previous day's raid, but the attackers' targets were wider and their aim even more deadly. On May 3, 673 deaths were recorded, and 1,608 houses destroyed. On May 4, 3,318 people were killed, and 3,803 houses destroyed. These air raids brought international attention to the fate of Chongqing, and the Chinese government in exile based there. At the same time that the Spanish Republic was in equally desperate combat against the Nationalist forces of General Franco, diplomats, reporters, and businessmen from many countries were able to witness the devastation of the Chinese Nationalist capital. Worse yet, the raids of May 3 and 4 were just examples, albeit the most savage, of a continuous battering that Chongqing would endure for years. During the most intense period of bombing, between May 1938 and August 1941, there would be some 218 separate raids using incendiary and fragmentation bombs, resulting in 11,885 deaths (mostly of civilians).[4] The air-raid signals became part of everyday life in the wartime capital. One man who spent his childhood in Chongqing recalled decades later: "The whole of my life, I have remembered the sound of the air-raid sirens howling in my ears; the whole of my life, I have retained the memory of the red air-raid warning balls hoisted above the Meifeng Bank building."[5]

Sitting high above the city in his hilltop retreat at Huangshan was one man who had particular reason to be alarmed by the arrival of death and destruction in the city. Chiang Kai-shek, China's wartime leader and head of the Nationalist Party, wrote in his diary on the evening of May 3 that "More than forty enemy planes came to Chongqing today and bombed the area around the Military Affairs Commission building. A lot of people in the city have been killed and wounded." The next day he displayed more emotion: "The enemy planes came [again] this evening to bomb Chongqing, and it's still burning. This is the most terrible thing I've seen in my life. I can't bear to look at it. God lives — why does he not swiftly bring some disaster to our enemy?"[6]

Yet some Chinese saw hope among the ashes. The great Chinese novelist Lao She had also been in Chongqing during the raids. He resided, along with various other cultural figures who refused to live under the Japanese occupation, in the suburb of Beibei. From there, he had a clear view of the fires' red glow in the city center. Lao She recognized the symbolism in the date of the raid. For his generation of writers and artists, the date "May Fourth" had a particular, highly meaningful resonance. On May 4, 1919, a student demonstration against imperialism had broken out in central Beijing, becoming symbolic of a wider current of freethinking. This new strain of thought envisioned a Chinese culture based on "science and democracy," those twin beacons that would rescue China from its political weakness. And no educated Chinese would have missed the significance of the terror raids on Chongqing on May 4, 1939, exactly twenty years after the legendary protest. Lao She declared:

> If we are to seize . . . a free, liberated "May Fourth," we cannot accept the threats of fire and blood. We must seize with our whole hearts the new life of our great China! Our lives, our struggle, our victory, this is our new "May Fourth" slogan![7]

Most Westerners have scarcely heard of the bombing of Chongqing. Even for the Chinese themselves, the events were concealed for decades. Yet they are part of one of the great stories of the Second World War, and perhaps the least known. For decades, our understanding of that global conflict has failed to give a proper account of the role of China. If China was considered at all, it was as a minor player, a bit-part actor in a war where the United States, Soviet Union, and Britain played much more significant roles. Yet China was the first country to face the onslaught of the

Axis Powers in 1937, two years before Britain and France, and four years before the United States. And after Pearl Harbor (December 7, 1941), one American goal was to "keep China in the war." By holding down large numbers of Japanese troops on the mainland, China was an important part of the overall Allied strategy. China had much less ability to make its own decisions than the other Allies because it was so much weaker than they, both economically and politically. Yet the war still marked a vital step in China's progression from semi-colonized victim of global imperialism to its entry, however tentative, on the world stage as a sovereign power with wider regional and global responsibilities.

Nor has the outside world ever fully understood the ghastly price that China paid to maintain its resistance against Japan for eight long years, from 1937 to 1945. Some 14 million deaths, massive refugee flight, and the destruction of the country's embryonic modernization were the costs of the war.[8] The road to victory for the Chinese Communist Party in 1949 lay within the devastated landscape of China created by the years of war with Japan.

In recent years the sheer scale of the war in China has become apparent. What began on July 7, 1937, as an unplanned local conflict between Chinese and Japanese troops near Beijing, known as the "Marco Polo Bridge Incident," escalated into an all-out war between the two great nations of East Asia; it would not end until August 1945. In the eight intervening years China's Nationalist government was forced into internal exile, along with millions of refugees. Huge tracts of the country were occupied by the Japanese, who sponsored collaborators to create new forms of government aimed at destroying the authority of the Nationalists. In other parts of the country, the Chinese Communist Party grew in influence, burnishing its credentials through resistance to the Japanese, and vastly increasing its territorial base through policies of radical social reform. The toll that the war inflicted on China is still being calculated, but conservative estimates number the dead at 14 million at least (the British Empire and United States each lost over 400,000 during the Second World War, and Russia more than 20 million). The number of Chinese refugees may have reached more than 80 million. The greater part of China's hard-won modernization was destroyed, including most of the rail network, sealed highways, and industrial plants created in the first decades of the twentieth century: 30 percent of the infrastructure in the rich Pearl River delta near Canton, 52 percent in Shanghai, and a stagger-

ing 80 percent in the capital, Nanjing.[9] The war would undo two empires
in China (the British and the Japanese) and help to create two more (the
American and the Soviet). The narrative of the war is the story of a people
in torment: from the Nanjing Massacre (widely known as the Rape of
Nanking, December 1937–January 1938), when Japanese troops murdered
and looted in the captured Chinese capital, to the blasting of dikes on the
Yellow River in June 1938, which bought time for the Chinese Army but
at a terrible price for hundreds of thousands of compatriots.

At the same time, China's war is also a story of heroic resistance against
massive odds, of a regime and a people who managed, despite everything,
to pull off victory against the enemy in a "war of resistance to the end,"
proving wrong the journalists and diplomats who predicted, over and
over again, that China could not possibly survive. For over four years,
until Pearl Harbor, China fought the Japanese practically alone. During
this time a poor and underdeveloped country held down some 800,000
troops from one of the most highly militarized and technologically advanced societies in the world.[10] For another four years after that, the success of the Allies in fighting on two fronts at once, in Europe and Asia,
was posited in significant part on making sure that China stayed in the
war.

The war was also a turning point for three men, each of whom had
his own vision for the future of China. During the war, all eyes, whether
admiring or critical, were on Chiang Kai-shek, leader of the Chinese Nationalist (Kuomintang or Guomindang) Party. At the outbreak of war in
1937, almost everyone, even Chiang's Communist enemies, acknowledged
that he was the only figure who could represent all of China in its resistance to Japan. Chiang dreamed that the war might be a cleansing fire:
China would rise from the ashes and become a sovereign, prosperous nation, able to take a leading role in the postwar order in Asia and the world
beyond.

In the end, Chiang won the war, but lost his country. For Chiang's great
rival, Mao Zedong, chairman of the Chinese Communist Party (CCP),
the war against Japan was the making of a leader. When the war broke
out, he was the head of a small party on the run that had been forced into
a hideout in the dusty hill country of northwest China. By the end of the
war, he would control vast areas of China with its population of some 100
million people, as well as an independent army of nearly a million men.[11]

In contrast, the war was the unmaking of a man whose name is little remembered outside the ranks of China historians: Wang Jingwei. Wang's story is one of the great tragedies of twentieth-century history. He was a more prominent nationalist and revolutionary in his youth than either Mao or Chiang, and served as second in command to the legendary revolutionary Dr. Sun Yat-sen. But during the war against Japan, Wang authored a decision that would condemn him, to this day, as "a traitor for a thousand generations" against the Chinese people. These three men — Chiang, Mao, and Wang — would use the war to propose and debate, often with great violence, their visions of what a modern, free China should be. The war forced them to take sides and exposed the fundamental disagreements among them that would eventually lead to the victory of Mao Zedong.

The story of China's war with Japan is also crucial to understanding the rise of China as a global power. To interpret the changing Chinese sense of identity, and the country's role in a rapidly changing world order, it has become profoundly important to understand one long-hidden aspect of its past: the story of China's experience during the Second World War. The war's legacy is all over China today, if you know where to look. In Nanjing, a huge combined museum and memorial commemorates the occupying Japanese army's massacre of many thousands of Chinese civilians in December 1937. In Chongqing, visitors are now welcomed into the house once occupied by "Vinegar Joe" Stilwell, the American chief of staff whose tempestuous relationship with Chiang Kai-shek would shape US-China relations for decades to come. On television, documentaries remind viewers of the record of the Communist Eighth Route Army and its resistance against Japan in north China, and soap operas with a wartime setting tell the stories both of the Nationalist army and of the Communist.

But the legacy of the war is also powerful in less tangible forms. The Chinese Communist Party (CCP) that continues to rule more than seventy years after Mao's victory in 1949 gained strength and then power precisely because the war against Japan had weakened and divided China. In today's international society, as China seeks to portray itself as a "responsible great power," the country's analysts and diplomats recall the days when China fought alongside the US, Russia, and Britain as one of the Allies. They draw a powerful parallel between a time when China cooperated against the forces of reaction, and the present day, when China wishes to portray itself as an integral and positive part of a new order.

Today, when relations between China and the United States grow tense, the Chinese side is motivated in part by a belief that its wartime contributions, its efforts to defeat America's enemies, have been forgotten — and that it is time for America, and Europe, to remember.

China's most fraught international relationship is still with Japan, and the war remains central to the present friction between them. Even for generations born many years after 1945, Chinese nationalist pride is shaped by anger at Japan's invasion of their country. In the 1990s the journalist Fang Jun, then only in his forties, made a personal journey of discovery to Japan to interview veterans of the war against China. "When [our motherland] was not rich and strong," he concluded, "we lost the Northeast [Manchuria] . . . we retreated from Shanghai, and the blood flowed in Nanjing."[12] Japan's wartime record in China is still capable of engendering deep emotions.

In recent years Chinese youths have continued to express anger at Japan: many of them feel that the country has never apologized fully for its actions in China during the war. Anti-Japanese resentment can flare up suddenly, and seemingly without immediate cause. A news report in 2003 detailed an "orgy" organized in a northeastern Chinese city by Japanese businessmen hiring Chinese sex workers. The incident led to riots in the streets because the date of the salacious events was September 18, the anniversary of the Japanese invasion of China's Manchuria region in 1931. In 2005 rioters, including educated college youths, surrounded the Japanese consulate in Shanghai and threw missiles, including glass bottles, at the building. They were protesting Japan's attempt to gain a permanent seat on the UN Security Council, but the subtext of this rage was a six-decades-old hatred, the legacy of Japan's war against China. In the summer of 2012 disagreements over disputed islands (known as the Diaoyutai to the Chinese, and Senkaku to the Japanese) in the East China Sea flared up into anti-Japanese demonstrations in numerous Chinese cities. Nor does this anger only affect Chinese-Japanese relations. Through the US-Japan Security Alliance, the United States has maintained a powerful position in the Asia-Pacific ever since the Second World War, shielding Japan under its defense umbrella. Continuing Chinese anger at these arrangements stems in large part from the sense that China, not the US, should be the major power in the region today. But the historical basis of that anger comes from the shared memory of Japan's role in the region during an era when China was weak and vulnerable.

Memories of the war against Japan can also heal scars left by another conflict, the painful civil war between Mao's Communists and Chiang's Nationalists. One of the most startling sights for anyone who remembers Mao-era China is the villa at Huangshan that once belonged to the chairman's old foe Chiang Kai-shek. Today the villa is restored to look as it did during the war years, when Chiang lived there, writing of the Chongqing bombings in his diary. The displays inside give plenty of details of Chiang's role as a leader of the resistance against Japan, all of them very positive, and none painting him as a bourgeois reactionary lackey. Of the Communists, there is very little mention. A generation ago, one might have seen this kind of praise for Chiang on Taiwan, but it would have been impossible to find on the mainland.

In the West, however, the living, breathing legacy of China's wartime experience continues to be only poorly understood.[13] Many do not realize that China played any sort of role in the Second World War at all. Those who are aware of China's involvement often dismiss it as a secondary theater. China's role was minor, this assessment goes, and its government was an uncertain and corrupt ally that made little contribution to the defeat of Japan. In this view, China's role in the war is a historical byway, not worthy of the full examination that is the due of the major powers involved.

One might guess that the West knows so little about China's wartime experience because the events of the conflict took place far from American and European eyes and had little relevance for anyone other than the Chinese themselves. But this was not true at all. The reverberations of the all-clear signals wailing in Chongqing after the massive raids of May 3 and 4, 1939, were heard far beyond China's borders. The agony of "Chungking," as the city was then known in the West, became a symbol of resistance to people around the world, who were now certain that a global war could not be far off. At the time, the conflict between China and Japan was one of the most high-profile wars on the planet. W. H. Auden famously wrote a series of "Sonnets from China" in 1938, and one of them linked places "Where life is evil now. / Nanking. Dachau." For many progressives in the West, the war in China was linked inextricably with the Spanish Civil War, and many observers — Auden, along with his companion Christopher Isherwood, the photographer Robert Capa, and the filmmaker Joris Ivens — went seamlessly from one war to the other, reporting on them as connected sites in an overarching global struggle by democratic (or at least progressive) governments against fascism and xenophobic "ultranationalism." In Britain, the China Campaign Committee raised funds for the defense of China. Even *Time* magazine's Theodore White, later one of Chiang's most powerful detractors, declared that the battle for Chongqing "was an episode shared by hundreds of thousands of people who had gathered in the shadow of its walls out of a faith in China's greatness and an overwhelming passion to hold the land against the Japanese."[14] And unlike Spain, where the war ended in 1939, the war in China became part of a global conflict that would engulf Asia and Europe too.[15]

For almost any major country in the Americas, Europe, or Asia — the US, Britain, France, Germany, Japan — it would be ludicrous to suggest that the experience of the Second World War was *not* relevant in shaping that society in the years since 1945. From the United States' sense of itself as global policeman, to Britain's attempt to find a post-imperial role as a reluctant European state, to Japan's desire to recast itself as a peaceful nation still living in the shadow of the atomic bombs, the war's present-day legacy is clear. In contrast, the role of China, the very first country to suffer from hostilities by an Axis power, has remained obscure in the decades since 1945. Contemporary China is thought of as the inheritor of Mao's Cultural Revolution, or even of the humiliation incurred by the Opium Wars of the nineteenth century, but rarely as the product of the war against Japan. Today, the names of battles and campaigns where China's fate was at stake — Taierzhuang, Changsha, Ichigô — lack the immense cultural resonance of Iwo Jima, Dunkirk, the Bulge, Saipan, Normandy. Why did China's wartime history fade from our memories, and why should we recall it now?

Put simply, that history disappeared down a hole created by the early Cold War, from which it has only recently reappeared. The history of China's war with Japan became wrapped in toxic politics for which both the West and the Chinese themselves (on both sides of the Taiwan Strait) were responsible. All sides aligned their interpretations of the war with their Cold War certainties. Japan and China traded places in American and British affections between 1945 and 1950: the former moved from wartime foe to Cold War asset, while the latter changed from ally against Japan to angry and seemingly unpredictable Communist giant. The question of what had happened in wartime China became tied up in the US with the politically charged question of "Who lost China?," and in the poisonous political atmosphere of the time it became nearly impossible to make a measured assessment of the contributions and flaws of the various actors in China. After 1949, in the newly formed People's Republic of China (PRC), on the other hand, official histories were quickly revised to attribute the victory over Japan to the "leading role" of the Chinese Communist Party. The role of Nationalists was dismissed: it was stated that the wartime government had been more obsessed with fighting the Communists than the Japanese, and was anyway badly run, corrupt, and exploitative of the Chinese people. Scholars in Taiwan, where the Nationalists had fled after 1949, did argue against this view, but in turn their views were often perceived as suspect because they were produced under a dictatorship ruled by Chiang Kai-shek, who was still concerned to rescue his tarnished reputation. Furthermore, archives from the wartime period on the mainland were closed to scholars. As a result, the nuances required for an understanding of the period never emerged. Instead of tragedy, the war in China was painted as melodrama, with villains and heroes cast in black and white. All sides became convinced that the war was an embarrassing period, irrelevant to the supposed glories of Mao's New China, but also of no interest to the West, which sought to forge a peaceful postwar world. Few wished to recall a depressing period that seemed to mark a low point in China's long modern history of disasters.

Of course, it was not unique for any society to stress those parts of the wartime narrative that helped to build its own national self-esteem. Until the 1970s many Western histories of the war concentrated on the Western European front, downplaying the crucial contribution of Russia. In turn, Russia made extensive use of the "Great Patriotic War" of 1941–1945 at all levels of society to remold itself in the postwar era and to seek gains in the international community. In contrast, the war against Japan was used very selectively as a national rallying point in postwar China. When the wartime period was referred to in public, the only parts of the experience that were discussed in detail were the events in the revolutionary base area with its capital at Yan'an (Yenan), where Mao had pioneered a peasant revolution. There was no mention of the bombing of Chongqing; of wartime collaboration with the Japanese; or of the alliance with the US or Britain. There was not even much discussion of Japanese war crimes such as the Nanjing Massacre.

This situation changed radically in the 1980s, however. The People's Republic of China reversed most of the key parts of its narrative about the war years. The party decided to revive memories of the wartime period, when Nationalist and Communist fighters had stood together to battle a foreign invader, regardless of party differences. New museums of the war sprang up to commemorate Japanese war atrocities, including Nanjing; movies and other museums gave the Nationalist military a much more prominent role, moving away from the ahistorical position that the CCP had been in the forefront of wartime resistance; and huge amounts of new scholarship poured forth, using archives and documents that had been locked away for decades.

This book is a beneficiary of the remarkable opening-up process in China. The new understanding of China's role in the Second World War is not the product of a Western historical agenda being imposed on China, but draws on major changes within China itself. It is high time for a comprehensive and complete reinterpretation of China's long war with Japan, and of China's crucial role in the Second World War. Now that the Cold War is over, the question is no longer "Who lost China?," with its implication of Communist infiltration and McCarthyism; but rather, "Why did the war change China?," a more open-ended and fruitful question that avoids questions of blame and instead looks for causes. It also moves the debate away from being primarily about the American role and places the emphasis much more on China itself.

The ability to reinterpret the story of China's war with Japan enables us to move away from melodrama. Instead, the war should be understood as a disruption to a much longer process of modernization in China. By the 1930s, after nearly a century of foreign invasion, domestic strife, and economic uncertainty, both the Nationalists and Communists wanted to establish a politically independent state, with a government that penetrated throughout society, and a population that was stable, healthy, and economically productive. It was the Nationalists who first tried to achieve those goals, in the decade before the war broke out in 1937. But the Japanese invasion made it almost impossible for them to succeed: from tax collection to provision of "food security" to the ability to cope with massive refugee flows, the problems were probably too great for any government to manage successfully. The war, then, marks the transfer of power to the Communists, but there was nothing inevitable about the process. And for much of the early part of the war, before Pearl Harbor, there was an alternative: the possibility that Japan might win, and that China would become part of a wider Japanese Empire. A new history of China's wartime experience must take account of the three-way struggle for a modern China: Nationalist, Communist, and collaborationist.

Such a history must also restore China to its place as one of the four principal wartime Allies, alongside the US, Russia, and Britain. China's story is not just the account of the forgotten Allied power, but of the Allied power whose government and way of life was most changed by the experience of war. Even the massive loss of life in Russia that followed the German invasion in June 1941 was less transformative than what happened to China in one fundamental sense: the USSR was pushed to its ultimate test, but did not break. It fought back and survived. In contrast, the battered, punch-drunk state that was Nationalist China in 1945 had been fundamentally destroyed by the war with Japan. Western condemnations of the Chinese war effort, and the role of the Nationalists in particular, have been based on accusations that the regime was too corrupt and unpopular to engender support: a popular American wartime joke declared that the Chinese leader's name was really "Cash My-Check." The truth was more complex: the Europe First strategy meant that China was to be maintained in the war at minimum cost, and Chiang was repeatedly forced to deploy his troops in ways that served Allied geostrategic interests but undermined China's own aims. The crippled and unsympathetic Nationalist regime that limped to peace in 1945 was not a product of blind anti-communism, refusal to fight Japan (a bizarre accusation considering the Nationalists' role in resisting alone for four and a half years before Pearl Harbor), or foolish or primitive military thinking. The regime was overwhelmed by external attack, domestic dislocation, and unreliable Allies.

China's war with Japan also repays reexamination because wartime conditions shaped society in ways that have persisted even to the present day. Constant air raids made it imperative that people should live and work in the same spot, as it was dangerous to move around; after 1949, "work units" would impose a similar system across China which would not be dismantled until the 1990s. Chinese society became more militarized, categorized, and bureaucratized during the harsh years of war, when government struggled to keep some kind of order in the midst of chaos. These tendencies, along with an almost pathological fear of "disorder," continue to shape the official Chinese mind-set. The greater demands that the state made on society in wartime also created a reverse effect: society began to demand more from government. The war saw extensive experiments in welfare provision for refugees, as well as improvements in health and hygiene. Other societies at war, notably Britain, found that they had to promise a welfare state to repay the population for the suffering it had endured during the war. But in the end, the Nationalists had created demands that only the Communists would be able to satisfy.[16]

In the early twenty-first century China has taken a place on the global stage, and seeks to convince the world that it is a "responsible great power." One way in which it has sought to prove its case is to remind people of a time past, but not long past, when China stood alongside the other progressive powers against fascism: the Second World War. If we wish to understand the role of China in today's global society, we would do well to remind ourselves of the tragic, titanic struggle which that country waged in the 1930s and 1940s not just for its own national dignity and survival, but for the victory of all the Allies, west and east, against some of the darkest forces that history has ever produced.

MAPS

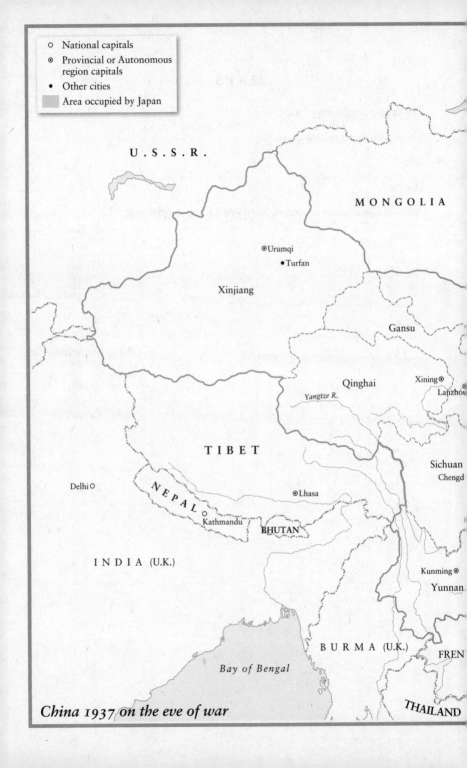

China 1937 on the eve of war

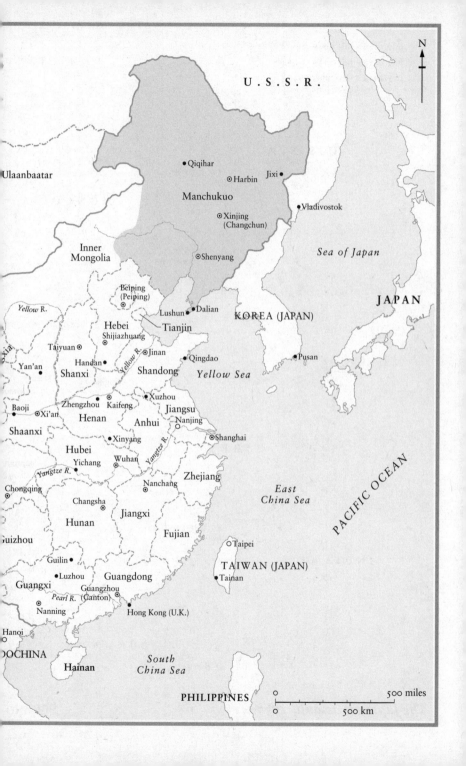

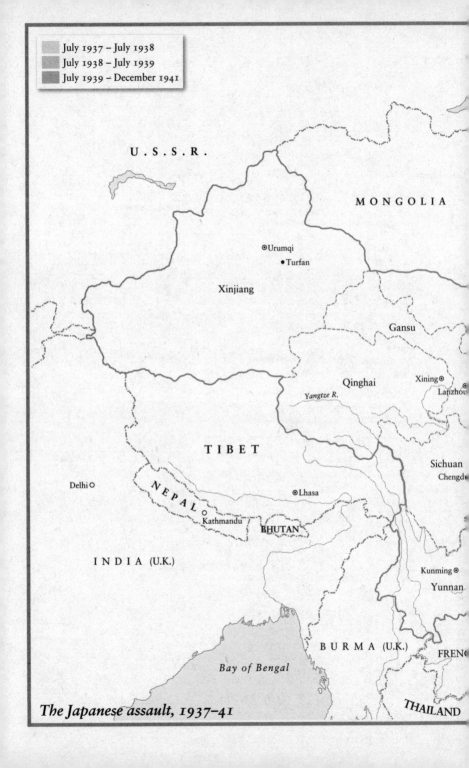

July 1937 – July 1938
July 1938 – July 1939
July 1939 – December 1941

U.S.S.R.

MONGOLIA

⊙Urumqi
• Turfan

Xinjiang

Gansu

Qinghai   Xining ⊙
          Yangtze R.   Lanzhou

TIBET   Sichuan
                                Chengdu

Delhi ○   N E P A L
              ○ Kathmandu   ⊙Lhasa
                    BHUTAN

INDIA (U.K.)
                                        Kunming ⊙
                                        Yunnan

                    BURMA (U.K.)   FREN

    Bay of Bengal

The Japanese assault, 1937–41   THAILAND

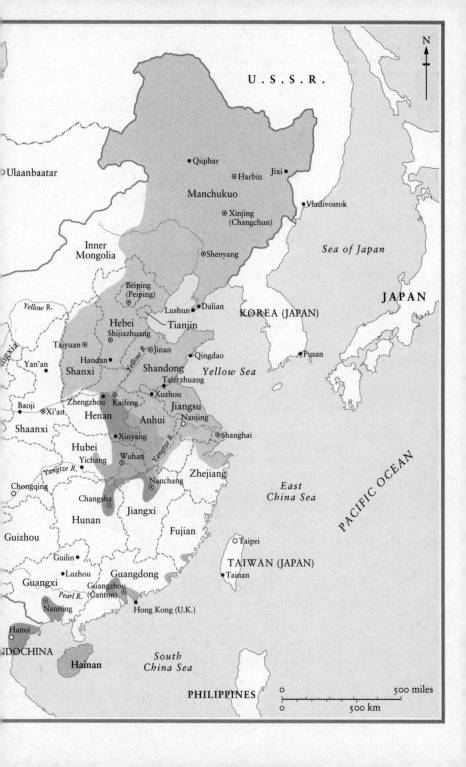

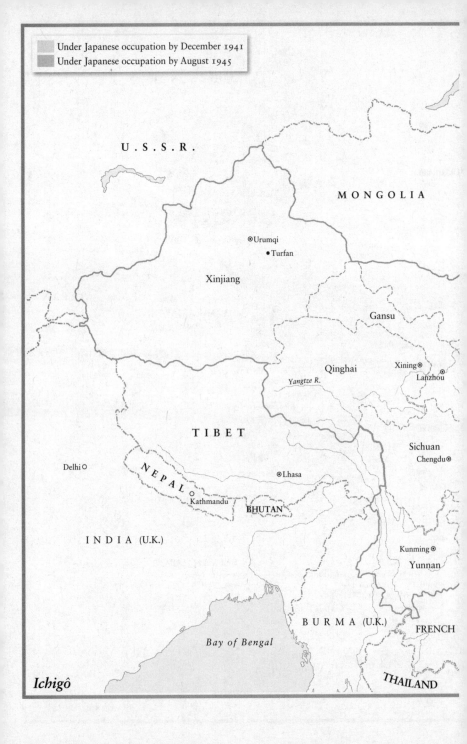

Under Japanese occupation by December 1941
Under Japanese occupation by August 1945

U.S.S.R.

MONGOLIA

⊙Urumqi
• Turfan

Xinjiang

Gansu

Qinghai   Xining ⊙
                        Lanzhou
        Yangtze R.

TIBET

Delhi ○   Sichuan
                                               Chengdu ⊙
        NEPAL
              ○   ⊙Lhasa
           Kathmandu
                    BHUTAN

INDIA (U.K.)
                                        Kunming ⊙
                                        Yunnan

                            BURMA (U.K.)   FRENCH

        Bay of Bengal

Ichigô   THAILAND

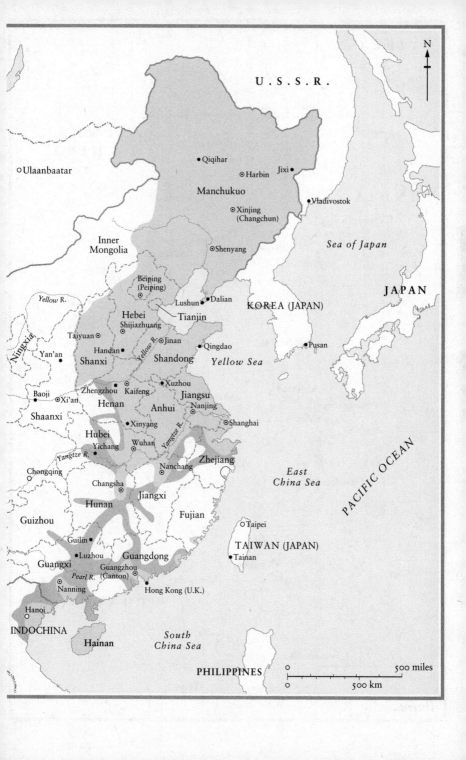

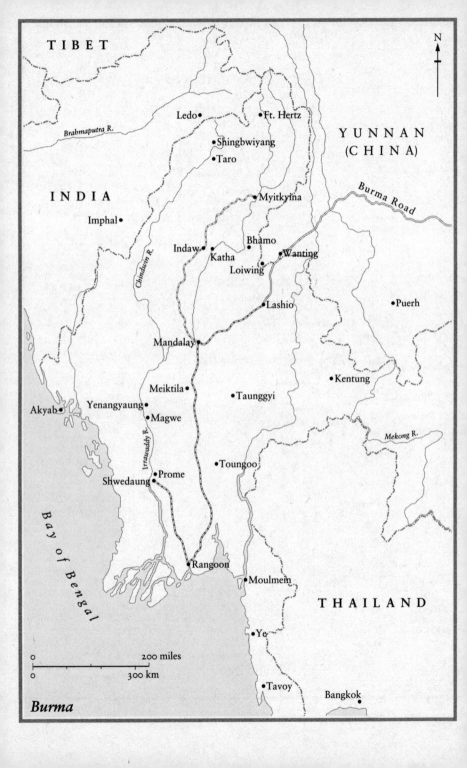

TIBET

Brahmaputra R.

Ledo •   • Ft. Hertz

YUNNAN
(CHINA)

• Shingbwiyang

• Taro

INDIA

• Myitkyina

Burma Road

Imphal •

Indaw •   • Bhamo

Chindwin R.

Katha •   • Wanting

Loiwing

• Lashio

• Puerh

Mandalay •

• Kentung

Meiktila •

Yenangyaung •   • Taunggyi

Akyab •

• Magwe

Irrawaddy R.

Mekong R.

• Prome

Shwedaung •   • Toungoo

Bay
of
Bengal

• Rangoon

• Moulmein

THAILAND

0
200 miles

0
300 km

• Ye

• Tavoy   Bangkok

Burma

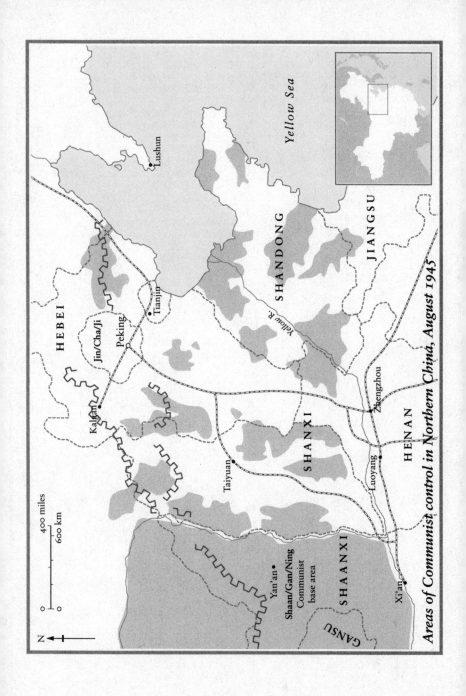

Areas of Communist control in Northern China, August 1945

PART I

THE PATH TO WAR

Chapter 1

AS CLOSE AS LIPS AND TEETH: CHINA'S FALL, JAPAN'S RISE

THE CLASH BETWEEN CHINA and Japan did not begin in 1937. It had been brewing for decades. The story of the first half of China's twentieth century is the story of its love-hate relationship with its smaller island neighbor. The hatred became more prominent as the years went on, reaching its climax with the devastation visited on China's territory by the atrocities of the 1930s and 1940s. But in earlier years, Japan had been mentor as well as monster. It was an educator: thousands of Chinese students studied there. It was a refuge: when Chinese dissenters such as the prominent revolutionary Sun Yat-sen were threatened by their own government, they fled to Tokyo. And it was a model: China's reformist elites looked to Japan to see how an Asian power could militarize, industrialize, and stand tall in the community of nations. For good or ill, a large proportion of the history of twentieth-century China was made in Japan. It became commonplace in both countries that Japan and China were "as close as lips and teeth."[1]

But if they were so close, how did the two nations come to fight one of the bloodiest wars in history? To understand the origins of their conflict, we must return to the late nineteenth century. To be Chinese during this period was to face a depressing range of political problems — floods, famines, and foreign invasions among them. And looming over all of these challenges was the greatest existential crisis in China's history. The country's elites had come to realize that they were no longer in charge of their own destiny. What had once been a self-confident civilization was now the victim of a new international system in which industrialization and imperialism shaped the world. That decline was doubly difficult for many Chinese to understand because it seemed to have come about so quickly. Just a century earlier, many observers in the West had felt that China's empire was surely the greatest on earth: Voltaire, for one, had criticized his native France by comparing it unfavorably with China. For centuries China's imperial dynasties had ruled over one of the most populous and sophisticated societies on earth, and for nearly a thousand years China had used a system of competitive examinations to recruit government bureaucrats, long before such a system operated in the West.

The cultural influence of China was at its zenith during this period. The orderly, conservative philosophy of Confucianism, which underpinned Chinese statecraft, spread across East Asia, shaping societies beyond China's borders, including Japan, Korea, and Southeast Asia. Chinese calligraphy, painting, and metalwork became renowned across the region, and the country developed a dynamic commercial economy: goods such as exotic fruits from the warm south made their way onto the sophisticated palates of the prosperous merchants in the cities of central and northern China. The rulers of Japan, in contrast, began to feel vulnerable. Concern about the arrival of Spanish and Portuguese missionaries eager to convert the Japanese to Christianity led the Tokugawa family, who ruled on behalf of the emperor, to impose a policy known as *kaikin* or *sakoku* from 1635: on pain of death, no Japanese were permitted to leave the country, and foreign trade was heavily restricted with Dutch, Chinese, and Korean traders permitted only on the artificial island of Dejima in Nagasaki Harbor and on outlying islands.[2] The Chinese court was much less concerned about the threat from abroad. When the British diplomat Lord Macartney attempted to open up trade between China and Britain in 1793, the emperor sent him away empty-handed, declaring loftily: "We have never valued ingenious articles, nor do we have the slightest need of your manufactures."[3] Still, despite this imperial insouciance, China was highly integrated with the world economy and was very far from being closed or isolated. During the Qing dynasty (1644–1912) the distinctive blue-and-white pottery of Jingdezhen in central China graced elegant homes in eighteenth-century Britain and France. The spread of New World crops such as sweet potato and maize enabled the Chinese to move west and cultivate large parts of their territory that had previously been considered barren. Between 1700 and 1800 China's population doubled, from 150 million to 300 million people.[4]

The best example of China's cultural power over its neighbors is the founding of the final dynasty, the Qing, in 1644. The dynasty was established by ethnic Manchus who rode into the Chinese heartland from the lands of the northeast. Even though the Manchus, like the Mongols and other non-Chinese invaders before them, had conquered China's territory, they still respected China's powerful social norms. The greatest emperors of the Qing, Kangxi (r. 1661–1722) and Qianlong (r. 1735–1796), sponsored large scholarly encyclopedias and wrote poetry to show how attuned they were to traditional Chinese culture (even though they maintained many customary Manchu forms at court and in wider society).

Yet China's success contained the seeds of its future problems. Although the country's territory expanded during the eighteenth century, its bureaucracy remained small, as did its ability to extract taxes. The lack of government revenue meant that military spending was low. This problem would be highlighted when a new threat appeared in the early nineteenth century: imperialism from the West. The new arrivals were different from previous conquerors who had established new dynasties. They did not share a Chinese view of the world, nor of China's central place within it. They were led by the British, who were invigorated by the economic gains of industrialization and their final defeat of Napoleonic France at the Battle of Waterloo in 1815. British traders had established the East India Company in 1600 and now sought a market for the products that emerged from their possessions in southern Asia.[5]

One crop that grew particularly well was the opium poppy, which produced a sticky black paste that could be smoked for a powerful narcotic effect. The drug quickly took off when introduced to China. Opium had in fact been known in China for centuries, used largely as a medicine and aphrodisiac by elite consumers. Mass-market opium was a British innovation. The imperial court became convinced that a powerful and destructive force was being unleashed upon the population, and Lin Zexu, a high official of the Qing, was sent to the port of Guangzhou (Canton) to destroy the stocks of the drug held by the British traders there. Lin was successful in the short term, capturing the opium after besieging the traders in their "factories," but he unwittingly provoked a war. Lord Palmerston, the British foreign secretary, authorized the use of force to punish the Chinese for their supposed insolence toward the British Crown, and the first Opium War (1839–1842) began. Chinese defenses turned out to be no match for destructive British firepower, backed up by gunboats, and the court was forced into humiliating surrender.

In 1842 representatives of the Qing dynasty signed the first of what are still known today as the "unequal treaties," the Treaty of Nanjing. It forced open new ports for foreign trade, including Shanghai, and ceded the island of Hong Kong to Britain, without any reciprocal benefits for the Chinese themselves. The treaty marked the start of the "century of humiliation," during which China lost control of its sovereignty and was at the mercy of foreign powers; even today, the phrase has the power to call up collective memories of a dark period in China's history. Over the next few decades the Western powers—first Britain, then the United States and France—would launch further assaults against China, each victory gaining them greater concessions and territory. For the Chinese, the greatest source of resentment was the establishment of "extraterritoriality," a provision designed to overcome the supposed inadequacies of Chinese law. It decreed that foreigners from nations covered by the treaties could not be forced to settle legal disputes or face criminal charges in Chinese courts, even if the events in question had taken place on Chinese soil. Instead, the two sides would have to go to a "Mixed" court under foreign authority.[6]

Shanghai was the key. A small trading city for most of China's history, and eclipsed for all that time by nearby Nanjing and Yangzhou, modern Shanghai was created by imperialism. Trading rights there were granted under the terms of the 1842 Treaty of Nanjing, which had followed the first Opium War. Although the treaty was a humiliation for the Chinese, it allowed the growth of a unique port. At the center of the city were two "concession" areas (that is, territory under foreign sovereignty). The French Concession was a small French colony within the city. The International Settlement was more complex. Not a formal colony, it was controlled by the Shanghai Municipal Council, to which until 1928 no Chinese could be elected; the majority of its councilors were British (although Americans, and then Japanese, also served). The settlers, who called themselves "Shanghailanders" (as if the city were its own country), were not directly accountable to London but were widely identified with British interests. Outside the concessions, the Chinese government of the day had control. Gangsters took advantage of the split sovereignty of the city to maximize revenues from drugs, prostitution, and gambling, most famously the notorious Green Gang under Du Yuesheng. Yet the city's colonial history also provided an opportunity for young nationalist Chinese to see modernity at close quarters. The neon lights and fancy department stores of Shanghai became legendary, even many thousands of kilometers inland.

The Qing dynasty had to reconsider its whole strategy of dealing with the Western world. Two years after the Treaty of Nanjing was signed, the senior courtier Qiying tried to reinterpret the situation for the Daoguang emperor in terms suited to the old imperial world. The foreigners "are constantly making arbitrary interpretations of things," he explained, "and it is difficult to enlighten them by means of reason." The court must not "fight with them over empty names," but rather aim to "achieve our larger scheme" of making them behave according to Chinese norms.[7] Qiying hoped that the British could be conciliated as previous foreign invaders from central Asia and the steppes had been appeased in centuries past. But it became clear that this tactic underestimated the fundamentally different nature of the new threat. The imperialists sought to occupy not just land, but minds.

The treaties allowed Christian missionaries to travel extensively in the interior of China. Missionaries were not always welcome, as their presence was often backed (implicitly at least) by the presence of foreign gunboats. Yet Christianity did find many converts in China, particularly as the faith also brought new educational and medical teaching in its wake.

However, nobody could have foreseen the terrible consequences of one particular conversion in the 1850s. A young man named Hong Xiuquan from Guangdong province had repeatedly failed the examinations for the civil service bureaucracy. After his fourth failure, he fell into a trance, in which he recalled various Christian tracts distributed by an American missionary many years previously. Hong's visions led him to believe that he was the younger brother of Jesus Christ, sent to earth to drive the Manchus from China and establish the *Taiping Tianguo* — the "heavenly kingdom of great peace." Hong founded a movement that became known as the Taiping, and despite its unpromising beginnings, it snowballed into the greatest civil war that China, and perhaps the world, has ever seen. Between 1856 and 1864 the Taipings established what was effectively a separate state within China; its capital was at the great city of Nanjing, and millions of people lived under its rule. The Taiping was nominally a Christian regime, but it espoused variations in doctrine (such as acknowledging Hong Xiuquan as Jesus's younger brother) that put off most missionaries and other foreigners from joining forces with it. The Taiping also enacted strict reforms such as the abolition of opium and made moves to redistribute property and land. "Nowhere will inequality exist," one Taiping notice declared, "and no one not be well fed and clothed."[8]

The Qing dynasty was desperate to put the rebellion down. But decades of atrophy meant that the official Qing armies, inheritors of the Manchu warrior tradition, were no longer capable of defeating a large and fanatical rebel group. Instead, the court decided to contain the problem by putting it in the hands of trusted local officials, who raised "New Armies" to defeat the Taiping. The New Armies were highly successful, and the rebellion was finally defeated, although not without massive bloodshed: some 100,000 people were reported killed at the last Battle of Nanjing, in 1864. The Qing had also exacerbated another weakness in their rule. Although the immediate problem of the Taiping was solved, the devolution of military authority from the center to the provinces had laid the grounds for a culture where autonomous militarists, often known as "warlords," rather than a central Chinese government could lay down the law.[9]

This fractured, militarized China would become more and more vulnerable, creating a political system that opened the way for the eventual war with Japan. Without the diffusion of power in the years after 1860, it seems far less likely that Japan would have invaded in the 1930s. Militarization and the loss of control by the central government led to a wider culture of violence that rocked the country for the last fifty years of the Qing dynasty's rule. That violence found one target in the increasingly resented foreign imperialist presence. Although China never formally lost its own sovereignty, foreigners were free to roam across its territory with little fear of legal consequences for actions they took, and this led to many troubling encounters between the Chinese and the intruders. In the streets of Shanghai scenes of rickshaw drivers being abused by British customers were everyday occurrences. In 1900 the Boxer uprising broke out, a peasant rebellion that gained its name from the religiously influenced martial arts practiced by its proponents. The rebellion was spurred on by a great drought that came on top of widespread, grinding poverty, and it saw immense violence against foreigners and Chinese Christians in the villages of north China, culminating in a two-month siege of the foreign legations in Beijing. The rebels whipped up feeling in drought-ridden districts with xenophobic slogans such as "When the foreign devils have all been killed, a heavy rain will fall."[10] Drought and famine also increased the level of local violence, as militias formed in communities that no longer trusted the state to defend them against marauding bandits or corrupt officials.

It was into this vulnerable, post-Taiping China that Chiang Kai-shek was born in 1887. Chiang remained an enigma even to many of his closest associates for the whole of his life. He was stubborn, manipulative, and callous, but also had firm commitments coming from his experience as a Bible-reading Confucian firmly committed to revolutionary anti-imperialism. From his earliest years, he was seized by the conviction that China must be reunited, and that the power of foreign imperialism must be eradicated from its territory. All his military and political life was spent in pursuit of this goal. But his tactics could lead him to adopt intricate and often deceptive strategies: Chiang was a master at playing off his colleagues against one another. Chiang, observed one British journalist in the 1930s, "has never hesitated to forgive his enemies . . . or to betray his friends."[11] Born to a family of salt merchants near Ningbo, in Zhejiang province, the prosperous central coastal area around the Yangtze delta, Chiang received an education which was highly traditional in many ways, and learned the values of the Confucian system of thought, including ideas of propriety, righteousness, and shame. But he would also be shaped by a very new institution in the early twentieth century, the military academy. In addition he would be China's first leader to have experience of the outside world: a youthful visit to the newly formed Soviet Russia shaped a lifetime of visceral hatred for communism, and a Japanese military academy gave him insights into the enemy he would face one day. During the Second World War itself, his visits to India and Egypt would shape his conviction that a postwar China must fight imperialism and stand tall among the family of nations. Li Zongren, an ally with whom Chiang would have a turbulent relationship, confirmed that he had one key quality for leadership: "he loved to make decisions."[12]

In the second half of the nineteenth century, while China floundered, its traditional "little brother" had taken a very different path. After the first Opium War, it was Japan's turn to confront the West, this time led by the United States. In 1853 Commodore Matthew Perry sailed into Tokyo Harbor, requesting that Japan abandon its centuries of near-isolation and open itself to a wider range of trading partners. Perry's demand was politely issued, but it was backed up by the force of gunboats. The next decade and a half saw a major crisis in Japan as the shoguns, the Tokugawa family who acted as regents on behalf of the emperor, found they had no solutions to offer to ward off the foreigners. One scion of the family, Tokugawa Nariaki, advocated all-out war. "If we put our trust in war the whole country's morale will be increased," he claimed, "and even if we sustain a defeat we will in the end defeat the foreigner."[13]

But few agreed with him, and the political turmoil caused by the foreign threat led not to a war against the Americans but to a coup against the shoguns. After a short civil war in 1868, the Tokugawas were replaced by a very different sort of aristocratic elite, who decided that the way to repel Western imperialism was to embrace wholesale modernization. "Knowledge shall be sought throughout the world," declared the Charter Oath of the new regime, "so as to invigorate the foundations of imperial rule."[14] The reformers carried out their actions in the name of the emperor, whose reign title was Meiji ("brilliant rule"), and the period has therefore become known as the "Meiji restoration." In reality, it was nothing less than a revolution. Japan had been a feudal aristocratic society, largely agrarian, with little foreign contact. Christianity and firearms, both dangerous influences that might upset the social order, had been outlawed. By 1900, within just three decades, Japan had been transformed. It had a disciplined, conscripted army, and a constitution and parliamentary system. It was Asia's most heavily industrialized society, exporting goods around the world. By the start of the twentieth century, Japan had nearly 6,000 kilometers of railway tracks and 700,000 tons of shipping. Its leaders had created a modernized, industrialized state in record time.[15]

Japan had also secured another essential element of a powerful modern nation-state in the late nineteenth century: an empire. In 1894–1895 Japan took on China for control of the Korean Peninsula, traditionally an area of Chinese influence. Twenty thousand Japanese troops made a daring assault on the fort of Weihaiwei, on the coast of China's northern Shandong province, and turned their guns on the ships of the Chinese navy, sinking five of its finest vessels. China had to send diplomats Prince Gong and Li Hongzhang to the city of Shimonoseki in Japan to sign a humiliating treaty; as Gong put it, he was "piecing together the cup which the present ministers had smashed to the floor."[16] The Japanese not only claimed control of Korea (which they annexed formally in 1910), but the island of Taiwan as well (which remained a Japanese colony until 1945). In 1904–5 Japan pulled off an even greater coup. It fought for influence in Manchuria, the northeastern province of China, where Russia had established a colonial presence. Japan paid a heavy price: over 80,000 of its troops were killed by wounds or disease. But thanks to Japan's military skill, the war ended with Russia's defeat. It was the first time that an Asian power had overcome a European one, and the achievement drew admiration from colonized and vulnerable peoples around the world.[17]

In September 1905 the two powers met at Portsmouth, New Hampshire, to sign a treaty mediated by President Theodore Roosevelt (who would later win the Nobel Peace Prize for his efforts). Russia had to hand over the rights to the Liaodong Peninsula, a strip of land on the east coast of Manchuria that contained the strategic port of Dalian. The Japanese then built on their gains by setting up the South Manchurian Railway. Much more than a transport network, this was a commercial semi-governmental organization modeled in part on the British East India Company. It gave Japan a strong foothold on the Chinese mainland. The Russo-Japanese War also had a powerful impact on the Japanese public. Songs such as "Comrade" became popular hits, with lines such as "Here, many hundreds of leagues from home,/The red setting sun of distant Manchuria/Shines down on a stone at the edge of a field,/Beneath which my friend lies."[18] Such songs fueled a growing feeling that Japan had earned its territories in China at a high cost and that this sacrifice gave the Japanese a special role in their neighbor's land.

This special status was spelled out most clearly by the stationing in Manchuria of the Kwantung Army. This force, initially made up of some 10,000 men, was supposed to protect the interests of Japanese citizens and business interests in the region, in particular the South Manchuria Railway Company (SMR, or *Mantetsu*), which was the primary instrument of Japanese colonialism in the region. By 1933 its numbers had increased dramatically to over 114,000, and it gave Japan a powerful advantage in its quest to control north China.[19]

By the early twentieth century, Japan was an Asian power that had remodeled itself as an empire with continental ambitions. In stark contrast, China had been thoroughly humiliated. It had lost its first all-out war with its "little brother," and then had to accept that rival imperial powers, including Japan, could occupy large parts of its territory with impunity. Feelings of resentment at Japan's actions were mixed with respect for that nation's ability to regenerate itself. Even the Chinese Guangxu emperor expressed his admiration for the Meiji reforms in a conversation with Japanese prime minister Ito Hirobumi in 1898: "The government of your honorable country has been praised by all nations . . . we request Your Excellency [Ito] to tell our princes and great ministers . . . the process and methods of reform, and give them advice."[20] Just a few decades earlier, it would have been unthinkable that the emperor, the "Son of Heaven," would ask an official from the small islands to the east for advice on any topic whatsoever.

The growing strength of Japan led many Chinese intellectuals to think of new ways out of the crisis, drawing on the political philosophy of the West, the region that had dominated China so successfully. Yan Fu, who studied naval technology in London, became the first translator into Chinese of Herbert Spencer, the Victorian social scientist who coined the term "survival of the fittest." Spencer argued that races and peoples, not just species, were competing for mastery. His central ideas were later characterized as "social Darwinism" and are now dismissed as pseudoscience, but they proved very popular in East Asia in the late nineteenth and early twentieth centuries, as they seemed to provide a rational explanation for the decline of the Asian powers, as well as a potential solution. (The young Mao Zedong, among others, was deeply influenced by such ideas. He used them to voice his opposition to the traditional Confucian respect for order, harmony, and hierarchy, instead embracing the idea that violence might be the necessary transformative power that would drag China into modernity. What China needed was a man who would "charge on horseback amid the clash of arms . . . to shake the mountains by one's cries."[21])

Despite such new thinking, the Qing's grip on power became ever weaker even as Japan gained strength. Attempts at reform were half-hearted and were stymied by conservative figures at court, including Cixi, the empress dowager who acted as a force behind the emperor's throne and was vehemently opposed to political change. The Boxer uprising of 1900 had proved a disaster for the dynasty: Cixi and the court had come out in support of the rebels and their antiforeign campaign, only to see the Boxers crushed by a 20,000-strong force made up of the soldiers of eight nations (including Japan). The dynasty was made to agree to a massive indemnity payment to the foreign powers. There was a final effort to turn things around in the first decade of the twentieth century. From 1902, the dynasty instituted the Xinzheng (New Government) reforms, which drew strongly on the Japanese example. These were designed to turn China into a constitutional monarchy, with elections steadily being introduced at a local, then provincial, then national level.

The reforms late in the Qing might have had some chance of success in a country that was already more unified and prosperous. However, the dynasty was running low on people who had a vested interest in its survival. There was a serious agricultural crisis in the countryside; military power had now been diffused to the local level; and the newly emergent middle classes, visible in new institutions such as chambers of commerce, formed a locus of power that owed little to the central government. For nearly a thousand years, Chinese dynasties had held sway through their control over the bureaucracy, entry to which was dependent on a series of examinations. But the examinations themselves had become ossified, demanding knowledge of classical precedents that seemed to have little relevance to the pressing problems of the day. In 1905, in one of its boldest moves, the Qing abolished the traditional examinations in favor of a new system demanding study in sciences and foreign languages. However, this alienated large numbers of elites who had spent years — in some cases, decades of their lives — studying for the bureaucratic examinations, and now found their ladder of opportunity snatched away.

The end of the old system created new opportunities for learning that had never been available to an older generation of Chinese. Some 30,000 Chinese students traveled to Japan for further study in the three decades leading up to 1937. This was a sharp reversal of past practice: Asians had always come to China to learn, but now Japan was the mentor. Chiang Kai-shek, for instance, attended the Shimbu Gakkô in Tokyo, a school set up to enable Chinese students to study military strategy. Among his fellow students was He Yingqin, who would become his minister of war during the conflict with Japan. Chiang was not a popular student, regarded as aloof and withdrawn, but he was respected for his capacity for sheer hard work. Chiang's three years in Japan would instill in him admiration for that country's sense of order, discipline, and commitment to modernization; but its imperialist intentions would also make him deeply wary.[22]

By the late nineteenth century, many Chinese despaired of the possibilities of gradual reform and began to plot nothing short of an overthrow of the Manchu dynasty. A new political philosophy was on the rise, personified in the revolutionary leader Sun Yat-sen, a Hong Kong–trained physician who was also a practicing Christian. Sun became convinced that the Qing would never revive China's fortunes, and spent much of the 1880s and 1890s moving among Chinese communities overseas and forging links with traditional secret societies, fomenting opposition to the dynasty. He even led a secret organization in China, the Tongmenghui,

aimed at overthrowing it. The Qing, in turn, put a price on his head, forcing him to flee to Japan. He failed to ignite an uprising, but his patriotic
credentials and charismatic presence inspired many Chinese nationalists,
including the young Wang Jingwei.[23]

Wang Jingwei is less well remembered today than his contemporaries
Chiang Kai-shek or Mao Zedong, who would also seek to lead China during the war with Japan. Yet in the first decade of the twentieth century,
he was better known than either. When he met individuals, Wang often
appeared diffident, but in front of a crowd he was transformed. A Japanese journalist who knew him declared: "He always spoke in a very, very
low voice in small groups . . . But in a crowd of three thousand, he was
just like a crazy lion! He was a great orator!"[24] Wang was born in 1883 in
Guangdong province, although his family originated from Zhejiang, the
same province as Chiang. Like his two contemporaries, Wang was seized
by an early conviction that China needed salvation and that he was the
man to do it. In 1905 Wang joined the Tongmenghui and quickly rose in
influence. Unlike Chiang or Mao, he gained national prominence early
with his daring public persona, and his public-speaking skills brought
him great fame. Wang enjoyed his glamorous image: he was startlingly
handsome and would build on his charismatic good looks by writing poetry in which he portrayed himself as a selfless patriot who cared little for
his own life. Wang Jingwei likewise chose Japan for his further studies,
arriving in 1904 for a course in law and politics. While there, he served
as one of the editors of the *Minbao* newspaper, whose passionate rhetoric
called for revolution in China, and one of whose readers was the youthful
Chiang Kai-shek.

Aged only twenty-two, Wang had emerged from his Japanese experience as a fully committed revolutionary comrade of Sun Yat-sen. Sun
and Wang both hailed from the southern province of Guangdong, and
throughout his life Wang would associate with other figures from this
region, which had always looked askance at rule from the northerners
in far-off Beijing. Wang traveled extensively with Sun in Southeast Asia,
using his rhetorical skills to inspire the region's ethnic Chinese to support the overthrow of the dynasty. But revolution seemed unlikely. In
1910 Wang decided that he would substitute action for words: he masterminded a plot to assassinate the prince regent, Prince Chun, with a bomb
timed to go off under his carriage. He was assisted by a young woman
named Chen Bijun. Chen was the daughter of a trader from Southeast

Asia, and she was a feisty and provocative figure as dedicated to revolution as Wang himself. Soon after meeting, they were married, and Chen
took a full role in all Wang's activities. Some years later Wang would re-
mark, "She is my wife, but she is also my revolutionary comrade, and
for that reason, I don't find it easy to make important decisions without
considering her views."[25]

The plot was discovered, and Wang was arrested and sentenced to
death. His sentence was then commuted to life in prison. The reasons for
his reprieve remain unclear, but one factor must have been the extraordinary fame that his action brought him. (Some more fanciful suggestions
hint that a highly placed lady at court was swayed by his extraordinary
good looks.) To many patriots, the assassination attempt gave him the
status of a true national hero, and the dynasty could not afford to have
him become a martyr. Wang wrote poetry that burnished his own image
as a patriot willing to die to save China from the dynasty which oppressed
it.[26] To explain his turn to violence, Wang referred to the newspaper edi-
torials he wrote as a young man studying in Japan. "These articles were
written in ink," declared Wang; "I wanted to translate them into blood."[27]
The combination of melodrama and commitment was typical of the
man. Driven, ambitious, vain, and also shaped by a streak of recklessness,
Wang's willingness to throw the dice when the odds were long would
shape his political life all the way into wartime.

Young Chinese like Wang took great inspiration from the activities of
the Russian nihilists and terrorists, with their anarchistic philosophy. Not
all Russian anarchists were violent, but those who were glorified their use
of violence. Sofya Perovskaya, the Russian revolutionary who had masterminded the assassination of Tsar Alexander II in 1881 and was subsequently executed, was so much an inspiration to the young Chinese
writer Ding Ling in the 1920s that she named the lead character of her
most famous story, "The Diary of Miss Sophia," after her. Wang Jingwei, as a thrower of bombs at Manchu princes, was a direct inheritor of
Perovskaya's legacy, although he was fortunate enough to escape her fate.

Despite the upheavals in society in the late Qing, there was no certainty that revolution was in the wings. Few could have foreseen the consequences of events in the central Chinese city of Wuhan in the autumn
of 1911. The city was alive with rumors that the Qing government wished
to sell railway rights in the region to foreign interests. In this atmosphere
of unrest, a small group of revolutionary soldiers in the local garrison

were discovered (but not captured) in the midst of their bomb-making preparations for rebellion. They had been planning attacks on local officials, but realized that they must seize their moment or be arrested. They marched to the military headquarters and made their demands to the commander. They gave him a choice: be killed, or announce on their behalf that on that day, October 10, he was declaring the city's independence from the Qing dynasty. He did so, and within days there was a chain reaction as city after city declared independence from the regime. Provincial assemblies, filled with the representatives of the new, politically empowered gentry class, all declared themselves part of a new republic and named Sun Yat-sen as their chosen president. (Sun himself was not in China but in America on a fund-raising trip when the revolution broke out.) The news quickly spread among young patriots ready to bring down the dynasty. Chiang rushed home from Japan and gained his first experience of combat by commanding hastily assembled revolutionary troops in his home province of Zhejiang.

The rule of the Qing proved highly brittle. A local uprising quickly ignited and was sufficient to bring the whole system down. By the end of the year, the dynasty was on the brink of collapse. Yuan Shikai, the leader who controlled the Beiyang army, the biggest in north China, went to the court with a proposal. In return for the abdication of the six-year-old emperor, Puyi, Yuan would ensure that the imperial household was given suitable accommodation and an income. On February 12, 1912, the last emperor of China abdicated, and China formally became a republic.

At first, there were high hopes for the republic. But from the earliest days, it was clear that power lay not with the political parties and Parliament, but with the militarists. Yuan Shikai swiftly used his military strength to force Sun Yat-sen's resignation and install himself as president, with the complicity of foreign powers that favored a military man in charge rather than the less predictable Sun. Wang Jingwei was released from prison just after the revolution broke out, and Yuan offered him the premiership of the new republic. Wang declined; rather in the manner of a traditional Confucian scholar, he chose to withdraw from political life rather than be corrupted by a flawed system. Others carried the mantle. General elections were set for late 1912, and Sun ran at the head of his newly formed Nationalist Party (Guomindang or Kuomintang). He handily gained the largest grouping in Parliament, with 269 out of 596 seats. But China's experiment in electoral democracy, while real, was very short lived. On March 20, 1913, an assassin walked up to Song Jiaoren, the Nationalists' brilliant young nominee for prime minister, and shot him. Song died of his wounds soon afterward. Everyone assumed the assassin had been sent by Yuan Shikai. Yuan quickly dissolved Parliament and banned the Nationalist Party. Sun fled to Japan, deeply disillusioned.

China's new republic was plunged into turmoil. Europe became caught up in its own crisis just a year later, as the Great War broke out. This gave Japan, now unquestionably the strongest power in the region, the opportunity to bolster its own position in China while the Europeans were distracted. In January 1915 the government of Prime Minister Okuma Shigenobu presented Yuan Shikai with a set of territorial and political demands that would give Japan immense advantages in everything from trading rights to the placement of Japanese "advisers" within the Chinese government. Yuan's position was still weak, and in May thirteen of the original demands were formalized by treaty. Yuan remained president until 1916, when he died of uremia. For the next decade, China was split among warring militarist factions. Although the international community recognized whichever government was installed in Beijing at any given moment, many felt that China was a geographical expression rather than a country.

The early republican era was not all bleak. Despite the chaos, it led to one of the finest flowerings of culture in China's modern history. In 1915 progressives launched a "New Culture" movement that aimed to liberate China from the constraints of outdated thinking. The movement gathered pace after Yuan's death, sparked by the 1919 signing of the Treaty of Versailles, which ended the Allied campaign against Germany in the First World War. Under the treaty, Germany had to give up its territories on Chinese soil, along with all its other colonies around the world. The Chinese assumed that the territories would be restored to the young republic, as a reward for the efforts of the nearly 100,000 Chinese workers who had been sent to the Western Front in Europe to assist the British and French. But the territories were awarded instead to Japan. The Western Allies turned out to have made simultaneous secret agreements with both China and Japan in order to bring them both in on the Allied side. Once again, Japan's actions on the international stage were wreaking havoc with China's internal politics.

The reaction to this news in Beijing was swift and angry. One student at a public meeting threatened to kill himself with a knife in protest. His fellow students quickly mobilized, and on May 4, 1919, three thousand students from the capital's finest colleges marched through the Legation quarter of the city and set fire to the house of a government minister whom they condemned as a "traitor to the nation" — an apologist for Japanese interests. The students sparked a wider movement that vowed to use "Mr. Science and Mr. Democracy" to revive a society suffering from "warlordism within, and imperialism from outside." The demonstration was over in a few hours, but the aftershocks helped to transform Chinese society and culture for decades to come. The New Culture movement became intertwined with the "May Fourth Movement"(commemorating the demonstration). Patriotic Chinese demanded technological development and political reform that could rescue China from its seemingly eternal weakness.[28]

In 1921, amid this upheaval, a fledgling group — the Chinese Communist Party — held its first congress. Socialism was one of the many Western ideas that had flowed into China late in the Qing dynasty, and radical exponents of the doctrine were further inspired by the outbreak of the Russian Revolution in 1917: Li Dazhao, head librarian of Peking University, declared: "The victory of Bolshevism . . . is the victory of the spirit of common awakening in the heart of each individual among mankind of the twentieth century."[29] Chen Duxiu, the university's dean of humanities, was at the meeting (as was one of Li Dazhao's library assistants, a young man named Mao Zedong). The assembled figures all felt that China's social problems, not least the burning question of foreign imperialism on Chinese soil, needed a radical solution. Yet even these optimists could not deny the size of the crisis that faced the country. The revolution seemed to have failed. How could China save itself?

Chapter 2

A NEW REVOLUTION

T HE REACTION OF CHIANG and Wang to the crisis of the republic was typical of the many young men and women of their
age. They had all been supporters of the 1911 revolution, and to
see their bright hopes for the country disappear into a sea of warlordism
was wrenching. Wang Jingwei took the most radical step in response. He
and his wife Chen Bijun traveled to France (soon to be a political training
ground for figures such as Ho Chi Minh, Deng Xiaoping, and Pol Pot)
and remained there for five years as the republic went from bad to worse.
Chiang and Mao both remained in China, but the continuing grip of the
warlords seemed to allow little scope for their dreams of a new politics
and society.

Wang's action was an extreme version of a wider feeling among the
politically conscious in China that the country was suffering from imperialism and warlordism. The Nationalist Party seemed to be dead and
buried. Sun Yat-sen, in exile again from his beloved China, spent the
next few years in Japan, that ironic place of refuge for an anti-imperialist
revolutionary. But the aftermath of Yuan Shikai's demise in 1916 made it
safer for Sun to return to his homeland. By 1921, with the assistance of
a sympathetic warlord, Chen Jiongming, Sun was based in Guangzhou
(Canton), where he set up a revolutionary government. The Nationalists
were in power, even if only in one region of China. Wang returned from
his self-imposed exile in France and stood by Sun's side as they sought to
recapture the revolution.

Yet Sun was now fifty-eight and in poor health. Who among his followers would take over from him? In the early 1920s, if one had to choose
a young man likely to lead a revolution in China, the most logical choice
might well have been Wang Jingwei. Wang was effectively second in command to Sun, and had helped shape a program of vigorous social reform.
He was a political star, with his near-martyrdom to burnish his reputation. Yet despite the talent that Sun and Wang brought to the Nationalist
Party, their prospects seemed limited unless they could find some powerful supporter who would arm them. Sun Yat-sen had had no success

in persuading the European powers to back him. He had more hopes of Japan, declaring in a speech at Kobe in 1924 that since Japan's victory over Russia in 1905, the peoples of Asia had cherished the hope "of shaking off the yoke of European oppression."[1] However, Sun's idea of pan-Asianism, the philosophy of Asian unity, meant something rather different in governmental circles in Tokyo: not cooperation, but domination by Asia's major power.

Then, in 1923, Sun made a decision that would help shape the path of Chinese history. For years, he had been seeking foreign support for his dream of launching a revolutionary army that would unify China, with him as its president. The Western powers had all turned him down flat. But there was another hand to play in the early 1920s. By 1921 the Bolshevik Revolution in Russia had been secured after a bloody and vicious civil war. Leon Trotsky, the fiery foreign minister of the new regime, was eager to find opportunities to use the Comintern, the agency responsible for spreading revolution abroad. In 1923 Sun held talks with Adolf Joffe, the representative of the Comintern, for a formal alliance between the Nationalists and the Soviets. In the Soviet view, China was too backward for a socialist revolution. Instead, a "national bourgeois" party, the Nationalists, should carry out the first revolution. Sun agreed, content to ally with Russia, believing that alone among Western nations she had shown "benevolence and justice."[2] To show his commitment, he sent a delegation of Nationalist representatives to Russia, Chiang Kai-shek among them. Being tapped by Sun raised the young officer's prestige greatly within the party, and was a sign that he was a rising star. Chiang met many prominent Bolsheviks, including Trotsky, but was not overly impressed, calling them "conceited and autocratic."[3] Chiang's sour memories of Moscow and the political system he saw forming there would come to shape his views when he returned home.

The new alliance changed the fate of the Chinese Communist Party. During the first couple of years of the party's history, it was a tiny and marginal political grouping (as well as being officially illegal). It made grand claims about fomenting a revolution among urban workers, Bolshevik-style, but in reality it had little prospect of doing so. Cooperation between Sun and the Soviets gave the CCP a crucial opportunity to expand. On Soviet advice, many Communists also joined the Nationalists, forming the United Front, making the two parties hard to distinguish during this period. The alliance made sense ideologically for Sun as well.

His political philosophy, which he termed the "Three People's Principles," consisted of democracy, nationalism, and the idea of "people's livelihood," a vague social welfarism that was sometimes rendered as "socialism" in English. He was not a Communist, but he and the Soviets had enough in common to make the alliance useful for both sides. Sun's prestige was also enough to calm the more conservative elements in the Nationalist Party who were wary of the Bolsheviks.

Revolutionary politics were forged on a small island in Guangzhou (Canton) Harbor. The nerve center was the Whampoa (Huangpu) military academy, where the Soviets tutored China's revolutionaries. For both the Nationalists and Communists, the experience of working with the Soviets between 1923 and 1927 on the National Revolutionary Army (NRA) was crucial. Wang Jingwei worked in the political education department of the academy, and alongside him was a rising star of the CCP, Zhou Enlai (later to become China's premier under Mao). On the military side, Chiang Kai-shek rose rapidly in the officer corps as his organizational skills became better known and better valued, along with his comrade from his Japan days, He Yingqin. Also at the Academy were Hu Zongnan and Xue Yue, both of whom would provide crucial military service to Chiang during the war years.[4]

The alliance was of particular interest to the young Communist Mao Zedong, as it meant a much larger party base which he could use to plan radical revolution. Mao's influence as a political activist was growing. In October 1925 he replaced Wang Jingwei as the Nationalist Party director of propaganda, providing a chance for him to hone his techniques of rhetoric and mass mobilization which would prove so vital in the decades to come.[5]

Mao Zedong was born in 1893, in a large village named Shaoshan in Hunan province, deep in the interior of China. Chiang seemed stolid and hard to read to many of his contemporaries; in contrast, Mao appeared mercurial, outgoing, and exuberant. Chiang had little small talk, whereas Mao loved to talk for hours with friends and visitors. Mao was always seeking a bigger stage for himself, and had little but contempt for the old ways of thought and behavior that he felt were holding China back. In one of his angriest articles as a young man he attacked the tradition of arranged marriage: "Chinese parents," he wrote, "all indirectly rape their sons and daughters."[6] Also characteristic of the young Mao was a personal exercise plan ("While squatting, the heels should more or less touch the buttocks. Three times.")[7], part of his youthful intention to exercise both body and mind as a building block for the establishment of a revitalized nation, an idea that would be echoed some six decades later when he launched the Cultural Revolution in 1966 with a public swim in the Yangtze. Throughout his life, Mao was shaped by early violent disagreements with his father, a conservative, well-off peasant farmer; their clashes eventually drove Mao to leave home and to take up political journalism. Mao was also shaped by romantic ideas of heroism drawn from the traditional Chinese classics, including tales of adventure such as *Outlaws of the Marsh* and *The Romance of the Three Kingdoms*. He was always driven by the idea of a strong China, but unlike Chiang, he demanded a complete overturning of "heaven and earth": nothing less than a complete social as well as political revolution would serve his purposes.

The American writer Edgar Snow met Mao in 1936, when he had just achieved national prominence. Snow was deeply impressed: "He had the simplicity and naturalness of the Chinese peasant, with a lively sense of humor and a love of rustic laughter . . . He was plain-speaking and plain-living, and some people might even have considered him rather coarse and vulgar. Yet he combined curious qualities of naïveté with incisive wit and worldly sophistication." Snow also noticed that there was more to Mao. "Something about him," he thought, "suggested a power of ruthless decision when he deemed it necessary."[8] Clearly Mao and Chiang had more in common than either would admit. Like Chiang and Wang, Mao wanted to embrace the possibilities of the new, more open world of thought and experience. In 1911, when he was eighteen years old, Mao had joined a group of revolutionary soldiers in his home province. This was his earliest taste of the warfare that would define his life for another seven decades.

By the spring of 1925 China seemed ready for revolution. On May 30 demonstrators gathered in front of a Japanese-owned factory in Shanghai's International Settlement, protesting their dismissal from work there. As the crowd grew to tens, then hundreds, chants of "Kill the foreigners" became louder. Panicking, an officer of the British-run Shanghai Municipal Police force directed his men (Chinese constables led by Indian Sikh officers) to shoot into the crowd. They shot eleven workers dead, and in doing so, sparked a national protest movement of demonstrations and boycotts. All across China, in Shanghai, Guangzhou, and Beijing, workers and students rallied against the imperialists who could wantonly shoot

Chinese citizens in their own country. On June 23 the situation spiraled, as British troops fired at a crowd in Guangzhou that included school-children and students, killing 52 people. Professors at Peking University spoke for many when they expressed their shock at what had happened: "The tragedy which has taken place . . . has filled the Chinese nation with horror and indignation . . . Some Chinese students, who were merely young boys and girls, paraded as a manifestation of protest . . . Would any right-minded person regard these boys and girls as rioters and treat them with bullets and rounds of machine guns?"[9] Anger against foreign imperialism appeared to have reached boiling point.

But Sun Yat-sen was not there to see that anger. On March 12, 1925, aged fifty-nine, he had died of cancer, succumbing just as his dream was about to be realized. The sudden likelihood that Sun's dream of unification might be fulfilled now brought the growing tension within the party leadership to a head. On July 1, Wang Jingwei was named head of the Political Council that controlled the new National Government declared at Guangzhou in 1920.[10] The same meeting also elected Chiang Kai-shek to the Military Council, an important recognition of his growing status. Over the next few months, rapid changes in the febrile political atmo-sphere would allow Chiang to concentrate more and more power, par-ticularly as key figures such as the Soviet adviser Mikhail Borodin came to mistrust Wang, whom they regarded as flashy and out for personal glory. The quieter, more solid-seeming Chiang appeared an increasingly attractive candidate for their support.

Wang Jingwei's leadership was formally confirmed by the party's Sec-ond National Congress in January 1926, but it was clear that Chiang's star was also continuing to rise.[11] Chiang's political direction was changing, too. Up to this point, he had been associated with the left of the Nation-alist Party, even allowing his son to go to Moscow to study. But by early 1926, Chiang had started to cater to the more conservative elements in the party, who had become convinced that the Soviets were planning to use the Communists to undermine the Nationalist leadership. Chiang be-came convinced that his own life was in serious danger from leftist plot-ters. In March Chiang placed Guangzhou under martial law, disarming the strong Soviet and Chinese Communist presence in the city. Although he swiftly released the senior Chinese Communists (including Zhou Enlai) and Soviet advisers who had been held under arrest, it was clear that the Nationalist troops supported Chiang and that power had shifted to him. Wang Jingwei, enraged, tried to use the party's military to reverse Chiang's position, only to find that his ideological preeminence counted for nothing against Chiang's force of arms.

On June 5, 1926, Chiang was officially placed in charge of the National Revolutionary Army (NRA), the military force that served the Nationalist Party. In an ironic echo of the way in which Sun Yat-sen's own power and prestige had been rendered null by the greater military power of Yuan Shikai in 1912, Chiang's ability to command force now brought him victory over Sun's supposed heir. That military power was important, for there was a great deal for the NRA to do. Over the next two years the Nationalist army fought or coerced its way to control over most of China's central and eastern provinces, a campaign termed the Northern Expedition. In fact, it was a drive to complete the national unification that had been lost in the wake of the 1911 revolution.

Month by month, the major coastal provinces fell to the Nationalists and their army, and despite Chiang's increasing suspicion of the Communists, they also continued to play a major role in the new revolution. Mao Zedong was one of those who undertook his political apprenticeship in the fervor of the Northern Expedition, trying out policies that would eventually dominate all of China. Early on, he made it clear that he regarded the alliance as merely temporary:

> As for the vacillating middle bourgeoisie, its right wing must be considered our enemy; even if it is not yet our enemy, it will soon become so. Its left wing may be considered as our friend — but not as our true friend, and we must be constantly on our guard against it. We must not allow it to create confusion within our ranks![12]

Mao was also beginning to develop ideas that were at odds with those of the party leadership. He was convinced early on that China needed a peasant revolution, rather than an urban one, although he was not the first revolutionary to think of the idea. In 1927 he wrote one of his best-known pieces, "A Report on the Peasant Situation in Hunan," which described the way in which the CCP had managed to foment a genuine class war in the rural areas of Mao's home province. The Hunan Peasant Provincial Association, which claimed some 5 million members, mobilized the poor peasants, arming them and encouraging them to attack the richer landlords. But the violence in Hunan merely mirrored the conflict that now gripped all of China.[13]

The NRA continued its advance, terrifying many foreigners who assumed that this Soviet-backed, Communist-allied army would upend their comfortable lives. Greater success increased the real tensions between the left and right wings of the alliance. Chiang Kai-shek's military supremacy over the other leaders was clear, as was his increasing distaste for the Communist presence within the United Front. The Soviets were bankrolling the Expedition, making it impossible for Chiang to end the alliance with them, but he had already begun to put plans in place to tip the balance of power when the moment was right.

That moment came in April 1927, when the greatest prize, the city of Shanghai, fell to the Nationalists. The British had already anticipated the rise of a more coherent nationalism in China and while they did not welcome it, they were prepared to deal with the country's new, more assertive face. The British settler community in Shanghai was less sanguine, and armed itself against what they feared would be leftist marauders. Some even termed Chiang "the little red general."

But in fact the greatest victims of the capture of Shanghai were not the foreigners (who were anyway mostly safe in the concession areas), but the Communists. They had infiltrated much of the city, awaiting the joyous moment when the NRA would arrive. What they did not know was that Chiang had used his secret society contacts with the Green Gang, the largest criminal outfit in the city, to have all known Communists rounded up and murdered. Many thousands were massacred in the space of a few days; some were kidnapped and tortured first. In later years, Chen Lifu, one of Chiang's close associates, would admit, "It was a bloodthirsty way to eliminate the enemy within. I must admit many innocent people were killed."[14] The killings put a sudden end to the alliance between the Nationalists and Communists. Chiang was in power, and had formally established himself as the ruler of a Nationalist government, but his victory was stained with the blood of his former allies.

Wang Jingwei refused to accept Chiang's new preeminence. At first, he attempted to create his own separate Nationalist government in Wuhan, but it quickly became clear that there was no military backing for an alternative to Chiang. Wang, still believing himself to be the true heir to Sun Yat-sen, refused to serve under his rival. Mao Zedong, along with his Communist comrades, also rejected the idea of Chiang as China's leader. As members of the Communist Party, their lives were now in danger. Mao, later followed by colleagues such as Zhou Enlai, slipped away to the rural hill country of Jiangxi province in inland China, seeking refuge from the new government's troops and hoping to rebuild their shattered revolution.

In 1928 Chiang Kai-shek formally established his government with its capital in the central Chinese city of Nanjing. Chiang moved the capital from Beijing (now renamed "Beiping" or "northern peace"), because he wanted to make sure that his seat of government was in the place where his military and economic control was strongest. For although China was formally united under Nationalist rule, the reality was that its control was partial at best. The provinces of the Yangze delta, such as Zhejiang, Jiangsu, and Anhui, were reasonably firmly under Chiang's command. But the further one went from Nanjing, the less secure the Nationalist government's control was. The Northern Expedition was supposed to have put an end to warlordism, but in many cases the Nationalists had had to reach uneasy agreements with the local militarists, lacking confidence in their ability to conquer them by force of arms. The coal-rich province of Shanxi remained effectively autonomous under the rule of Yan Xishan (a progressive militarist who had campaigned strongly against footbinding). The provinces of Manchuria in the northeast were the fiefdom of Zhang Xueliang, "the young Marshal." In northern China regional warlord Song Zheyuan attempted to solidify influence, while the Japanese sought to increase their influence from Manchuria into the areas south of the Shanhaiguan pass. In far-off Qinghai in western China, the feuding uncle and nephew Ma Lin and Ma Bufang ran the province, and from 1933, Xinjiang, to the north, was governed by Sheng Shicai. Xinjiang bordered the Soviet Union and was effectively under Soviet control from 1937 (although Sheng would turn suddenly and viciously anti-Soviet in 1942). Xinjiang was one of the areas of the country that looked vast on the map, but where very few people actually lived; the most populous parts of the country by far were the east and the south. Perhaps most crucially for a country that might face the threat of invasion from the east, the fertile western province of Sichuan was not under full Nationalist control. Its militarist leader, Liu Xiang, ruled from Chengdu and was deeply wary about allowing any further encroachment from Nanjing.[15] Chiang's shaky grip on large parts of China was an immense obstacle to achieving a genuine unification: Nanjing could not rely on tax collection or military recruitment from huge swathes of the country that it claimed to rule.

Chiang had built his new state at a time of international turmoil, and it had the chance to gain status on the world stage. President Woodrow Wilson's declaration in 1918 of the right of peoples to self-determination, as part of his Fourteen Points, was the trigger for much soul-searching about what modern, independent societies outside Europe might look like. This gave the Nationalist government a special role in the eyes of the imperialist world: until the end of the Second World War, it was a very rare example of a non-Western, nonwhite society that was at least partly independent. Three major powers in particular would be crucial in shaping the world's attitude toward China in the wartime years.

If Britain was the most pragmatic in its approach, this was probably because there was relatively little ideological content in the empire's presence in China. The British had forced their way in to trade, and trade they did; until the 1920s, Britain was the single largest investor in China. Unlike the British presence in India, cultural interaction with the Chinese was limited, and there were few efforts to convert them to British customs and habits, not least because the British had never had a full colonial structure in China. The British presence was deeply exploitative, racist, and often brutal, but British diplomats were also capable, on occasion, of a remarkable clarity of vision and were ready to recognize the Nationalists as different from the warlords who had preceded them.[16] In December 1926 a statement from the then British foreign secretary, Austen Chamberlain, was published which argued that the foreign powers should recognize the new potency and legitimacy of Chinese nationalism. Although the powers should still protest violations of their treaty rights, Chamberlain felt, they should realize that the time had come to make an accommodation with this powerful new political force.[17] At that point, the Nationalists had not yet won the power struggle, and the British position therefore showed a notable level of foresight.

The United States simultaneously maintained two contradictory views of China. On the one hand, the US shared in all the imperial rights that the European powers enjoyed there: they had extraterritoriality, as well as representation on the Shanghai Municipal Council, and had been important actors in the opium trade. Chinese migrants to the US were subjected to severe and often violent racial discrimination, and from 1924, under the Johnson-Reed Immigration Act, Chinese (and Japanese) immigration to the US was effectively banned. Yet within China itself, many Americans felt that they had a special role, and regarded themselves as somehow different from the imperialist powers of the Old World. The missionary influence was key to this belief. By the early twentieth century, funding from American missionaries in China had paid for some of the most important modernizing institutions in the country, such as the Peking Union Medical College, founded in 1906. In addition, missionaries spread throughout China, operating at a village level in a way that few other foreigners ever did. There were of course numerous European missionaries, but the attention of Britain and France tended to be focused more on their own colonies, and that left China's souls up for grabs. It also helped that influential figures in the US had connections with China. Henry Luce, founder of *Time* magazine, was born in China, and his magazines would prove a vital source of propaganda in favor of Chiang Kai-shek during the war with Japan. Pearl Buck was the daughter of Southern Baptist missionaries, and wife of the agronomist and missionary John Lossing Buck. She lived in China through much of the Nationalist era, and wrote novels that made her one of the most popular authors in America. Books such as *The Good Earth* (1931) and *Dragon Seed* (1942) told the stories of peasants fighting poverty and banditry to secure a better life. *The Good Earth* reaped the Pulitzer Prize in 1932 and then, in 1938, Pearl Buck won the Nobel Prize for Literature.

America's missionary presence in China led to many fruitful cultural encounters. But there was a fundamental misconception at the heart of much of the American thinking about China, and one which is not entirely absent from political thought today: a widely held belief that the Chinese aspired to become like Americans, and that it was the job of the Americans to train them to achieve that goal, whether in systems of government, education, or religion. Wealthy American families including the Luces and the Rockefellers established universities, hospitals, and other institutions whose ethos was to encourage ideas of scientific modernity and democratization on a distinctly American model.[18] A positive view took hold that China was indeed a fledgling America, a Christian nation in the making, and a potential liberal democracy. The disconnection between the fantasy and the reality would, in time, lead to fundamental clashes between the US and China during the war with Japan. The Nationalists themselves, of course, were often guilty of playing to this view of themselves as Western liberals in the making, assuring American visitors that they were building a new China that could stand proudly among the free and democratic nations of the world. The Nationalists had a very weak hand to play—China had not been truly pacified, and imperialist power remained strong—and had an interest in telling a powerful sponsor such as the US what they thought it would want to hear.

Japan, the third great power whose fate would affect China in wartime, viewed the establishment of Chiang's Nationalist government in Nanjing with great alarm. During the 1920s Japan had appeared to take a more moderate attitude toward China. Tokyo had learned important lessons from the aftermath of the First World War and the Paris Peace Conference that had followed it. The May Fourth demonstrations in 1919 showed that Chinese nationalism was an important force to be dealt with, and that Japan could not simply invade Chinese territory wholesale as it had done in the wars of 1894–95 and 1904–5. The international climate was changing; in the wake of Woodrow Wilson's Fourteen Points, elite opinion had begun to shift away from the notion of traditional empires. But Japanese delegates, including Prince Konoye, the man who would be premier when war with China broke out in 1937, learned a more cynical lesson from the West. Wilson's internationalist talk was undercut by hypocrisy and racism: Japan's desire for a racial-equality clause in the final peace settlement was rejected by Western politicians who could not bring themselves to declare openly that nonwhite peoples were formally equal. The attitudes of imperialism had not disappeared, only mutated.[19]

These discoveries fueled a contradictory set of impulses toward China. At one level, Japan became an active participant in the interwar global economic and political order, supporting international financial reforms that were supposed to strengthen China and help it gain greater economic autonomy. At the time, Japan's urban culture showed significant liberal trends, in everything from youth fashion to popular music and mass-circulation magazines. The country's huge industrial-financial concerns *(zaibatsu)* had a vested interest in exporting to a global market, and a parliamentary democracy with the rotation of parties became institutionalized during the 1920s.

But not all trends were liberal or pro-Western. Many Japanese thinkers argued that Asian nations could not hope for fair treatment from the West, and that the region should seek its own destiny. The poet Noguchi Yonejirô observed that "A state is not a state . . . if it is merely being supported by other nations, unable to support others. Therefore, I always think and wish that Japan could support other nations, be that India or China."[20]

At the same time, many politicians and military thinkers also became convinced that Japan was being surrounded by hostile powers that wanted to hem it in. Japanese intelligence agents used their network of trading and diplomatic posts throughout China to influence powerbrokers, financiers, and militarists to ally themselves with Japanese interests. If those allies showed too much independence, the results could be deadly: in June 1928 the warlord of Manchuria, Zhang Zuolin ("the Old Marshal"), was killed when a bomb planted by the Japanese military blew up his personal train. In general, the Japanese army was often much keener on hard-line measures than the Foreign Ministry officials, but for all of them, the Chinese mainland was both a buffer against invaders, specifically Russia, and also a source of vulnerability if it fell under the control of forces hostile to Japan. Memories of the victory over Russia in 1905 were still strong, and the term "lifeline" was used repeatedly to explain the region's importance. As one writer put it, "Japan . . . buried 100,000 souls in the Manchuria plain . . . These are the victory prizes won with the priceless blood and sweat of the Japanese race."[21]

The Japanese elites saw Chiang's Nationalist government, with its anti-imperialist rhetoric, as a hostile opponent. They refused to take the Nationalists seriously as a movement with popular legitimacy and an ideological agenda that demanded the eventual removal of imperialist power from Chinese soil. Instead, the Japanese acted as if Chiang was just another Chinese warlord to be bribed or browbeaten. Like the US in some ways, the Japanese were imperialists in China who thought of themselves as friends and mentors, rather than occupiers. Japan had indeed been a real haven for Chinese revolutionaries in the dying days of the Qing dynasty, and a refuge for Sun Yat-sen in 1913 after Yuan Shikai had destroyed China's new Parliament.

Drawing on the idea that the Asian nations needed to cooperate, Japan began to propagate the ideology of pan-Asianism in the first decade of the twentieth century, arguing that the nations of the "spiritual" East should differentiate themselves from the "material" West. The term "pan-Asianism" played into the irrational, romantic streak in Japanese nationalism that drew on Zen and Nichiren Buddhism as well as German ideas of "blood and soil" to give meaning to the national quest for power and glory.

Chinese nationalism, however, did not share much of that spiritual element. It was rooted in a much more secular and civic model of citizenship, and the Nationalists' propaganda, while fiercely patriotic and even xenophobic at times, did not stress ideas of spiritual purity in the way that Japan's (or Nazi Germany's) did. This distinction would prove crucial. China would not be ruled by ideologues who defined themselves by race or sought a system based on a fascist primordialism.

Japan's rage at China was all the stronger because the two nations shared a common cultural heritage, as well as elements of their written language and religion, and yet were set on different paths in their quests for modernity. As Chiang took power in Nanjing, the difference between the two countries' visions for East Asia foretold a deadly confrontation.

Chapter 3

THE PATH TO CONFRONTATION

O N SEPTEMBER 18, 1931, a bomb exploded on a railway line near the city of Shenyang (then known better in the West under its Manchu name of Mukden). Robert Lewis, an American adviser to the Nationalist government who was stationed in Manchuria, sent a telegram to the Ministry of Foreign Affairs in Nanjing saying what happened next:

> On Friday night September eighteenth the Japanese Army sent from Korea into Manchuria through Antung seven army railway trains fully loaded with soldiers. On Saturday night September nineteenth [sic] Japanese army sent four additional trains loaded with soldiers in to Manchuria at the same point . . . [The Japanese] arrested superintendent of schools and forbad [sic] teaching of Dr Sun Yatsen's principles . . . Troops and military cadets were disarmed when captured and the arms and munitions of the Chinese arsenal were removed by Japanese including modern rifles field guns heavy guns military motor trucks.[1]

The Japanese Kwantung Army, garrisoned in the region since 1905, declared that the blast had been set off by Chinese subversives, and that they had no choice but to launch an immediate military coup to protect Japanese lives and property. In fact, the Japanese had set off the bomb themselves. Two officers of the Japanese Kwantung Army, Ishiwara Kanji and Itagaki Seishirô, were behind the coup, which took place without the knowledge of the civilian government in Tokyo. Within weeks the Kwantung Army had occupied an area the size of France and Germany combined, placing 30 million people under their control.

The "Manchurian Incident" became one of the most notorious diplomatic crises of the interwar period, one of the first in a series of confrontational acts by militaristic governments that would shatter the fragile peace created after the Great War. But the events of September 18, 1931, would also forever change the fate of China under the leadership of Chiang Kai-shek and his Nationalist Party.

After his bloody start, Chiang had made huge strides in his attempt to establish a government that could modernize China and end the stain of imperialism on its soil. During the first half of the decade, the Chinese economy began to improve markedly and indigenous businesses, from textiles to tobacco, thrived. Chinese diplomats began to take an important role in organizations such as the League of Nations. Infrastructure in the cities expanded: in the decade up to 1937, China's paved roads doubled from 30,000 to 60,000 kilometers, and the railway system also improved. Still, Chiang's regime at Nanjing had major flaws. The government abused human rights on a significant scale, regularly arresting or assassinating political dissidents, reserving particular venom for Communists. The Nationalist Party structure also became highly corrupt, particularly at local levels where officials used tax collection as a means of extorting all sorts of unauthorized extra payments from farmers. The government's greatest failing — and one that gave the Communists a superb opportunity — was its failure to deal with the desperate poverty of the country's rural regions. The Nationalists' power lay in large part in its ties to wealthier elites, who had a vested interest in economic relationships not changing, whether in factories in the city or throughout the vast countryside.[2]

One witness to the hardships endured by rural Chinese under Chiang's government was the American Presbyterian missionary Katharine W. Hand, who lived for years in Shandong province in northern China. Shandong was a poor and drought-ridden place, which had been at the center of the Boxer uprising of 1900, and was the scene of horrific clashes between Boxer rebels and Chinese and Western Christians. Over thirty years later, there was little danger of an attack on Westerners stationed there, but the place was still remote. Hand wrote home to the US in 1935:

> . . . I do wish I could give you something of the atmosphere of this back-of-the-world place. One can hardly say interior, when it is barely seventy-five miles from the coast, but it is still living the life [of] the Old Testament pictures. I look out on a little threshing field and watch the stone being pulled around and around by the ox and the ass . . . When the grain has been threshed in this way it is tossed in the air, a shovelful at a time, to be winnowed by the wind. And they are very expert . . . Naked children dance around and old women sit on the edge of the floor, possibly gleaning a few grains . . . I feel that I am back historically several centuries, and at the same time seeing the West just beginning to crash in — for better or worse it is sometimes hard to say.

Hand also observed the modernization that was changing China: she wrote of her trip out in a Ford V8 automobile on a "dirt road for such length the best I ever travelled — 160 miles. Telephones, busses, bridges — all within so short a time." Yet disaster was ever present:

> Once we saw ahead of us in the road a great crowd — my heart som- ersaulted for a moment; then we learned that it was one of the groups of flood refugees that are being distributed throughout the province to be cared for — the government is trying to meet the situation as it has never done before, but of course it is a tragic drain on the people who must take them in and share with them their own next-to-nothing.[3]

Despite the desperate poverty in much of the country, most outside observers regarded the strength of the Nationalist government as a positive development for China after the years of warlord factionalism. But the Japanese regarded events on the mainland with dismay. What worried them most was the Nationalists' slow but steady move to reduce foreign privileges in China and become a more equal trading partner. In 1930 the government finally managed to restore tariff autonomy, the right to charge its chosen level of import taxes on goods coming into China. After nearly eighty years during which this right had been controlled by foreigners, a part of the "unequal treaties," it was an important milestone. During the Nationalist period, the Customs service that handled these tariffs started to replace foreign employees with Chinese, evidence that China would soon move to take charge of its own finances.[4] That greater autonomy caused deep concern in Tokyo, where the government was becoming almost manic in its conviction that China should be regarded as an area of special influence for Japan.

In 1922, General Utsonomiya Tarô had lain on his deathbed and pointed to a world map, declaring, "That must all become Japan's!," indicating territory that stretched from Siberia to New Zealand. Yet in making such declarations, Japanese imperialists felt that they were merely learning from their Western counterparts. "Haven't you ever heard of Perry?" asked General Ishiwara Kanji of an American prosecutor at the Tokyo war crimes trials in 1946, referring to the US commodore, Matthew C. Perry, who had forced Japan open in 1858. Japan "took your country as its teacher and set about learning how to be aggressive. You might say we became your disciples."[5]

The government that had so concerned the Japanese was a rather unusual creature. In theory, the Nationalist Party was a "vanguard party" which controlled society through a system of "tutelage" until it was enlightened enough to enjoy "democracy" (which had been one of Sun Yatsen's Three Principles of the People, along with nationalism and social welfare). Yet for a one-party dictatorship, the Nationalist Party was exceedingly diverse. The views of its members ranged from liberal to highly traditional and conservative. Often, all these people had in common was an allegiance to party leader Chiang Kai-shek. It was a mark of Chiang's skill that he was able to keep such disparate men together in one party and retain their loyalty.

Some of the most pro-Western members of the government were also Chiang's relatives, the children of a Shanghai merchant, Song Jiashu (nicknamed "Charlie" Soong), a well-heeled supporter of Sun Yat-sen from the days of the 1911 revolution. All had remarkable careers in Chinese Nationalist politics. Song Meiling (Soong Mayling), known in much of the West as "Madame Chiang Kai-shek," was one of Charlie Soong's daughters. She spoke fluent English, a product of her education at Wellesley College in Massachusetts.[6] Chiang had first proposed to her in 1920, as he was beginning to come to prominence in the Nationalist Party, but she declined him. He appeared undistinguished, had little facility for small talk, and was anyway already married. By 1927 things were very different. Chiang was clearly the leading force in the Nationalist Party, and he and Song Meiling courted for over a year. He fulfilled the two conditions she set him by obtaining a divorce from his previous wife, and by agreeing to study the Bible and consider converting to Christianity. They married on December 1, and from that point she became Chiang Kai-shek's face to the Western world. Diplomats frequently noted that if they met the "Gissimo" (Generalissimo), they would frequently meet the "Missimo" as well; the British diplomat Robert Howe noted early on in the war years that "it is a difficult matter to gather [a] definite impression from a Chinese of Chiang Kai-shek's stamp who is slow to make up his mind . . . Madame Chiang Kai-shek . . . is of a more volatile temperament."[7] Song Meiling's views were shaped by her cosmopolitan background, and she was able to give a wider picture of the West to Chiang (who had never been further west than Moscow). At her wedding, she had bowed down before a portrait of Sun Yat-sen. She would go on to play a significant part in the greatest test that Sun's Republic would endure.

Song Meiling's brother, T. V. Soong (Song Ziwen), also became a major figure in the government. Harvard-educated, and fluent in English, Soong's great talent was raising revenues, which he did for several years as minister of finance (1928–1931, 1932–1933). "T. V." was well known and liked by Western diplomats and financiers of the age. He was relatively liberal, which helped to keep channels open to the United States. Another of Chiang's brothers-in-law, H. H. Kung (Kong Xiangxi), also played a crucial role in the financial affairs of the government. Kung believed himself a 75th-generation descendant of Confucius, but his influence derived from a twentieth-century connection, his marriage to Song Ailing, the sister of Song Meiling. From 1933 to 1945 Kung served as governor of the Bank of China, as well as finance minister for most of that same period, taking over in the latter role from T. V. Soong. Kung, unlike Soong, was not well regarded in political or public circles, and was frequently accused of being the richest — as well as the most corrupt — man in China. Song Meiling had one other sister, Qingling (Song Chingling), who had married into the finest revolutionary pedigree possible, first as the wife and then widow of Sun Yat-sen.

But the Nationalist Party also contained elements who were much warier of the West. The initials of two brothers, Chen Lifu and Chen Guofu, gave their faction the nickname of the "CC Clique." They were two tough political operators. The Chens were nationalists and anti-imperialists, but did not believe in any fundamental change in the economic makeup of society and were strongly anti-Communist. Throughout Chiang's rule, the Chens would push for crackdowns on dissidents, and argue that China needed a more regimented society, rather than a more liberal one. And behind all of the party's activities was a man who was not a blood relative, but whose loyalty meant he might as well have been. Dai Li was later characterized by the journalist Oliver Caldwell as "China's Himmler." Dai was the head of the Nationalist Secret Service, the Juntong (officially the Military and Statistics Bureau). When assassinations or arrests were called for, Dai's men were selected for the job.[8]

Completely absent from the power structure was Wang Jingwei. Wang had never forgiven Chiang for his usurpation of power during the Northern Expedition, and he spent the first three years of Chiang's rule attempting to topple him, either from abroad or in alliance with militarist leaders opposed to Chiang. In 1930 Wang joined forces with the powerful northern warlords Feng Yuxiang and Yan Xishan in the Northern Plains War. Further factional battles between Wang and Chiang's other rival,

Hu Hanmin, followed in 1931. Sun Yat-sen's heir refused to relinquish his legacy.

In 1931 the atmosphere changed utterly with the Japanese invasion of Manchuria. At that moment, Japan became the single most pressing problem facing Chiang's government — greater than the Communists, or rival militarists, or other imperialist powers. Woodrow Wilson's internationalist ethic in the interwar period had dampened Japanese expansion in Asia. But in 1929 the Great Depression plunged Japan into an economic crisis and onto the path of authoritarianism and aggressive imperialism. The two-party system that had operated in interwar Japan had always been troubled, but the collapse of Japan's export economy during the Depression turned people's minds toward protectionism and away from liberal ideas of free trade. The United States had begun to close its markets with laws such as the Smoot-Hawley Tariff of 1930, and the British Empire embraced "imperial preference." Japan now tried to assess where it might create its own zone of economic autarky. The idea that Manchuria was Japan's "lifeline," and that Japan should have special and indeed exclusive rights on the Chinese mainland, was expressed in ever more strident terms. In September 1931 the Kwantung Army, directed by Ishiwara and Itagaki, declared that the locals had revolted against the corrupt warlord government of the then provincial leader, Zhang Xueliang, and that they had established in its place an independent state named "Manchukuo" (country of the Manchus), which would receive friendly "assistance" from the Japanese. Few believed this fiction, but nobody (including an investigative committee that the League of Nations dispatched in 1932) had the power or will to counter it — a lesson likely noted by Adolf Hitler, at that time a rising German opposition leader. Refugees from occupied Manchuria lobbied Chiang to resist Japan, but he insisted on limiting himself to official protests.

Over the next few years, Japan's policies would become a toxic series of interactions between the armies in the field and the civilian politicians. While there were differences of emphasis between various Japanese leaders, the overall ideological belief that Japan deserved special and exclusive rights in China was held throughout leadership circles. Senior Japanese generals took an active role in interfering in Japanese military maneuvers in north China.

Chinese diplomats did make repeated angry exhortations to the League. Chiang declared on September 23 that "If the League of Nations

. . . fail[s] to uphold justice, the National Government is prepared for the final and supreme struggle . . . I shall go to the front and if need be fall with other patriots."[9] But Chiang could not live up to this promise, at least, not yet. He knew that his armed forces were simply not strong enough to take on the Kwantung Army, never mind the whole Japanese Imperial Army.

The exiles from occupied Manchuria formed a lobbying group known as the Northeast National Salvation Society, which used everything from media campaigns to demonstrations to try and persuade the government to employ force to recapture the lost northeastern provinces. One of their public announcements in November 1931 chided the government for its inaction: "Only if we unite can we strive for our survival . . . Set up a strong government, bring about a united country, and make your minds up to declare war on Japan."[10] But in the mid-1930s there was still little popular enthusiasm within China for war, and while the fate of the exiled Manchurian Chinese engendered sympathy, it had to battle for attention against the other crises of the era, including the continuing economic crisis. Manchuria's geographical separateness meant that it did not form a central part of Chinese identity.

There was no doubt that atrocities were taking place under Japanese occupation: the massacre of the 3,000 villagers of Pingdingshan in 1932 (on the pretext that they had been harboring resistance fighters) was just one case that caught international attention. "Houses were put to the torch by Japanese soldiers," wrote one reporter, "and their inhabitants mowed down mercilessly by Japanese machine guns."[11] In spite of this crime, and others like it, there appeared to be little appetite for resistance within Manchuria itself. There was scant enthusiasm for the Japanese, but neither had the locals felt any deep attachment to the previous modernizing regime of Zhang Xueliang, nor to his father, Zhang Zuolin, who had been a classic warlord, illiterate, and addicted to opium. The Japanese combined threats of terror with a certain amount of spending on local infrastructure to appease the population. The invaders also found local officials who were willing to continue their previous roles under the Japanese, providing a sense of continuity. Collaboration with the occupiers may not have been enthusiastic in most cases, but it was widespread. The occupation of Manchuria helped the Japanese exercise control of the mainland and also taught them lessons on how the Chinese population might respond in the event that they ever expanded beyond the boundaries of Manchukuo.

Chiang was feeling pressure from all sides in late 1931. He was still being opposed by the southerners within the Nationalist Party, Wang Jingwei and another veteran of the early days of the revolution, the Cantonese conservative Hu Hanmin. The Communists seemed well established in Jiangxi. To fight the Japanese as well would have been suicidal. Furthermore, the increasingly militarist government in Tokyo took every opportunity to argue that the Nationalist government was "insincere" about its relationship with Japan, and any provocation inevitably would allow them to demand more territory. (One such incident was the arrest and summary execution of one Captain Nakamura, who had been traveling undercover near the Mongolian border and had been suspected of spying by local Chinese soldiers.)[12] Chiang's prestige had been damaged by the loss of Manchuria, and he desperately needed to restore his standing. And so, on December 15, 1931, he resigned.

With this bold gamble, Chiang aimed to prove that no other leader could take his place in the midst of a crisis. Within days, it was clear that he was correct. Top military leaders declared that they would not serve under his replacement, Sun Fo (the son of Sun Yat-sen); tax offices would not transmit funds to the new government; there were public demonstrations demanding that Chiang come back. By early January 1932, Chiang had agreed to return, his position much strengthened. He was also now able to draw in one of his most constant rivals, Wang Jingwei. The threat from Japan now appeared too great to ignore, and after uneasy negotiations Wang agreed to serve in Chiang's government as the president of the Executive Yuan (the equivalent of prime minister). This was a highly prestigious position, theoretically putting Wang in charge of the major executive body in the government, but it had no military authority at all. Chiang had managed to bring his opponent into the government without allowing him any autonomy, though Wang's grouping, known as the "Reorganization Faction," was at least given a significant role in the government. Chiang was now the undisputed leader of the party, and his rivalry with Wang was subdued, if not buried.

However, Chiang's decision not to challenge the Japanese occupation had serious repercussions, as it encouraged ever greater boldness from his opponents. In February 1932 fighting broke out in Shanghai between

Chinese factory workers and Japanese monks, and escalated quickly. A Japanese naval commander, Rear Admiral Shiozawa Kôichi, seized the opportunity to demand an apology and compensation, along with the suppression of anti-Japanese demonstrations in the city. The navy was jealous of the Kwantung Army's success in Manchuria, and this was an opportunity for them to gain prestige. In public, Chiang offered a compromise, but in private, he encouraged the Chinese 19th Route Army, under the command of Cai Tingkai, to fight back. China and Japan were at war. It was a short conflict, but a real one: the inhabitants of Shanghai were surprised to see trenches dug in the alleys and boulevards of the great city as missiles and bullets flew. In three weeks, there were some 14,000 Chinese casualties, and over 3,000 Japanese; civilian deaths were 10,000 or more. Eventually the two sides reached a truce, an agreement which restricted the ability of Chinese troops to operate in Shanghai and was therefore highly unpopular with the Chinese public. With his stated opposition to Cai's resistance (even if he had a different position behind the scenes), along with the policy of nonresistance in Manchuria, Chiang developed a reputation for appeasing Japan. He was further embarrassed by the Communists, who trumpeted their determination to resist the occupation, but most of the party was in Jiangxi province, sixteen hundred kilometers away from Manchuria. Unlike Chiang, the CCP were not called upon to make good on their threats.[13]

Even if the Chinese were not unified, they had to be militarily prepared. Seen in this context, the continued battles against the CCP and the various regional militarists seem more logical: from Chiang's point of view, opposition to unification, whatever the reason, contributed to China's continuing weakness in the face of an external threat. To criticize Chiang for attacking the CCP in the face of a threat from Japan, as many have done, assumes that had he stopped fighting, his opponents would have too. This seems unlikely: only a decade earlier, Mao had declared that neither the left nor right wings of the Nationalists were true friends of the CCP, even though he had been allied with both at the time.[14]

Chiang truly understood that the assaults from Japan were a real threat to the stability of his regime. From the early 1930s onward, the Nationalists made concrete plans based on the idea that there would eventually be a war with Japan. Governments around the world were making similar calculations. Germany and Japan had both brought themselves out of the Depression by massively increasing their military spending. Along with Italy, they became corporatist states: key parts of the economy came under state control, but unlike in the USSR, private firms still maintained a role. The primary goal of the fascist powers was military conquest. Chiang's government did not share that goal, nor would it have had the resources to pursue it. But Chiang realized that mobilizing for war would provide an opportunity to develop China's infrastructure and technology, perhaps leading it out of its desperate poverty.

Discreetly, the Nanjing government began to ramp up the war effort. A key move was the establishment of the National Defense Planning Council on November 29, 1932, which undertook thorough and detailed surveys to measure just what China's capacity was in terms of coal mining, railway infrastructure, crop cultivation, electricity production, and metals. The Council also investigated the impact of education and the importance of currency reform. A crucial conclusion was that China's geography made it vulnerable in the event of a major war, because the vast majority of the country's infrastructure was on the east coast, the area most likely to be invaded. Plans were drawn up for the state to ensure sufficient supplies of iron, coal, and chemicals should war break out. There needed to be more production in the interior of China: iron and steel in Hunan, copper and iron in Sichuan, and coal mines in south and southwest China.[15] The seeds of the planned economy that would mark Mao's China were sown by Chiang's government, stimulated by the Japanese threat.

Chiang also knew that China's security depended on the strength of its army. Despite his own military victories, he was aware that the National Revolutionary Army was a patchwork of troops, some of high quality, others barely trained and only marginally loyal to the central government. In 1934 Chiang brought in a new adviser, the German Hans von Seeckt, a senior officer during the First World War who had been instrumental in retraining the Reichswehr (German Army) during the years of the Weimar Republic, instituting one of the most rigorous military training regimes in the world. From 1935 von Seeckt was succeeded by Alexander von Falkenhausen, who had also been an officer during the Weimar Republic. Both men were supporters of a professional army that would be controlled by the bureaucracy, rather than a political force in its own right. Neither man was a Nazi sympathizer, although they both agreed to serve under Hitler's regime. Overall, the aim of the reforms was to provide a relatively small, well-trained Chinese Central Army that would be supplied through a mandated period of national service (as in Japan). By the mid-1930s some 80,000 men had experienced German-style training.[16]

Chiang's policy of avoiding public confrontation with Japan while quietly preparing for conflict was only partially successful. He stayed clear of war, but was forced into humiliating surrenders of territory. Following the full occupation of Manchuria in February 1932, and Manchukuo's subsequent "declaration of independence" from China, in February 1933 the Japanese invaded and occupied the province of Rehe (Jehol). Zhang Xueliang's troops in the province showed little inclination to fight, and the province fell quickly. Chiang's government decided it must seek a compromise with Japan, and on May 31 the two countries signed the Tanggu Truce. The terms of the treaty were designed to save face on both sides, but they marked a de facto recognition of Manchukuo. Under the terms of the truce, there would be a demilitarized zone between the Great Wall and an area north of Beiping and Tianjin. The Japanese were allowed to maintain observation rights in the area, and Chinese troops were forbidden from engaging in "provocations." It was clearly an embarrassment for China, but in the short term it was a very useful agreement for Chiang, as it provided a temporary breathing space in which he could focus on other priorities, notably his campaigns against the Communists.[17] The years 1933–35 would see a significant lessening of tension in Sino-Japanese relations. Indeed, if the Japanese had stayed content with their already powerful control over north China in 1933, and not sought to advance further into the mainland, the war that would eventually consume much of the continent of Asia might have been averted.

Beginning in 1933, Chiang was faced with an exquisitely difficult task: simultaneously to rearm China against Japan, avoid provoking the Japanese into further military aggression, and placate growing anti-Japanese public feeling. The need to maintain these contradictory aims meant that public figures who advocated resistance to Japan could find themselves in trouble not only with the Japanese but also with their own government. A prominent example was the journalist Du Zhongyuan. In 1935 Du's journal published an article entitled "Loose Talk about Emperors," which made disparaging comments about the ruler of Japan, saying that he was an "antique" who "actually does not have the real power, though everything is done in his name."[18] Du had not actually written the article himself, but he was put on trial for authorizing its publication, and was sentenced to fourteen months in prison.

Wang Jingwei proved a particular challenge to Chiang in this regard. After their wary reconciliation in 1932, Wang supported Chiang's policy of strengthening China's defenses, but also advocated a policy of close relations with Japan. Wang was still an ardent nationalist, and wanted to see a vital, independent China, yet he shared Chiang's belief that the armed forces were too weak to mount a war of resistance, and agreed that China must play for time. In 1934 he wrote that "as a matter of plain fact, the Government is prepared to admit it is weak and powerless" in international affairs. For the moment he dismissed talk of fighting back against Japan, but in terms that made it clear he regarded Japan's demands as unacceptable:

> the present Government refuse to be carried away by popular clamour for war against Japan. High-sounding words are anathema. Pride kills victory; modesty averts defeat . . . Japan's apparent object is to reduce China to the status of a Japanese colony, but to this ignominy the National Government . . . will never consent.[19]

Wang, like most Chinese nationalists, regarded all foreign imperialism as enemy action. He did not see any intrinsically greater merit in allying with Britain or the US — both of which also maintained significant colonial power on Chinese territory — than with Japan, a country that at least had cultural connections with China. Wang was in the unhappy position of advocating close ties with Japan (which was government policy, after all), but being associated in the public mind with a uniquely pro-Japanese stand. And he was detested for it.

On November 1, 1935, members of the Chinese government gathered for a group photograph. Suddenly, one of the photographers revealed a Browning machine gun hidden under his camera, and fired three times at Wang Jingwei. Wang barely survived the attack. It left him with wounds that affected him for the rest of his life, embittering him further against Chiang (who was supposed to have attended the event where Wang was shot, but had canceled at the last minute). Wang maintained that Chiang had ordered the attempted assassination, but this was probably unjustified. Being perceived as pro-Japanese had become dangerous by the mid-1930s; another minister in the same faction, Tang Youren, was shot and killed on December 25, 1935. In fact, Wang's death would not have served Chiang's purposes: the impression among the public that Wang was biased toward Japan was very useful to distract attention from the fact that Chiang did not himself hold a significantly different viewpoint on how to deal with Tokyo. Wang's injuries led him to withdraw from government and he soon left the country for a tour of Europe. As policy hardened in Tokyo, the "pro-Japan" faction had been marginalized in the government.

Although the threat from Japan preoccupied minds in Nanjing, it was less immediately visible in the hill country of remote Jiangxi province, where the remnants of the CCP had fled after Chiang's purge in 1927. While Chiang had been consolidating power, the Communists had been plunged into a bitter series of recriminations about why the United Front had failed so dismally. The changes that they made in the decade that followed, while Chiang was in power in Nanjing, would equip them with ideas of military and economic self-sufficiency that would shape their efforts in the war with Japan a decade later.

Among the younger Communists who had made their way to Jiangxi was Mao Zedong, not yet in charge of the party, but rising rapidly. Mao quickly took a leading role in debates about why the party had been so comprehensively outmaneuvered by the Nationalists. One of the main reasons was that they had had no military of their own. On Soviet advice, Communist troops had been subsumed within the National Revolutionary Army, but when the confrontation came, the NRA remained loyal to the Nationalists. Therefore, one of the earliest acts of the Communists in Jiangxi was to establish the Red Army. Zhu De, a former warlord commander who had also spent time training in Germany, took the lead in training the fledgling force.

While in Jiangxi, Mao took the opportunity to try out radical social policies, including the redistribution of land from richer peasants to poorer ones. "A landlord is a person who owns land. . . . and lives entirely by exploitation," Mao declared baldly. "Warlords, bureaucrats, local bullies, and bad gentry . . . are particularly ferocious elements among the landlords."[20] The party's leaders were cautious at first, since they realized that gaining the support of local elites was necessary for mobilizing the wider population. But several factors began to weaken the Communists. Factional fighting within the party became savage, particularly as clashes emerged between Mao and his colleague Xiang Ying, and Wang Ming's "Returned Bolsheviks," younger Chinese ideologues who had been sent to Moscow for training under Stalin. Land-reform policy became much more violent, and alienated many of the middle-level peasants who were condemned as rich even though they sometimes had only marginally more than those defined as "poor." As the CCP began to turn in on itself, events outside Jiangxi started to plague the party too. The Tanggu Truce of 1933 had created a breathing space in Sino-Japanese relations that allowed Chiang more time and space to direct his armies against the CCP. His initial Suppression Campaigns, as they were uncompromisingly termed, had been failures, but by 1934 the army reforms were beginning to have an effect. The Communists in Jiangxi found themselves under siege. It was time to leave.[21]

In June 1934 the Red Army began a trek to the northwest that has become known as the Long March. The party's position in Jiangxi had become untenable, and thousands of men and a smaller number of women made the winding journey westward through central China. In January 1935 the Politburo gathered in the small town of Zunyi, in Guizhou province. The meeting turned into a showdown between the party's leadership (including their Soviet advisers) and rivals, including Mao, who had been kept away from the top levels of power up to that point. Mao attacked the leaders for using misguided military strategy and allowing the Nationalists into the Communists' base area; they should have followed Mao's advice on tactics. Otto Braun, the chief Soviet adviser, said little, but he "turned white when Mao began to attack him. At no point did he lose physical control, but he smoked cigarette after cigarette . . . He looked more and more depressed and gloomy."[22] When the meeting ended, it was clear that Mao's devastating indictment of the existing leadership had turned him into one of the preeminent personalities in the party. He now had the momentum that would propel him to the very top.

In October 1935 the weary Long Marchers finally reached the dusty yellow earth of Shaanxi province, where a Communist base had been founded in the small city of Bao'an. Of the more than 80,000 who started out, only around 7,000 reached their destination: the others had died, or had to abandon the trek in the face of hostile armies and immensely difficult terrain including marshes, mountains, and swamps. But the end of the Long March was a crucial staging post for Mao's rise to paramount power. Up to that point, Mao had been an important member of the party (he had been at its first congress in Shanghai in 1921), but not the leader. The very fact that the party had been forced onto the Long March suggested that his rivals' strategies had failed, and his criticisms of the CCP's dominant ideological line, including the attention to urban over rural revolution, had real substance. Although Mao still had rivals, the march to Bao'an was an important stage in Mao's ascent.

The Long March was to become a glorious foundation myth of the Chinese Communist Party. In reality, it was a desperate retreat. Even after it was over, it still seemed likely that the ever more effective tactics of the Nationalists would have a good chance of finally crushing the Communists. But within months a series of secret dealings and double-crosses would change the political reality completely.

In 1935 the dictatorships in Europe stepped up their aggression. In Italy, Benito Mussolini, fired by visions of re-creating the Roman Empire, invaded Ethiopia, one of Africa's last independent states. In Germany, Hitler defied the provisions of the 1919 Treaty of Versailles that prevented rearmament, announcing that the army would be increased to half a million troops. In Moscow, Joseph Stalin observed these moves with alarm. The USSR had been weakened by political purges and mass starvation, and was in no shape to deal with an invasion either from Germany in the west or Japan in the east. On August 1, 1935, the USSR and its international organization, the Comintern, declared a worldwide front against fascism. The CCP was to abandon its policy of opposition to Chiang and give him its full support.[23]

Chiang and Mao both understood that Moscow's new line had the potential to change Chinese domestic politics utterly. For the Communists, it was galling to have to embrace a former ally who had turned on them without warning just a decade earlier. And Chiang also knew that his hope of finally crushing the CCP might well be slipping away. A war with Japan was now likely, and if it happened, he would need Soviet assistance to defend China. To serve that end, he might have to abandon any hope of destroying the final Communist holdouts, even though the party had been greatly weakened by the Nationalists.

Parallel negotiations among Chiang, the Soviets, and the CCP continued through the summer and autumn of 1936. Officially, the CCP obeyed Stalin's demand for unification with the Nationalists. Chiang, in turn, publicly declared that the Communists were nearly routed, and that he had no need to deal with them. But negotiations between the sides for a joint effort against Japan, with Zhou Enlai in the lead for the CCP, continued in secret. By early December both parties had agreed in principle that the Red Army would come under central military command and that the most radical Communist policies, such as confiscation of land, would be ended. The agreement had been made verbally, but not in writing, when Chiang Kai-shek decided to inspect troops at the northern city of Xi'an.[24]

On December 12, 1936, China awoke to extraordinary news: Chiang Kai-shek had been kidnapped. Troops serving under the militarist leaders Zhang Xueliang and Yang Hucheng had surrounded his villa and were holding him hostage. (Zhang had ruled Manchuria until the Japanese invasion of 1931. After that, although he had had to flee his home provinces, he had remained in command of substantial forces below the Great Wall.) The militarists demanded that Chiang cease attacking the Communists, and instead lead a united front against the Japanese.

For the next two weeks the Chinese public remained transfixed as a series of frantic negotiations took place. Chiang's old fellow-student He Yingqin now threatened to launch an attack on Xi'an to rescue the Generalissimo. James Bertram, a New Zealand journalist sympathetic to the CCP, was in Xi'an at the time, and recalled feeling a civil war was about to break out: "A fleet of Government planes roared low over the roofs of Sian [Xi'an]," he recorded. "The sound of their engines cannot have been very reassuring to the Young Marshal's prisoner."[25] However, Chiang's wife Song Meiling vetoed the idea of a full-scale assault on the city, fearing that her husband might be killed in the battle (and wondering whether that was He's intention, a ploy to seize power himself). She traveled to Xi'an and was able to stay with Chiang while he remained captive. Meanwhile, back in Nanjing, H. H. Kung took to the airwaves, "asserting that there could be no dealings with armed rebellion, no truce with the 'Communist bandits,' and assuring the nation that the dignity of the Government would certainly be upheld."[26] But Kung's reference to the Communists hid a more complex reality, as it emerged that Zhang Xueliang had made a terrible error.

In the previous months' confusion, Zhang had not been privy to the secret talks that had already laid the ground for an alliance between the Nationalists and Communists, and far from being hailed as a new leader for the nation, his actions were viewed as treachery by the Nationalist government and the wider public. Negotiations continued for two weeks, with both Chinese and foreign observers completely at a loss to know whether the country's leader would be released or killed.

Zhang Xueliang is today seen in China as a patriot who was shocked by the Generalissimo's unwillingness to face the "real" threat of Japan, and his insistence on fighting his fellow Chinese, the CCP. In this version of events, Zhang kidnapped Chiang in order to force a change of direction. In fact, Zhang's motivation may well have been more straightforward: Chiang was likely to deprive him of his military command. But the most important factor that saved Chiang was quite simple: few Chinese leaders would have benefited from his death or deposition. Many high-level members of the CCP, such as Mao, were very keen to execute Chiang after he was captured. But other figures were more wary, including former warlord opponents of Chiang such as Yan Xishan of Shanxi province. They realized that if Chiang was killed, there was nobody else of his stature to rule China. Chiang's great success, and his key to maintaining his own position, was in keeping control over a Nationalist Party that consisted of factions in strong disagreement with each other. If Chiang died, potential successors such as T. V. Soong were unlikely to command wide support. And if Wang Jingwei took over, there was a greater likelihood of accommodation with Japan.

One actor who found the prospect of Chiang's death terrifying was Stalin. His support for the Communists had been variable in quality and consistency, and had plunged the party into trouble as often as it had helped. Yet his advice was still taken very seriously. Now Stalin made it clear that the CCP had to settle its disagreement with Chiang and obtain his release. Stalin knew that Chiang's death would not be to the advantage of the small, beleaguered Communist Party. Instead, someone like Wang, assisted perhaps by He Yingqin, might well take over. A pro-Japanese China would place the USSR in grave danger. By 1936 the Anti-Comintern Pact (which Chiang had seriously considered joining) threatened to encircle the USSR with a hostile Germany on one side and Japan on the other. If China also turned toward the Axis, then the Soviet Red Army might have to fight a war — without allies — on two fronts. Since Stalin had spent much of the 1930s purging the Red Army of its best officers, this could have been disastrous. Whatever else happened, Chiang must be restored to power. He was anti-Communist, but had swallowed his principles enough to establish diplomatic relations with the USSR in 1933. More important, he was implacably anti-Japanese.[27]

The abduction of Chiang mesmerized China. Had Zhang Xueliang realized that his goal of a united front had in effect already been agreed, he might never have kidnapped Chiang at all. In that sense, Zhang was a victim of the tendency of both Chiang and the top CCP leaders, including Mao and Zhou, to keep their plans secret and also to pursue several lines of strategy simultaneously and sometimes contradictorily. In the end it was Zhou Enlai who negotiated Chiang's release. Chiang gave his assurance that he would now lead an all-party resistance against Japan. To the public, it looked as if Chiang had been compelled into an alliance against the Japanese, but in fact the terms of this arrangement were very similar to those agreed upon in secret before the kidnapping took place.

When Chiang was released, there was an outpouring of national rejoicing. Despite the many flaws in Chiang's government, the public had been forced to contemplate China without the Generalissimo and realized that it would be a weak and vulnerable country indeed. By escaping the threat on his life, Chiang had made himself indispensable. The American ambassador, Nelson T. Johnson, wrote of the startling boost to Chiang's fortunes in a report to Secretary of State Cordell Hull just a month after the kidnapping. "Whereas the outstanding developments during the first half of 1936 increased the precariousness of China's position," Johnson suggested, "the significant events of the second half, in their larger aspects, have had the opposite effect." He suggested that several factors had "tended to unify and strengthen the Republic and even to cause the Japanese, at least temporarily, to adopt a decidedly less aggressive policy towards China." Among those factors were Chiang's success in putting down an attempted uprising by the southwestern faction of militarists, as well as a strong defense of Suiyuan province in north China against Japanese attempts to expand into the area, which provoked "an amazing manifestation of nationalism." But entirely unpredictably, the other factor was the outcome of the Xi'an crisis, which "fostered another spontaneous outburst of nationalism throughout the country and caused universal rejoicing when the Generalissimo was released on Christmas Day."[28] Chiang's moment of greatest peril turned out to be his most triumphant.

Chiang did exact retribution on his kidnappers: Zhang was placed under house arrest and only released on Taiwan in 1990, more than half a century later. But Chiang did not go back on the idea of a new united front. It was clear to him that the threat from Japan was simply too great to allow another civil war to break out. Under the terms of the new United Front between the Nationalists and Communists, the armed forces of both sides would cease action against one another and would make preparations for war against a foreign invader.

The atmosphere on the other side of the Sea of Japan was becoming yet more turbulent. On February 16, 1936, young army officers attempted to overthrow the government, which they claimed was doing too little to relieve poverty at home and build up Japan's military strength. They managed to assassinate senior figures including Finance Minister Takahashi Korekiyô. Prime Minister Okada Keisuke only escaped because the plotters murdered his brother-in-law by mistake. Although the coup failed and its ringleaders were executed, there was much sympathy for their cause in high circles, leading to greater political tension.[29]

Japanese politicians became yet more determined to show a strong hand in China. Hirota Kôki became prime minister just two weeks after the attempted coup. His government became more and more concerned that if China were not pacified, it would stand in the way of a future Japanese confrontation with the Soviet Union. In late 1935, the Comintern had made Japan one of the areas of key concentration for their activities, and clashes had begun to arise on the border between Manchukuo and the eastern USSR. "Japan is destined sooner or later to clash with the Soviet Union," said Itagaki Seishirô (then chief of staff of the Kwantung Army) to Foreign Minister Arita Hachirô, "and the attitude of China at that time will gravely influence operations."[30] "Japan is extremely concerned over the current situation in north China," stated one army spokesman on May 15, "particularly the menace of the Communist army, which is advocating an anti-Japanese campaign . . . If . . . it became necessary to cope with an emergency, we are concerned that we could not . . . be able to carry out our full responsibilities." It was true that there had been thrusts into the area by Communist armies, as well as fears about the safety of Japanese residents. But these fears now gave the Japanese army an opportunity to place a new force in north China whose commander would be appointed directly by Tokyo.[31]

By spring of 1936, the Japanese increased the number of their troops in north China from 2,000 to a permanent brigade of 5,600, with troops based around major cities including Tianjin and Beiping. Throughout 1936, further incidents of violence took place against Japanese in various parts of China, all of which further fueled Japanese demands to increase their armed presence in China. In August 1937, the top Japanese civilian and military leadership agreed to a fundamental set of demands that they would make of China, including an anti-Communist military pact, the lowering of tariffs on Japanese imports, and the employment of Japanese military "advisers." The demands were part of a more wide-ranging general statement of policy, which included the longer-term conviction of the army that they must go to war with the USSR and the determination by the navy that Japan should expand its influence in Southeast Asia.[32] However, discussions between Chinese foreign minister Zhang Qun and Japanese ambassador Kawagoe Shigeru over the next few months ended with no agreement between the two sides. The first months of 1937 saw a more moderate civilian prime minister in Tokyo, Hayashi Senjûrô, but military commanders in the field remained strident in their opposition to China's Nationalist government.

On March 3, 1937, the Chinese foreign minister, Chiang's old classmate and friend Zhang Qun, perceived as moderate in his attitude toward Japan, was replaced by Wang Chonghui, a former judge at the World Court in The Hague, who seemed to endorse a tougher line toward Tokyo. The perceived change of mood in China then filtered back into Japan, souring public faith in the moderate Hayashi Senjûrô government (which had replaced Hirota's in January 1937), particularly as a string of isolated anti-Japanese incidents in China in the spring of 1937 were interpreted by Japanese politicians and public as part of a wider conspiracy.[33] On June 4, 1937, the Tokyo government fell, and a new government was appointed in which Prince Konoye Fumimarô became premier, and Hirota Kôki, a hard-liner, was now made foreign minister. Meanwhile, Japanese influence in north China continued to consolidate. While the region was technically under Chiang's government, in practice it was the Japanese who controlled it, mostly through uneasy agreements and understandings with local Chinese commanders who were as wary of Chiang as they were of Tokyo. Central Army troops whose commanders were based in Nanjing were forbidden to move north of the Huai River.

China was still at peace. But just a month later, on July 7, 1937, reports came in of clashes between the Chinese 29th Army and the Japanese North China Garrison Army, at a small village named Wanping.

Although neither side knew it, the Second World War in Asia had begun.

PART II

DISASTER

Chapter 4

THIRTY-SEVEN DAYS IN SUMMER:
THE OUTBREAK OF WAR

WANPING DOES NOT LOOK like the sort of place where the destinies of nations are decided. Even today, it is an unremarkable village about 15 kilometers southwest of Beijing (Beiping). Back in 1937 it was practically countryside. It does, however, have one impressive feature, a granite bridge decorated with the carved heads of nearly five hundred stone lions, which drew the attention of the Venetian traveler Marco Polo, who called it "one of the finest bridges in the world." This endorsement gave it the name by which it is best known in the West, the Marco Polo Bridge. In Chinese, it is known as Lugouqiao.

In the summer of 1937 the area around Lugouqiao was heavily populated by rival troops. The Chinese 29th Army was under the command of local strongman Song Zheyuan. Also positioned nearby were soldiers of the Japanese North China Garrison Army. The Japanese were allowed to deploy their military in the area because of agreements made after the Boxer Rebellion of 1900, permitting foreign powers to station troops that would protect them against another uprising. The relationship between the two sides was very uneasy, and Song himself was in a difficult position, caught between the government in Nanjing and the Japanese. Chiang's government wanted Song to refuse to cede any further ground to Japan, but at the same time not to provoke a diplomatic incident; and Song needed to compromise with the Japanese to preserve his own base of power.[1]

In July 1937 diplomats stationed in northern China sensed something in the air. "Rumors have been current in Peiping [Beiping] during the past week of possible disorders being created by disgruntled Chinese or Japanese Nationals," wrote the counselor in the US Embassy. "The rumors seem primarily due to the uneasiness which has developed among local Chinese as a result of Sung's lengthening absence."[2] The counselor's judgment was that General Song [Sung] was away from base because he was trying to avoid the Japanese, who wanted to pressure him into allowing them to dominate more of north China.

On the evening of July 7 Japanese troops started firing in the area around Wanping. This was not surprising in itself: the foreign powers in north China had been granted the right to carry out military maneuvers when they chose. But this time the Japanese troops went further. The local Japanese commander declared that one of his men had gone missing, and demanded entry to Wanping to search for him. The accusation was clear: the Chinese must have kidnapped or killed him. Over the past few years, the Japanese had become used to making demands of Chinese troops, and their orders were generally obeyed. But this time Song's troops refused, and low-level skirmishes broke out. It seemed likely that they would die down again; many such clashes had dissipated before, usually after the Chinese had made some concession. However, in distant central China, Chiang Kai-shek decided that it was time for a different sort of response.

When he heard the news of the fighting near Beiping, Chiang was not in Nanjing, but at the resort of Guling at Mount Lushan, in Jiangxi province. Chiang used Lushan as a country retreat during the hot summer months, and throughout the 1930s he invited his advisers there to plan for a future war with Japan. By the summer of 1937, this preparation had become urgent. "China has a responsibility to strengthen itself," he wrote in his diary. "Only if we develop the psychology that having to fight is inevitable may we perhaps avoid fighting."[3]

Chiang was meeting with his Military Council when he heard the news that Song's troops had clashed with the Japanese. "The dwarf bandits have attacked at Lugouqiao," he added in his diary, using the derogatory term for the Japanese that had first emerged in the imperial era. "This is the time for the determination to fight."[4] In his diary, Chiang also reflected on the meaning of the fighting at the Marco Polo Bridge: "Is there going to be trouble for Song Zheyuan? Are the Japanese trying to bring about independence for north China?"[5] He then added, more pensively still: "Is this the time to accept the challenge?"[6]

At first, three of Song Zheyuan's senior officers cabled Nanjing, telling Chiang that they could not comply with Japanese demands to withdraw from the bridge, "because of the consequences for national sovereignty."[7] However, despite a show of defiance, the Chinese and Japanese local commanders at Wanping began to discuss a cease-fire. It seemed possible that the Marco Polo Bridge skirmish would be resolved quickly.

Chiang was confronted with a fateful question: Was the two-day struggle really just a minor skirmish, like so many before it, or did it herald the start of another major Japanese assault on Chinese territory, like the Manchurian crisis of 1931? If he decided that it was the former, then tensions would quickly cool. After all, north China was not really under Nationalist control, but dominated by a patchwork of regimes run by Chiang's Chinese rivals and the Japanese military. By letting the fighting go, Chiang would not be immediately worse off. But if he decided that the incident was more serious, a push by Japan to invade and occupy yet more of northern China, leaving the Nationalist heartland in central China vulnerable, then Chiang had a grave decision to make: whether or not to declare war.

The choice was not entirely Chiang's. Indeed, since the occupation of Manchuria, his options had been narrowing. As Chiang received the news in Lushan, he had to weigh up a complex range of factors, domestic and international, confronting him that hot July.

First, and most immediately, it seemed likely that any compromise settlement would involve his government formally ceding control of the former capital. This was not like giving up Manchuria. The establishment of Manchukuo had been a huge blow to China's prestige, but not a disaster. Chiang had all but recognized the Japanese client state by 1933. Beiping was a different matter. Under its former name of Beijing, the city had been a national capital for centuries. Although its political importance had waned, it was still a place of immense cultural and emotional significance to many Chinese. The city also had strategic importance: it was the major rail interchange for northern China, connecting the north of China to the inland commercial city of Wuhan, and allowing rail traffic to travel in all four directions of the compass. If Beiping fell under Japanese control, then an order from Tokyo could send thousands of troops from Korea and Manchukuo into the heart of the mainland. If Chiang surrendered the city, he would cede north China for a generation, and put the Nationalist heartland in great danger. Chiang recognized this in his diary entry for July 10: "This is the turning point for existence or obliteration."[8]

If it were just Beiping, that would be one thing, but Chiang feared that the city would be just one more conquest in an ever-lengthening list of Japanese provocations in China. Ever since 1931 the journalist Du Zhongyuan (who had been imprisoned for publishing anti-Japanese rhetoric in 1935) and his fellow exiles from occupied Manchuria had used their power in the press to argue that Chiang should be more active and launch a military campaign to recapture the northeast. Despite the rhetoric of "30 million compatriots" under the "iron hooves" of Japanese imperialism, Chiang had not changed his position on resistance: although the Chinese public felt sympathy, Manchuria was simply too distant to arouse the sentiments of the wider population for all-out war. Then, between 1933 and 1935, it had seemed possible that Japan would be content with its gains so far, and that Nationalist China could live, at least for a while, with Manchukuo on its borders. But from 1935 Japanese influence in north China had grown, and it had become clear that they regarded the entire region as their own territory. Chiang was increasingly convinced that Japan would not rest until all China was a client state. If he did not confront them now, then the moment would surely have to come soon. The influential Chinese newspaper *Shenbao* had published an editorial on July 9 starkly entitled "Yet Another Invasion," and warning: "This act is clearly a planned invasive action by the Japanese. This act is of a truly serious nature, and should shock the world."[9]

Yet challenging Japan would be a highly risky venture — possibly a suicidal one. Chiang could expect very little support from the wider world. The year 1937 was a grim one around the globe. In Europe, the political momentum appeared to be with the dictatorships. Hitler's Nazi Party had re-created Germany as a strong tyranny instead of the weak Weimar democracy that had collapsed in 1933. Mussolini's Italy likewise seemed orderly and powerful. Many observers ignored the violence and racism that underpinned these regimes to draw the conclusion that authoritarian government was the way of the future. In the USSR, Stalin's regime had turned its rage inward, and the country had been devastated by a series of purges against its own elites, leading to the execution or exile of millions of citizens, from top military leaders to ordinary schoolteachers. Although most of Europe remained in a sullen peace, the world was also riveted by the Spanish Civil War, in which the Republican forces of the elected government were battling the Nationalist forces of General Franco. The Republicans relied on minimal assistance from the USSR, while Nazi Germany and fascist Italy provided support for Franco. On the sidelines were the democracies, Britain and France, and Chiang could see clearly that they would be offering no help. Spain had already learned that the United States was in no mood for international intervention.

Franklin D. Roosevelt had been reelected president just a few months earlier, but had spent much of early 1937 engaged in a wounding and unsuccessful struggle to give himself greater powers to change the composition of the US Supreme Court, while the Depression continued to haunt American life. To return to a war in Europe would be unpopular; to enter a conflict in China was close to unthinkable. So if Chiang wanted to fight back against Japan, he would have to do it on his own. He would also need to calculate how long China could last alone in a war against Japan.

Chiang's hopes lay with his best troops. Cabling his son Ching-kuo, Chiang told him not to worry about an invasion from Japan, because he had "the means to counter them."[10] Chiang was referring to troops trained by von Seeckt and von Falkenhausen, his two German military advisers.[11] It was certainly true that improvements had been made. However, Chiang's cable was laced with bravado. The reforms needed much longer to bed in, and the number of officers who had gone through training was still small, only 30,000 in number.

Instead, much of Chiang's strategy would have to rely on troops provided by his supposed subordinates. He not only had to assess how useful such troops would actually be, but also how many commanders would in fact be loyal to him. Song Zheyuan had extensive contacts with the Japanese, and seemed to miss no opportunity to bolster his own position at the expense of Chiang's.[12] Yan Xishan, who led the major inland province of Shanxi, had been known as a progressive warlord. But he had also been part of an anti-Chiang alliance during the 1930 Northern Plains civil war, and had played the Communists and the Japanese off against the Nationalists in the years leading up to 1937. The alliance with the Communists was also very fragile; despite the official message of cooperation, neither side truly trusted the other, and memories of the debacle at Xi'an were still powerful on both sides.[13]

This unappetizing menu left Chiang with a stark choice: either he acknowledged that north China was lost, or he fought back. But by fighting, the war would undoubtedly expand from a local conflict to an all-out confrontation between the two powers.

The problem was that Chiang did not have time on his side. China did not — as Chiang would have wished — have sufficient time to professionalize more of its military, neutralize the separatist tendencies of its militarist leaders, and strengthen the economic and fiscal base of the country.

And the scale of preparation for war in Japan by 1937 made the Chinese efforts look minor indeed. During the attempted coup of February 1936, Japan's finance minister, Takahashi Korekiyô, had been assassinated. A consequence of his death was a major increase in military spending.[14] Japan's government and public were both increasingly fueled by a desire to "teach China a lesson," and regarded its increasing unification and the growing sense of nationalism with alarm. Unlike in Nazi Germany or fascist Italy, there was no single figure in Japan, no *Duce* or *Führer*, whose personal megalomania lay at the heart of foreign policy. Instead, Japan had ended up with a toxic situation where most of its politicians, military and public, had become infected by "war fever."

Military spending now took up nearly half Japan's total budget. Furthermore, recovery from the Depression was fueled in part by growth in heavy industry, much of which made products that would be useful to any future war effort. At home, the media publicized the idea that Japan was being surrounded by hostile powers who wished to prevent its rise. In 1934, the Tokyo government abrogated the 1930 London Naval Treaty, which was supposed to restrain the size of Japan's navy in comparison with those of the US and the British Empire. Now nothing but budget would prevent Japan expanding its naval capabilities.

In June 1937, after some six years of Japanese policymakers blowing hot and cold toward China, a new man was appointed as prime minister. It fell to Prince Konoye Fumimaro to decide how to respond to the Marco Polo Bridge incident.

Konoye was an aristocratic civilian with abundant diplomatic experience. He had attended the Paris Peace Conference in 1919 and come away from it convinced that the nations of Asia would never receive a just settlement from the Western powers. Konoye came from one of the noblest families in Japan, so close to the emperor that he even spoke in the rather stilted language that was reserved for the royal family and a few close courtiers. He was a cultured man, who had translated works by Oscar Wilde in his youth, and he had an aristocratic temperament. He rarely held meetings before eleven o'clock in the morning (a stark contrast to Chiang, whose military training and natural asceticism meant that he regularly rose at 5:00 a.m.). Yet Konoye was also a weak man, unable to stand up to people who opposed him. His secretary recalled him as "Hamlet-like" and "lonely." The aristocratic veteran politician Prince

Saionji Kinmochi declared that Konoye lacked the one thing he needed in dealing with the army: "strength" *(chikara).*[15]

Konoye's first test on the "China question" came just a month after his appointment. He found his cabinet split on the matter of how to respond to the Marco Polo Bridge incident. The senior General Staff officer Mutô Akira and the chief of the military affairs department of the Ministry of War, Tanaka Shin'ichi, advocated an escalation of hostilities: now was the time to strike hard at China and destroy Chiang Kai-shek's regime. Ishiwara Kanji, who headed the operations division of the General Staff, was much more cautious. This was ironic, as Ishiwara had been the mastermind behind the invasion of Manchuria in 1931, but he now argued that Japan was not ready for war with China, and that opening a war with the Nanjing government might even make Japan more vulnerable to the USSR. One should not exaggerate the difference between the two sides — even "moderates" in the Japanese government believed that China should ultimately come under Japanese influence, but they disagreed on the timing. On July 9 Sugiyama Gen, the minister of war (known as "the toilet door" because it was said by his colleagues that one could push him in any direction, like the door in a Japanese-style bathroom stall), asked for five divisions to be mobilized for deployment in north China. The request was denied — but only for the moment.[16]

Back at the Marco Polo Bridge, the local Chinese and Japanese commanders were beginning to discuss a cease-fire. The Shanghai press was still trying to determine who was responsible for the incident. "Who started the firing is still not clear," the *North-China Daily News* of July 10 declared, "but it is considered probable that the Chinese, guarding the railway bridge-head, seeing an armed party advancing along the embankment in the dark, challenged them and on receiving no reply, opened fire, thinking them to be plain-clothes men or Japanese staging a real attack."[17] But by now, the fate of a bridge near Beiping was beside the point. The leaders of both China and Japan were seeing the events through a much wider lens. On July 10 Chiang noted: "The Japanese have attacked at Lugouqiao, but their goals don't stop there. We've already sent troops north; perhaps we can restrain their ambitions." He went on: "If we don't show preparation and determination, then we can't resolve this peacefully."[18]

On July 11 an American diplomat met He Yingqin, Chiang's minister of war, and asked him whether the confrontation at Lugouqiao meant war. He Yingqin replied that it was up to the Japanese, and that if they continued their "bandit methods" then war would be inevitable. The diplomat put it to He that "even at a sacrifice" it was worth postponing war for a couple of years to strengthen preparations. But He was firm: it would be hard to know exactly when China was truly ready, and if they were attacked, then they would fight.[19]

It was not just the Americans who urged caution on Chiang. Plenty of his colleagues did too. Wang Jingwei had spent most of the 1930s trying to find a way to avoid war with Japan. Now he advised Chiang not to escalate the conflict. Another voice advocating patience belonged to Zhou Fohai. In 1937 Zhou was deputy director of propaganda for the Nationalists. But he had taken a tortuous path to get there; as a young man, Zhou had been a founding member of the Chinese Communist Party, but had swiftly left it to join the Nationalists. Even so, he retained friendships with prominent Communists. When one of the CCP's founders, Chen Duxiu, was released from prison in August 1937, Zhou was one of his first visitors. However, during the Nanjing decade, his politics drifted much more closely toward Wang Jingwei's. Within a few months, their association would have huge consequences for both men.

In the days after fighting broke out on July 7, Zhou was on his way to join Chiang at Lushan. On arrival, he wrote in his diary: "I fear that an external issue will evolve into a domestic issue, which makes it harder for the central government to deal with. I'm disappointed."[20] Even as he took in the atmosphere at Lushan, Zhou continued to hope that matters would be settled peacefully. The mood was convivial, as he attended a banquet given jointly by Chiang and Wang. Even though resistance was discussed at a meeting on July 17, there did not seem to be a desire for war. "About seven people spoke," Zhou noted, "but none of them was impressive." The next day, he wrote that he had heard that the Japanese ambassador to China, Kawagoe Shigeru, had been in contact with the Chinese Foreign Ministry, trying to calm the situation down and frame the conflict as a regional matter. "Based on this," Zhou wrote with a sense of hope, "I reckon the incident won't expand."[21]

Zhou also took the opportunity to greet "old friends" in Lushan, although the term was laced with a certain irony. For these friends were the CCP leaders Zhou Enlai and Lin Boqu, whom he had first come to know in the days of the first United Front. In less then twenty years, the twists and turns of Chinese politics had meant that Zhou Fohai was now firmly allied with Chiang and Wang, until very recently sworn enemies of the CCP and all it stood for. Although they were all temporarily united against the new enemy, the fundamental differences between them could not be resolved even by long-standing friendships. Still, Zhou hoped that war might be put off, at least for a while.

But Chiang wrote in his diary on July 19 that he would not back down:

> Everyone believes it's dangerous to make a public declaration of war . . . but to turn danger into safety, this is the only way . . . I don't care about safety or danger; this is our very last remedy against the Japanese dwarfs. But only my wife agrees with me.[22]

As events escalated in July 1937, the Marco Polo Bridge fighting began to resemble the shooting of the Archduke Franz Ferdinand at Sarajevo in June 1914. It was not inevitable that that particular incident would escalate into continental war. But if it had not, the balance of power and wider tensions within Europe would probably have precipitated war shortly afterward. In the same way, even if the fighting near Beiping had been resolved at a local level, it had become clear that China and Japan were heading toward conflict sooner rather than later. From July 7, events would no longer be driven by patched-up deals between local Chinese strongmen and trigger-happy Japanese officers tussling with each other in towns and villages in Hebei and Chahar provinces. Instead, the national capitals — Nanjing and Tokyo — would make the decisions that would commit their nations to war or peace.

Far away, in Washington, DC, the Chinese ambassador to the US, the former premier and foreign minister Wang Zhengting (C. T. Wang), held a luncheon at his home in Twin Oaks for Stanley K. Hornbeck, the State Department's top specialist on East Asian affairs and a close adviser to Secretary of State Cordell Hull. Also present on that afternoon of July 10 was H. H. Kung, China's minister of finance (and Chiang's brother-in-law). Hornbeck made a comment that was flattering, but that also constituted a warning. He acknowledged the modernization of China under the Nationalists, and observed that progress in "finance, in road building, in railway construction" meant that "in general, things in China seemed to be going along extraordinarily well." Therefore, he wondered aloud, would it not be better "to continue along this course of concentrating its attention and energies upon reconstructive effort rather than for China to start arguments with foreign governments?" If China just took more time to strengthen itself, then other powers would have to take the Chinese position seriously. Hornbeck had a point. Just a few days earlier, Kung had been persuading a group of New York investors that the new Nationalist China was a sound place for their investments: "China is no longer the disunited, disorderly China of the war lord days."[23] But now, Kung quickly shot back with a rather different message. "China was preparing for what he felt was an inevitable war with Japan," Hornbeck reported, inevitable because with each year, "Japan would become as compared with China comparatively stronger." Wang and Kung both made a prescient observation: "some day the United States would have to face Japanese aggression, unless that aggression should be checked by China"; therefore, the US should help China now.[24] But Hornbeck, while sympathetic, was careful to point out that the US would only intervene where its own national interests were at stake. It was clear that as far as the US government was concerned, Japanese aggression in China was not a priority issue in the summer of 1937.

Meanwhile, the temperature rose in Tokyo. On July 11 Prince Konoye announced at a press conference that Japan was mobilizing troops in north China. Ironically, on the same day, the local Chinese and Japanese commanders announced that they had agreed on a cease-fire. But it was no longer a local issue; Chiang's decision to move troops northward had become a signal for the Ministry of War to dispatch troops from Korea and Manchuria. Japanese public opinion was now in a frenzy. Three days later, Konoye addressed a meeting of prefectural governors. In his remarks he advised the Japanese public to be ready for the "worst eventuality." "Our strenuous efforts to reach an amicable settlement of the north China incident have to all appearances failed," Konoye declared. "Thus, the lives and properties of our co-nationals in Peiping, Tientsin, and the neighboring areas are in danger." The minister of war, General Sugiyama Gen, added that the "real cause" of the affair was "the anti-Japanese campaign and education, strenuously carried on by the Nanking government for years."[25] A spokesman for the Kwantung Army added his own menace: "We are prepared to resort to the most extreme measures if further provocation is given." As the Kwantung Army had occupied Manchuria in a lightning strike in 1931, this was a warning worth heeding.[26]

The Chinese government made it abundantly clear that it was mobilizing for a major war. On July 13 "large-scale air-raid defence manoeuvres designed to test the immunity of the Peiping–Hankow and the Lunghai Railways to air raids" were staged in Zhengzhou, in central China. A few days later, practice gave way to reality, as it was reported that "Japanese military planes . . . made three separate attacks on Chinese trains at various points on the Peiping–Hankow Railway."[27]

The Chinese public was becoming increasingly incensed. Shanghai's civil society began to demand resistance to the Japanese: "Numerous Chinese public bodies here dispatched telegrams to the 29th Army in the north, expressing their sympathy and urging the soldiers to defend the country . . . The Civic Association, the Chinese Bankers Association, the Native Bankers Association, and the Chinese Chamber of Commerce have sent $1,000 to the defenders of Lukouchiao [Luguoqiao]."[28] Even small incidents could suddenly flare up. The tensions between the two sides meant that a dispute between a Chinese rickshaw driver and a Japanese client over a fare in early July led to mob violence in Shanghai.[29]

By late July the situation had moved far beyond a few locally garrisoned soldiers taking potshots at each other. Japan's Imperial Army Staff headquarters gave orders to mobilize, while offering its final ultimatums to Chiang's government. The increasingly worried Shanghai community observed the lines being drawn in north China:

> Although it was at first hoped that the Sino-Japanese crisis was yielding to moderating influences, the situation developed on July 18 on unfavourable lines . . . It was felt that the next two days would see the issues of peace or war decided . . . In a virtual ultimatum, delivered to the Nanking government at 11.30 o'clock last night, Japan requested the immediate cessation of "provocative activities" as well as the discontinuance of "interference" with the execution by the local authorities of the terms for a settlement of the Lukouchiao incident of July 7.[30]

The Japanese were reluctant to declare war openly. But they wanted to neutralize China fast, and they hoped that they still had a chance to confine the conflict to the north: the Japanese Army had stated in a resolution that its aims were to eliminate the northern Chinese armies "in one go," and occupy the region north of the city of Baoding, some 140 kilometers south of Beiping.[31] At the disposal of the Japanese was the Kwantung Army, along with local forces that would either collaborate with them or at least not stand in their way, some 130,000 troops in total or more.[32]

On July 26 the Japanese struck. Beiping came under attack, as did Tianjin, about one hundred kilometers away:

> Tremendous fires were started as incendiary bombs struck the principal Chinese buildings [in Tianjin], including Nankai University, the Central Station and the headquarters of the Peace Preservation Corps between the East Station and the International Bridge. The flames were visible for miles . . . As [Japanese bombers] performed their mission, a terror-stricken mass of Chinese fled from the Chinese City to the security of the concession.[33]

The cities fell swiftly, Beiping on July 28 and Tianjin on the 30th. Chiang was shaken. "The dwarf bandits took Beiping and Tianjin with great ease," he wrote in the monthly reflection section of his diary. "This was not what I expected. But if they gained it with such ease today, then how do we know they won't lose it again with ease on another day? . . . When it comes to diplomacy with the dwarfs, you have to be firm."[34]

Chiang did not deploy his own Central Army, instead leaving the fate of the north in the hands of the generals who had dominated the region, including Yan Xishan and Song Zheyuan. Chiang did put one of his personal allies into the army: General Tang Enbo, who, like Chiang, had been trained in Japan. Yet Chiang also hampered Tang; he refused to allow first-rate troops to serve under him, saving them for the coming war in Shanghai and the Yangtze valley. As the best troops were very limited in number, this was perhaps understandable, but it put Tang in an almost impossible situation. The Japanese Kwantung Army deployed more than 90,000 of its troops, vastly outnumbering the Chinese, and were supplemented by more than 60,000 other troops, including those of the Mongolian Prince De (Demchugdongrub). With inferior forces, Tang fought hard at Nankou in Hebei province, losing 26,000 men, but he was unable to defend the city even with Yan Xishan's support. The fighting in north China went on into August, although it soon became clear that the region was lost.

Chiang did have another option, albeit a very risky one: he could now enlist his former enemies, the Communists. On July 13 he received those visitors whose arrival would have been unthinkable just a few months earlier: top-level Communist officials including Zhou Enlai, Bo Gu, and Lin Boqu. They had been tasked with negotiating a more concrete agreement between the Nationalist and Communist armies, and had come to meet senior Nationalists including Shao Lizi, Zhang Zhonghui, and Chiang himself. The Lugouqiao fighting now made this task all the more urgent. Immediately after the Marco Polo Bridge incident, Mao Zedong and several senior colleagues had issued a statement urging Chiang to stand firm and fight, and pledging their support:

> The Japanese bandits have attacked Marco Polo Bridge as a step in carrying out their established plan of taking North China by military force. Our grief and indignation upon hearing this news are beyond description! . . . We respectfully implore you to issue strict orders to the Twenty-ninth Army to put up resistance with all its courage and might, and to carry out a general nationwide mobilization . . . The officers and men of the Red Army sincerely wish to give their all in the service of their country under your leadership, Mr. Chairman, to fight against the enemy.[35]

Yet both sides were cautious. Chiang did not want yet more troops who would not obey his commands, and the Communists, still wary after a decade of persecution by Chiang's forces, were unwilling to lose any control over the Red Army, which had been formed under conditions of great difficulty as the party fled from its Nationalist enemies. The Communists wanted cooperation, whereas Chiang's preferred term was "assimilation." Chiang wrote on July 27: "We mustn't let [the Red Army] be too independent."[36] Mao, in turn, had let his negotiators at Guling know that they must not cede too much: "We have decided to adopt the policy of holding no more talks with Chiang if he refuses to compromise."[37] Finally, the urgency of the moment forced an agreement. Chiang compromised, allowing the Communists to set up their own military headquarters. Mao then confirmed that reorganization would be completed before August 15, and specified that the CCP would provide three divisions of 45,000 men, along with 10,000 local troops who would defend various key points in the north, including the front in the northwestern province of Suiyuan.[38] On August 2 Chiang legalized the Red Army.

Of all the concessions that Chiang made to the Communists, the most important was permission to establish their own armed forces. Following their legalization, the Communist troops based in the northwest were renamed the Eighth Route Army. Under their commanders, including Lin Biao and He Long, the army would stand at the heart of the Communists' ability to maintain autonomous control of armed force. There were also a smaller number of troops in the south. In the summer of 1938, they would be designated the New Fourth Army. However, they were a guerrilla force initially so few in number that they struggled to reach their authorized troop level of 12,000 men, although within two years they would number 30,000.[39]

By now, Chiang had returned to Nanjing and called a meeting of the Military Affairs Commission, the forum in which the decision to go to war would be discussed. To symbolize that the new politics of cooperation against the Japanese was real, three major CCP leaders took the precarious flight to Nanjing to attend the meeting: Zhou Enlai, Red Army marshal Zhu De, and General Ye Jianying.[40] Mao instructed them to cooperate, but also to act with caution. He felt that in north China, the area of greatest CCP presence, the first line of defense should run through cities such as Zhangjiakou in Hebei and Qingdao, the seaport in Shandong. Cities such as Datong and Baoding would be the next priority. Mao also authorized the type of combat that would characterize the CCP's contribution to the war over the next seven years: "The Red Army and the other appropriate armed forces . . . may engage in guerrilla warfare." But Mao also sounded a wary note as he sent his comrades on their way into the camp of their former enemy, now reluctant ally: "You may come up with other ideas as opportunity offers, but not too many, and firmly grasp the essentials."[41]

Chiang then turned his mind to leveraging his new alliance with the CCP. His target was the Soviet Union. For years Chiang had been trying to bring the USSR into an alliance against Japan, even while he was attacking the CCP. (He assumed, rightly, that Stalin would regard Chiang's anti-Japanese stance as more important than his anti-Communist one.) Now, Chiang saw the agreement with the Chinese Communists as an opportunity to sign a nonaggression pact with the Soviets and hinder Japan's "dream" of further aggression in China; "otherwise not only will they control north China, but the whole country will become a second Manchukuo." Chiang was not starry-eyed about a pact with the Soviets. "Although there are dangers in allying with the Soviets," he reflected, if he did so, then "we would lose north China [to the Japanese] but not lose our national dignity, and they wouldn't be able to occupy it all. I'm choosing between two evils."[42]

Mao and the CCP also had to make a painful choice. They deferred dreams of revolution and entered an alliance with an old enemy. Mao's public statements at this time reflect the unease that he and his comrades felt at the sudden outbreak of conflict. "The authorities of north China from the very start resorted to the tortuous pursuit of compromise, without making sufficient preparations militarily," Mao declared at a rally on August 1, 1937. The "authorities" had also failed to harness popular anger against the Japanese. "The result of this behavior was that they lost Beiping and Tianjin!"[43] Clearly he was pointing a finger at figures such as Song Zheyuan, but he was also criticizing the Nationalists. He would not attack them openly on the eve of war, but he was doing his best to position the CCP as the "truly" patriotic party, and by implication associating Chiang with appeasement, weakness, and poor judgment.

The foreign community in China was not immune to the Nationalists' plight. They feared a war because of the disruption it would bring to their lives and businesses, but they could also see why Chiang had been forced to act. An editorial in the *North-China Daily News* made the point with biting sarcasm:

> It is impossible to withhold sympathy from the Japanese people. They have become so accustomed to the absence of any limit to the freedom with which their military . . . have been allowed to lay down the law and take action . . . that even the mild propositions now established by General Chiang Kai-shek must seem to them to constitute an astonishing defiance . . .
>   One thing is certain: if words mean anything, the Generalissimo has not stretched the sense of Chinese public opinion by a single letter . . . The sympathy of world opinion is with China. It recognizes that the choice of resistance by arms is not hers; it is being forced upon her by pressure which no nation could permit to proceed further unchecked without forfeiting whatever claim it might have to individual freedom.[44]

A later editorial also cast doubt on Japanese justifications. Konoye's explanation to the Diet (Parliament) that the Japanese expedition to China was to secure "cooperation in contributing to the development of Oriental culture" was met with hollow laughter by the Western press in Shanghai. The "blindness" of the Chinese government in refusing to cooperate with "the spread of Oriental Culture will, no doubt, be regarded in Tokyo as another example of Chinese 'insincerity.'"[45] Such sentiments might have persuaded Chiang that if he were to act, the foreign community would rally behind him against Japan, and that the move to war was a wise one.

On August 7 the Chinese government held a confidential Joint National Defense Meeting in Nanjing at the premises of the Lizhishe (the Society for Vigorous Practice of the Three Principles of Sun Yat-sen). The location was symbolic, reminding everyone present of the hard-won Chinese republic and its history, and what was at stake if the country were defeated by Japan. The participants represented the recent, tumultuous history of the Nationalist Party. All the major figures in Chinese Nationalist politics attended, including Wang Jingwei, former finance minister (and another of Chiang's brothers-in-law) T. V. Soong, and military strongman Yan Xishan, leader of Shanxi province.

The war minister, He Yingqin, gave a dry but necessary summary of the maneuvers made at Lugouqiao. The main event, however, was the address by Chiang Kai-shek, who was now uncompromising in his strong advocacy of war. Chiang made it clear that this was a struggle for the fate of the entire Chinese people. "If we can win this war," he declared to his elite audience, "then we can revive the country, and turn danger into security . . . but if China loses a war with Japan, then I fear it may take decades, or even centuries, to revive it." Objectively, he pointed out, the Japanese military was stronger than the Chinese; but the Japanese economy had real problems. "In spirit, the United States and Britain would help us," he added, "but as the Italian case shows, they're not reliable." (Chiang was referring to the failure of the Western democracies to prevent Fascist Italy's invasion of Abyssinia in 1935.)

Chiang then raised the question on everyone's mind:

> Many say that if we can resolve the problem in Hebei and Chahar [the two provinces of north China where the troops were being deployed], then China will be safe for fifty years . . . Some say that if we have a clear border around Manchukuo and Hebei-Chahar, then the Japanese won't invade further. This idea of a border is all right, and I dare say that if we did draw it up along the Great Wall then the Japanese wouldn't invade.[46]

But those who were trying to solve the problem with these makeshift ideas were missing the point, Chiang warned. The leaders should understand that they could not trust Japan, and that what Tokyo wanted was "to destroy China's international position in order to achieve its ambition of doing whatever it wants." Chiang reserved particular criticism for the "scholars" who advocated further appeasement: while he did not name them, it seems inevitable that he was thinking of Hu Shi and Jiang Menglin, both distinguished and prominent liberal intellectuals outside the government who had counseled Chiang to "bear the pain while seeking peace." Through late July into early August, Hu argued that Chiang should recognize the client state of Manchukuo. By doing this, he would win a further breathing space, and allow elements in Japan that were less enthusiastic about war, such as the interests of big business, to tip the scales away from conflict. It would also allow more time for Chiang to develop the Central Army and make it indestructible. A concession now, thought Hu, might guarantee fifty years of peace.[47] "I tell these scholars," Chiang warned, "that in a revolutionary war, the invaders will lose. The Japanese can see only materiel and troops; they can't see the spiritual aspect." Throughout the length of the war, Chiang would see the war as a spiritual, sacred trust, a continuation of the 1911 revolution symbolized by Sun Yat-sen. That trust inspired him to declare repeatedly that the war could be the making of a new China. It was also why, despite continued temptations in the darkest days of the war, he would refuse to surrender to Japan.

Chiang then issued the challenge in terms that were hard to turn down. "So, comrades, we need a decision. Do we fight, or shall we be destroyed?" Chiang may have been looking in the direction of the next speaker: Wang Jingwei. But Wang did not speak up in favor of peace. Despite his supposedly pro-Japanese reputation, he had always advocated a strong, independent China. Now, whether under pressure or out of conviction, he supported the war. Wang agreed that "China had come to a crisis point. Only through war can we seek survival; there's no possibility of a conditional peace." Wang then advocated the acceleration of military production, and echoed Chiang's thoughts on the contrast between the two sides: "Let us not worry about material losses. The spiritual effects will last forever." Wang was followed by Zhang Boquan, who echoed this sentiment. "This war is a symbol of civilization and progress," he said. "On the surface, it's destruction, but its significance is for a new, progressive reconstruction."[48]

Chiang had the room right where he wanted it. But he was not done yet. With characteristic moral fervor, he now proceeded to tell China's government how hard the task before them was, and how far they fell short:

> Compared with the Japanese level of preparation, it's not that we are not 10 percent as prepared, we're not even 1 percent as prepared. No wonder the general population is panicking . . . All generals and officials must face up to their responsibilities.

Chiang gave specifics: official reports were claiming that air-raid shelters in Nanjing were close to completion, yet an aerial inspection suggested that nine out of ten were in fact exposed and vulnerable to attack. "From the air-raid shelters," he scolded, "you can infer how other things have been done." Another example was the evacuation of bureaucrats' families from Nanjing; instead of being carried out in an orderly fashion, there was such chaos that the railway stations were jammed solid with people. Instead, the leaders should look at their enemy, the Japanese, and see how their "discipline" had helped them prepare for war. Furthermore, there would be problems of implementation; it was all very well to order people to build defensive walls or use sandbags, but were there the financial resources to supply the materials for these defenses? Chiang used a phrase — *shishi qiushi* — "seek truth from facts" — that would later be associated with the two most powerful Communist figures of the century, Mao Zedong and Deng Xiaoping. But the meaning was clear: the war could only be won if people paid attention to the situation on the ground, as opposed to sending out meaningless orders or reams of paperwork. "That's it," Chiang snapped, as he ended his diatribe.[49]

At the end of the meeting, those who favored war were told to stand up. Among those who stood were Liu Xiang, military commander of Sichuan province in the west of China, which would within months become the center of China's resistance. Liu had offered troops from his native province, declaring that over 5 million of them could be conscripted within two years. Also standing was Yan Xishan, another bitter military rival of Chiang, but one who now accepted his arguments that the war must come. And then there was Wang Jingwei, the man who had for so long tried to keep China out of a conflict with Japan.[50] He too voted for war. In fact, everyone stood up. In truth, it would have been hard not to.

The next few days saw frantic military preparations. Chiang had finally abandoned any hope that the conflict in north China might be contained, and peace restored. His own best troops were located in central China, under the control of his government in Nanjing. It was time to take the war to the Japanese, and in a place of Chiang's choosing: the great port city of Shanghai.

Chapter 5

THE BATTLE FOR SHANGHAI

I N LATE OCTOBER 1937 all of Shanghai's inhabitants, Chinese and foreign alike, looked out on a city transformed. Within the space of three months, China's most open, lively, and cosmopolitan center had been turned into a charnel house. A report of October 28 described the scene:

> Stunned Shanghai watched with shocked horror yesterday the awful aftermath of hostilities in Chapei, appalled as fire after fire broke out, from before dawn all through the day, until the whole of its northern Chinese city was wrapped in flame. Numbed crowds gazed upwards at the four-mile-long cliff of smoke, towering many thousands of feet into the air and drifting in the light southerly wind, throwing its gloomy pall over the countryside as far as Woosung, and beyond over the Yangtze River where Japan's mighty fleet lies concentrated.[1]

It had been clear for weeks that both China and Japan were squaring up for a war in central China. The Japanese had been diverting naval troops from the north to boost their numbers in Shanghai, and by early August they had assembled over 8,000 troops. A few days later, some thirty-two naval vessels had arrived. On July 31 Chiang declared that "all hope for peace has been lost."[2] Chiang had been reluctant to commit his best forces to defend north China, an area that he had never truly controlled; Shanghai, on the other hand, was central to his strategy for the war against Japan. Chiang would use his very best troops, the 87th and 88th Divisions, units trained by generals advised by the German von Falkenhausen, who had high hopes that they would do well against the Japanese. In doing so, Chiang would show his own people and the wider world that the Chinese could — and would — resist the invader.

Chiang had not taken the decision to open a new front in Shanghai lightly. Built on two banks of the Huangpu River, the city was the junction between the Pacific Ocean to the east and the great Yangtze River that wound thousands of kilometers inland to the west. Shanghai was a distillation of everything that made China modern, from industry, to labor relations, to connections with the outside world. And although foreign diplomatic presence was concentrated in nearby Nanjing, the capital, it was in Shanghai that the foreign community took the country's temperature. Foreigners in the city's two "concession" areas — the French Concession and the British-affiliated International Settlement — often dismissed towns beyond Shanghai as mere "outstations."

On August 13, 1937, Chiang Kai-shek gave orders to his armies to defend Shanghai: "divert the enemy in the sea, block off the coast, and resist landings."[3] Even before Chiang had mobilized troops, panic had hit Shanghai. The iconic photograph of that period, taken by the journalist Randall Gould, shows refugees in uncountable numbers crossing the Garden Bridge in the hope of being admitted into the foreign areas of safety. On August 6 the *North China Daily News,* the voice of the British community in Shanghai, reported the influx:

> . . . the exodus from Chapei and Hongkew reached alarming proportions on Aug. 5 when thousands of people streamed into the Settlement and the French Concession with their belongings throughout the day . . . So heavy was the traffic at every bridge along the Creek that motor cars had to crawl for some distance before being able to get through . . . a conservative estimate put the number of refugees [between July 26 and August 5] at 50,000.[4]

The foreign community did not welcome its new guests. Another commentator in the same paper fussed about the unwillingness of the Chinese to accept their inevitable fate without inconveniencing others: "The responsible authorities will, it is hoped, take measures to stem the apparently quite unnecessary and highly dangerous exodus [of Chinese refugees]." It added forlornly, "The admirable co-operation of the local Chinese and Japanese authorities has so far succeeded in preserving calmness and an absence of panic in Shanghai."[5] Still, the appearance of the city's waterfront became ever more menacing: "Arms, ammunition, and supplies poured out of a number of Japanese cruisers and destroyers yesterday afternoon onto the O.S.K. wharf in an apparently unending stream . . . In addition, a large detachment of men, in full marching kit, tramped ashore . . . A cruiser, the Idzumo [*Izumo*], two destroyers, and nine gunboats arrived here a short while ago."[6] A week later, the headline to an editorial asked the question that occupied the foreign community most: "WILL SANITY WIN?"[7]

One terrible event would shatter the illusion that calm might be restored. The Nationalist military command decided to knock out one of the greatest Japanese naval assets in Shanghai and bomb the *Izumo*, harbored with support craft on the Huangpu River in the center of the city. On Saturday, August 14, the atmosphere in the center of Shanghai was already anxious; a public health official recorded at 1:45 p.m. that day, "Refugees streaming up Nanking Rd. from the East! Shops closed and barred!"[8] That afternoon, bombers of the Chinese air force set out from airfields in the Yangtze delta toward Shanghai, targeting the Japanese ship. But for two of the pilots, something went very wrong. "From one of the four monoplanes making up the rear four aerial torpedoes were seen to drop as the planes passed over the Bund far from their apparent objective . . . Two others fell in Nanking Road."[9] Either the pilot had misjudged his target, or else there was a problem with the release mechanism. Whatever the reason, the bombs had fallen on one of the busiest civilian areas in the whole city, where thousands of people were walking, shopping, and strolling on a hot August Saturday. At 4:46 p.m. the public health department's work diary recorded "Palace Hotel hit! — many injured and dead in street! — Nanking Road opposite Cathay Hotel."[10] A reporter captured the horror of the scene:

> A bomb curved through the air, struck the Palace Hotel a glancing blow and dealt carnage indescribable. A scene of dreadful death was uncovered as the high explosive fumes slowly lifted. Flames from a blazing car played over distorted bodies. In shapeless heaps where they had been huddling in shelter bodies in coolie cloth turning scarlet lay piled up in the entrances to the main doorways and arcades of the Palace and Cathay hotels. Heads, legs, arms lay far from smashed masses of flesh . . . Dead in his tracks as he had been directing the corner traffic lay the corpse of a Chinese policeman with shrapnel through his head. A disembowelled child was nearby.[11]

To make matters worse, another pilot had released his weapon over the Avenue Edward VII, another major shopping street. When the numbers were tallied, over 1,000 people had been killed, Chinese and foreigners alike. The bombs had hit the International Settlement, politically neutral and supposedly safe.

Although the *Izumo* did sustain damage, the incompetence of "Black Saturday" could not have come at a worse time for the Nationalists, who needed to rally public support for their cause at home and abroad. In addition, Chiang's forces had lost the element of surprise. Now, as August drew on, both sides began to dig in for battle — literally so, as trenches were formed in the streets. Chinese troops under some of the major commanders, including Hu Zongnan and Chen Cheng, were moved toward Shanghai. The Japanese responded; by early September some 100,000 troops had been moved in from north China and even from as far as Taiwan (at that time a Japanese colony).

Meanwhile, Shanghai society responded to the sudden outbreak of war. In July the city's residents worked, ate, drank, and played as they had done for decades. Beginning in August, they had to remake their entire lives. Local institutions started to relocate; in late September it was announced that four local universities would open joint colleges with institutions in China's interior.[12] In the country's premier commercial city, business was being destroyed: "Like a nightmare octopus flinging cruel tentacles around its helpless victims," the *North-China Daily News* reported, "the local hostilities are slowly strangling Shanghai's trade." A shopkeeper lamented: "We obtain a lot of business, of course, from tourists who visit Shanghai. What tourists are there these days?"[13]

Attempts to capture the city street by street led to intense fighting, with massive aerial bombing by the Japanese to wear down resistance. From the beginning, Chiang knew that the city's fate was part of a wider set of calculations and gambles. In his diary for September 14 he asked: "Are we gathering our forces for a decisive battle at Shanghai?"[14] Already, just a couple of months into the war, Chiang was preparing himself — and his party and people — for the likelihood that the war would not be over in weeks or even months, but years. This view was still not shared by the Japanese, at least not officially. They continued to regard the events in north China and Shanghai as "incidents" that had flared up and would be damped down with a firm hand.

But Chiang's purpose in opening up the Shanghai front was to make it clear that the two battles were part of the same conflict. Chiang knew there was a high chance of losing Shanghai. Von Falkenhausen had advised him that the crowded streets of the city were less favorable territory for the Japanese than the open plains of northern China, and that there was a reasonable chance of success. Nonetheless, Chiang's German-trained troops, however good, were limited in number, and large proportions of the Nationalist Army were under the control of generals who were only occasionally reliable allies, such as Li Zongren, leader of the military clique based in the southwestern province of Guangxi. As a precaution, there had been plans in place since 1932 to move the government and industrial production into the interior, in case of foreign occupation of the eastern seaboard.[15]

However, bringing the war to Shanghai was important both for domestic and international political reasons. Despite the appalling performance of its bomber pilots, the Central Army had thrown itself fully into the defense of Shanghai. The era of avoiding military confrontation and political concessions was over. The decision to attack the Japanese in Shanghai also drove home that this was now a national war. Up to that point, it had been possible to argue that Manchuria was a separate issue from Chinese sovereignty as a whole — there was plenty of rhetoric but little action. The Chinese exiles from Manchuria had become deeply frustrated at their inability to force the issue of the recapture of the northeastern provinces.[16] Even north China, around Beiping, felt remote when viewed from the populous Yangtze delta, where Shanghai lies. The Japanese also had a vested interest in fueling the idea that China was not one entity, but a patchwork of regimes, referring to the conflict not as a war but as a "North China incident." They would maintain this strategy of division throughout the war, sponsoring a variety of client Chinese regimes, many at odds with one another. Now Chiang made it clear that an attack on north China would mean retaliation in the south, and that the country was engaged in one "war of resistance to the end" (Kangzhan daodi), a phrase that quickly came to define the conflict, and remains in use even today.

By bringing the war to Shanghai, Chiang forced the world to take notice. Clashes in north China could be seen as part of the wild activity in the "outstations," a very long way from Shanghai's foreign concessions. Chiang's great hope was to gain foreign cooperation for the war: in his diary he wrote that he hoped "every country would be angry at the enemy, and . . . encourage the US and Britain to take part in the war along with the USSR."[17] On September 12 Song Meiling made a radio address to the US in which she lambasted the West for its unwillingness to support the Chinese cause: "If the whole Occidental world is indifferent to this and abandons its treaties . . . we in China, who have labored for years under the stigma of cowards, will do our best."[18] The League of Nations, which had shown itself so supine in the face of the occupation of Manchuria in 1933, again offered words instead of concrete assistance, unanimously adopting a resolution condemning the open bombing of Chinese towns by the Japanese. There was especial poignancy about one particular expression of support. The foreign minister of Spain, another country whose government was fighting to survive and which had found liberal internationalism a weak reed, declared: "Spain sends the great Chinese people the warmest expression of their solidarity."[19]

Among foreign powers there was also an early, if grudging realization, that the resistance to Japan was a sign of Chinese determination, even when it seemed at times that it might be more realistic to seek negotiations with Japan. The British diplomat Robert Howe noted, "The difficulty which I found in Nanking was that no one in authority appeared to be able or willing to formulate terms which would serve as a basis for approach to Japanese either for an armistice or peace."[20] On November 27 Howe went on to say that "unwillingness to surrender is practically confined to the military and intelligentsia, whilst the agricultural and mercantile mass of population are apathetic and would welcome peace on almost any terms."[21] It was Chiang's challenge to change this view, both among his own people and in the eyes of the world.

Chiang used Shanghai as a challenge to his militarist rivals. They all billed themselves as patriots, but would they actually provide troops to defend China? In many cases, the answer was "yes": Cantonese general Xue Yue and Sichuanese general Liu Xiang were two of the most prominent regional commanders to send troops, supplementing Nationalist generals directly loyal to Chiang who commanded sections of the Central Army, such as Hu Zongnan and Chen Cheng. Military leaders who would not previously have favored sending troops outside their areas of control were now operating, however sporadically, on a national scale. In the last weeks of the fighting in Shanghai, more than 200,000 Chinese soldiers from all parts of southern and central China fought there.[22] The process of unification that had eluded Chiang for so long in times of relative peace was, ironically, being patchily strengthened by the war.

The assault on Shanghai had also enabled Chiang to move ahead with his only successful attempt to gain support from a foreign power: that surprising ally, the Soviet Union. Having saved Chiang Kai-shek during the Xi'an Incident, the Soviets now had a strong interest in keeping China engaged in a war with Japan. Now the situation in Shanghai made it clear to the rest of the world that Japan was a real threat to global peace. On August 1 the Soviet ambassador to China, Dmitri Bogomolov, agreed to a mutual nonaggression pact with the Nationalist government. In fact, it involved more active assistance than the term "nonaggression" implied: by mid-1938 the Soviets had supplied nearly 300 military aircraft, along with ammunition and aid of some 250 million US dollars.[23] Despite his anticommunism, Chiang was now dependent on Moscow for his survival, an irony not lost on his old rival Wang Jingwei. Chiang made no secret of his new alliance. In September deputy propaganda chief Zhou Fohai, then living in the increasingly vulnerable capital city of Nanjing, declared in his diary that Chiang was "wise" to publicize the agreements with the CCP and the USSR. Zhou had been concerned that the alliance with the CCP might raise eyebrows among foreign observers, but there was little reaction and he congratulated Chiang on his judgment. Yet as the fighting worsened, Wang Jingwei told Zhou that the government should not move so quickly to end diplomatic relations with Japan. Zhou agreed, and criticized T. V. Soong for a speech whose defiant nature he felt was "naïve" and harmful to China's greater interests.[24]

In Shanghai the destruction in September stretched on into October. The foreign community looked on in disbelief, finally realizing that the war was not a temporary interruption. Early in the month there were reports of "severe hand-to-hand fighting in the maze of streets between North Szechuen and Paoshan Roads." Familiar buildings were suddenly taking on frightening new roles. One reporter declared that he had "exchanged salutes with a tattered Chinese soldier who stood back from one of the windows of the [Pantheon] theatre, waved a potato-masher bomb in a friendly manner, then peeped cautiously out of the window . . . and threw the potato-masher at some unwelcome visitor who was evidently lurking in the alley."[25] Nor did the bombing campaign let up. On October 13 it was reported that "Chinese areas and military positions around Shanghai" had been subjected to "the most severe aerial bombardment since the beginning of local hostilities. Japan's aeroplanes yesterday took to the air over a wide area."[26] Two days later the Japanese committed an act reminiscent of the Nationalists' Black Saturday disaster: they bombed a tramcar within the neutral International Settlement and killed many Chinese travelers, including an eighteen-month-old girl. On October 20, Shanghai's North Station was attacked, leaving the railway terminus in ruins and palls of black smoke billowing up, visible across the city. The next day the government escorted groups of foreign and domestic reporters to the station so that they could see the destruction in detail. Photographs of the destruction were printed in newspapers around the world.

The final phase of the battle for Shanghai began on October 24, when the Chinese forces retreated to the Suzhou Creek, only to face two weeks of attack from the Japanese, who had sent in 120,000 troops to finish the job. The Japanese piled on further pressure on November 5, when they landed an amphibious force at Hangzhou Bay, some 150 kilometers southwest of Shanghai. Chiang had withdrawn troops from the area to defend the city itself, but in doing so, he had left the approach to Shanghai vulnerable.[27]

By early November, Chiang faced the inevitable. His forces could not hold Shanghai. Rather than sacrifice more of his best troops, he decided to pull out, substituting a more achievable aim: to "defeat the enemy's plan of a rapid decision in a quick war by carrying out a war of attrition and wearing out the enemy."[28] Secretly, on November 8, orders were sent to Chiang's military commanders to prepare to move out of the city. The order was not, for obvious reasons, made public. Instead, the next day, the newspaper *Zhongyang ribao* reported that Chiang was offering "direct negotiations between China and Japan to prevent any deepening of China's crisis."[29] The following day, November 10, the Nationalist government misleadingly declared that "Shanghai's south city will be defended to the death in this war of resistance." The *North-China Daily News* told a rather different story:

> Having watched hostilities on its eastern, northern, and western boundaries for nearly three months, Shanghai faced southward yesterday as China's armies swiftly withdrew from the Soochow Creek regions during the night and Japanese armed might threw an encircling force after them and captured Lunghwa in the afternoon.[30]

The next day more wrenching details were revealed in the headlines: "Shanghai's South City Grievously Attacked in General Assault by Enemy Army." The article praised the patriotic effort of the Chinese Army, but admitted that it had been "destroyed" by the invading force. On November 12 the inevitable was finally made public: "The lone army in the south city has been given orders to retreat." The "defense to the death" to save Shanghai would not take place. Nine days later, on November 21, the people of Shanghai learned that the "National Government" would be mov-

ing "to Chongqing for long-term resistance."[31] Now that Shanghai was
lost, Nanjing could not be defended either. The military command would
move upriver to Wuhan, and base its defense of central China there. The
government bureaucracy would move further upriver, to the hilltop city
of Chongqing in southwest China, a last redoubt against an invasion by
land.

Insiders had found out the news earlier than newspaper readers did,
among them Zhou Fohai, a few hundred kilometers away in the government offices at Nanjing. On November 13 Zhou met Chen Bulei, Chiang
Kai-shek's political secretary and ghostwriter, who told him that the government would have to relocate immediately. Zhou's first fear was that the
government would collapse as a result of the military disaster. "This day,"
he wrote on November 16, "was the beginning of my new life." He continued: "I am extremely pessimistic . . . China will have no more history.
Why should I keep my diary any more?"[32] Zhou sought out one of the
few comforts left to him: alcohol. Along with love affairs and trips to the
movies (he would sometimes go twice a week), drinking had long been
one of Zhou's addictions, and he indulged as he waited for the capital to
fall. One night he heard the sinister sound of the wind whistling. In his
alcohol-befuddled mind, it seemed to recall the winds that had whipped
around the collapsing Ming dynasty when it had fallen to invaders from
the north in the mid-seventeenth century. As he and his wife packed their
bags to flee for Wuhan, about 450 kilometers to the southwest, he felt like
an official of the old Qing court escaping from Beijing as the Eight-Power
Army advanced on the capital in 1900 to attack the Boxer rebels who held
the foreign legations under siege. These historical allusions were natural
ones for Zhou, who was a well-educated son of the affluent upper classes.
But the devastation that this invasion would wreak was on a scale un-
imaginable to his predecessors.

Still, as late as November 28, the press reported continued fighting for
the city: "Fierce battle starts in Changxingshan area." This was the last
edition of the newspaper.[33] Just why the supply of war news stopped so
abruptly mattered little to the residents of the area. What was abundantly
clear was that the government had left them at the mercy of the Japanese
Imperial Army.

Yet the sacrifice made by the Nationalist armies was real. Chiang had
taken a great gamble at Shanghai. By early November he had more than
half a million troops on the ground there, but some 187,000 of them were

killed or wounded in the first three months of the war, including some 30,000 of the officers who had been so painstakingly trained by Chiang's German advisers.[34] The Communist armies had not been involved in the battle.

The Western powers, despite wringing their hands about the fate of China (and the markets they wished to exploit), did almost nothing to help at this stage. The outbreak of war put British power and goodwill under the spotlight. One British diplomat wrote to the British foreign secretary, Anthony Eden, from Wuhan that the Chinese government showed:

> resigned acceptance of unpalatable fact that there is no immediate hope of foreign intervention. In no case have I heard a sharp criticism of England's attitude ... Regret is nevertheless expressed that we should not be in a position to defend our vital political and economic interests in the Far East which Chinese are convinced will be entirely obliterated once Japanese gain control over China.[35]

A further memo debated the wisdom of sending the fleet to East Asia:

> Had there been a powerful British fleet in Far Eastern waters in July Japan would never have dared to ride roughshod over all our established rights in Shanghai for the purpose of attacking and destroying the Chinese Government . . . Japan was admitted to share in these privileges [within the International Settlement, by the British and the Americans] and His Majesty's government are entitled therefore to insist that she does not grossly abuse them.

This diplomat viewed the deteriorating situation purely in terms of British interests, and noted explicitly that the situation in the Yangtze valley was to be treated as part of an international situation. In particular, the establishment of "puppet" client governments serving the Japanese in the surrounding areas was a crucial part of the Foreign Office's concern. The summary went on to state, among the six key objectives, that Britain should "restore the status quo in the Yangtze Valley and South China . . . namely a regime under the control of the Chinese Government providing for the open door," but that they should also "protect particular British interests in North China, but otherwise stand aside [except Tianjin Customs]."[36]

The fate of Shanghai deeply shocked the West even after the guns ceased firing and a sullen peace returned. The British poet W. H. Auden and the writer Christopher Isherwood, both fresh from seeing the carnage of the Spanish Civil War, arrived in Shanghai some months after the fighting had ended. Isherwood recorded in graphic terms the destruction that lay before him, made more eerie by the fact that the foreign concessions remained almost intact while the Chinese-controlled parts of the city had been demolished:

> The International Settlement and the French Concession form an island, an oasis in the middle of the stark, frightful wilderness which was once the Chinese city. Your car crosses the Soochow Creek: on the one side are streets and houses, swarming with life; on the other is a cratered and barren moon-landscape, intersected by empty, clean-swept roads. Here and there a Japanese sentry stands on guard, or a party of soldiers hunts among the ruins for scrap-iron. Further out, the buildings are not so badly damaged, but every Chinese or foreign property has been looted — and no kind of wild animal could have made half the mess . . . books and pictures have been torn up, electric-light bulbs smashed, wash-basins wrecked.[37]

Zhou Fohai, now safely in Wuhan, had been even more pithy, if no less despairing, in his assessment of the retreat from the Yangtze delta. "Our fate has been decided," he wrote. "Where will our burial places be?"[38]

Chapter 6

REFUGEES AND RESISTANCE

T HE PROSPEROUS CITY OF Wuxi, about 80 kilometers west of
Shanghai, like much of the Yangtze delta, was heavily bombed
during the initial months of the war. Mrs. Yang, a Chinese Christian, was one of thousands who prepared for evacuation, along with
her husband and children. On November 16, 1937, she set out, carrying with her only a few essentials, including two big turnips with two
hundred banknotes hidden inside, and some jewelry in a hollowed-out
egg. The party had to make a terrifying choice: should they flee via the
Grand Canal, the most obvious route, or across Taihu Lake, and the less
well-known canals? If they chose the Grand Canal, then they would be
traveling parallel to the railway and main highways, which were major
targets for Japanese bombers. But if they went via the lake, they would
likely be robbed — and "robbery meant death, too." A sudden sighting
of a bomber overhead forced them to choose, but arriving at the Grand
Canal, they "met thousands of people, rich and poor, in small fishing
boats like ours fleeing from their homes . . . The Grand Canal was simply jammed with boats." Among the horrors they saw were "dead bodies
on the shore, dead babies in the river, and . . . bombed ships sunk here
and there."

Conditions on the boats were bad, and made worse by the very soldiers
charged with defending them. "Every boat was so crowded that it was
almost impossible for us to move," despaired Mrs. Yang. They all had to
share just one basin for washing, and "sometimes a mother would almost
suffocate her baby in order to stop the noise to reach the soldiers' ears."
Chinese soldiers, supposedly there to protect them, in fact were more interested in seizing the boats for their own use, or stealing valuables from
the refugee passengers.[1]

They finally reached Zhenjiang (Chinkiang), 219 kilometers northwest
of Shanghai, on November 22, and managed to fight their way onto a
British steamer, after an air raid had interrupted boarding. The group of
refugees were sprayed with water to prevent the crowd rushing forward

("we were as wet as ducks"), but they were still lucky, as they did at least manage to board: "Thousands who were left on the pontoon were in despair and many got aboard by throwing away all of their possessions and even children."[2]

They then traveled over four days around 520 kilometers to the southwest from Zhenjiang to Wuhan. In mid-November the Nationalists were making preparations to leave Nanjing and move the military headquarters there, and Wuhan was in a frenetic state.[3] But for Mrs. Yang the visit was a brief respite, before the strains of refugee life hit once more. As the capital moved, and the foreigners were evacuated in large numbers to Wuhan, Mrs. Yang was among the many Chinese refugees who felt pressured to move further inland. The next stage of their journey, by rail, was to Changsha in Hunan province, 350 kilometers south of Wuhan, but they soon found that the chaos of the boats was to replay itself on the train:

After staying at the station for seven hours the train arrived at eleven o'clock in the night. Being so unfortunate that we were waiting at the place where the first class car stopped, that when we ran to the third class many of us were almost overtrodden to death and especially with those [sic] children and old ladies even with people helping them. I found I missed three people in my family, then I feared that they might have been hustled down to the railway track [that is, denied the chance to board the train] after my husband and servant came back to say that no response came to their calling in each car "Is there any Wusih [Wuxi] people here?" I worried until the next morning when the lost people came to look for us.[4]

Having suffered ordeals by water and rail, the Yangs entered the final stage of their nightmare once they made it onto the roads. Members of the group negotiated to hire trucks to take them to Guangxi, around 500 kilometers southwest of Changsha, but the vehicles were endlessly delayed. Eventually, the trucks arrived on January 3, 1938, and the refugees were ordered in at once. Salvation came with its own discomforts. "I felt that I was not used to the smell of the gasoline," Mrs. Yang remembered, "and the jolting of the truck upset me so much that I could not suppress myself from vomiting [sic]. I opened my eyes and poured out all what [sic] I ate and [another passenger] immediately followed. Now only five persons out of twenty one [sic] on our car behaved themselves."[5] Chiang Kai-shek and his government might have decided on an orderly retreat in the autumn of 1937, but for Mrs. Yang, like millions of others, there had been no warning. Nor was it just China's cities that were under attack. More than nine out of ten Chinese at the time lived in rural areas, following a way of life that had changed only gradually over hundreds of years, focused on religious rituals, agriculture for subsistence and sale, and ever-continuing struggles against taxation or other requirements of the state. Chiang's plans for resistance centered on the idea of a unified national effort, but the circumstances of war seemed to be destroying everything that had defined the Chinese sense of shared stability and community.

Once the Japanese had captured Beiping and Tianjin at the end of July 1937, they drove westward, scattering ill-equipped and loosely coordinated local Chinese armies. The railways were also shaping the pattern of war in northern China. The Japanese military depended on its ability to move large numbers of troops fast, along with their technologically superior weaponry. To do this, they had to dominate the railways in the north, which they did with increasing success through the summer of 1937.[6]

There were two wars being fought in the autumn of that year. In central China, the struggle for power was between the Nationalists and the Japanese, mainly in Shanghai, but stretching down as far south as Guangzhou (Canton). In northern China, the situation was much more complex: armies aligned with Chiang, but not under his control, dominated the area. In addition, the Communists were a powerful presence. Their armies had not been involved in the battle for Shanghai, but their leaders were deeply concerned with the defense of other cities in northern China, which were nearer to their Yan'an base in Shaanxi province. Theoretically, Chiang Kai-shek was now their supreme commander, but in practice he had no control over their actions. Mao had little to say about events in the Yangtze delta, but he issued a string of commands from Yan'an in an attempt to shape events in the north. The city of Taiyuan, 350 kilometers to the northeast in Shanxi province, now became a center of resistance as the local militarist, Yan Xishan, tried to defend it against the ever-increasing numbers of Japanese troops pouring into north China. Through the autumn of 1937 the fate of Taiyuan and Datong (250 kilometers further north), the major cities of Shanxi province, would dominate the battle for the north. Taiyuan had a major arsenal and Datong had crucial coal mines: both were important prizes for the Japanese.

The maneuvering among the Nationalists, the militarists, the Communists, and the Japanese had real and devastating effects on the wider population. Should they remain where they were, at the mercy of clashing armies? Or should they gather all their belongings and flee to places unknown for a life lived out of a suitcase, with no clear means of support? For the very poor, there was often no choice at all; they simply had too few resources to leave their homes. For the middle classes, the question was often more pressing.

Not all those traveling around China at this time were so helpless. One person who found himself absolutely in his element was the journalist Du Zhongyuan, who had been imprisoned in 1935 for publishing anti-Japanese screeds. Upon his release in 1936, he had been adopted by powerful Nationalists who had admired his stance. The outbreak of war gave Du his chance to use his skills where they were most valuable: in reporting the unfolding war against Japan. As the north collapsed and the Nationalists tried desperately to hold onto territory between the autumn of 1937 and the spring of 1938, Du traveled extensively in northern and eastern China, telling his readers the story of the war in near real time. He had arrived in Shanghai on the afternoon of August 13, the day that fighting in the city had started in earnest. Du's writing, sent in regular dispatches to the *Resistance* [*Dikang*] newspaper, gives a powerful sense of the chaos that was enveloping China as the invasion started. Ironically, Du himself was clearly having the time of his life, exhilarated and shocked in equal measure by what he saw. Free now to report on the resistance to Japan as he wished, he haggled for rides in military convoys or hitched rides. As he said himself, when the enemy was invisible and the day was clear and cloudless, it was as if they "were all going for a holiday in the hills."[7] But the most notable part of Du's wartime odyssey was his reporting from China's besieged rail network.

He started in central China, and began a tortuous journey that would first take him to the battlefields of the north. In mid-August, Du and his traveling companion Li Gongpu were unable to find a train to take them out of Shanghai and had to get a ride to the nearby city of Suzhou, 120 kilometers to the west, avoiding the attention of enemy aircraft along the way. When they reached Suzhou station, Du and Li looked for the stationmaster to find their prearranged booking, only to be told that "there were no more passenger carriages [coaches], and he could only prepare an iron-roofed carriage, which was normally used for cattle."[8]

Over and over again, Du would find himself dealing with trains that were delayed, or missing a connection, or canceled. His detailed accounting was more than a diary of personal frustration. (In fact, Du seemed to take some delight in finding ingenious alternative ways of getting to his destination.) It was evidence of the wider disruption that the war had brought to China. Railways were one of the most potent and glamorous representations of modernity in early twentieth-century China. They had only been operating on a wide scale for some quarter of a century by the time war broke out, and their speed and power were widely used as a metaphor for development in the region. The Japanese-controlled South Manchurian Railway regularly used advertising that featured modernist images of speeding coaches, a symbol of the sleek, futuristic face of the Japanese Empire, which was, by implication, superior to backward Chinese society. The Nationalists too had taken pride in the great increase in railway tracks that had been laid during their decade in power — doubling from 30,000 to 60,000 kilometers. Now modernization was under siege.

Enough of the system was working for Du to see how the country was preparing for war. One notable feature of the landscape was the air-raid shelter. In the mid-1930s air war was still relatively new, although there was plenty of evidence of what it could do. The Spanish Civil War was still under way, but it was already clear by 1937 that German and Italian bombers were providing powerful assistance to General Franco against the Republicans. Among Western politicians, including British prime minister Stanley Baldwin, the fixation on the idea that "the bomber will always get through" provided a powerful motivation to pursue policies of appeasement. And for China in the 1930s, even less used to technologically advanced warfare than was Europe, it was shattering to have to deal with death from the sky.

Some areas were well prepared. Taiyuan in Shanxi province was ruled by the militarist Yan Xishan, one of the many militarists with whom Chiang had a wary relationship. Du had succeeded in his precarious journey north, and arrived at Taiyuan in early October 1937. On arrival, he reported "everywhere, we saw air-raid defense preparations, which had been started a year previously to get to this stage, proving the authorities' early determination to set up resistance." Less impressive, but more typical, was the scene in the city of Datong, some 250 kilometers north. Du grabbed a ride from Taiyuan in a car that was subsequently held up by military traffic and horse carts. The journey took him the best part of a day:

Datong looked very different from Taiyuan. Because enemy aircraft come many times every day, the whole city had a dead air, but apart from some long tunnels dug near the city, air-raid preparations were nil. The officials in the city would grab a few bread rolls for breakfast in the morning, and then hide in the tunnels all day from the aircraft, all the way until about 7 p.m., and only then would they dare to move freely . . . As for ordinary folk, there was no organization for them at all . . . even when the planes had flown off, the people still didn't dare move . . . Even hiding in the tunnels, they did not dare to talk in a loud voice as they were afraid they could still be heard by the planes!⁹

Within weeks all the normal patterns of life were utterly disrupted. People had to work by night rather than day, remain quiet and still for long hours, and endure the constant fear of death. Shortly before Du arrived in Taiyuan, 180 people had been killed in a single air raid.

Chaos enveloped China, and it affected all levels of society, from shopkeepers and peasants to soldiers and government officials. Some jaundiced foreign observers expressed doubts about the government's capacity to survive: one British diplomat, Douglas MacKillop, was particularly pessimistic in a note sent to London from Wuhan:

The strongest impression which one forms here is of the supineness, incapacity, disunion, irresponsibility and ill-founded optimism of the Chinese Government — optimism based almost wholly on hope that other countries including prominently our own will be willingly or (?unwillingly) [sic] involved in war and that a great catastrophe will save something out of the wreck for the Chinese government.

It can be stated fairly in their defence that their machinery of government and even their centre of gravity has been forcibly displaced, that they have never before been called upon to discharge full normal obligations of centralised sovereignty over this territory, that it is a difficult country to administer on modern lines, and that they are deprived of foreign advice and of the wealth of Shanghai to which they formerly had access. But the real question for us is surely not respective deserts of blame or sympathy but whether they are capable of existing

... In my opinion [the] answer is that they will disintegrate as soon as they are forced to leave Hankow [Wuhan] ...

I have spoken of Chinese Government and not of China. Latter unlike the former is probably indestructible.[10]

The British military attaché in Wuhan, W. A. Lovat-Fraser, sent a similarly worded note, which warned that the "Chinese army is irreparably smashed and air force is eliminated"; that the government, "most of whom are men with unsavoury records," was trying to draw out resistance so as to attract British help; and that:

The Chinese are not serious about fighting our war and have done nothing but harm to our interests having brought about serious international situation in Shanghai and gravely jeopardised our commercial interests in Central China.

Central Government should therefore receive no encouragement to continue ...[11]

These gloomy notes summed up the contradictory attitudes of the British and other Western diplomats in China. The view that "China" would last while its government would not was a clear expression of the longstanding Western idea that somehow modern government was alien to a more traditional and unchanging "Cathay." For some, the idea that the Nationalist government was an indigenous product of a new, modern China still seemed hard to swallow. MacKillop's note also grudgingly recognized that the problems of the Nationalists were not all of their own making, and that a would-be modernizing government had been forced to abandon its sources of finance and foreign expertise. However, this was uncomfortable ground for all the Western powers, because it suggested they were culpable. The last thing Britain needed was a war in China. The European situation was darkening and in a few months the British prime minister Neville Chamberlain would make his ill-fated trip to Munich and end up appeasing Hitler by handing over parts of Czechoslovakia. But MacKillop's note, precisely because of its self-contradictory tone, betrays the unease in the minds of the diplomats on the ground. MacKillop was finding excuses for British inaction. The challenge for Chiang's government was to prove MacKillop's gloomy prediction wrong. And in fact there were British officials, such as Robert Howe, who wrote to British foreign secretary Anthony Eden about MacKillop's views and stated his disagreement with them, arguing that China should not receive "special facilities," but that British neutrality should also not restrict the Nationalists' ability to import arms.[12]

Repeatedly, outsiders' assessments of Chinese resistance rested on their perception of public morale. As a prominent figure in China's press, Du Zhongyuan sought to shape that morale, and inspire his readership to continue the struggle against Japan. However, he also did not hesitate to criticize what he saw as weakness in the war effort. During his stay in Datong, he encountered a group of three or five wounded soldiers who had been serving under General Tang Enbo, a close ally of Chiang Kai-shek. Tang's army had fought valiantly at Nankou, 150 kilometers northwest of Beiping, in mid-August, and had lost 26,000 men. But he had had little support from the Central Army; once again, Chiang had reserved his best troops to fight the war in central China, sensing that the north was already lost. The soldiers gave Du a critical account of how their efforts had been undermined by lack of material support, and Du tried to explain the defeat to his readers:

> It was a pity the 29th Army was garrisoned there, as they had set up no defence works. So our army opened up Nankou, but we had to set up defences and do the fighting at the same time, so how could we achieve the task? Furthermore, our side had no aircraft nor cannon, so when the enemy aircraft came on raids, all they could do was wait to die . . . I don't know how many times this sacrifice was made. Each day they only got one meal, because the supply transport corps were so often bombed by enemy aircraft. But what I felt saddest about was that when our side withdrew, a lot of our seriously wounded brothers had no-one to look after them. Some were crawling by the roadside, some shot themselves, and although ultimately our troops did manage to get back by luck, all the shops just opened up as normal and nobody took any interest in them. Please tell me — who are we fighting for? Who are we sacrificing for?

Du was clearly depressed by the lack of enthusiasm for the war that he detected all across China. He did offer some practical help to the soldiers he had encountered, paying for a car to take them to Taiyuan, but reflected on the "terrible situation of the wounded soldiers and the lack of popular understanding, and the general corruption of the military and the officials," asking — not entirely rhetorically — "how can we make war like this?" His journey back to Taiyuan did not improve his mood: "the further we went, the worse the road got . . . we almost slid down the cliff," and the travelers ended up walking for part of the journey and only getting to the city at one o'clock in the morning. He headed for the Shanxi Hotel: "I really felt as if I'd got out of hell and entered paradise, and pen and ink can't describe the sweetness of my night's sleep."[13]

Hair-raising car rides, trains that would not function, discomfort: these might seem like small matters compared to the devastation of battle. But battles — crucial for changing the path of the conflict, but marginal to its lived everyday experience — were only a small part of the kind of total war that characterized the twentieth century. The press was a powerful weapon for the Nationalists in shaping the way that war was understood, and Du's own newspaper columns were part of that strategy. China did not have a widespread broadcasting network in the 1930s, but it had a rich and lively press culture, and its readers would have understood and empathized with Du's experiences precisely because they were themselves enduring similar privations. The great newspapers of China — for example, the Tianjin *Da gongbao* — followed their readers into exile, constituting a new civil society that grew up as China itself fought for survival.

Du Zhongyuan had witnessed the gallant preparations that Yan Xishan's troops had set up in Taiyuan, hundreds of kilometers west of Shandong. The Japanese had captured major railheads including the city of Shijiazhuang in Hebei province, which gave them the bases they needed to launch an assault on Taiyuan. From October 13 the Japanese attacked in three separate groupings. Yan's troops resisted valiantly, but after taking tens of thousands of casualties, the line finally broke, and the troops fled west. The Japanese took the city as terrified crowds of Chinese soldiers and civilians tried to escape the aerial bombardment. The Communist Eighth Route Army was not directly involved in the defense of the city, although Mao positioned troops nearby. However, he told close comrades, including Zhou Enlai and Zhu De, that they should be prepared for the city to fall, and that if necessary, "be prepared to burn the city of Taiyuan."[14]

The fall of Taiyuan now convinced Mao that the CCP must engage in a long war, making fuller use of guerrilla combat that could excite the Chinese people. He wrote, in typically earthy style, "The essence of the contradiction is that those who have seized the latrine pit can't shit, while the people of the whole country, who suffer acutely from bloating, have no pit. Resistance by the government and the army alone can never defeat Japanese imperialism."[15] Instead, the Communist forces would be used to harass the enemy: "A guerrilla war should be mainly in the enemy's flanks and rear."[16]

The CCP's efforts in guerrilla warfare were in stark contrast with some of Chiang's other commanders. Most notorious was Han Fuju, governor of Shandong province (where the missionary Katharine Hand was located), who tried to make a deal with the Japanese and then flew to Kaifeng at the end of December 1937, abandoning his armies. Chiang had him arrested, and he was later court-martialed and executed as an example to other generals who might feel tempted to leave their command.[17]

Meanwhile, on December 14, as Chinese troops fled Shandong, the bombing began. Katharine Hand wrote: " . . . the barracks just south of us were bombed, my house shook . . . It is an experience I don't care to repeat often. I found I could scarcely speak when it was over. 7 bombs were dropped, not all exploding. 2 men were killed and several injured." The next few weeks saw constant bombardment. On December 25 Hand wrote ruefully: "And such a Christmas! I was so thankful for the happy service in the Church in the morning. Then in the afternoon eleven bombs." She noted that she "had to have a stool lest my knees give way and I add to the fright of the group." The following day she wrote "there was no rush for shelter" as the bombers came back, but the fear remained.[18]

Du Zhongyuan noted in one of his reports that the wider population feared the enemy aircraft as if they were "ghosts and spirits."[19] Superstitious beliefs were just one of the obstacles that stood in the way of efforts to institute a rational civilian response in the face of constant aerial bombardment. The rhetoric in China, as it would be in wartime London three years later, was of defiance, and for many, that defiance was fierce and real. But it coexisted with a fear that death might come from above at any time, unannounced and terrifying.

The scenes that Katharine Hand witnessed as the Chinese armies withdrew from Shandong were reproduced countless times as the battlefront moved further west. The military campaigns in north China and central China had become distinct from one another, but refugees were not subject to military discipline, and they traveled in panic from one zone of conflict to the next. Nobody knew how fast the Japanese would move, and what their occupation would be like when they arrived. The Nationalists quickly created an official portrait of a defiant retreat into the interior, in which large numbers of patriotic Chinese chose to follow their government into exile rather than live under Japanese oppression. And this was indeed the motivation of many.

For those fleeing central China, the lifeline was the Yangtze River, the waterway that could bring them to safety in Wuhan, or further west upriver 800 kilometers away, in Chongqing. The government made arrangements for some 25,000 skilled workers to be brought west to staff the arsenals. Factories were also broken down and shipped, as it would be nearly impossible to build new plants from scratch in the midst of war.[20] Some of the most prominent refugees were businessmen from Shanghai, desperate to bring their factories with them. The owner of a pencil factory recalled:

> During the constant air raids, my employees and I seized every minute to take apart and ship things. We put the machine parts in a wooden boat, and camouflaged them with wood and sticks. Then along the way, we met enemy air raids, so we hid in the reeds along the side of the river; then we came out and went on, all the way through Zhenjiang to Wuhan.[21]

Another former refugee remembered the practical difficulties of the river voyage. As they moved upriver, refugees needed to move to smaller boats, particularly where there were dangerous shoals, which required towlines and great rowing skills. There were other perils, too:

> One day, on the eve of Chinese New Year, it was very cold; we were travelling to Shibaozhai (village), in Wan county, when we met two warships that caused big waves and made the wooden ships bump into rocks and sink . . . only the tops of the bargepoles were still above water. Later we asked around and found that about 30 *li* [i.e., about 15 kilometers] away there was an old man who was very skilled in the water. He had a lot of apprentices who were known as the "water-rats." They specialized in getting back property from sunken boats . . . they took turns diving in, hooking and clipping wooden boxes, and then the people on the surface would pull them up, and as the weight reduced, the boat would slowly begin to float up . . . after ten days, they floated it to the surface, but the hole was too big to repair, so we had to hire another boat to go west.[22]

In later years, Mao never wished to commemorate those who had gone to Chongqing, only those (rather fewer) who had traveled to the Communist headquarters at Yan'an. That situation finally changed after Mao's death. In a 1991 interview, former refugee Yan Yangchu declared, referring to the transfer of the factories: "This was Chinese industry's Dunkirk," and Xu Ying, a former journalist for *Da gongbao,* declared that "there was no difference between our Dunkirk and the British one — ours may have been worse."[23] Another historical comparison also stands out. Both the Long March and the move upriver were retreats in the face of a stronger enemy. But the Long March was carried out by a party, the Communists, that would finally come to rule all China, and as a result, their retreat became a world-famous legend. The equally wrenching retreat to Chongqing, associated with Chiang Kai-shek, was wiped out of the official memory.

The refugees who had followed Chiang's government upriver would soon prove the greatest organizational problem to face the Nationalist government in exile. Some 9.2 million were officially registered with government relief agencies during the war years in Sichuan province alone.[24] Many knew that they would have to live in squalid conditions for years on end, with no assurance of return to their former homes, and no guarantee that China would even win the war.

For centuries, the Chinese had experienced refugee flight. Every conquering dynasty had scattered thousands of terrified civilians in its path. But the twentieth century allowed movement at high speed for the first time across the vast distances of central China, and this changed the way the Chinese people imagined their own geography. For many, these internal migrations would in turn help forge a national consciousness that would shape the country for decades to come. In happier days, Du Zhongyuan had worked as a travel writer, reporting to the readers of *Shenghuo* [*Life*] magazine on parts of the country that he had reached on the ever-expanding railway. Now, he used his experience of travel writing to craft one unified narrative of China's torment out of the stories of numberless local disasters. Mrs. Yang, fleeing from Wuxi, also observed that "the man [sic; that is, her traveling companions] had meetings everyday and studied the map in such a way that they never had since they could remember." In the later stages of her journey, on the boat from Guilin, she even mused ironically, as she looked out at the scenery along the Yangtze,

"I wonder whether we should be thankful to the Japanese for they made us travel so far and see so much."[25]

Mrs. Yang's journey also ended in a way that was very different from the narrative of defiant exile that the National Government was propagating. For she and her family made their way to Hong Kong and from there took a roundabout trip back to Shanghai. In the end, Mrs. Yang had ended up essentially where she had started some three months before. She was not alone. Now that eastern China had been conquered, it was no longer an area at high risk from bombing. The Japanese did not bomb areas that they controlled. And the continuing presence of the foreign settlements in Shanghai meant that there was at least some brake on destructive behavior by the Japanese. However, her choice was not a popular one either for the government or for her many fellow countrymen and -women, for whom even the thought of returning to live under enemy occupation was unacceptable. Du Zhongyuan observed an aspect of this phenomenon that would become common across China during the war: the attempt to root out collaborators, or *hanjian,* implying that these people had lost the right even to be seen as Chinese. He was told in Taiyuan about squads whose job it was to root out traitors:

> One day they brought forward eight collaborators, and each collabora-
> tor was wearing a high paper hat, on which was written clearly each
> one's name, personal details, and his treacherous behaviour. They were
> placed in a vehicle and taken through the streets, and the squad used a
> really big drum, beating it as they went along . . . The streets were full
> of people watching these collaborators, and all of them with one voice
> yelled and cursed them.[26]

Suddenly, the circumstances of war made the concept of the nation, and personal identification with it, more urgent and meaningful for many Chinese. At the same time, it also painted people's choices — in particular, whether to resist or collaborate with the Japanese — in black-and-white moral terms. This tendency was an intensification of the already strong sense of crisis in early twentieth-century China. The politics of that era had been modernizing and progressive in various important respects, but the early Nationalists had failed to build on the atmosphere of relative political freethinking that had surrounded the May Fourth Movement of the 1910s and 1920s. Partly as a consequence of the many crises that China faced, the politics of the time became polarized and confrontational, with neither side willing to allow that disagreement could be productive or even legitimate. Neither the Nationalists nor the Communists sought a genuinely pluralist political culture, although they both made gestures toward allowing minor parties that would not undermine their rule.

In addition, the culture of constant warfare had led to a deep and pervasive violence permeating Chinese society. The outbreak of war with Japan, where the stakes were perceived to be immensely high, exacerbated these tendencies. The public humiliation of criminals was common practice in China, but the use of it during wartime created a stark division between brave resistance and cowardly collaboration that obscured the more complex realities facing many Chinese, such as the dilemma of whether to leave family, property, and businesses.

Yet the war also provided an opportunity for successful mobilization of society at a level that had not previously seemed possible in China. From this point on, mass mobilization would become the norm. The endless campaigns in Maoist China, from the public humiliation and killing of landlords in the land-reform campaign of the 1950s to the ritual public torture of teachers and doctors in the Cultural Revolution, had their roots in practices forged in wartime, turning the indifferent and unsure in society into true believers.

During his visit to Taiyuan, Du had been invited to speak to the troops:

> [I] told them how we had united and unified the country, how great the valour of our armies had been at the battle of Shanghai, and how the enemy's bravery had been reduced . . . And then I talked about how during a long war, China must organize the whole of the masses to resist the enemy, and we people of the lost provinces [Manchuria] would do well to take the opportunity to return beyond the Great Wall and act as guides, uniting with the national army to form a rearguard to cause chaos for the enemy . . . After I had spoken, everyone was very excited, and their clapping was like thunder. They weren't welcoming me; they were welcoming the war of resistance.[27]

Du was from a borderland region of China and had seen for himself what the fracturing of Chinese identity had wrought. When Manchuria was invaded in 1931, there had been a swell of popular outrage, at least for a while, but it was still politically feasible for the government of Chiang Kai-shek to pursue a policy of nonresistance. Du's overriding commitment was to create a sense in the population that China was one entity, united by the war. Later in the war, he would become head of an academy in the remote northwestern province of Xinjiang, inspired by the vision of a stronger, centralized China, where air and road networks served to bring the country together (as well as his strong affinity with the CCP). Du's aspirations reflected Chiang's intentions. Chiang believed that Chinese society would come through the war more united and better governed. But were these hopes realistic? It was true that the call of national unity allowed the Nationalists to consolidate rule in parts of the country where they were still in control (and the majority of territory, at least technically, remained part of what the Nationalists called "Free China" throughout the period). But the Nationalists found it hard to make good use of their greater authority. In reality, the disintegration of China in the autumn of 1937 seemed like a deadly blow to their hopes.

By the end of 1937 the cities of north China lay in Japanese hands: Tianjin, Beiping, Taiyuan, Datong, and Ji'nan had all fallen. The invaders had less control in the countryside, where guerrilla fighters, many controlled by the CCP, ambushed and harassed them. Central China lay vulnerable, but Wuhan, the city where the temporary Nationalist military command was located, remained secure for the moment. Still, the fear that the Japanese would conquer yet more of the country meant that the numbers of refugees continued to grow.

No robust statistics have ever been put forward for the number of Chinese who became refugees during the war. So many people fled in so many directions, and the governments under which they lived were so consumed by the struggle for survival, that keeping meaningful records became a secondary task. Nonetheless, the best estimates put the number very high: at some point during the war, some 80 million or even close to 100 million Chinese (approximately 15 to 20 percent of the entire population) were on the move.[28] Not all of them spent the whole war in exile; many returned home soon after they fled. But the mass migration had destabilized society in ways that would reverberate throughout the war period and beyond. Nor was the worst over as 1937 ended. In the first winter of war there would occur an incident so shocking that it still shapes the relationship between China and Japan more than seven decades later.

Chapter 7

MASSACRE AT NANJING

O N DECEMBER 1, 1937, Chiang Kai-shek and Song Meiling celebrated their tenth wedding anniversary in Nanjing. It was not an auspicious occasion. "We've been married ten years," wrote Chiang, "but the future for the party and the country looks very difficult. In the next ten years, I don't know what changes there may be." Chiang also noted that the city itself looked deserted.[1]

In fact, for some months, an eerie quiet had blanketed the capital at Nanjing. In mid-August the war had taken the city by surprise:

> Nanking had its first taste of aerial warfare when twelve Japanese machines appeared at two this afternoon to bomb the capital and were engaged by ten Chinese planes . . . Sirens throughout the city sounded the alarm half an hour before the arrival of the Japanese planes . . . Since the capital had never been subject to an air raid before, the populace were unaware of the dangers, and many people were talking and laughing in the streets while the aerial engagement was in progress.[2]

But people learned quickly. Du Zhongyuan passed through Nanjing in late August, just a few days later. Already, he reported, much of the city's population had gone. He stayed at the Central Hotel, where because "the catering staff were frightened of [bomber] aeroplanes, most of them had resigned." Du was reduced to searching for snacks in the kitchen, then heading out to beg a meal from friends in town. The fears of the hotel staff were well founded. Du recorded, as he headed to Datong:

> I'd stayed three nights in Nanjing, and every night, the enemy's aircraft had invariably lit up the sky three or four times. But fortunately Nanjing's air-raid shelter facilities were still good, and when [the planes] came, there was a warning siren which wailed. They used searchlights to shine into the distance. When the light lit up the aircraft's body, they fired high-altitude mortars, or sent out a squadron in pursuit. In the night, it was fiery all around . . . the brilliance was unbelievable. I had the strong emotions I get seeing the lights at New Year.[3]

While the night sky lit up over the capital, 260 kilometers to the east, Shanghai was in the middle of a pitched battle as the Nationalist armies carried on their doomed defense of the great port city. As Nanjing came under fire, Zhou Fohai also had to get used to the frightening new world of constant bombing: as his house had a basement, various of his friends ran to visit him whenever an air raid took place, and those underground meetings soon led to more organized activity based on disillusionment with the progress of the war.[4] But Zhou would not stay long in Nanjing. Chinese and foreigners alike had made the same decision that he had, and begun to leave the city for Wuhan or other points inland.

In October 1937 Chiang's government began its westward march, relocating its military command to Wuhan, and the administration to Chongqing. A Reuters report from late November reported the gloomy scene: "In a steady downpour the evacuation of the Chinese Government was almost completed to-day. Offices and factories are now being stripped of all valuable equipment . . . If the city is taken it will be only an empty shell." The report did add that "there is absolutely no sign of civil disorder or impending collapse. The general opinion among the Chinese is a resolute determination to carry on resistance, and feeling against capitulation is very strong."[5] Chiang was aware of that feeling. His priority now was to defend central China. But even though the coastal regions were given up for lost once Shanghai fell, Chiang felt he could not leave the east of his country until the last possible moment. He knew that the abandonment of the capital was a devastating blow to the prestige of his regime, and his public statements remained defiant. "It is our fixed policy to resist to the last inch and to the last man," he declared on November 25.[6]

Nanjing held immense cultural resonance for all Chinese. Until 1421 the city had been China's capital under the Ming dynasty. Its great city walls had taken over twenty years to build with the labor of 200,000 workers, and they towered above Nanjing as a symbol of imperial power. Even after the capital moved to Beijing, the city was renowned for its fine architecture and the gracious lifestyle of its merchant class. Nanjing had also been the Taiping capital during the bloody civil war of 1850–1864. The city came to prominence again starting in 1928, when it had become the national capital under Chiang's government. The Nationalists used the city to project a vision of urban modernity that would rival the great colonial city of Shanghai. A mighty boulevard named after Sun Yat-sen (Zhongshan Road) was bulldozed through the city's ancient center; grand pillared government buildings were thrown up to house ministries; and plans were made—never fulfilled—for a new party headquarters that would combine features of the Temple of Heaven in Beijing and the US Capitol building. Beautification began with the planting of trees on the city's main streets. (Even today it is one of the few Chinese cities that benefits from the shade and greenery of trees.)[7] Nanjing became a symbol of the kind of environmental and technological modernity that the Nationalists desired for all of China. Much of this remained a dream. By the late 1930s the economic crisis meant that large building projects were difficult to fund. And when war broke out, Nanjing's status changed from a capital city at the heart of the Nationalists' project of renewal to a place terribly vulnerable to invasion.

The Japanese high command had not initially intended to capture Nanjing. When fighting broke out in northern China, the Japanese were mainly concerned with consolidating their grip there, rather than taking over the areas under Nationalist control. But Chiang's decision to widen the war by opening up a front in the Yangtze valley forced the Japanese to rethink their plans. They set up a new entity, the Central China Area Army (CCAA), which was established in some haste on November 7, 1937. The CCAA was the product of two preexisting forces, the Japanese Tenth Army and the Shanghai Expeditionary Army, and its formation reflected the rapidly changing nature of Japan's campaign in the region. From the start of the war in July, the Japanese had hoped to use one forceful strike to eliminate Chinese resistance. But the escalation of the war surprised them, as did the determination of the defending Chinese forces. Although the landing of Tenth Army troops at Hangzhou Bay just south of Shanghai on November 5 proved an important turning point, contributing strongly to the Japanese victory at Shanghai, the Japanese took many more casualties than they had expected, some 42,202 killed and wounded.[8]

Indeed, Nanjing was never a strategic target for the Japanese. Shanghai gave them mastery over China's greatest port. The capture of Nanjing was purely a matter of symbolic power. By taking the capital, the Japanese would finally demonstrate their victory over Chinese nationalism, a force they considered pernicious and alien to their vision of East Asia's future. "Unless the Nanking Government reconsiders its attitude and ceases its resistance," declared General Matsui Iwane, "Japanese troops will continue to advance to Nanking, Hankow, and even Chungking, China's new capital." From Matsui's viewpoint, shared by others in the Japanese leadership, the apathetic European powers were somehow propping China up, and only the Japanese had China's true interests at heart:

> The first point is to make the Nanking Government abandon the policy of depending on European countries and America . . . The second point is to make the Chinese people recognize that Japanese troops are the real friends of China, and have been sacrificing themselves in the current incident to rescue 400,000,000 Chinese correcting the latter's misconceptions brought about by the anti-Japanese policy pursued by the Nanking Government.[9]

The idea that the Nationalist government was "dependent" on Europe or America was a reference to the way that Chiang's government had tried to counter the threat from Japan before 1937 by seeking support from the Western powers, although those powers remained reluctant to offer much substantial help. It was also, more broadly, a recognition that China had started to participate in a world where transnational organizations such as the League of Nations were trying to overcome the frictions caused by bilateral conflicts between countries.[10] Japan regarded China as its backyard, and these developments were deeply unwelcome.

Most foreigners had left Nanjing by early autumn. Embassies evacuated their staff, companies sent their employees home. One of those who stayed on was John Rabe, a German businessman working for the Siemens Corporation.[11] The German noted that by mid-October most of the hotels, shops, and all the cinemas in Nanjing had already closed.[12] For most foreigners, this had been a signal that it was time to leave, but Rabe was one of a small group of foreigners who decided they must do something to help the Chinese population left behind by the Nationalists. Aside from Rabe himself, these foreigners included Nanjing University professor Lewis Smythe; Minnie Vautrin, missionary and director of studies at the Ginling Women's College; and George Fitch, head of the city's YMCA. This group decided that in the event of a Japanese capture of Nanjing, they would establish an International Safety Zone that would be deemed neutral and that Chinese who sheltered there would be safe.[13]

• • •

Chiang Kai-shek welcomed the idea, and even offered 100,000 dollars to support the Zone (although only 40,000 dollars was ever paid).[14] Tang Shengzhi, the general whom Chiang had placed in charge of the last-ditch defense of Nanjing, was also in favor. The Japanese, however, found the idea unacceptable. They suspected that the Zone would become a hiding place for Chinese soldiers defending the city. Tang confirmed these fears when he made it clear that Chinese troops would be stationed in the Zone, and that trenches and defenses would be drawn up around it.[15]

By early December, Shanghai had fallen. Chiang knew that the abandonment of the capital would be seen around the world as a humiliation for his government. He had to withdraw to the interior, but he wanted to make it clear that the capital had died hard, and that troops had fought to the last man. It was not just a matter of honor, but also of good public relations. If China could not provide victories, it could at least provide an impressive narrative of its courage.

As November turned into December, Chiang made last-ditch attempts to prevent what now seemed like the inevitable fall of Nanjing. He cabled Stalin, asking him to dispatch troops to help China; Stalin, who had no intention of launching a land war in China, refused. Chiang's distrust of the Soviets, and the CCP by implication, increased. On December 6 Wang Jingwei held talks with the German ambassador, Oskar Trautmann, hoping to mediate a peace agreement, but it came to nothing. On that day Chiang assessed his chances: Japanese arms were superior, the Chinese forces were weak, and morale within Nanjing had already been destroyed.[16]

At 4:00 a.m. on December 7, Chiang rose and said his prayers. At 5:00 a.m. he and his wife left the doomed capital by airplane. They flew first southward to Nanchang, in Jiangxi province, and then on to Lushan. The situation left Chiang "broken-hearted."[17] He made it clear that the city must fight to the last. But he had always been a strategist, and his first instinct was not to think about the city he had abandoned but to calculate what should happen next. In the planning notes in his diary Chiang reflected on the need for a "wartime educational strategy" as well as a "national mobilization plan." The most important thing, he felt, was that the Nationalist Party "must not lose its revolutionary spirit." These reflections may seem almost willfully optimistic in the face of the disaster that Chiang had just left behind. But they surely helped him cope with the horrors that had been visited on China so far. By proposing education, or any other social policy, Chiang was able to build up the idea that the War of Resistance was a positive enterprise, aiming to reconstruct a nation, not merely a terrified flight into the interior before an all-conquering enemy.

He also invoked "revolutionary spirit" because he knew that there were other claimants for the term's prestige. If communism were permitted to gain a hold, he wrote on December 11, then "China could become a second Spain." Many Western progressives saw the wars in Spain and in China as linked, both being examples of progressive forces being attacked by reactionaries and fascists.[18] However, Chiang's thinking was in many ways close to Franco's. For Chiang, the civil war in Spain showed how communism could use national disunity to infiltrate itself into power. Spain also gave Chiang another melancholy parallel. As he left Nanjing, he was not at all hopeful about the prospect of swift intervention by the foreign powers. He thought, with some prescience, that it was likely to come after three years of "hard struggle" by China on its own.

Even if he had wanted to put Nanjing's fate behind him, Chiang could not just forget the city. Since the outbreak of fighting at the Marco Polo Bridge in July, Chiang had spent five exhausting months in eastern China trying to defend the region against Japan. For a man who identified his own fate with that of China as a whole, the loss of his capital, the seat of his hopes and dreams for the Nationalist government, was deeply wrenching. On the morning of December 14, Chiang traveled on a commandeered pleasure steamer down to Lushan, where he gave a speech on the reasons for the retreat from Nanjing. From there, he flew to Wuhan, the new headquarters of the Nationalist military command. He was full of plans: refugee relief for people who had had to flee Nanjing; a complete restructuring of the military command. The only thing his diary does not record in those days immediately after his departure are any thoughts on what might be happening in the capital he had left behind.[19]

The man who volunteered to take charge of Nanjing's last stand was General Tang Shengzhi, yet another "ally" with whom Chiang had an ambivalent and complicated relationship during China's turbulent warlord era. Tang was from Hunan, the prosperous and restive province in central China that was also the birthplace of Mao Zedong. In the 1920s Tang had switched sides more than once, joining the National Revolutionary Army in its Northern Expedition to unify China, then turning against Chiang, before backing him again. Of course, other prominent leaders, including Wang Jingwei and Feng Yuxiang, had acted similarly. Now, Chiang had to work out how to fight a war against Japan while the loyalty of his own leaders was in question. This prompted him to place commanders in positions where their loyalty and willingness to fight would have to be tested in public. Chiang's tactics also drove him to place less well-trained troops in hopeless positions, such as the defense of Nanjing. As a result, the very best troops from Chiang's own Central Army, along with the Guangxi troops of Li Zongren, were preserved for battles that could actually be won during the long war. But this was of little comfort to the commanders and soldiers who had to fight when there was no chance of success. Tang was now in a nearly impossible position: he was in effect being asked to conduct a suicide mission, or else be publicly disgraced.

By the second week of December 1937, the atmosphere described by the few foreigners who remained in Nanjing was unnatural in the extreme. John Rabe, half ironically, noted in his diary on December 8 that he was now effectively the mayor of Nanjing, because the actual mayor, Ma Zhaoqun, had left the city the day before. The Chinese military, however, continued to dig in and give every impression of wanting to defend the city to the last man. F. Tillman Durdin, who reported for the *New York Times,* noted:

> Opposed to the Japanese forces as they closed in on Nanking were a number of Cantonese divisions, a few Kwangsi [Guangxi] troops, some Hunanese and — within the city itself — the Thirty-sixth and the Eighty-eighth Divisions and a number of other so-called Nanking divisions. The Cantonese troops had been decimated by weeks of shelling as they retreated before the Japanese from around Shanghai.
>
> The Thirty-sixth and Eighty-eighth Divisions, former crack troops of Generalissimo Chiang Kai-shek, had been badly shattered around Shanghai. Withdrawn to Nanking, they had been replenished with raw recruits.[20]

Meanwhile, residents began to panic. Cheng Ruifang (Mrs. S. F. Tsen) was a member of the Emergency Management Committee set up at Ginling Women's College, under the directorship of Minnie Vautrin. Cheng's diary recorded the way that public buildings inside the Safety Zone — colleges in particular — were beginning to fill up as people sought shelter from the inevitable arrival of the Japanese army. On December 10, shortly after Chiang's departure but before the city's fall, Cheng recorded the chaos that was engulfing Nanjing. "No cars," she observed, "but men, women, old, and young were carrying everything themselves. They paid no attention to the noise of aircraft or artillery. It was truly miserable."[21] The college was a prime target for the fleeing population; in the men's part of the college, even the library was full of people. On the buildings and on the ground, there were hanging "old ragged clothes, ragged blankets and diapers, and on the trees too." Even the ornamental ponds on campus served a purpose: one was for washing clothes and food bowls, and one for cleaning chamber pots and soiled infant clothes.

The commerce that normally kept the capital fed suddenly collapsed. As people fled their own homes for the Safety Zone, measures had to be initiated to feed them. Cheng Ruifang set up a kitchen dispensing rice porridge just outside the main gate of the college. On the first day of operation, it would be free, after which those who could afford it would pay a small fee. The original plan had been to allow no more than 2,700 people to relocate to the campus, but within days this number ballooned. By mid-December, Vautrin had instituted a new system by which a red cloth tag was sewn to the poorest refugees' clothes, which would enable a fairer distribution of food, making sure that only the truly destitute obtained it for free.[22] There was a long-standing tradition of members of local elites providing public relief in the face of emergencies in China, notably at times when the imperial dynasty appeared unable to cope.[23] The actions of the committee at Ginling College echoed and built on that tradition.

Panic and disruption could literally be smelled in the air. One of the clearest signals that things were not normal in Nanjing was the sudden rush of sewage. As Cheng put it ruefully, "food going in is a small thing, but coming out, it's a big thing." She described unsparingly the reality of life lived in crammed quarters with no adequate sanitation, not even the traditional stool buckets (or "honeypots") which were used instead of flush lavatories in poor Chinese homes: "They just do it anywhere, so there's excrement and urine everywhere." Within days, things got worse: "You can't even go into the stool bucket room [because of the smell] and there are people with no buckets, so they just use other people's." To make it worse, "there are people living in the toilet."[24]

The ubiquity of human waste was not just an immediate health hazard.

It marked a reversal of a trend that had been central to Chinese self-perception over the past few decades. Technology and new forms of government had been among the most prominent ways in which the Chinese state had demonstrated its modernity, and therefore its right to reject imperialism on its own territory. Another was "hygienic modernity," the idea that using scientific techniques could make a society cleaner and healthier.[25] As Chinese cities modernized, they used sewage and drainage to show the world the progress that the country had made. Now the impact of war had reversed that tendency in the most arresting, and noxious, way. As it had been for Mrs. Yang, fleeing Wuxi just a couple of months previously, it was the stench of war that brought its reality home most clearly.

On December 12 the Japanese carried out an act that shocked the outside world: they sank the American gunboat USS *Panay*. American and British ships were stationed on the Yangtze outside Nanjing, and served as a reminder to Japan that the Western powers had not yet abandoned their interest in China, even if they remained neutral in the conflict. Japanese aircraft swooped over the ship without warning and bombed it, killing three sailors and wounding forty-eight people.[26] The Japanese government took responsibility and quickly issued compensation of $2.2 million to the US government, all the while maintaining that the incident had been unintentional. A confrontation that had had the potential to open hostilities between Japan and the US was therefore avoided. But the *Panay* affair was a clear warning that the West could not rely on neutrality to shut itself off from the ever-spreading war.

Within Nanjing itself, though, December 12 was clear and still. Although the artillery kept firing, Cheng Ruifang noted, there was "no aerial bombing. The weather's been good. This is good for the refugees, but it also has helped the enemy."[27] The shops were all shut, and refugees continued to gather in the Safety Zone. But after dark, matters took a more sinister turn. For the city was now in flames. As it became clear that they could not hold Nanjing, Tang Shengzhi's men had begun to burn buildings across the capital. John Rabe was told by a senior Chinese official that Tang himself had left the city by eight o'clock.

While the refugees huddled in the Safety Zone, Tang Shengzhi's troops had made their last stand. They did resist with vigor. The troops had been fighting hard for the two days since Chiang's departure, and Tang had refused a formal request for surrender.[28] But on the evening of December 12 he decided that the city could no longer be defended. Tang gave orders to his divisions to break through the CCAA's siege via a gate in the city's northern wall, and abandon Nanjing to the Japanese.

Immediately, Chinese soldiers fled, looted, and squeezed through the wall, in some cases drowning in the Yangtze in their haste to escape. Some 70,000 had already been killed trying to defend the city. The night sky was lit up by flames; this was not the doing of the Japanese, but of the Chinese troops who had set further major buildings ablaze. Durdin of the *New York Times* wrote that "the Chinese burned nearly all suburbs, including fine buildings and homes in Mausoleum Park. Hsiakwan [Xiaguan] is a mass of charred ruins . . . The Japanese even avoided bombing Chinese troop concentrations in built-up areas, apparently to preserve the buildings. The fine Ministry of Communications building was the only big government structure destroyed inside the city. It was fired by Chinese."[29] The burning of buildings was a constant feature of the war. In a desperate attempt to deny anything of value to an advancing enemy, the Chinese forces, both Nationalist and Communist, would set buildings on fire. Back in October, Mao had advised his colleagues to think about burning Taiyuan in the event of that city's capture.

Early on December 13 the Japanese army entered the capital. General Matsui Iwane led the CCAA, but illness meant that his deputy, Prince Asaka, was the acting officer in command when the Japanese took the capital. The city was in desperate shape. Durdin noted the change in Zhongshan (Chungshan) Road, the boulevard that symbolized the Nationalists' hopes for modernity: "Chungshan Road was a long avenue of filth and discarded uniforms, rifles, pistols, machine guns, fieldpieces, knives and knapsacks. In some places the Japanese had to hitch tanks to debris to clear the road."

Cheng Ruifang recorded the arrival of the invaders in her diary too: "Yesterday evening our army retreated. This morning we heard no return fire. At 2 p.m. today the Japanese army entered through the Shuixi gate." The policeman who guarded the college gates saw the Japanese marching through the city and tried to tear off his uniform while running down the road: "He fell over and his face was white; he's such a coward." But in the next couple of days Cheng recorded good reasons for the policeman's terror. More and more people arrived at Ginling College:

because Japanese soldiers were arriving in broad daylight to steal their money and to rape. In the streets, a lot of people have been bayoneted to death, even in the Safety Zone. Even more [have been killed] outside [the Zone]; nobody dares go outside. Most of the dead are young men.[30]

Less than a week after the city surrendered, there were more than 9,000 people sleeping in the college's corridors, "like sardines in a tin."[31] And not long after, Minnie Vautrin recorded: "Great fires are now lighting the sky to the northeast, east and southeast, each night these fires light the sky and by day clouds of smoke make us know that the work of looting and destruction still continues. The fruits of war are death and desolation."[32]

In many places in China foreigners were bystanders to the conflict between the Chinese and the Japanese. In Nanjing the tiny group of Westerners, fewer than thirty, who remained in the city, found themselves thrust suddenly into the midst of events, providing a buffer between the Japanese army and a Chinese population left defenseless. The Westerners who formed the Safety Zone committee were not trained bureaucrats or public servants. Rabe was a businessman, Robert O. Wilson a doctor, Smythe and Vautrin were university teachers. The committee members made an assumption that the Japanese army would behave, overall, according to the laws of war. They also assumed that it would have an interest in restoring order, something that would also benefit the Chinese and the foreigners in the city. As they were citizens of neutral countries (including the US and Germany), the committee members also hoped that they would gain authority by virtue of their third-party status. And there were hopeful precedents. Beiping and Tianjin had been occupied without major chaos. Even Shanghai, pounded to destruction that same autumn, had fallen into a deathly calm once the Nationalist government had retreated.

But something utterly different happened in Nanjing. From the first hours of the occupation, the Japanese troops seem to have abandoned all constraints. For the next six weeks, until the middle of January 1938, the soldiers of the Japanese Central China Area Army embarked on an uninterrupted spree of murder, rape, and robbery. Far from establishing a new, if temporary, order in the city, the army seemed determined to reduce Nanjing to utter chaos.

In the days after the Japanese entry into Nanjing, Rabe was asked by senior Japanese officers to try to bring together a Chinese workforce that could restart supplies of electricity. Rabe was keen to preserve order in the city, and so agreed to help, but found it impossible to recruit workers in the atmosphere of constant terror: "The Japanese soldiers are completely out of control. Under the circumstances I can't find the workers needed to get the electricity works running again."[33]

The foreign observers witnessed deeply disturbing sights from the very first day of the occupation. At first, the targets seemed to be civilian men suspected of being soldiers who had abandoned their uniforms, although it seemed that little discrimination was being used. Any Chinese man might be a victim. The sounds of rifle fire were heard over and over again in those days, but those who were shot were perhaps fortunate. George Fitch, head of the city's YMCA, noted on December 19:

> I . . . went to the house of Douglas Jenkins of our Embassy. The flag was still there; but in his garage, the house boy lay dead . . . There are still many corpses on the streets, all of them civilians as far as we can see. The Red Swastika Society [the Buddhist charitable organization; it had no connection with Nazism] would bury them, but their truck has been stolen, their coffins used for bonfires, and several of their workers bearing their insignia have been marched away.[34]

Three days later, Fitch wrote, "Went . . . to see fifty corpses in some ponds quarter of a mile east of headquarters . . . All obviously civilians, hands bound behind backs, one with the top half of his head cut completely off. Were they used for sabre practice?"[35]

Fitch saw for himself what might happen to those suspected of being soldiers. On December 23 a man was brought to headquarters, "head burned cinder black — eyes and ears gone, nose partly, a ghastly sight."[36] He said that he had been part of a gang of some one hundred men, all of whom had been tied together, covered in gasoline, then set on fire. Some workers, Cheng observed, had shaved their heads to disguise themselves. To their regret, the tonsure made them look more like soldiers, not less.

The Japanese of course claimed that they were simply rooting out military opposition, but no such explanation could make sense of another crime that was visited upon the civilian population: rape. Day by day, hour by hour, reports came in of women being sexually assaulted. On December 17 Rabe wrote: "Last night up to 1,000 women and girls are said to have been raped, about a hundred girls at Ginling College alone. You hear of nothing but rape."[37] Two days later Fitch reported: "Some houses are entered from five to ten times in one day and the poor people looted and robbed and the women raped. Several were killed in cold blood for no apparent reason whatsoever."[38]

Minnie Vautrin's diary reported the victims of rape who sought refuge at Ginling College. "A stream of weary wild-eyed women were coming in," she wrote. "Said their night had been one of horror; that again and again their homes had been visited by soldiers. (Twelve-year-old girls up to sixty-year-old women raped. Husbands forced to leave bedroom and pregnant wife at point of bayonet . . .)."[39] Working under Vautrin at the increasingly crowded refugee station at Ginling College, Cheng Ruifang saw the city's women becoming victims over and over again. Women were raped in the living quarters of one of the buildings. Vautrin did her best to intervene but was unable to be everywhere at once, and she appeared "tired to death." An entry in Vautrin's own diary for December 19 was typical: "was frantically called to the old Faculty House where I was told two soldiers had gone upstairs. There, in room 538, I found one standing at the door, and one inside already raping a poor girl."[40] On one occasion Japanese soldiers demanded to know whether Chinese soldiers were being concealed in the building. When Vautrin told them that there were no soldiers present, "he then slapped me on the face and slapped Mr. Li [her Chinese colleague] very severely."[41]

Yet Cheng Ruifang felt that Vautrin still failed to understand the nature of the invaders. In late December Vautrin said of Japanese military policemen who had been sent to the college: "They really seem like clean, well-disciplined men, and in the main have kind faces."[42] But Cheng had reason to doubt this assessment. On December 21 more Japanese soldiers had turned up at the college. "Miss Vautrin thought he was a good man," Cheng observed, "but actually he hates us [Chinese] because he has lost face [when previously reprimanded]. So although we still take in girls from outside, the soldiers come at all times to drag them away." The next day "two soldiers came and dragged out two girls on the grass [and raped them]. I'd heard how immoral they were, but now I see it." Cheng despaired of Vautrin's desperate attempts to mediate by reporting these acts to the Japanese consulate: "I tell her, the more you report them, the more they will keep doing this." Yet Cheng also noted that without the few Americans and Germans in the city assisting them, even more Chinese would be on "the road to death."[43]

On December 20 Cheng's frustrations came together in a howl of anger at the Japanese, at her American protectress, at her compatriots:

Today at noon two soldiers came to snatch two girls; as it happened, a senior officer came to inspect them, and Miss Vautrin told him to look and see what his soldiers were doing, so he was embarrassed. But this doesn't really matter to him. The Chinese are his enemy, but Miss Vautrin doesn't understand this. She is really busy, driving soldiers away as she receives their superior officers. Chen Feiran [head of a local governmental district] is terrified and for two days has not wanted to come outside. I'm tired to death. And these refugees don't *listen* to anything you say — they shit and piss everywhere, there's nowhere to walk, you don't dare *move* after dark.[44]

Cheng added: "In one week, one baby died, and ten were born." A couple of days later this thought darkened her mood yet further. "Every day a child is born. I can't handle it, I feel very disturbed." She was angry, too, because she had not washed for two weeks, in part because she was worried that Japanese soldiers on the lookout for women to rape might enter the bathhouse and seize her, and also because there was a blackout after dark. The Japanese had destroyed the college's electricity generator. Those sheltering inside did not even dare light candles in case it attracted unwelcome attention at night. Sometimes, ironically, it would be the squalor of the circumstances that would lead to salvation: Cheng managed to save one girl from an attempted rape by a Japanese soldier because the girl was in one of the many parts of the college where the ground was covered in excrement, and in the struggle, her clothes became covered in feces, making her no longer so desirable.[45]

The desperation of the times led both Chinese and foreigners into judgments that sit very uncomfortably by present-day standards. On December 23 Cheng observed a girl who had been brought back after suffering multiple rape by Japanese soldiers, so badly injured that she was unable to walk. Cheng observed in her diary that there would soon be a lot of mixed-race babies in Nanjing: "Hateful!" The next day she described how Japanese officers had come with Chinese collaborators looking for prostitutes. Minnie Vautrin had agreed to a deal. On Christmas Eve in an attempt to protect the "innocent and decent women," she allowed Japanese officers to search for prostitutes. (They obtained twenty-one of them in the end.) Cheng's reaction was that if the prostitutes were taken away and forced to work outside the college, then the soldiers would not come in and rape the "good women"; this seemed "reasonable." But apart from making a moral judgment about sex workers that few would endorse today, Cheng's idea of what was "reasonable" was tied to an expectation of rationality that the Japanese army showed no signs of displaying. By Christmas Eve some 600 people were camping in Rabe's garden.[46] Rabe told Cheng that it was Christmas. Cheng replied that it was like a "holiday in hell."

The Safety Zone committee and their Chinese colleagues were on the same side, but there were still tensions between them (perhaps unsurprising in the hysterical atmosphere of those weeks). In the first few days Japanese soldiers repeatedly raided houses and buildings, stealing cigarettes, alcohol, and food (even the chickens held at Ginling as part of the animal science laboratory). Cheng noted with a certain black satisfaction after one raid: "They even took the wine and cigarettes of the International Committee. The Committee lost face; they had feared *our* [the Chinese] army looting, and said that the Japanese would behave very well. Now they know this isn't true. The Japanese don't even recognize the Safety Zone."[47] For many Chinese, the foreigners were allies, but even so, the hierarchical relationship between Westerners and Chinese cast a shadow, and clichés about the Japanese being more ordered than the chaotic Chinese persisted. It is easy to see why Cheng took bleak comfort from the committee's embarrassment about their mistaken judgment.

There seemed to be no letup in the intensity of the atrocities. Just after Christmas the Japanese set up public stages where they called upon former Chinese soldiers to confess, saying that if they did so, they would not be harmed, but if it were later discovered that they had been soldiers, they would be executed. Over 200 former soldiers did come forward, and were promptly killed. Men then stopped identifying themselves as soldiers, but the Japanese rounded up a group of young men who had aroused suspicion. Some of the women refugees were asked to identify them: if they were recognized as relatives, then they would be freed, but "people left unrecognized were just taken away" to their deaths. "There was a brave old lady who identified three people she didn't know to save them," Cheng recorded, "and a young woman who identified her brother then came out again having changed her clothes and identified other relatives . . . this was really admirable."[48] A few days later Cheng reported that her colleague Wei had come back from the Xiaguan district of the city. He said "you couldn't walk . . . without treading on corpses; what he saw was terrifying, and he was scared to death."[49]

The members of the Safety Zone committee were conscientious in their recording of the events. They knew that they were the only outside witnesses to a major war crime (indeed, some would later be called to testify at the Tokyo War Crimes Trial), and that they had to record details that few others would be able to. But even though few Chinese were able to document their experiences at the time, the entire population was witness to the horrors being visited on the city. The judgment of the International Military Tribunal for the Far East (IMTFE), held in Tokyo after the war, described what happened in the city over the next few weeks:

> [T]here were many cases of rape. Death was a frequently [*sic*] penalty for the slightest resistance on the part of a victim or the members of her family who sought to protect her . . . Many women were killed after the act and their bodies mutilated. Approximately 20,000 cases of rape occurred within the city during the first month of the occupation.[50]

The IMTFE also found that 20,000 Chinese civilian men were killed on the false grounds that they were ex-combatants, and that 30,000 genuine combatants were killed and their bodies thrown in the river. Since then, controversy has raged about the exact number of people killed, with the Chinese government maintaining that 300,000 is the correct figure, and other estimates ranging from the tens into the hundreds of thousands.[51] This dispute should not obscure the fact that a very large number died as the out-of-control Imperial Army exacted revenge on a population that had stood in the way of its advance.

The anarchy in Nanjing showed very clearly that there was a crippling division between the rhetoric (and possibly the intentions) of the Japanese civilians in the city and the behavior of the military. Over and over again, Japanese Embassy officials and senior officers declared that they would calm the situation down. But in the streets the rape and murder went on. Japan was at the time a very hierarchical society. Still, over the previous two decades, it had become clear that lower-level actors in Japan were quite capable of defying their supposed superiors, and that as long as they acted quickly, those superiors would not question their acts, at least in public. The occupation of Manchuria in 1931 had not been approved by the government in Tokyo, but once it had happened, the government (led by a relative liberal) felt unable to condemn it.

Orders from officials counted for little in Nanjing that December. Fitch visited the Japanese Embassy, frustrated by the inability of Japanese officials to do anything about the endless rapes and murders. "The victorious army must have its rewards," he wrote, "and those rewards are to plunder, murder and rape at will, to commit acts of unbelievable brutality and savagery . . . In all modern history surely there is no page that will stand so black as that of the rape of Nanking."[52] The embassy staff soon proved unable even to cope with their own needs: Fitch observed wryly that at one point the three Japanese diplomats he met asked him whether he could help them find transport in the city.[53] On one occasion a drunk Japanese soldier who threatened two Germans with a bayonet was caught by a visiting general, who "soundly slapped" his face a couple of times, "but I don't suppose he got any more than that."[54]

Things did improve, albeit very slowly. The fury of the army eventually began to fade, and the Japanese began to turn their minds to co-opting the city's inhabitants rather than merely terrorizing them. By December 30, 1937, Japanese guards had been placed at the foreign embassies; up to that point, Japanese soldiers had been breaking into them on a regular basis. By late January 1938 the arbitrary murders and rapes were lessening in number. Cheng had noted that as refugees began to leave Ginling College, layers "of dirt and piss" were left behind.[55] At the start of the year, a new city government under Japanese command was set up, which slowly began to restore some sort of order. Food also became a little easier to find.[56]

The Japanese made some attempts to create a belated impression of benevolence in the conquered city. Just after the New Year, Japanese women associated with the army called on Minnie Vautrin, who brought them to Cheng Ruifang. Cheng "couldn't bear to look" at the "devils," but she reserved her greater contempt for her fellow Chinese. When the Japanese visitors unwrapped some "mouldy apples and sweets, the refugees immediately ran and snatched the food." "For children this would be acceptable," Cheng fumed, "but for adults, it's not right to eat Japanese food." She reflected gloomily: "there is very little hope for China's future. When you think about how many intellectuals have become collaborators, then we can understand why this uneducated group behaves this way."[57] Chiang Kai-shek felt similarly about the country as a whole. How could the population be persuaded to resist when nationalism was still patchy and unformed, and when everyday needs, such as food and shelter, were much more pressing? And who should be judged a collaborator, and on what grounds?

Nanjing slowly returned to a sort of deathly calm. It was a city under occupation, and atrocities continued into the spring and beyond. But by mid-February, the initial frenzy of murder and rape had ended. Now the city waited to find out what years of Japanese occupation would bring.

It is one of the peculiarities of the massacre in Nanjing that so much of what we know about it comes from reports by foreigners. But that is not surprising. Chiang had stated clearly that Nanjing would be defended to the end, so Chinese newspapers were constrained from reporting fully the reality of social breakdown and mounting panic in the city. After the city fell on December 13, with the Chinese press gone, there was no chance that Japanese reporters would expose what had happened, and very few foreign journalists were able to enter Nanjing and move around freely. Furthermore, Nanjing itself was in limbo after the Nationalists' withdrawal: there were no Chinese government officials there, and therefore the agencies that would normally deal with welfare and relief simply did not exist. They were replaced by a shadowy self-government set up with great haste, working alongside local charitable organizations. The structures that would allow full reporting of crimes were also absent. The members of the Safety Zone committee nevertheless kept as complete a record as they could.

The fall of Nanjing also showed the Nationalists in a bad light. Chiang could not have held the city, but the inaction of the government suggested it had little concern for the fate of the thousands of Chinese stranded there. Tang Shengzhi's actions also made things worse; not only was the city set on fire, but in the end the defenders fled without trying genuinely to defend the city's population. News reports about Nanjing in China itself were muted, and there were few foreign reporters in the city. Durdin, one of a handful who did report on the conquest of the capital, blamed Chiang for insisting that the army should make a stand at Nanjing: "Generalissimo Chiang Kai-shek was responsible to a great degree because against the unanimous counsel of his German military advisers and the opinions of his chief of staff, General Pai Chung-hsi [Bai Chongxi], he permitted the futile defense of the city."[58]

But in the end the focus must be on Japanese terror, not Chinese faults. Chinese missteps were the result of a war they had never sought. In contrast, the Japanese behavior was inexcusable. As Durdin pointed out,

"The Japanese appear to want the horrors to remain as long as possible, to impress on the Chinese the terrible results of resisting Japan," adding, "Nanking today is housing a terrorized population who, under alien domination, live in fear of death, torture, and robbery. The graveyard of tens of thousands of Chinese soldiers may also be the graveyard of all Chinese hopes of resisting conquest by Japan."[59]

William Edward Dodd, the US ambassador in Berlin, noted on December 14 that his Japanese counterpart boasted of having "killed 500,000 Chinese people," and that Tokyo expected the West would do nothing to intervene.[60] Ambassador Johnson in Wuhan had his own theory about what the Japanese were doing. Despite the noises of peace emanating from Tokyo, he felt, the actions of the Japanese on the ground suggested that they intended to make China a purely Japanese area of influence: "I am even convinced that the actions of Japanese soldiers at Nanking . . . [were] partly motivated by a desire to convince the Chinese that they must not depend on white intervention."[61] Western observers, both diplomatic and journalistic, saw the fall of Nanjing as a terrible blow for hopes of continued Chinese resistance to Japan. So too did some around Chiang Kai-shek, notably Wang Jingwei.

Why did the atrocity happen? Few believe that there was a preplanned conspiracy to massacre the population of Nanjing. What made it shocking was the violent manner in which the looting and killing took place, not its cold calculation. In fact, Nanjing was just one, albeit the most prominent, of a series of atrocities carried out by the Japanese during their invasion of eastern China. The Japanese Army was deeply angry. It had assumed that it would conquer China fast, and that the lack of resistance that it had met on earlier incursions between 1931 and 1937 would be repeated. The strength of opposition, and the length of time it took to secure Shanghai, had enraged troops who were already whipped up by propaganda about the rightness of their cause, and who had themselves been brutalized by their military training in Japan.

Ever since the early twentieth century, the conscript army had been at the center of Japan's reinvention of itself as a modern state. By the 1930s, the army and navy dominated Japanese life almost to the exclusion of other more liberal sections of society; public life, business, and the media all came more and more under the military project. The Imperial Army had entered an echo chamber in which its mission to subjugate China could not be opposed either within Japan or outside it.

When the war broke out, Chiang had criticized his own countrymen for the poor state of many of China's troops, in contrast to Japan's sophisticated military training. But the troops who served in the CCAA were a long way from being Japan's finest. Many of them were older soldiers (in their thirties or even forties) who were resentful at having been called up. The goal of capturing Nanjing only emerged as the temperature of the conflict rose during the summer and autumn of 1937.

The lack of external witnesses was another factor. But news reports of what had happened at Nanjing did leak out, even if the scale of the killings was not clear. The *North-China Herald* ran an editorial entitled "Nanking Horror" and lamented "If every city which may be captured by the Japanese is to be transformed into a bath of blood the world will be repelled with horror and dismay." There was more detail, although not much: "Grim tales of massacre, looting and rape during Nanking's capture were received yesterday," ran the report:

> . . . in two days the whole outlook has been ruined by frequent murder, wholesale and semi-regular looting, and uncontrolled disturbance of private homes, including offences against the security of women . . . any one who was caught in streets or alleys after dusk by roving patrols was likely to be killed on the spot . . . the terror is indescribable.[62]

Even if there was no meticulous plan for the massacre in Nanjing, the wider ideological clash between Japan and China was a central cause of the tragedy. Japanese Pan-Asianism had metamorphosed in the decades between 1900 and the 1930s, and the Japanese were seized with a sincere, if deluded, belief that they had a duty to lead their Asian neighbors, including China, in a journey of liberation from Western imperialism. The notion that China might have developed its own vision of nationalism, in which Japan was as much an aggressor as the West, did not fit into the worldview of the invaders. This cognitive dissonance did a great deal to fuel the contempt of the troops for their victims and their consequent savagery.[63]

Chiang Kai-shek did not immediately know the enormity of what had been done in Nanjing in the name of the emperor. But Chiang's departure from the city had left him deeply shaken. His attempt to turn immediately to matters of state worked for a few days. Then he was hit by a high fever. For four days he lay prostrate, and even when the symptoms had subsided a little he declared: "My spirit hasn't recovered. I've had to stay in bed."[64]

He continued to reflect on negotiations with Japan and with the CCP, even while ill. But in his diary he wrote nothing about Nanjing.

At least, not until January 22, 1938, when Chiang recorded: "In Nanjing, the Japanese dwarfs have been killing and raping. [They're stuck where they are] — but it's our compatriots who are in extreme suffering."[65] Why did Chiang not write about the massacres before this, even to himself? One scholar, certainly, has suggested that perhaps none of his subordinates had told him about what had happened. That is possible.[66]

But sometimes it is hard, even in a supposedly private diary, to admit the truth. Chiang had seen what the Japanese had done to Shanghai, even with the entire international community watching. He knew that Nanjing was a great prize; why else would he have insisted that it must be defended to the death? He would have had some inkling of what the Japanese would do to a defenseless city. And he was the one who had abandoned it. His reason for doing so was understandable. Without Chiang, the defense of Wuhan would have lost its key commander. Leaving Nanjing was just one of the horrific choices he had been forced to make. He would be forced to make many more before the war was over.

Or perhaps Chiang wrote nothing about Nanjing in his diary for a month because he simply had no idea what he could possibly say.

Chapter 8

THE BATTLE OF TAIERZHUANG

O N MARCH 8, 1938, the British author Christopher Isherwood recorded the following words in his diary: "Today Auden and I agreed that we would rather be in Hankow at this moment than anywhere else on earth."[1] His sentiments were echoed by progressives all over the Western world. For a brief moment, the battle between the forces of enlightenment and darkness seemed to be symbolized by events in that city, which housed the temporary Chinese military headquarters located halfway up the Yangtze River.

In November 1937 Chiang Kai-shek had moved his command to the great tricity of Wuhan. For the Nationalists there could have been no more symbolic place than Wuhan to make a stand. The city was really three municipalities in one — Hankou, Wuchang, and Hanyang — which had grown prosperous over the centuries as it became a gateway for trade between coastal China and the interior. Westerners tended to refer to the whole city as "Hankow." On October 10, 1911, the discovery in the city of a bomb plot against the government had ballooned into a nationwide protest, the revolution that would topple the last emperor and see the establishment of the republic. That revolution had been underpinned by a new phenomenon in China, the rise of politically active merchants, who were not only involved in republican politics but also helped to grow the city's industries, including new steelworks and cotton mills. The city had developed a new modern look in the early twentieth century, with Western architects designing imposing, pillared buildings in brick and stone set alongside wide boulevards.[2]

The Nationalist revolution of 1926–1928 had brought the city to wider attention when it became the capital for the Nationalist Party's left wing, then led by Wang Jingwei in alliance with prominent Communists. The revolutionary government did not last long, as Chiang outmaneuvered Wang and sent in troops to attack his Wuhan government, which fell in late 1927. Mindful of the city's rebellious past, Chiang made sure that the Chen brothers (leaders of the "CC Clique") kept firm political control in Wuhan once the capital had moved to Nanjing.[3]

But the disasters of autumn 1937 thrust Wuhan into new prominence, and just a decade after it had been stripped of its status as temporary capital it once again became the seat of military command and resistance. Leading Nationalist politicians had been seen in the city in the months before war broke out, fueling suspicions that Wuhan would play a major role in any imminent conflict, and by the end of the year the generals and their staffs, along with most of the foreign embassies, had moved upriver. Yet as 1937 slipped into 1938 the Japanese advance seemed practically unstoppable. From the destruction of Shanghai, to the orgy of violence in Nanjing, to the increasing vulnerability of Wuhan, the government appeared powerless against the onslaught.

In January 1938 there was a new escalation of hostilities. Until that point, Japan had not officially declared war, even during the Shanghai campaign and the massacre at Nanjing. But on January 11 an Imperial Conference was held at Tokyo in the presence of Emperor Hirohito. Prime Minister Konoye set forth a "Fundamental Policy" to deal with the "China Incident." In fact, it was an ultimatum to the Nationalist government. Its terms were harsh, including reparations payable to Japan, and new political arrangements that would formalize the separation of north China under Japanese control. Chiang's government would have seventy-two hours to accept the demands. If they refused, then Tokyo would no longer recognize the authority of the Nationalist government and would seek to destroy it. The Chinese government was still considering its response when at noon on January 16, Konoye publicly declared that "Hereafter, the Imperial Government will not deal with the National Government." In Japanese, this became notorious as the *aite ni sezu* ("absolutely no dealing") declaration. Over the next few days, the Japanese government made it clear that this was a formal breach of relations, "stronger even than a declaration of war," according to Foreign Minister Hirota Kôki. The Chinese ambassador to Japan, who had been sitting ineffectively in Tokyo for six months since hostilities broke out, was finally recalled.[4]

At the end of January, Chiang summoned a military conference, at which he declared that the top strategic priority would be to defend the east-central Chinese city of Xuzhou, about 500 kilometers north of Wuhan. This was yet another decision, like the one to mobilize troops near Lugouqiao, that was influenced by the railway: Xuzhou was located at the midpoint of the Tianjin–Pukou (Jinpu) line, and if seized, would give the Japanese mastery over north–south travel in the populous area of central China. The Jinpu line also crossed the Longhai line, China's main cross-country rail artery, running from Lanzhou in the west to the port of Lianyungang in the east, north of Shanghai. The Japanese military command marked the Jinpu line as a target in the spring of 1938.

Control over Xuzhou and the railway lines that ran through it were key to the defense of Wuhan, to the city's south. Chiang's defense was part of a larger strategy that had been evolving since the 1920s, when the military commander and thinker Jiang Baili had first introduced the idea of a long war against Japan. His foresight earned him a position as an adviser to Chiang in 1938. Jiang had run the Baoding military academy, a predecessor of the more famous Whampoa academy, which had trained some of China's finest young officers in the first decade of the republic (1912–1922). Now, many of the generals who had trained under Jiang had gathered in Wuhan, and they would play a crucial role in defending the city: among them, Chen Cheng, Bai Chongxi, Tang Shengzhi, and Xue Yue. They were loyal to Chiang, but also sought to avoid his tendency to micro-manage all aspects of their strategy.[5]

Nobody knew whether Wuhan would be able to resist the Japanese advance, and the predictions of outside observers were gloomy. Yet the uncertainty in Wuhan created a remarkable, and perhaps unique, oasis of freedom in modern China. The writers Lao She, Mao Dun, and Guo Moruo, along with artists such as Xu Beihong and Feng Zikai, had all been deeply affected by the liberal moment of freethinking that had emerged around the time of the May Fourth demonstrations in 1919. In the years that followed, the increasing censorship and centralization of the Nationalist government had had a stifling effect on their ability to work creatively, but now the disintegration of political power caused by the war had, paradoxically, given them a new arena. Many of China's most important cultural figures had retreated to Wuhan. Lao She spearheaded a movement through the All-China Writers' Association to spread what he termed "old wine in new bottles," using traditional forms such as folk songs and popular stories to embody a message of resistance against the Japanese. He found a willing audience for his work, such as the play *Defend Wuhan.*[6] It was this spirit of resistance that had also attracted Western writers such as Isherwood.

The press, too, was freer than it had ever been before, giving rise to a wide range of competing viewpoints. Zou Taofen published his left-oriented *Shenghuo (Life)* magazines, already well known in prewar China, not least because of Du Zhongyuan's controversial columns. War correspondents such as Fan Changjiang also became celebrities because of their incisive front-line reporting. Overseas journalists were dealt with by Hollington K. Tong (Dong Xianguang), Chiang's vice minister of propaganda. Tong had trained in the US at the Missouri School of Journalism and at Columbia University, and also worked for various New York newspapers. He used his knowledge of the American press to encourage foreign correspondents to report from the battlefront. In doing so, he managed to create a strong feeling of sympathy for the Chinese resistance on newspaper front pages in the West.[7]

As Wuhan's inhabitants explored their unexpected new freedoms, the Japanese continued their conquest of central China. On February 9, 1938, they seized the city of Bengbu, some 400 kilometers northeast of Wuhan, giving them control of areas north of the Huai River. The next few weeks saw a savage campaign with Xuzhou as the target. The Japanese advanced in two columns from north and south, marching along the track of the Jinpu railway. The Chinese defenders stood their ground along the eastern end of the Longhai railway, near the port of Lianyungang. The Japanese aim was to crush the Chinese between the two halves of their pincer movement. At Yixian and at Huaiyuan, north of Xuzhou, both sides fought to the death: the Chinese could not drive back the Japanese, but the Japanese could not scatter the defenders either. At Linyi, some 50 kilometers northeast of Xuzhou, Zhang Zizhong, a general who had disgraced himself by abandoning an earlier battlefield, became a feted hero because of his determination to stop Japanese troops (led by Itagaki Seishirô, the conqueror of Manchuria).[8]

The Japanese hoped that their capacity to pour in up to 400,000 troops could destroy the Chinese forces holding eastern and central China.[9] Chiang was determined that this should not happen, recognizing that the fall of Xuzhou would then place Wuhan in immense danger. On April 1, 1938, he gave a speech to Nationalist Party delegates in which he linked the defense of Wuhan to the fate of the party itself. Although the Japanese had so far managed to invade seven provinces, Chiang declared, they had only taken the provincial capital cities and main transport routes: "villages and cities off those main communication routes, they have absolutely not been able to invade and occupy." The Japanese, he went on, might have more than half a million soldiers, but even so, they had found themselves bogged down after eight or nine months of hard fighting. Chiang went on to declare that as long as the Chinese held Guangzhou (Canton), then "it would be of no significance if [the Japanese] invaded Wuhan." Holding Guangzhou would enable China to keep its sea links to the outside world, and after all, "Guangdong province is our revolutionary base area": Guangdong, of course, had been the homeland of Sun Yat-sen. If the Japanese "dwarfs" attacked Wuhan and Guangzhou, it would cost them a great deal, and would threaten their ability to maintain order in the zones they now occupied. Chiang restated the plan: "I tell all of you here clearly: the base area for our war will not be in the zones east of the Beiping–Wuhan or Wuhan–Guangzhou railway lines, but to their west."[10] For that reason he had authorized the withdrawal of Chinese troops behind the railway lines.

Chiang's speech mixed defiance with an attempt to explain why the Chinese had to regroup. Evidently, he was trying to have it both ways, or at least put a brave face on what was turning into a military disaster. But his position was extremely difficult. At the time he made the speech, Chiang simply did not know whether Wuhan could be held. He had to declare that the city was important, and to show both the Chinese public and the wider world that his resistance was real, yet he could not afford to tie his reputation too tightly to a city that might fall.

Holding Xuzhou was the first priority. And doing so meant that Chiang had to place great trust in one of his rivals: the southwestern general Li Zongren. The relationship between Chiang Kai-shek and Li Zongren would be one of the most ambivalent in wartime China. Li came from Guangxi, a province in southwestern China that had always been regarded as half civilized by those who lived in China's cultural heartland in the east. Its people had never felt themselves to be fully a part of the empire ruled from Beijing (or even Nanjing), and in the early days of the republic there was a powerful impetus for autonomy in the region. Li was one of a group of young officers, trained in regional military academies, who fought to bring the region under national control, and he joined the Nationalist Party in 1923, the year that Sun Yat-sen announced his alliance with the Soviets. (Li was not a graduate of the Baoding Academy, but had trained in Yunnan's equivalent institution, which had similar views about military professionalism.) Li enthusiastically took part in the Northern Expedition of 1926–1928, and had a crucial role in the National Revolutionary Army gaining control over much of north China. But after the establishment of the Nanjing government, Li became wary of Chiang's desire to centralize power in his own person. In 1930 Li's "Guangxi clique" took part in the Central Plains war, the attempt by a group of militarist leaders to topple Chiang. Although they did not succeed, Li retreated to his own base in the southwest, ready to challenge Chiang again. It took the occupation of Manchuria in 1931 to change Li's position; now he believed that a Japanese invasion posed a greater threat than Chiang.[11]

The tension between the two men was clear from the earliest days of the war. On October 10, 1937, Chiang had appointed Li commander of the Fifth War Zone. Li agreed on condition that Chiang did not interfere with the way that Li commanded his own troops; in other words, Chiang was not to send any *shouling* (personal commands) to Li's subordinates. In fact, Chiang stuck to the agreement throughout the war, a sign of how much he valued his wary colleague. (He also treated Li's fellow Guangxi commander, Bai Chongxi, with great caution.)[12] Chiang was conscious that he needed a commander who could produce some sort of victory in the midst of endless retreat and destruction.

As part of the public-relations battle, journalists were given open access to the commanders on the Xuzhou front. Li and his associates were keen to burnish their own images and give the impression of efficient, competent command to the newsmen who came to visit them. One of those journalists was, of course, Du Zhongyuan. Du spared no effort in praising the "formidable southwestern general, Li Zongren." He was "elegant and refined" and "vastly magnanimous." In language that echoed the way the Communist armies presented their troops to the public, Du also suggested that Li's armies were under strict instructions:

> The most important point in the people's war is that . . . troops do not harass the people of the country. If the people are the water, the soldiers are the fish, and if you have fish with no water, inevitably they're going to choke; worse still is to use our water to nurture the enemy's fish — that really is incomparably stupid.[13]

In Xuzhou itself, Du claimed that the local population all expressed great enthusiasm for Li, calling him "Duke Jiang" in a classical reference to a renowned warrior. Li talked at some length with Du, and invited him and his companions to dine with him. The evening was spent in banter, and Du praised Li's abilities as a raconteur. All this served to boost Li's image as a calm, effective commander who represented the true face of the Chinese Army.[14]

Sheng Cheng was another journalist who traveled to the Xuzhou front. Sheng, like his contemporary Du Zhongyuan, was a product of the turmoil of early years of the republic. He had traveled to France, and on returning to China had been at the iconic May Fourth demonstration of 1919, even taking part in the burning of the house of a minister who was considered overly close to the Japanese. Now he was part of the All-China Cultural Committee on Resistance to Japan, which aimed to use the media to inspire people for the long war. He kept copious notes drawn from interviews with soldiers who were taking part in the Xuzhou campaign.

Despite the outward calm reported by the media, a frightening reality was on the horizon by late March 1938: the Japanese were close to victory on the Xuzhou front. The North China Area Army (led by Generals Itagaki Seishirô, Nishio Toshizô, and Isogai Rensuke) was to link up with the Central China Expeditionary Force (under General Hata Shunroku), in a combined drive on central China.[15] Li Zongren and his senior colleagues, including generals Bai Chongxi and Tang Enbo, decided to confront the Japanese at the traditional stone-walled city of Taierzhuang. The town was not big, but it was strategically significant, lying not only along the Grand Canal, China's major north–south waterway, but also on a rail line that linked the Jinpu and Longhai lines, bypassing Xuzhou. Chiang Kai-shek himself visited Xuzhou on March 24. While that city was still in Chinese hands, the Japanese troops in the north and south remained separated from one another. The loss of the city would close the pincer. By late March, Chinese troops appeared to be gaining ground in Taierzhuang, but then the Japanese started to increase the number of troops, drawing men from the column led by General Isogai Rensuke. The defending generals were no longer sure whether they could hold the position, but Chiang made it clear in a telegram of April 1, 1938, that "the enemy at Taierzhuang must be destroyed."[16]

Even by the savage standards set by the war so far, the fighting at Taierzhuang was brutal, with the combatants confronting each other face-to-face. Sheng Cheng's notes reflect the battle memories of Chi Fengcheng, one of the star officers of the campaign:

> We had a battle for the little lanes [of the town], and unprecedently, not just streets and lanes, but even courtyards and houses. Neither side was willing to budge. Sometimes we'd capture a house, and dig a hole in the wall to approach the enemy. Sometimes the enemy would be digging a hole in the same wall at the same time. Sometimes we faced each other with hand grenades — or we might even bite each other. Or when we could hear that the enemy was in the house, then we'd climb the roof and drop bombs inside — and kill them all.[17]

The battle raged for a week. On April 1, General Chi asked for volunteers for a near-suicide mission to capture a building: of fifty-seven chosen, only ten survived. One soldier claimed to have fired at a Japanese bomber and to have succeeded in bringing it down; he and his comrades then set it on fire before another aircraft could come in to rescue the pilot. On April 2 and 3, Chi called the Chinese defenders at the town's north station to check on the situation. They were all crying and sneezing because the Japanese had used tear gas. The Japanese had superior technology, including cannon and heavy artillery, but for once the cramped conditions in Taierzhuang gave them no advantage. The Chinese command managed to resupply their troops successfully (this is what so often undermined Chinese defenses on other occasions), and also prevented the Japanese from restocking their own dwindling supplies of arms and bullets. Slowly, the Japanese were worn down. On April 7 they finally broke and fled, leaving behind thousands of dead; the Chinese later claimed that 20,000 Japanese had been killed, although the number was probably closer to 8,000. For once, the Chinese had won a decisive victory.

There was an explosion of joy all over unoccupied China. Du Zhongyuan wrote of "the glorious killing of the enemy," and even Katharine Hand, stuck out in Japanese-controlled Shandong, heard the news.[18] The victory provided a much-needed morale boost for the army as well as the wider population. Sheng Cheng recorded evening conversations with soldiers of General Chi Fengcheng's division, who traded banter with their senior officer. At one point, the men claimed, Chi had given them "the secret of war": "when you get food, eat it; when you can sleep, take it." These sorts of familiar, slightly glib-sounding truths were much more resonant when the Nationalist forces had shown that they were capable of more than retreat.

The victors may have described the battle in terms of glorious success, but they did not forget that their enemies were human. Chi recalled one scene he came across: he had picked up a Japanese officer's helmet, the left side of which had been scorched by gunpowder, with a trace of blood, the marker of a fatal wound taken from behind. Elsewhere in Taierzhuang they found religious and personal trinkets: images of the Buddha, wooden fish, and flags decorated with slogans. A makeshift Japanese crematorium in the north station had been interrupted partway through its work: "Not all the bones had been completely burned." After the battle, Li Zongren asked Sheng if he had picked up any souvenirs on the battlefield. Sheng replied that he had found love letters on the corpses of Japanese soldiers, as well as the photograph of a girl (perhaps a hometown sweetheart) marked "19 years old, February 1938."[19] These sentiments stood in contrast to news coverage in which the Japanese were portrayed only as demons, devils, and "dwarf bandits."

The foreign community noted the new, optimistic turn of events and the way it seemed to have revitalized the resistance effort. US ambassador Nelson Johnson wrote to Secretary of State Cordell Hull from Wuhan just days after Taierzhuang. He passed on reports from his American military observers: one had spent time in Shanxi, where he had been impressed by Communist success in mobilizing guerrilla fighters against the Japanese; and another had spent three days watching the fighting at Taierzhuang, and had confirmed that "Chinese troops in the field there won a well-deserved victory over Japanese troops, administering the first defeat that Japanese troops have suffered in the field in modern times." This confirmed Johnson's view that Japan would need to use a great deal more force than it had anticipated in pacifying China. He noted that the mood in unoccupied China had been similarly transformed:

> Conditions here at Hankow have changed from an atmosphere of pessimism to one of dogged optimism. The Government is more united under Chiang and there is a feeling that the future is not entirely hopeless due to the recent failure of Japanese arms at Hsuchow [Xuzhou] . . . I find no evidence for a desire for a peace by compromise among

Chinese, and doubt whether the Government could persuade its army
or its people to accept such a peace. The spirit of resistance is slowly
spreading among the people who are awakening to a feeling that this
is their war. Japanese air raids in the interior and atrocities by Japanese
soldiers upon civilian populations are responsible for this stiffening of
the people.[20]

The British had always been wary of Chiang Kai-shek, but Sir Archibald
Clark Kerr, the British ambassador in China, wrote to the new British
foreign secretary, Lord Halifax, on April 29, 1938, shortly after the Taierzhuang victory, and gave grudging credit to China's leader:

[Chiang] has now become the symbol of Chinese unity, which he himself has so far failed to achieve, but which the Japanese are well on the
way to achieving for him . . . The days when Chinese people did not
care who governed them seem to have gone . . . my visit to Central
China from out of the gloom and depression of Shanghai has left me
stimulated and more than disposed to believe that provided the financial end can be kept up Chinese resistance may be so prolonged and
effective that in the end the Japanese effort may be frustrated . . . Chiang Kai-shek is obstinate and difficult to deal with . . . Nonetheless [the
Nationalists] are making in their muddling way a good job of things in
extremely difficult circumstances.[21]

In the euphoria of a rare victory Chiang pushed Tang and Li to build on
their success, and increased the number of troops deployed in the area to
450,000. But the Chinese Army was still afflicted by fundamental problems. The parochialism that had crippled Chiang's armies repeatedly in
the past half year reared its head again. Although the various generals had
agreed to serve together in a war of resistance, they still looked out for
the safety of their own troops first, concerned with protecting themselves
from any attempt by Chiang to usurp their power. Li Zongren did not use
his top Guangxi provincial troops at Taierzhuang, for instance, and tried
to deflect the bulk of the fighting onto Tang Enbo's men. Chiang's generals were aware of the fates of two of their colleagues: Han Fuju of Shandong had been executed for his refusal to fight, while Zhang Xueliang
of Manchuria had allowed Chiang to reduce the size of his northeastern
army, and had ended up under house arrest. They were right to distrust
Chiang. He truly did believe, after all, that their provincial armies should
come under the control of a national military command, which he would

lead. From the point of view of national unity, Chiang's aspiration was not unreasonable. But it made other military leaders suspicious that taking part in the anti-Japanese war would lead to the dilution of their own power. The split nature of the military command also prevented logistics operating efficiently; supplies of ammunition and food to the front lines were unreliable and easily cut off.

The glow of Taierzhuang faded within days. The Japanese commanders learned from their defeat. They renewed their war plans and reinforced the numbers of troops, moving soldiers from Japanese armies in north and central China to enclose Xuzhou in a vise. Tang Enbo's troops fought valiantly to the north and east of Taierzhuang, forcing the Japanese to battle for territory through the rest of April. But a Japanese advance in late April and early May managed to cut off Chinese access to the Long–Hai railway, severing the flow of Chinese troops who were trying to hold Xuzhou. Nor did Chinese troops to the south of the city show the persistence of Tang's troops to the north. By mid-May the remaining Chinese troops in Xuzhou were about to be encircled. On May 15, Chiang Kai-shek authorized a withdrawal. "Duke Jiang," along with Tang Enbo and Bai Chongxi, had to retreat. Somehow, forty divisions managed to escape from Xuzhou and slip past the Japanese, helped by a fortuitous sandstorm and fog on May 18.[22]

As in Nanjing, this Chinese army may have lived to fight another day, but the effect on Xuzhou itself was horrific. The city had experienced Japanese bombardment beginning in August 1937, and the mood of the population had fluctuated between cautious hope and utter despair. In March, Du Zhongyuan had visited the city. Before he left Wuhan, he had been told by friends that "the city was desolate and the people were terrified," but in fact "all the inhabitants of Xuzhou were quietly getting on with their business . . . sometimes it was even calmer than Wuhan."[23] The Australian journalist Rhodes Farmer observed something similar in a book published at the end of the war, noting the "ordinary townsfolk who became wardens, fire-fighters and first-aid workers during the raid and then went back to their civil jobs."[24] But the departure of Nationalist troops in mid-May left the city and its outskirts at the mercy of an angry Imperial Army. Bombing continued throughout the final days of battle, and 700 people were killed in a single raid on May 14, 1938. In the area around Xuzhou itself, buildings and bridges were destroyed, some by the retreating Chinese troops, some by the advancing Japanese. One

of the towns that was utterly destroyed was Taierzhuang, the setting of
the iconic Chinese defense just a few weeks earlier. The scene in Xuzhou
itself was recorded by Canadian Jesuits who remained in the city after it
fell: more than a third of the houses were destroyed, and most of the local
population had fled in terror. In all the rural areas around the city, there
were repeated reports of massacres, many of them witnessed by missionaries. Aside from the atrocities committed by the Japanese themselves,
the local population found that they were assailed by bandits in the absence of local law enforcement, and that none of the vital agricultural
tasks, such as planting seed, were being carried out.[25]

The loss of Xuzhou was both strategic and symbolic. Its fall marked
another terrible blow to Chiang's attempt to hold central China and
control the transportation of troops in the region. Morale, built up so
suddenly by the Taierzhuang victory, was now battered again, though it
did not collapse. The fall of Xuzhou was also a sign, if one supported
the resistance, that the war would be a long one and that a swift victory
against Japan was no longer a possibility. Mao Zedong's Yan'an base area
was many hundreds of kilometers northwest of Xuzhou, but he understood the meaning of defeat there. In May 1938 he gave one of his most
celebrated lectures, "On Protracted War," in which he chided those who
had been overly optimistic: "After the Taierzhuang victory, some people
maintained that the Xuzhou campaign should be fought as a 'quasi-de-
cisive campaign' and that the previous policy of protracted war should
be changed." Such people had been made "giddy" by Taierzhuang. Mao
had no doubts that China would ultimately prevail (he could hardly say
otherwise), but "it cannot win quickly, and the War of Resistance will be a
protracted war."[26] In the meantime, the development of guerrilla warfare
was an essential part of the long-term strategy, which the Communist
armies would seek to develop in north China.

Yet the loss of Xuzhou did not necessarily portend a long war. It could,
rather, suggest that the war would be terrifyingly short.

Chapter 9

THE DEADLY RIVER

ON JUNE 7, 1938, the first secretary at the US Embassy in Wuhan
reported that the Japanese had taken the city of Kaifeng, 450 kilometers to the north. Slowly but inexorably, the Japanese army
was moving westward, holding close to the railway lines that brought tens
of thousands of its troops across the plains of central China. "The second
phase of the Lunghai [Long-Hai] campaign is now nearing a close," he
declared. "A direct campaign for the capture of Hankow [Wuhan] will
ensue."[1]

But before they could strike at Chiang Kai-shek's center of command,
the Japanese needed to take the city of Zhengzhou, where two major
railway lines, the west–east Long–Hai and the north–south Ping–Han
(Beiping to Wuhan), intersected. If the Japanese captured the city, then
Wuhan and the northwestern city of Xi'an would in turn become vulnerable. Once they had recovered from the shocking defeat at Taierzhuang,
the Japanese had advanced deep into central China by the end of May
1938, and were just 40 kilometers from Zhengzhou.

By the spring of 1938 the Chinese defenders were desperate. There was
a serious chance that the entire Chinese war effort would collapse. The
Nationalist armies' most significant success as defenders of a shrinking
area of "Free China" had been their avoidance of complete disaster. The
government had undertaken highly successful propaganda efforts with
the foreign press to persuade the world that the Nationalists had some
plan other than constant retreat. If the Japanese had taken Wuhan in the
spring, then the Chinese Army would have had to retreat at high speed,
giving an even greater impression of disintegration. However much sympathy there might be from progressives around the world, it was clear that
Western governments would do nothing to save China unless they were
persuaded that doing so was in their own interests.

Ambassador Johnson, writing from the temporary embassy at Wuhan
in July 1938, did not believe that the Nationalists could hold the tricity.
But he commended Chiang's strategy to Washington. Controlling the
huge territory triangulated by Beiping, Nanjing, and Wuhan put pres-

sure on the Japanese armies. Johnson drew on the expertise of colleagues including Frank Dorn, an American military observer, to argue that if the Japanese were to relieve that pressure, they needed to capture Wuhan. Johnson also noted that the political effect of the loss of Wuhan would be to concentrate Nationalist strength much more in southern China, leaving the north to the Japanese and the CCP. The fall of the city would be an economic blow for Chiang, as the customs revenue that had flowed through the city would no longer be received by the government. In addition, the city was the largest major industrial center left under Chiang's control. Yet Johnson also stressed that "the Chinese intend to make the taking of Hankow as expensive as possible." Finally, he added the key vote of confidence: "It is our conclusion that serious as the loss of Hankow will be it does not mean the collapse of Chinese resistance."[2] The Japanese, he said, wanted to treat the capture of Wuhan as the end of the war in China; for the Chinese, however, it would mark merely the end of a phase.

Further American correspondence over the summer of 1938 showed how important the Wuhan question was in gauging the seriousness of Chinese resistance. John Carter Vincent of the State Department's Division of Far Eastern Affairs wrote to Stanley K. Hornbeck, adviser to Secretary of State Cordell Hull, declaring that he had talked to an American close to the Japanese government and that "the Chinese do not appreciate the strength of their own position," adding "if the Chinese can maintain resistance in a reasonable degree of effectiveness" (this meant holding down some half a million Japanese troops), then the Japanese would be compelled to "withdraw from China within a year." Vincent's assessment of the length of the war was clearly very wrong, but he was astute to point out that "very much now depends on the strength of the Chinese will and ability to continue effective resistance." Vincent stressed to Hornbeck: "I believe, as I think you do, that it is vitally important not only for China but for us and other democratic nations that Chinese resistance not collapse." Vincent recognized that the US could not become directly involved in the war at this point, but urged Hornbeck to consider encouraging financial support for China, as well as trade restrictions on Japan.[3]

There were competing instincts at play within the Nationalist government. The state was making demands of the wider population, and had consequently accepted the necessity of doing more for the people's welfare. The recent period in Wuhan had seen one of the biggest refugee relief efforts in Chinese history, supported by the Nationalist government. In 1937–1938 government-run shelters housed about 60 percent of the refugee population (some 20,000 people), assisted by local charitable organizations as well as the International Red Cross.[4] Yet there was also a more callous streak in the government's collective psyche, leading officials to regard the lives of individuals as expendable. This side would come into play as Chiang's government debated whether it could stop the Japanese.

Over the centuries the force that had shaped central China more than any other was a waterway known as "China's Sorrow": the Yellow River (Huang He). The loess silt that floated in the river gave it its distinctive name, and rendered it far less navigable than its southern counterpart, the Yangtze. The Yellow River also made the surrounding land rich and fertile, and the region had been the cradle of China's civilization. However, the nurturing river could be treacherous too. Every few centuries the Yellow River would burst its banks and change direction without warning, flooding land and drowning thousands of peasant farmers. Eventually, the Chinese had learned to control the river, and it was held in check by massive dikes that prevented the river from leaving its bed. Many of those dikes were located near Zhengzhou, across the path that the Japanese would have to take to approach Wuhan by land. There was one way to stop the Japanese advance, at least for a while: to breach the dikes. But to do so would unleash incalculable suffering on those who lived nearby. A major flood on the Yellow River in 1887 had taken nearly a million lives.

The idea of using the river as a military tool was not entirely new. In 1935 Chiang's German military adviser, Alexander von Falkenhausen, had suggested as part of a much longer general military survey that "the Yellow River is the final line of defense, and it would be a good idea to plan . . . to extend its defensive strength."[5] But the German was not the author of the suggestion, in the desperate days of 1938, to "use water instead of soldiers [*yi shui dai bing*]." Cheng Qian, commander of the First War Zone, was one of those who put the idea to Chiang, who had flown to Zhengzhou and realized that a military assault could not repel the Japanese now. The only choice was to let the Japanese capture the city within days, or else unleash the only weapon that would stop them, at least for a while: the river's implacable force.

A leader more humane than Chiang might never have considered the dilemma, choosing to spare the dams and let the Japanese take Wuhan.

But Chiang knew that if he did not break the dikes, and Wuhan fell within days, the Nationalist government might not be able to relocate to Chongqing in time and would be even more likely to surrender, leaving Japan in control of almost all China. Perhaps the nearest equivalent during the Second World War would be the decision of the French high command to surrender to the Germans in June 1940.[6] As in France, Chiang's decision was being made in the face of the most terrifying assault that the country had ever seen, and China's armies were much weaker and less well trained than the French. The dilemma over whether to break the Yellow River dikes was the product of desperation.[7]

Chiang made his decision. He gave orders to General Wei Rulin to blow up the dike that held the Yellow River in place in central Henan. There was no doubt about what this meant. Floods would inundate much of central China, turning it into a vast expanse of water and mud, and the Japanese advance would be forcibly stopped. However, to make this strategy work, it had to be done fast. Nor could the government give any public warning, in case the Japanese found out and accelerated their advance.

Xiong Xianyu was chief of staff in the 8th Division at the time, and he reported the urgency of those hours in his diary. The Japanese were already on the north bank of the Yellow River. They had been temporarily delayed when the Chinese army blew up the railway bridge across the river. The destruction of the dikes was the next step: if the area became a sea of mud, then there was no way that the Japanese could even attempt to reconstruct the bridge.

Blasting the dikes proved easier in theory than in practice. To hold back as massive a body of water as the Yellow River had required very substantial engineering work, and the dams were thick and well fortified. The army made its first attempts to blow up the dike at the small town of Zhaokou between June 4 and 6, 1938, but the structure there proved too durable. Another attempt nearby failed also. Hour by hour, the Japanese were moving closer.

Then division commander, Jiang Zaizhen, asked Xiong Xianyu his opinion about where they might try and breach the dams. "I discussed the topography," Xiong wrote, "and said that two places, Madukou and Huayuankou, were both possible." But Madukou was too close to Zhaokou, where the attempted breach had failed, and there was a danger that the Japanese might reach it very shortly. The village of Huayuankou was further away, however, and on a bend in the river: "To give ourselves enough time, Huayuankou would be best."[8]

At first, the soldiers regarded their task as purely an assignment in military engineering, and, in Xiong's word, an "exciting" one. Xiong and Wei Rulin made their first inspection of the site after dark, late on June 6. The surroundings lent a deceptive calm to the proceedings. "The wind blew softly," recalled Xiong, "and the river water trickled pleasantly." But it was hard to gauge the water level, and they were not helped by the murky moonlight and the burned-out bulbs in their flashlights. They spent the night in their car so that they could work out just where to break the dike as soon as day dawned.

But daylight seemed to bring home the consequences of what they planned to do, and the soldiers became more and more worried. Wang Songmei, commander of the 2nd Regiment, told the workers about to breach the dike, "My brothers, this plan will be of benefit to our country and our nation, and will lessen the harm that is being done to the people." He added, "In the future, you'll find good wives, and have plenty of children." Wang's words were meant to reassure the men of the political necessity of what they were about to do, and that fate would not curse them — in traditional Chinese style — by denying them a family because of the enormity of the acts they had committed.

General Wei confirmed that Huayuankou was the right spot, and on June 8 the work began, with some 2,000 men taking part. The Nationalist government was keen to make sure that it was done quickly. Xiong recorded that the "highest authorities" (*zuigao dangju* — undoubtedly a reference to Chiang or his immediate colleagues) kept making telephone calls from Wuhan to check on progress. In addition, the party sent performers to sing and play music to give heart to the workers. Senior general Shang Zhen announced to the laborers that if they could break the dam by midnight on June 8, they would each earn a reward of 2,000 yuan. If they managed it by six the next morning, they would still be given 1,000 yuan. They needed encouragement, for the diggers were given no artificial assistance. After the failure of explosives to open the dikes at Zhaokou, Wei's troops used "not an ounce of explosive:" all the backbreaking excavation was done by hand. But the workers earned their 2,000 yuan payment. The dike was breached in just a few hours.

On the morning of June 9, Xiong recorded, the mood had changed rapidly, and the atmosphere was tense and solemn. At first, the flow of water was small, but by around 1:00 p.m. the water was "fierce," flowing "like 10,000 horses." Looking into the distance, Xiong felt as though a sea had appeared before him. "My heart ached," he wrote. The sheer force of the water widened the breach in the dike, and soon a deadly stream, hundreds of feet wide, making up some three-quarters of the volume of the river, flowed southeast across the plains of central China.[9]

"We did this to stop the enemy," reflected Xiong, "so we didn't regret the huge sacrifice, as it was for a greater victory." But as he and other soldiers began to talk, they made a crucial observation. The troops had taken on the task of destroying the railway bridge and the dikes, but it would be for "the government and the compatriots of the whole country" to provide relief for the countless people whose houses and property would be destroyed by the flood. In fact, on the previous evening, commander Jiang had telephoned to ask that assistance be sent for the local people who would be flooded out of their homes.

Wei, Xiong, and their troops managed to escape in wooden boats. Hundreds of thousands of farmers caught in the floods were not so fortunate. *Time* magazine's correspondent Theodore White reported on the devastation just a few days later:

> Last week "The Ungovernable" [i.e. the Yellow River] lashed out with a flood which promised to change not only its own course but also the course of the whole Sino-Japanese War. Severe breaks in the dikes near Kaifeng sent a five-foot wall of water fanning out over a 500-square-mile area, spreading death. Toll from Yellow River floods is not so much from quick drowning as from gradual disease and starvation. The river's filth settles ankle-deep on the fields, mothering germs, smothering crops. Last week, about 500,000 peasants were driven from 2,000 communities to await rescue or death on whatever dry ground they could find.[10]

Chiang's government had committed one of the grossest acts of violence against its own people, and he knew that the publicity could be a damaging blow to its reputation. He decided to divert blame by announcing that the dike had been broken, but blaming the breach on Japanese aerial bombing. The Japanese, in turn, fiercely denied having bombed the dikes. White's reporting reflected the immediate response of most foreigners; having heard about the atrocities at Nanjing and Xuzhou, he was disinclined to give the Japanese the benefit of the doubt. Furthermore, at the very time that the Yellow River was flooding central China, the Japanese were heavily bombing the city of Guangzhou (Canton) in the south, causing thousands of casualties. To White, the Japanese counterargument — that the Chinese themselves were responsible — seemed unthinkable: "These accusations, foreign observers thought, were absurd. For the Chinese to check the Japanese advance at possible sacrifice of half a million lives would be a monstrous pyrrhic victory. Besides, dike-cutting is the blackest of Chinese crimes, and the Chinese Army would hardly risk universal censure for slight tactical gains."[11] But, of course, that is exactly what they had done.

During the war the Nationalists never admitted that they, not the Japanese, had breached the dikes. But the truth quickly became widely known. Just a month later, on July 19, US Ambassador Johnson noted, in private communication, that the "Chinese blocked the advance on Chengchow [Zhengzhou] by breaching the Yellow River dikes."[12] Eventually some 54,000 square kilometers of central China were inundated by the floods. If the Japanese had committed such an act, it would have been remembered as the prime atrocity of the war, dwarfing even the Nanjing Massacre or the Chongqing air raids in terms of the number of people who suffered. Accurate statistics were impossible to obtain in the midst of wartime chaos and disaster, but in 1948 figures issued by the Nationalists themselves suggested enormous casualties. For the three affected provinces of Henan, Anhui, and Jiangsu, the number of dead was put at 844,489, with some 4.8 million becoming refugees. More recent studies place the numbers lower, but still estimate the dead at around 500,000, and 3 million–5 million refugees.[13] In contrast, the devastating May 1939 air raids on Chongqing killed some thousands.

Xiong reflected in his diary that the breaching of the Yellow River dikes was a sacrifice for a greater victory. Even to some Japanese it seemed that the tactic had been successful in the short term. The first secretary at the US Embassy in Wuhan reported that the flood had "completely checked the Japanese advance on Chengchow" and had prevented them taking Wuhan by rail. Instead, he predicted, the attack was likely to come by water and along the north shore of the Yangtze.[14]

Supporters of the dike breaches could argue that these acts saved central China, and Chiang's military headquarters in Wuhan, for another five months. The Japanese were indeed prevented from advancing along the

Long–Hai railway line toward Wuhan. In the short term the floods did what the Nationalists wanted. But the flooding was a tactic, a breathing space, and did not solve the fundamental problem, that China's armies needed strong leadership and rapid reform. Some historians suggest that Chiang's decision was pointless anyway, since it merely delayed the inevitable.[15]

Theodore White was right: no strategic advantage could make the deaths of 500,000 of China's own people a worthwhile price to pay. However, Chiang Kai-shek's decision can be partly explained, although not excused, by the context. We can now look back at the actions of the Nationalists and argue that they should not have held on to Wuhan, or that their actions in breaching the dam were unjustifiable in the extreme. But for Chiang, in the hot summer of 1938, it seemed his only hope was to deny Japan as much of China for as long as possible, and create the best possible circumstances for a long war from China's interior, while keeping the world's attention on what Japan was doing. The short delay won by the flooding was itself part of the strategy. In the struggle raging within the soul of the Nationalist Party, the callous, calculating streak had won, for the time being. The breaking of the dikes marked a turning point as the Nationalists committed an act whose terrible consequences they would eventually have to expiate.

In the summer of 1938, in the midst of all this turmoil, one of Chiang's most important alliances ended. On June 22 all of the Nationalist government's German advisers were called home; any who disobeyed would be judged guilty of high treason. Ever since the First World War, there had been a special relationship between those two fledgling republics, the German Weimar and the Chinese. Both were weak and not in full control of their own sovereignty. As part of the Versailles Treaty of 1919, the Germans had lost their extraterritorial rights on Chinese soil, but that disadvantage meant that they could deal with the Chinese as noncolonialist equals, and therefore found themselves more welcome in many business and political circles than other Westerners. Chiang's military reorganization had been dependent on von Seeckt, then von Falkenhausen, and even the rise to power of Hitler in 1933 had not immediately broken the bond between the two countries. Chiang had no ideological affinity with Nazi Germany, but his government regarded it as a potential ally, and put significant efforts into trying to persuade Berlin to choose China and not Japan as its principal East Asian, anti-Communist partner. In June 1937 H. H. Kung had led a delegation to Berlin that had met Hitler and made the case for an alliance with China. But the outbreak of war and the retreat of the Nationalists to Wuhan convinced Hitler's government that they should throw their lot in with Japan, and the recall of all German advisers was one immediate consequence. Chiang gave a speech praising von Falkenhausen, declaring that "our friend's enemy is our enemy too," and declaring that the loyalty and ethics of the German Army were an example that the Chinese Army should follow. "After we have won the War of Resistance," Chiang declared, "I believe you'll want to come back to the Far East and advise our country again."[16] (Von Falkenhausen would go on to become the governor of Nazi-occupied Belgium during the Second World War, but would be praised after the war for having clandestinely saved the lives of many Jews.)[17]

As the Germans left, they made sure the roof of the train coach transporting them sported a prominent German flag, complete with swastika. This was a wise precaution, as Wuhan was already being subjected to serious aerial bombardment. The Japanese were beginning the campaign to capture the city, and some 800,000 Chinese troops had been gathered to oppose them. But the Yellow River floods made it impossible for the Japanese to approach the city from the north. Instead, they decided to use the navy to approach the city along the Yangtze River, supported by some nine divisions of troops. The Chinese fought with immense bravery, but their defenses were simply too weak to resist the pounding from the technologically advanced Japanese navy. They had only one welcome element of external assistance: Soviet pilots flying aircraft purchased from the USSR as part of Stalin's plan to keep China in the war against Japan. (Between 1938 and 1940 some 2,000 pilots would offer their services to China.)[18] Between June 24 and 27, Japanese bombers furiously pounded the fortress at Madang, on the banks of the Yangtze, until it surrendered. A month later, on July 26, the Chinese defenders abandoned the city of Jiujiang (250 kilometers southeast of Wuhan), whose population was then subjected to a spree of murder and rape by the invaders.

The news of Jiujiang's terrible fate stiffened military resolve. So did a highly critical address that Chiang gave to his troops on July 31. "Our achievement in our first year has been to bog down the Japanese," he declared, pointing out that if Wuhan were lost, the country would essentially be split into north and south halves, which would cause great complications for moving men and supplies across the country. But Wuhan would also be "a great spiritual loss," since the place had such strong connections to "revolutionary history." The world's sympathy for China's case was growing, Chiang assured his listeners, and as people became aware of Japanese atrocities, the invaders' reputation would suffer. However, Chiang was deeply concerned about the behavior of the Chinese troops. Men were not under the control of their officers; this was "the suicidal act of a doomed country." Raiding the population would destroy the trust between citizens and the military. "Not only should you not steal," Chiang declared, "you should be giving things *to* the people." Commanders must stay at their posts; he reminded his listeners that the commander who had let Madang fall had been shot. Chiang's message was aimed at the officers in particular. Unlike in Shanghai, he pointed out, there were proper air-raid shelters in Wuhan, but "we shouldn't just jump into them and abandon our men!" or behave as some officers had in Xuzhou when they left their troops behind. If officers did not show loyalty, they could expect none in return.[19]

The pep talk — along with the feeling that the army was making a desperate last stand — may have had some effect. The Japanese then had to fight much harder to advance up the Yangtze in August. Under General Xue Yue, some 100,000 Chinese troops pushed back Japanese forces at Huangmei. At the fortress of Tianjiazhen, thousands of men fought until the end of September, with Japanese victory assured only with the use of poison gas. Yet even now, top Chinese generals seemed unable to work with each other. At Xinyang, Li Zongren's Guangxi troops were battered to exhaustion. They expected that the troops of Hu Zongnan, another general close to Chiang Kai-shek, would relieve them, but instead Hu led his troops away from the city and the Japanese captured it without having to fight. The capture of Xinyang gave the Japanese control of the Ping-Han railway, which spelled the endgame for Wuhan.[20]

Chiang once again spoke to the troops defending the city. Knowing how desperate the situation was, he combined encouragement with an acknowledgment that the city might soon be lost. Although Wuhan was a city well connected to the outside world because of its large foreign population, the army must not expect any foreign assistance. Therefore, if it became necessary to leave Wuhan, they should have a proper plan for doing so. Chiang went on to specify which routes they should take. He then touched on one of the most affecting subjects possible: the disastrous retreat from Nanjing in December of the previous year, where "foreigners and Chinese alike had already turned it into an empty city." The soldiers had been tired and too few in number. "So why did I order that it should be defended?" Chiang said he had asked the soldiers at Nanjing to "sacrifice themselves for the capital and for Sun Yat-sen's tomb," and they had "looked upon death as if it were just like going home." If the army had retreated, Chiang declared, it would have been the worst shame in five thousand years of their history. The loss of Madang, too, had been a humiliation. Now, by defending Wuhan, "we avenge our comrades and wash away our shame." Otherwise, Chiang said, "we cannot face our martyrs, or our own consciences."[21]

In giving this explanation Chiang had both to rewrite the past and build up political capital for the future. In this version of recent history, Nanjing *had* been defended to the death; it was the loss of the city, not the performance of the soldiers there, that caused the "shame." In fact, Tang Shengzhi's troops had fought hard for two days, but they had not been there when the Japanese arrived to overrun the city and kill and rape its citizens. By stressing the heroic element of the defense of Nanjing, and ignoring the story's less creditable end, Chiang made it a scene of "martyrdom" that could inspire his troops for their last stand at Wuhan. At the same time, he had to make it clear that the defense of Wuhan would not be a defense to the death. It was a very difficult tightrope to walk. It must have helped that Chiang had a gift for self-deception; having constructed this version of the truth, he probably believed it quite sincerely.

Mao Zedong, observing the situation from his far-off base at Yan'an, agreed strongly that Chiang should not defend Wuhan to the death. "Supposing that Wuhan cannot be defended," he wrote in mid-October, as the Nationalists made their last stand at the city, "many new things will emerge in the situation of the war." Among these would be the continued improvement of the relationship between the Nationalists and the Communists, a more intense mobilization of the population, and the expansion of guerrilla warfare tactics. "The purpose of the struggle to defend Wuhan is to drain the enemy, on the one hand, and win time, on the other," Mao continued, "so that the work in the whole country will make progress, and not a last-ditch defense of a strong point." In a long war of resistance, it was quite "permissible" to give up certain strongholds temporarily so as to be able to sustain the wider struggle.[22]

Scenes from Shanghai in October 1937 were now repeated, nearly a year later, in Wuhan. The government made frantic moves to ship the most important industrial plant upriver before the Japanese reached the city. As he had done in Nanjing, Chiang remained in command until the very last day. On October 24, Wuhan was unusually cold, and snow was falling on the city. Chiang called his senior officers and told them to depart. "You must go first," Chiang told them, "I'll leave soon after." That evening, at ten o'clock, Chiang and his wife Meiling traveled to the city's airfield. The weather had turned cold and snow was falling. The Chiangs' airplane was delayed, so after some confusion, they boarded a civilian aircraft and left for Hengyang, 450 kilometers south of Wuhan. As they were leaving, guns sounded and Wuhan burned. They had departed just in time. On October 25, 1938, the city was surrounded on all sides, and fell to the forces of the Imperial Army.[23]

There was one further tragic consequence of Chiang's hasty judgment that the Japanese would not only take Wuhan, but swiftly drive further inland. He decided that the city of Changsha, to the south in Hunan, was vulnerable, and gave the impression (if not a direct order) that the city should be burned to the ground to prevent it falling to the enemy. Local officials consequently set fire to Changsha, and it burned for two days. But the Japanese did not reach the city: they stopped nearly 80 kilometers away, at Lake Dongting. Chiang denied responsibility for the destruction, but in reality it was his command that had led his subordinates (some of whom were then executed) to act.[24]

All eyes now turned to the new center of resistance, the temporary capital at Chongqing. Chiang's "Free China" now meant Sichuan, Hunan, and Henan provinces, but not Jiangsu or Zhejiang. The east of China was definitively lost, and along with it China's major customs revenues, the country's most fertile provinces, and its most advanced infrastructure. The center of political gravity moved far to the west, into country that the Nationalists had never controlled and where everything was unfamiliar and unpredictable, from topography to dialects to diets. On the map, it might have looked as if much of China was still under Chiang's control. But vast swathes of the north and northwest were very lightly populated; the bulk of China's population was in the east and south, where the Nationalists had either lost control or held onto it only very precariously. In the north, meanwhile, the Japanese and the CCP were in an uneasy stalemate. Mao's army could make it impossible for the Japanese to hold the deep countryside, far from the railway tracks that enabled them to transport hundreds of thousands of men into China's interior. But the Communists could not defeat the occupiers.

In the dark days of October 1938, fifteen months after war had broken out, one fact remained constant. Repeatedly, observers (Chinese businessmen, British diplomats, Japanese generals) had predicted that each new disaster must surely see the end of Chinese resistance and a swift surrender, or at least a negotiated solution in which the government would have to accept yet harsher conditions from Tokyo. But even after the defenders had been forced from Shanghai, from Nanjing, and from Wuhan, despite the terrifying might that Japan had brought to bear on the Chinese resistance, and despite the invader's manpower, technology, and economic resources, China was still fighting. Yet it was fighting alone.

PART III

RESISTING ALONE

Chapter 10

"A SORT OF WARTIME NORMAL"

T HE THREE YEARS BETWEEN the fall of Wuhan in late 1938 and Pearl Harbor at the end of 1941 may at first glance give the appearance of a stalemate in the history of the Sino-Japanese War. It is true that the three major parties settled in for a long war, a strategy acknowledged by both Chiang and Mao. But there was nothing calm or stable about China's situation during those three years. For a start, China had to fight practically alone without any assurance that help from the outside world would be forthcoming. It took massive military commitments on all sides to maintain a division of China among the Nationalists in the south and center, the Communists in the north, and the Japanese in the east. The nature of the war changed from offensive to defensive. The dramatic battles of the first year of the war were fewer in number: instead, China's fate became tied up with shifting alliances, diplomatic intrigues, and social change that would permanently alter the country's course. Central to those changes were new ideas of social provision. Traditionally, the Chinese state had taken little responsibility for the direct day-to-day welfare of its inhabitants. Now, the circumstances of war forced the new regimes into competition with each other. Nationalists and Communists would strive to demonstrate that as the state demanded more of its people, so they should demand more of their government. Meanwhile, the regimes under Japanese occupation would show that the new masters would have to confront many of the same old problems.

The people looked first to Chiang Kai-shek's new capital, Chongqing. As millions of refugees fled west, the city became a microcosm of the nation itself.[1] "I had been to Chongqing seven years previously," Du Zhongyuan reflected. "It was an utterly feudal place full of opium and gambling." So he was impressed at the transformation. "The roads have been newly repaired," he noted, "the face of the city has changed, and government agencies have filled up the town."[2] Many of the "downriver people" who had come from prosperous eastern China were disparaging of what they saw as a backward and filthy place. The writer Lao She recalled the experience of smoking local cigarettes made with inferior tobacco:

> The first puff gave off yellow exhalation — I thought that it was a firework! But I didn't hear an explosion, so I kept smoking. After four or five exhalations, I saw mosquitoes fleeing, so I was very happy. Smokable *and* drives away insects — truly valuable!

But over the course of the war years, representatives of every province found themselves forced to work and live alongside each other. The very location of Chongqing itself was also important in changing China's sense of its own geography. For years, the west of the country, particularly Sichuan province, had been at the outer edge of what was considered to be China, and had never been properly under Nationalist control. Now it was the center of government operations while the eastern heartland was under occupation. Rather as the invasion of another borderland region, Manchuria, in 1931, had helped to stimulate a much stronger sense of centralizing nationalism, the forced move west turned the government's mind to solidifying unification with areas like Tibet and Xinjiang, both of which had edged out of Chinese influence because of the weakness of the republican governments.[3] Anthropologists at the universities in the Nationalist areas began to study the peoples of the western borderlands, bringing them (at least ideologically) into the wider embrace of Chinese nationalism.[4] Moving the entire government 1500 kilometers up the Yangtze River helped to consolidate ideas of a united China that spanned the whole of the country's landmass.

It was not just the Chinese themselves who now looked at the wartime capital as a beacon of resistance. Theodore White, who would become one of Chiang's most trenchant critics in the last days of the war, noted of "Chungking" that it was a "moment in time," when people fought to "hold the land" through a belief in "China's greatness."[5] The English-language magazine *China at War,* managed by the shrewd head of Nationalist propaganda, Hollington K. Tong, told tales for a neutral American public of brave Chinese fighter pilots seeking to land on Chongqing's precarious Shanhuba airfield, a sandbar exposed only at high tide. (These magazines anticipated a very similar effort by British propagandists to tell tales of London during the Blitz in an effort to persuade isolationist Americans to enter the war.) The selling of the resistance was evident in the name given to the provinces of western and central China that Chiang ruled from

Chongqing: "Free China." This was a geographical designation primarily for foreign consumption.

Although within China and in the outside world Chongqing was painted as a fierce center of resistance, roaring defiance at the Japanese invaders from the top of the cliffs that sat above the confluence of the Yangtze and the Jialing rivers, the reality was rather less impressive. The city was ill-equipped for the massive refugee flight and quickly became dotted with different types of temporary housing. Some were structures made of bamboo poles tied together with steel wire, around which wooden boards were placed. Mud and clay were slathered on the outside, and a thin roof of tiles or straw covered the top. Another type was made of clay, with up to three layers of wooden boards. The famed literary critic Hu Feng (who would later be the victim of one of Mao's most vicious campaigns in the 1950s) lived in one of the latter, which proved little protection when an air raid punched a hole in the top, nearly killing him.[6]

Such hastily built dwellings were hardly a surprise in a desperately poor city suddenly thrust into national and international prominence. Chongqing's population had soared as refugees poured into Free China: a city of nearly 474,000 people in 1937 had expanded to over 700,000 by 1941 and would rise to some 1.05 million by the end of the war.[7] Sichuan province served as a major base for the government's plans for resistance and reconstruction, and its population (at its highest point in 1944) was some 47.5 million people.[8]

The newcomers were not used to their new conditions of life. Many were from the emergent middle class that had been growing up in China's cities in the republican era, and were used to a higher standard of living than they could find in war-torn Chongqing. Drinking water was often scarce: citizens would sometimes have to travel several miles to find spring water, and during droughts, particularly during Sichuan's scorching summer, there would be lines. Even when water was available, it was often highly polluted, needing chemical treatment. For dwellings that were not on the electricity grid, there was no household power, and therefore no light at night. Instead, people would put out plates of oil with wicks in them, perhaps adding a wick or two when the children were doing their homework.[9]

Still, the city's transformation was remarkable. The other great wartime capitals all had decades of experience as seats of government, as well as a long-standing cadre of trained politicians and bureaucrats; Washington, Moscow, London, Paris, Berlin, and Tokyo were cities used to the pressures of ruling. Chongqing was not even the capital of Sichuan, the province where it was located. (The provincial seat of government was in Chengdu, some 160 miles away to the northwest.)

Because of its mountain topography, Chongqing is enveloped in fog for most of the autumn and winter, a deterrent for any enemy aircraft seeking to raid the capital. The lack of reliable power supplies also meant that there were few bright lights to attract the attention of visitors from above. But spring brought with it warmer weather and an end to the protective mist. The city then became a clear target.

Many aspects of life in the city were beyond the Nationalist government's control, and none more so than the terrifying new reality of constant bombings. In the winter of 1938 there were a few "trial raids" on the city. The attacks began in earnest from the spring of 1939, and it was the destruction that rained down on May 3 and 4 that year that really marked the arrival of a new campaign of terror. Yet the "great raids" *(da hongzha)* that had so cruelly marked the twentieth anniversary of the nationalist May Fourth demonstrations were just the start of a stream of destruction from the sky that would be part of everyday existence for years to come.

A new communal space entered Chinese consciousness: the air-raid shelter. For many, everyday routine had to be reshaped around the need to run suddenly for protection. "Your everyday plans were decided by the weather," remembered one inhabitant of the city. "If you needed to travel a long way, then you'd choose a cloudy day. If it was a clear day, you would get up early before it got light." People became used to carrying air-raid emergency packs: they might contain food, water, and perhaps essential medicines. Richer families might store their valuables in such a way that they could be moved quickly. For the shelter itself, some people had chairs and stools ready so they would not have to spend long hours standing.[10]

Like so much else in wartime China, the rhetoric of shared distress concealed the reality of class differences. Richer or better-connected citizens of Chongqing had access to better shelters. Government officials were given special access to reserved shelters, and were given certificates that allowed them to take their immediate families also. For those who could afford true luxury, at some 2,000 yuan a year, there were top-of-the-line shelters. For most, however, there were basic shelters carved out of the rock cliffs.[11]

The raids happened in spring and the height of the summer, when the city was at its hottest, with temperatures reaching more than 40 degrees Celsius. In the shelters, as the Chongqingers awaited the raids, the atmosphere was stifling, and people brought hand fans to keep themselves cool. When the bombers were still miles away, people chatted away normally, and children called out to their parents. Some of the more casual even put their chairs out to sit at the shelter entrance, waiting in the cooler air until the police forced them inside.

Then the planes came. People felt "a very strange wind" which foreshadowed the impact to come: after the bombs were released from the aircraft's fuselage, they created an airstream that would force its way into every empty space. People had to be very careful: if they were unprepared, the force of the pressure could throw them violently against the wall of the shelter. "Then," recalled one local, "you'd hear a noise . . . like the sky and the earth being smashed, like thunder on your head." Sometimes an enemy aircraft would be shot down; if it was, then the silence in the shelters could be broken by cheering and clapping. The whole experience made the population intensely fatigued. Day after day waiting for the air-raid sirens, and then the all-clear signal, meant disruption to patterns of work and family life. As the May 1939 raids showed, even if the all-clear had sounded, another raid might be imminent, and people became used to the idea of settling down in the hot, dark shelters for days at a time. Their emergency kits and toilet arrangements would last for a couple of days, but after that, they were at the mercy of enterprising vendors who were willing to brave the raids to sell overpriced essentials to the families trapped in stifling, lightless conditions. Emerging after five or six days in the shelter was a painful process for some, as their eyes simply were not used to the bright sunshine.[12] The authorities tried to reshape regulations to accommodate the new realities. On days when the all-clear was sounded after midnight, workers' hours were reduced for the next day. Some shops which sold essential goods were ordered to stay open, and were given government subsidies for doing so.[13] "For months," wrote Theodore White in *Time*, "Chungking merchants have done their business late in the afternoon, opening shop at 4 p.m., in order to limit the danger from air raids." Adjusting to the possibility of sudden peril from the sky, he wrote, had become "a sort of wartime normal."[14]

After the raids of May 1939, the authorities recruited professional body-carriers to deal with the corpses of people killed in the raids, and they would be paid the equivalent of one *jin* (half kilogram) of rice per body carried. The corpses would be buried together at a spot named the "new coffin mountain," having been transported on one of the boats shipping bodies out of the city. (At the height of the raids, more than a hundred boats operated at a time.) The boatmen would take whole bodies but, after a while, would dump partial corpses overboard or bury them at the riverside. This was not callousness or superstition, but practicality. At the bottom of each boat, the fluid from the corpses could flow a foot deep. For workers without rubber boots, just sandals, it was neither pleasant nor hygienic to work with their feet soaked in the body fluids of the dead. The stack of corpses also attracted hordes of flies, against which the workers were protected only by a thin face mask. When the stench became too horrific, whole corpses might even be buried by the side of the river.[15]

Chongqing's air-raid defenses remained weak, largely because the alternative would have required a swift increase in China's aerial warfare capacity, as well as antiaircraft weapons and other equipment that the country simply did not possess. Chiang's wife Song Meiling addressed the problem in 1937 by recruiting one of the more remarkable figures to work in wartime China: retired US Air Force Major General Claire Lee Chennault. A strong advocate of airpower, Chennault took over the training of China's still minimal air force (the official number of 600 aircraft was probably an exaggeration). As well as giving combat training to the small cadre of Chinese pilots, Chennault also recruited pilots from the US who might be better able to take on Japanese fighters. The group was officially known as the American Volunteer Group (AVG), but it soon became much better known by its nickname, the "Flying Tigers." The group was a real morale-booster for the beleaguered capital, even though the Tigers never actually flew in combat over its skies. But the real significance of Chennault's presence and views would not be made clear for several more years.[16]

However, even if it could not prevent the frequent air raids, the state did start to cope with the aftermath. In doing so, it began to remake the relationship between the government and the people in China as it developed a new system of social welfare provision, partly through planning and partly through improvisation in the face of sheer necessity.

The National Government knew that its techniques of mass mobilization were impressive in appearance but not always convincing in practice. The rhetoric of China's resistance to Japan was based on genuine popular

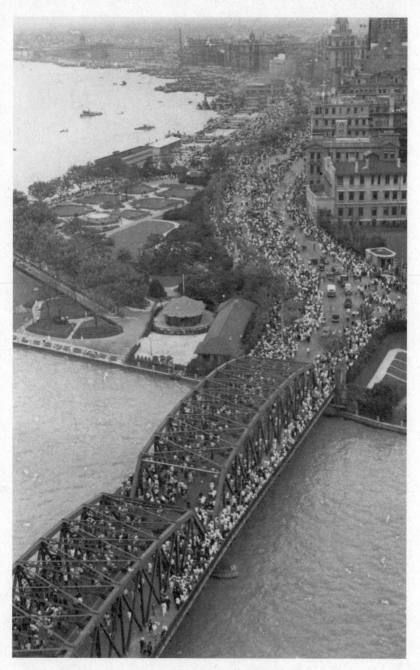

Refugees stream across the Garden Bridge, Shanghai, August 18, 1937.
Just six weeks previously, war had broken out suddenly in North China.

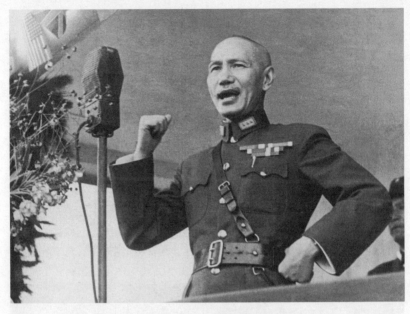

Chiang Kai-shek, thrust into the role of war leader, broadcasting in 1937.

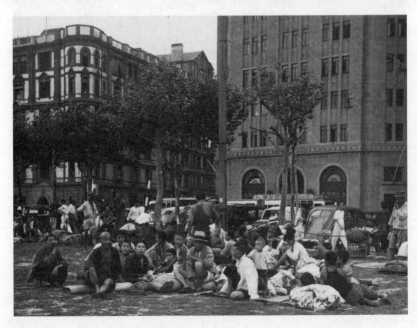

Refugees on Shanghai's Bund, 1937. Even neutral zones in the city were flooded with Chinese desperate to escape the Japanese invasion.

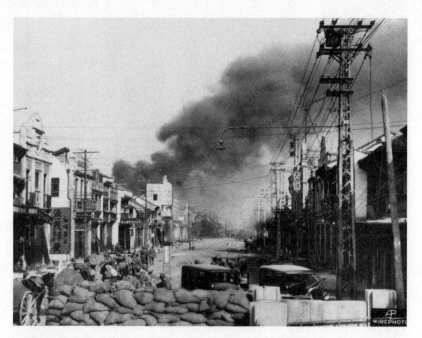

Retreating Chinese troops set fires in Nanjing, December 1937. The Chinese capital would soon be the scene of a horrific massacre.

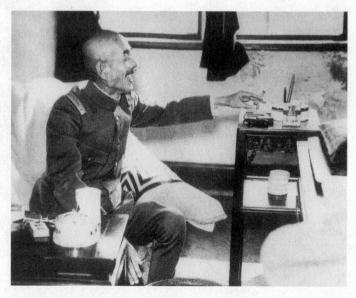

General Matsui Iwane at his headquarters, Shanghai, 1938. Just a few months earlier, Matsui had allowed his troops to kill and rape at will in occupied Nanjing.

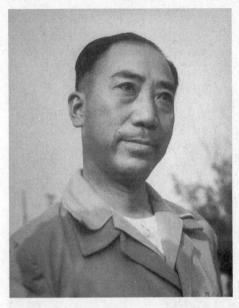

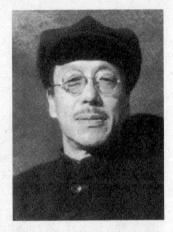

Kang Sheng, security chief and mastermind of terror in Mao's Communist base area in northwest China.

Dai Li, the Nationalist security chief, working with special police forces. Dai Li intended his agency to be Chiang Kai-shek's "eyes and ears."

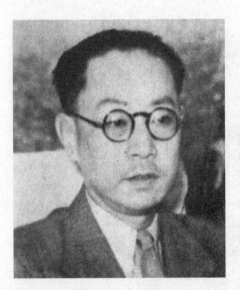

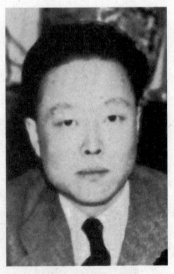

Zhou Fohai. The senior Nationalist minister was intimately involved with Wang Jingwei's defection and collaboration with the Japanese in 1938.

Li Shiqun, Wang Jingwei's vicious security chief, whose reign of terror operated from Shanghai's "Badlands."

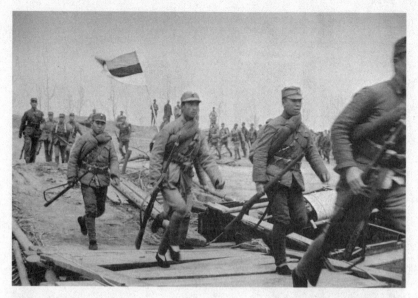

The Battle of Taierzhuang, April 1938. This rare Chinese victory boosted spirits in the face of the Japanese assault.

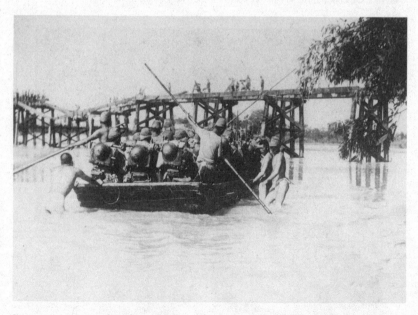

Japanese troops using a boat during the Yellow River floods, July 1938. Chiang's decision to break the river dikes temporarily stopped the Japanese but took numerous lives.

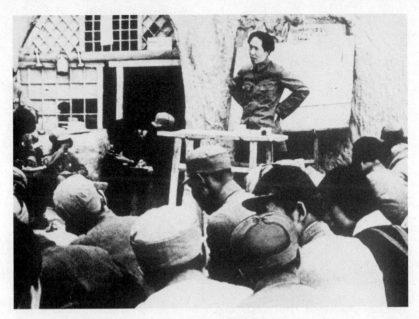

Mao Zedong speaks at the Lu Xun Arts Institute in Yan'an, May 1938. During the early war years, the Communists sought to widen their sources of support.

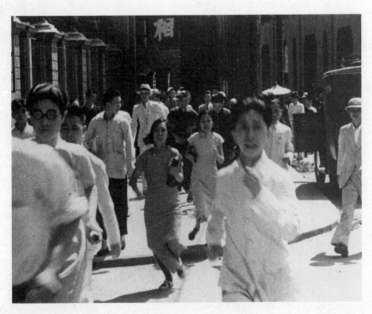

Civilians in Guangzhou (Canton) take flight, June 1938. Air raids were a constant danger in Nationalist China in the early war years.

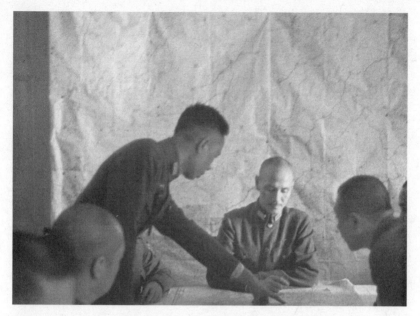

Chiang Kai-shek at a Supreme War Council meeting in Wuhan, July 1938. Chiang was faced with an immensely difficult decision on whether to abandon the city to the Japanese.

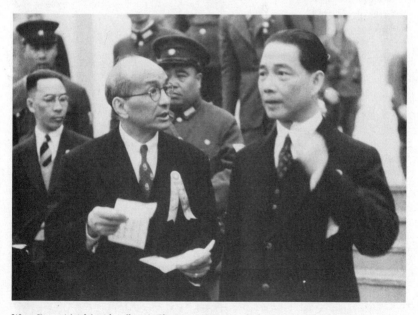

Wang Jingwei (*right*) with colleague Chu Minyi in Nanjing before Wang's inauguration, 1940. Wang set up a rival Nationalist government in collaboration with the Japanese.

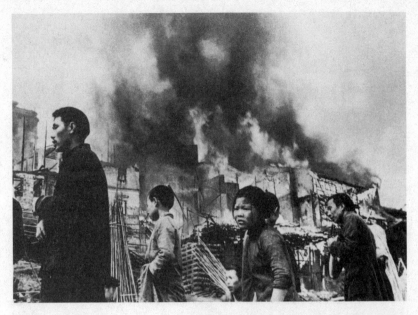

Homeless people in
the aftermath of air raids,
Chongqing, 1939. On May 3
and 4 the city suffered
a wave of devastating attacks by
Japanese bombers, highlighting
its vulnerability.

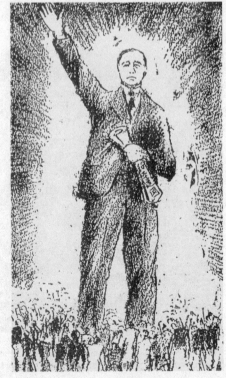

A cartoon depicting
Wang Jingwei on the date of his
inauguration as president of the
collaborationist government,
March 30, 1940. Wang is portrayed as a
giant radiating light to his grateful
people at the moment when Chinese
resistance seemed most futile.

feeling. However, it also raised expectations among the wider population that, having followed their government into the interior of China, they would be supported by that government through the troubles that war brought with it. The National Government used the circumstances of war to continue the project of modernization that had begun when it was in Nanjing. In particular, it gathered information. As the war situation disintegrated, the feeling of control that came from having statistics and data was at least some comfort to those who were trying to make the state work. It became important to stress that even if air raids could not be prevented, the government was competent in dealing with the aftermath.

The effort had already begun during the months that the government had spent in Wuhan, and figures such as the Nationalist activist Shi Liang became central to the hasty construction of relief provision.[17] However, the arrival of the government in Chongqing enabled the system to become more clearly organized. A major innovation was the establishment of an identity document (ID) scheme for refugees. Different types of ID allowed different levels of access to assistance, including assignment to jobs. The regulations showed concern about the potential that the new system allowed for corruption: refugees were forbidden from using their IDs to do "dubious deals."[18]

As well as refugee work, the city authorities in Chongqing sought to find a more systematic way of dealing with the aftermath of air raids. On January 16, 1939, representatives of bodies including the Chongqing city Public Works Office and the city Relief Committee discussed the most important preparations needed for the air raids. Organizations including the local New Life Movement and the Red Swastika (the traditional Buddhist relief organization) were to be brought into the arrangements.[19] Police reports also recorded air-raid damage after the terrible raids of May 1939.[20] Other public servants were also given more incentives: one proposal was that the authorities should offer the sum of a month's salary upfront to employees of the Public Works Bureau, as an incentive for valued staff not to leave Chongqing.[21] Another, yet more comprehensive suggestion, argued that even greater provision of facilities and services had to be made for employees who were air-raid victims. First, employees of the Public Works Bureau who were injured in air raids should be granted free treatment in a hospital, although it was specified that treatment should not cost more than 100 yuan. The family of an employee killed in a raid whom it could not afford to bury, or an employee needing to bury a spouse or child who had been killed, should be given up to 200 yuan to cover costs.

The total scale of Nationalist government refugee assistance was well beyond anything previously seen in China. Prior to 1937 there had been relatively little officially sanctioned government welfare provision. Now the demands of wartime made it imperative to create such a system. Between 1937 and 1941 the government's national-level Development and Relief Committee (DRC, or *Zhenji weiyuanhui*), established in 1938, assigned some 214 million yuan to relief work, as well as creating jobs for 90,000 refugees. The DRC's identity-card plan created a network of transit stations that enabled the evacuation of refugees to take place even under the most unpromising conditions: by the end of 1941 there were 38 general stations and 1,059 substations, which had been used by 9.2 million registered refugees. The relief may have been inadequate to the need, but it was not trivial. [22]

The government knew that its treatment of refugees was being judged in comparison with the Communists and with the Japanese. For many in the middle class, particularly those of a progressive frame of mind, the clear alternative was the Communists. The refugees from poorer rural backgrounds were more inclined to consider living under Japanese occupation. To do so would mean at least enjoying the familiarity of home, and in some cases the Japanese may have seemed no worse — or even better — than the many militarists who had rampaged through China in previous decades. The Nationalist government was therefore reluctant to let refugees return home, not only for reasons of national pride, but also because the returnees might prove an excellent source of intelligence about conditions in Free China. The Japanese in turn made sure to offer incentives to return. One report from 1940 declared that refugees were being tempted by rumors of a bumper harvest in the occupied zone, and were being assisted by road maps and instructions being smuggled to them by agents of the Japanese, with very specific advice on where to obtain free vehicle rides, or how to find smugglers' boats to make the tricky journey downriver from Yichang to Wuhan. "If we do not root this out," noted one concerned government report, "this will have a grave effect on the War of Resistance." In response, the Nationalists put more resources into propaganda as well as relief efforts, trying to prevent the newcomers from being "deceived by the enemy."[23]

The propaganda effort was not simply aimed at the refugees. Beyond

Chongqing itself, immense demands were now being made on the local population, including army recruitment and the growing of food to supply the cities and armed forces. The government tried to combine modern propaganda techniques with the reality that much of the countryside was still very traditional. One Sichuan county report from January 1939 described torchlight parades, political plays, and music (including traditional flower-drums and bamboo instruments) as ways of rallying the local population, some 3,000 of whom attended the public performance. On another occasion, the midautumn "Lantern Festival" was adapted so that the poetic couplets traditionally composed for the occasion were written to reflect wartime goals: "Our lights on the night of the lantern festival can reach even as far as [Japan]," read one couplet, "and set up the foundation for 10,000 years of the [Chinese] Republic."[24] Yet there were many signs that the message of mass resistance was only patchily successful at best. Confidential reports complained that efforts to redistribute rice to reward the families of men called up to the army were not being organized fairly.

Recruitment was key to the government's efforts to continue resistance. But initially conscription had been haphazard, and little had been done to explain to the wider population the significance of their participation in the war. As a result, there had been widespread desertion, as well as corruption by local officials who accepted government recruitment fees but then failed to sign up the troops as promised. In January 1938 new regulations were introduced that tried to regularize recruitment, which set monthly recruitment targets and (at least on paper) forbade forced enlistment. While recruitment was never popular, and continued to be plagued by endless numbers of abuses at the local level, in the first few years of the war it managed to hold steady (total recruitment to the Nationalist armies remained broadly steady at between 1.7 million and 2 million men a year between 1938 and 1941). In the initial years of the war, the system did not engender widespread, endemic social unrest.[25]

Another report attacked the failure to enthuse a huge section of the population: rural women. "Women are conservative, and their outlooks are rooted in clan and countryside," it declared. "They don't understand the meaning of the War of Resistance." The writer believed that the war provided an opportunity to mobilize women and increase their national consciousness, making use of the fact that the Japanese had "kidnapped children, burned property, and raped women." The role that was envisaged for women was not necessarily a liberating one — nursing wounded soldiers or making clothes for the troops — but the report acknowledged that women needed to be included in any modernization of society. War was supposed to create a nation-state from all of China's citizens.[26]

The Nationalist wartime economy did show promise. Prior to the outbreak of war, China had not been self-sufficient in food, and had regularly imported millions of tons of grain and rice, largely from Southeast Asia. During the first years of the war, rice imports were increased, the purchase price of rice in major cities in Free China remained broadly stable, and farmers were reasonably prosperous. Luck played some part in this; for the first two years of the war, fine weather meant plentiful harvests. However, the government also instituted reforms that contributed to productivity, including the use of refugee labor, the application of modern pesticides, and the supply of loans for agricultural collectives. The result was relative stability in food supply: up to 1940, crops of rice and wheat, as well as many other major crops, remained constant.[27]

Still, the Nationalists' efforts to create a state with welfare responsibilities while fighting a war were expensive, and Chiang's government was cash-strapped. Between 1937 and 1939 annual government revenues fell by 63 percent, whereas expenditure increased by 33 percent. Many of the major sources of state revenue, most notably import duties collected by the Chinese Maritime Customs, were lost when the National Government retreated from the east of the country. Instead, a new interport duty was established that taxed the movement of goods within China. Although a barrier to the free market, it proved a reasonably effective means of replacing a small proportion of the lost Customs revenue in the first two years of the war.[28]

The industrial economy of Nationalist China was also in a worrying state. Beginning in 1932, the government had concentrated on creating a "defense state," involving central government control of new military-oriented enterprises such as steel production and the manufacture of machinery. However, the new industries had not yet been fully constructed when war broke out, and most of the factories that were transferred upriver to Sichuan were privately owned. The region had just 4 percent of China's total electrical power-generation capacity; it held a similar tiny percentage of China's industrial capital. Sichuan lacked the railways, modern steel production, and highways developed elsewhere in the country in the decade before the war broke out.[29] This was therefore a pitifully small base on which to try to mobilize a wartime industrial economy. To make matters worse, the loss of eastern China meant that the best way that further industrial materials could be brought to Sichuan was to bring them in by sea from the south, or else to fly them in via the dangerous route over the Burma "Hump" from India to China. The alternatives to imports included ingenious but increasingly desperate measures such as refining industrial alcohol as an alternative to gasoline.[30]

The government responded in the way that would become typical of all societies in the modern period of total war: a major increase in the level of state control of the economy. A new Ministry of Economic Affairs was created, which incorporated the prewar National Resources Commission and was headed by that body's energetic chairman, Weng Wenhao. In 1938 Weng's ministry was given the power to nationalize crucial industries. By the end of the year, the ministry was running some sixty-three enterprises either by itself or in cooperation with other state organizations or private capitalists. Yet however great the efforts, the growth in wartime production was severely limited by the resources available in the underdeveloped southwest; even in the last years of the war, the total amount of electricity that could be generated in the Nationalist areas was only around 8 percent of what the occupied areas could produce.[31] The oil lamps would be a constant, dim glow through Chongqing's wartime years.

As the Japanese pushed deeper into eastern China, the American missionary Katherine Hand remained in Yizhou, in Shandong province. The Chinese soldiers had retreated hastily. Now the city was in the hands of the Japanese. "The army is passing through our city in thousands," Hand observed. Yizhou was captured with little initial violence, but the fear of it was always there, as Hand noted on May 2, 1938:

> It is most uncanny to stand guard in an empty street, with nothing to be seen but destroyed buildings, in front of the ruins of a house, the only sound odd bits of tin flapping in the breeze, knowing that there are men inside searching for grain or money in the ruins, and that any moment a band of soldiers may come up . . . We are probably safe so long as I am around with the [American] flag, but civilians have been shot without provocation in the city, and the men would not be safe for a moment without identification. We have also escorted groups of our refugees part way to places they can scatter in the country.[32]

Hand used the word "uncanny" more than once to capture what it felt like to be in a state of war but not in the midst of a battle. She was not alone. As more and more of eastern China fell under Japanese control, the region's Chinese population waited—with a mixture of terror and resignation in the face of Japan's seemingly inevitable victory—to discover the nature of the new regime.

The Japanese were almost as unprepared for the responsibilities of occupation as the Nationalists were for governing in retreat. The invaders had not expected the events of July 1937 to turn into an all-out war, and they had few concrete plans in place to deal with the extent of their sudden new conquests. There were precedents, however. In particular, the occupation of Manchuria in 1931–1932 had forced the Japanese to find ways to deal with the politics and economics of occupation. Their general technique had been to find collaborators, preferably people of some standing, to run local government for them. The Japanese wanted their conquests to pay for themselves, or better still, to provide revenue for Japan, but realized that in the short term they would have to spend money to restore order and gain the trust of the local population. These techniques had been easier to carry out in Manchuria, where there was little serious military resistance to occupation, in comparison to central China in 1937–1938, where the fighting had devastated the local infrastructure. Bringing order back was the best chance for the Japanese to claim legitimacy for their new regime.[33]

Strong government was necessary, yet no such government was available. The suppression of "banditry" became a common theme for the occupiers and their collaborators. This was not always simply a pretext. A middle-class Chinese Christian woman who had fled from a small village near Suzhou in January 1938 gave an account of being kidnapped by local Chinese criminals. After a month of negotiation, in which a ransom of 30,000 dollars was whittled down to 1,000, the woman and her two daughters were freed. All of the ransom demands were dealt with by the local community; there was no authority left to which they could appeal.[34] Kidnapping was not uncommon before the outbreak of war, but the withdrawal of the National Government from eastern China cleared the path for banditry. As the war went on, the Japanese and local authorities would blur the issue by using the term "bandit" to refer to groups ranging from criminals simply out for ransom to anti-Japanese partisans. Chiang, of course, had done the same thing by referring to the CCP as

"Communist bandits." And it was also true that many of those who used the title "resistance fighters" were, in practice, bandits, or at any rate accustomed to living off the exploitation of the locals (although in many cases, they may have had little choice).

While banditry was more a phenomenon of rural China, criminality and disorder also reigned in the cities. In Shanghai the first Japanese-controlled government was instituted on December 5, 1937, in the part of the city that had formerly been under Nationalist control. The "Great Way government" *(Dadao zhengfu)* lasted only until April 28, 1938, but it was the first attempt in the city to provide an alternative to the now-retreated Nationalist government.[35] A more ambitious replacement regime was the Reformed Government of China *(Weixin zhengfu)*. On March 28, 1938, the government was officially formed in the Great Hall of the National Government in Nanjing, and headed by Liang Hongzhi, who had been prominent in militarist politics in the 1910s and 1920s, but whose political career had been eclipsed under the Nationalists.[36] Having publicly declared their status in Nanjing, the entire government got on a train and returned to the New Asia Hotel, Shanghai. From there, they ran what became known to detractors as the "Hotel government" for the next two years. (A couple of years later, the Vichy government in France would go one better, commandeering not just a hotel but an entire spa resort). Very few people in Shanghai knew anything about the shadowy leaders who came and went at the top of their government.

With the weakness of the government in the occupied parts of the city, it fell to the rich network of other social organizations that China had built up over the centuries to deal with the aftermath. One such group, the native-place association *(tongxianghui)*, was an organization with branches in many cities: members of the Wuxi native-place association who found themselves in Shanghai on business, or migrating to seek a better life, could call on local members to provide them with financial or other assistance. Another source of relief was the powerful network of religious philanthropic organizations. One of the most prominent was the Red Swastika (which, as noted earlier, had no connection to Nazism, but rather used the traditional symbol of Buddhist practice), the equivalent of the Red Cross (which also had a powerful presence in China by this stage). Their documents from Shanghai in 1938 declared that they had no interest in politics, but rather, their most important desire was to relieve suffering in the wake of the outbreak of fighting in Shanghai.[37]

Meanwhile, even though the foreign concessions continued to operate as oases of neutrality, the war still forced itself into their imposing buildings and spilled out onto the streets. A natural instinct was to help the thousands of refugees who had flooded into the safety of the concessions and were now the charge of the British-dominated Shanghai Municipal Council or the French Concession authorities. "Camp No. 100," a typical temporary shelter in Shanghai, was based in an old isolation hospital that had been evacuated during the battle for Shanghai in the autumn of 1937, and held some 1,300 people. Conditions were clearly appalling: one volunteer's task was to help prevent the spread of disease because of the close proximity of so many displaced people. Her day involved trying to sterilize milk bottles for displaced refugee children, dealing with the distribution of new clothes, and bathing the refugees themselves. "Poor things," she observed, "they haven't had a real bath for months and months, and incidentally, it is astonishing, considering their lack of facilities, how clean their skins look."[38]

For the Shanghai Municipal Council (SMC) that ran the International Settlement, however, the provision of space and facilities for the refugees was a highly unwelcome task. SMC official R. C. Robertson drew up a report on September 6, 1937, noting with condescension that there was a continuing evacuation to the countryside, but that it was "chiefly the better classes of refugee who have gone, leaving a large number of refugees who are very difficult to evacuate . . . A glaring example of this is the 'squatter' type of Kompo low class population, who have practically commandeered the dilapidated foreign-style houses in the terrace on Sinza Road." He went on: "These refugees are apparently self-supporting by casual labour, thieving, etc. They have no desire to be evacuated. They keep the premises in a state of filth and are a menace to public health. The only measures to deal with this group are Police measures."[39] But Robertson realized that this was not the whole story. "This influx was of refugees who had been throughout the hostilities in hiding among shell-torn ruins, and had been exposed to all the terrors of fire and war fare [sic]," he noted. "From the medical point of view we had thus a shell-shocked and nerve-strained addition to our refugee population."[40] The arrival of refugees, and the disease that they brought with them, threatened to upset Shanghai's sense of itself as orderly, rational, and modern.

Suggestions were made for supplements to the refugee diet, including mass deliveries of cod-liver oil, but the "very large number of refugees in each camp" made this an expensive plan. The SMC also wished to encourage public donations: they did not see the provision of mass refugee welfare as part of their role.[41]

By April 1938 the French Concession authorities had to write to Sterling Fessenden, secretary-general of the SMC, to let him know that "since April 1, 1938, the number of persons who have arrived seeking refuge in the Settlements exceeds 150,000."[42] The French authorities suggested that no further ships be allowed to arrive in Shanghai, but the SMC police pointed out the practical difficulties in shutting down shipping to China's largest port. The Commissioner of Public Health, however, continued to stress that "the 80,000 refugees registered in Settlement camps are a mass of rather uniformly primitive and uneducated people from the country and from the poor suburbs of Shanghai which for this reason are unable to understand and to comply with the various necessities essential for a sound and orderly community."[43]

Terms such as "primitive" are revealing of the authorities' near-panic. It seemed that events were going to spiral out of control. Shanghai's status as an enclave of foreign privilege rested on its connection to a growing and prosperous China outside the Settlement borders, whether a weak imperial China or a Nationalist China growing in strength. But the "moonscape" of the battered Chinese city, or the refugee flight that destroyed the region's marketing and transport networks, or the collapsing Nationalist government, spelled doom for the huge financial — and emotional — investment that the Westerners had made in Shanghai.

Nor was Shanghai the only place where the Japanese assault had created chaos. On February 12, 1939, Katharine Hand reflected on the first year in Yizhou under Japanese occupation:

> The Japanese garrison is still here in the city and the guerillas [sic] in the country. Friction is frequent and inevitable. We never know when or where there may be a more or less serious battle. The bandits are taking advantage of the situation. The country people are in terror, frequently fleeing hither and yon. We still have so many refugees that we can't take all the students we would like into the dormitories. The refugees are many of them city people who have absolutely no place to go. The city remains a sort of military fortress, mostly in ruins, with no local business, and few inhabitants except the soldiers. The hospital is filled almost to capacity, but few can afford to pay for their treatment. Many of the people would have starved if we had not had relief funds

to give to them. Many, who were doing well before the war, are without jobs or the prospect of them . . .

What is the end and when? Would we be happy if we knew?[44]

When they wrote their memoirs, the outsiders who visited the Communist capital at Yan'an in Shaanxi province came back, over and over again, to the subject of food. Mealtimes were at 8:00 a.m., 11:00 a.m., and 3:00 p.m., and consisted of millet porridge or dried millet as a staple. In winter, there were no eggs, as it was too cold for the chickens to lay.[45] Food was rationed carefully and there was little variation, although mothers with children were given extra meat. The privilege system by which certain people in high standing with the party got better provisions meant that there could be discrimination within families: the writer Ai Qing got the medium-quality meal, whereas his wife and child obtained only basic-level food.[46] The meal regime was one facet of a larger way of life. Wartime Yan'an was stark and regimented, particularly for those who had accepted the discipline of the party. Even more than in Chongqing, Yan'an was the testing ground for a new social contract. The party and state promised deeper commitments to social provision, but demanded complete obedience in return.

One year earlier, in 1936, a group of 9,000 soldiers, bedraggled and exhausted, had reached this northwestern hill town. Their arrival marked the end of the Long March, an event that would become a legend in Chinese Communist mythology. In reality, the Long March had been a retreat, a reaction to the growing strength of the Nationalist campaigns against the CCP, as well as the party leadership's vicious infighting in Jiangxi. Yan'an became a symbol of an alternative political future for those who were increasingly angered by the dictatorial tendencies of the Nationalists. But the Communist experiment in government was in profound danger by the mid-1930s.

The threat of approaching war changed the fortunes of the Chinese Communist Party. No longer a band of rebels on the run, they were now officially regarded as a junior partner in the United Front against Japan. The development of Communist political policy in the years of the war was inexorably shaped by the demands of warfare itself.

The war also transformed the career of Mao Zedong. Mao had not been the only possible leader for the party when the war broke out, but his position had been greatly strengthened by the Long March; later accounts would play down the role of other Communist leaders whose feats of bravery on the March equaled or exceeded Mao's. The Zunyi Conference, held in Guizhou province in January 1935, was also a major turning point for Mao's fortunes, as it endorsed his tactics of mobile warfare and moved the party away from the conventional warfare strategies supported by the Comintern. Yet by the outbreak of war in 1937, there were still other contenders for leadership of the CCP, most notably the Moscow-trained Wang Ming (Chen Shaoyu) and rival Long March veteran Zhang Guotao.[47] But Mao's decisions were not made just in the context of other figures and ideas within the party itself. Despite the turn toward self-sufficiency, the CCP did not exist in a vacuum. Communist ideology had to change to fit the real, unpredictable, and very fast-moving events of the war itself.

Mao knew that the United Front with the Nationalists was an outstanding opportunity for the CCP to extend its power, but also one fraught with great danger. In particular, the Red Army would be placed under the overall command of Chiang Kai-shek. However, the CCP had no intention of allowing a repetition of 1927, when it had been left without armed forces of its own and vulnerable to Chiang's purges. The Communist armies numbered some 30,000 men at the start of the war, and during August and September they were reorganized as the Eighth Route Army, made up of three divisions which quickly expanded to around 80,000 troops. Not long afterward, the Communists were authorized to establish a second force of up to 12,000 men known as the New Fourth Army, which would operate in central China.[48] At least a third of the Communist forces would not fight the Japanese directly, but be retained at the base areas (by implication, to defend them against the Nationalists).

Mao observed that Chiang was genuine in his resistance to Japan. On August 13, 1937, the very day on which fighting broke out between China and Japan in Shanghai, Mao spoke to the sympathetic American journalist Nym Wales (the pseudonym of Helen Foster Snow) and acknowledged that the National Government had agreed to immediate war, with Communist troops as part of the national army.[49] On September 6 the Shaan-GanNing (SGN) Border Region government was officially declared. Its name derived from the first syllables of the three provinces where it was located (Shaanxi, Gansu, and Ningxia), with its headquarters at Yan'an. This was the key base area where Mao would spend the war and create a new vision of society, what a classic later analysis would call "the Yenan [Yan'an] Way."[50]

In the first years of the war, Mao's writings show a politician and thinker in the process of change. Mao took advantage of his relative isolation in Yan'an by reading extensively in Marxist literature. He had always been a voracious reader, but not being on the run allowed him space for the first time, perhaps since the heady days of the May Fourth Movement, to immerse himself in the ideology that he had embraced as a young man. Unlike Wang Ming and his followers, who had been able to learn at the hands of Stalin in Moscow, or the various urban sophisticates in the party, such as Zhou Enlai, Mao came from a rural background and was an autodidact. His intellect was not in doubt, but his training and theoretical suppleness were. By making it clear that he was in control of the ideological apparatus that shaped the party, he was strengthening his bid for leadership.

Mao's writings on the war in its first year show a thinker whose range of reference took him well beyond the caves of Shaanxi province.[51] Shanghai fell in November 1937, as did Taiyuan. Mao saw the fall of these cities as a sign that the positional warfare of the large Nationalist armies was over, and that guerrilla warfare would be the dominant strategic method, at least until the war became internationalized. As with Chiang's plans, this was a leap of faith, for there was no indication in autumn 1937 that the war was likely to become global. Nor was Mao correct in arguing that conventional pitched battle was no longer effective; Xue Yue's defense of Changsha in 1939, for instance, would preserve a key strategic city for Nationalist China for at least a few more years. Even had it been possible to wage the kind of mobile warfare Mao favored, it would have been politically very difficult for the Nationalists, with the world's eyes upon them, to abandon a conventional armed defense while continuing to call for international assistance. As the secondary partner of the Nationalists, Mao had the freedom to indulge in more radical strategic thinking, but it was Chongqing, not Yan'an, that had to lobby London and Washington for aid.

The powerful status of Yan'an as a beacon of radical resistance attracted large numbers of migrants, some 100,000 between 1937 and 1940.[52] These numbers were dwarfed by the millions who fled to Chongqing, but the types of people who came to Yan'an were disproportionately well educated: perhaps some 50,000 were middle-class, educated types such as students, journalists, and teachers. Many of them came in search of a new future for China, feeling that the Nationalists were already hopelessly compromised by the brutality of their government's behavior before 1937. For many, however, the reality of Yan'an did not measure up to the dream. The small city was in an economically deprived and backward area that made Chongqing look like a sophisticated metropolis. The surrounding areas of Shaanxi province were desperately poor — one reason the Communist message had resonated there — and still almost entirely agricultural. The total population of the region that the party ruled from Yan'an was only 1.4 million. The region was prone to natural disasters (earthquakes and drought) along with human-made ones (banditry and famine).[53] The harsh yellow loess soil had formed into cliffs into which cave houses were carved.

For those who wanted to make revolution, life was a strain, with scarce food and basic accommodation. The Yan'an College of Marxism-Leninism was a typical party educational institution: students lived in a hillside cave. There were desks and lamps so that they could study in the evenings, but no chairs. Duan Suquan recalled many years later: "Student life was very ordered. We studied, went to class, discussed things, then ate and slept. There was strict order, and a whistle was used as a signal [for instructions]."[54] Yet despite the stress on order, it was hard to organize a dynamic political movement. Chen Xuezhao, founder of the Yan'an hospital, wrote in *Liberation Daily*:

> When we hold a meeting, even if there are lots of people there, the waiting time is almost as long as the actual meeting time. For a meeting that lasts two hours, you wait two hours . . . so if I'm waiting to hear two hours of reports, and I've already been waiting an hour and a half, I'm exhausted and can't concentrate.[55]

In Chongqing the refugees from eastern China had found themselves at odds with the Sichuan locals. In Yan'an, too, the newcomers seeking a systematic Communist revolution came up against the centuries-old habits of the local farming population. One young worker activist, Yang Changchun, recalled that in the spring of 1938 he had taken part in a tree-planting exercise, and suggested arranging the trees to keep them neat. The official he spoke to, a veteran of the Long March, disagreed, saying that one shoved a tree into the ground and that was all there was to it. A shouting match broke out. Yang yelled that the man was "just an old peas-

ant," only to receive the reply that "you people who've come from the Nationalist areas are disgusting — you look like foreigners!"[56] Skilled industrial workers were at a premium in Yan'an and consequently could earn
higher wages and a better standard of living (by some calculations, twice
what they had before the outbreak of war), causing further resentment.[57]

In Yan'an men always outnumbered women. In 1938 there were some
thirty men to every woman; even by 1944 there were still eight men to
each woman.[58] For many women, this was a chance to escape stereotyped
roles; "revolutionary costumes" with "Lenin-style" open collars became
de rigueur at the Women's University, for instance. The activist Chang
Zhaogou recalled in a memoir nearly half a century later that the roman-
ticized image of Yan'an was misplaced:

> There were no women there with permed hair, and there were no lov-
> ers hand in hand. Few women comrades had a pretension toward femi-
> ninity. Their fashions were almost the same as the men's. In general,
> Yan'an was really not a sexy town.[59]

Women in Yan'an were also subject to profound social pressures. The lack
of contraception led to many unexpected pregnancies, but the primitive medical conditions meant that childbirth could be a dangerous and
traumatic experience. Nor were there sufficient facilities for childcare.
If women wished to continue their revolutionary careers, then they had
to consider the wrenching possibility of handing over their newborns to
local peasant families to bring up.[60] Hygiene was very poor: a local joke
held that lice were "revolutionary insects" because everyone who was
committed enough to stay in Yan'an would become infested by the insects
eventually.[61]

Nor was the town immune from Japanese attack. On November 20,
1938, some seven Japanese aircraft launched bombs on the old city. One
observer, Wang Guangrong, recalled "seventy or eighty dead or wounded,
flesh flying, terrible to see." The bombers came again the next day, hitting
Mao's own house, and killing thirty soldiers. But people learned fast. At
New Year and Chinese New Year, Yan'an was raided again, but this time
preparations were better and there were few injuries. The town's old Ming
dynasty tower was fitted out with antiaircraft guns, and the bell was tolled
as an air-raid warning.[62]

The Japanese did not target Yan'an in the way that they did Chongqing. In total, there were some seventeen air raids between 1938 and late

1941; the death toll was 214, a significant loss, but a much smaller number than the 5,000 or more killed in just the Chongqing raids of May 3 and 4, 1939.[63] The enemy was fiercely anti-Communist, but the prize target was Chiang Kai-shek; it was his resistance that symbolized the fact that not all of China was willing to succumb to Japanese dominance. The Nationalist regime was under constant bombardment and in the public eye not only of the Chinese media but the international community. This fact, along with the remote location of Yan'an and the smaller influx of refugees relative to Chongqing, allowed the Communists to develop their project free from outside observation or interference. Yan'an remained something of a mystery: no embassies were located there, and no journalists had bureaus in town. Foreigners were not unknown, but most of the invited guests from outside, such as the radical journalists Edgar Snow and Agnes Smedley, were Communist sympathizers who gave a generally positive account of Yan'an in their reports.

Being out of the international spotlight allowed Mao a much greater opportunity to create a new social order. In addition to being poor, the land was distributed unequally, with one estimate suggesting that 12 percent of the population owned some 46 percent of the land. In the SGN region, policies were designed to equalize the burdens on all living in the area, but were adapted according to local circumstances. In areas where a relatively small number of landlords owned a high proportion of the land, rent reductions became an important tool; in other areas where land was more evenly distributed, but poverty was widespread, the reduction of tax burdens was more important. The Communists did not attempt to control the whole of the base area's economy from Yan'an, but rather supervised the significant private economy, which included large private landholdings. Politics was also pluralized, with elected local assemblies, although the party continued to dominate them in practice.[64] In 1940 the Communists adopted another system of representation that would stress United Front policies: the "three-thirds" system *(san san zhi)*. This decreed that local assemblies (but not the party or the army) should be elected from three groupings: one-third CCP members, one-third leftist elements not in the party, and one-third middle elements neither from the left nor the right.[65]

Other leaders varied in the strength of their threat to Mao. In the spring of 1938, Zhang Guotao had realized that his hopes of dominance in the party were becoming ever weaker, and he defected to the Nationalists. Wang Ming was a more substantial challenger, particularly since his pedigree included prestigious training in Moscow. He advocated policy that was anathema to Mao, suggesting that the CCP might cooperate more strongly with the Nationalists, possibly even through a combined government. Since the Soviets were giving significant assistance to the Nationalists, this might also have been an opportunity for the Communists to share in some of the finance and materiel then flowing to Chiang Kai-shek. Wang Ming also clung strongly to the idea that a Communist revolution in China would take place in the cities, not the countryside.[66] Yet events conspired against him. The loss of Wuhan meant that his hopes of organizing an urban base for Communist power were no longer realistic. Instead, it was the rural areas where the CCP would make inroads, and Mao's vision prevailed over Wang Ming's. By the end of 1938 the Moscow-trained pretender was no longer a real threat. Mao was not the only noteworthy Communist leader, nor was his base area the only place where the CCP developed its ideas and strength during the war. But Mao's charisma, along with the geographical advantages of Yan'an, meant that the stories of the Communist resistance elsewhere in China were rather overshadowed.

The Communists also advanced in central China, setting up a base (the JinChaJi base) in the border lands between Shanxi and Hebei, as well as in northwest Shanxi (JinSui) and the Taihang mountains of southeast Shanxi (the JinJuLuYu base). In Shanxi province the provincial militarist Yan Xishan had formed an alliance of convenience with the Communists, despite (like Chiang) being hostile to the party by instinct. Yet in the first months Shanxi's capital city of Taiyuan became the headquarters for the CCP's North China bureau, overseen by Liu Shaoqi. Communist influence led to a significant military victory at Pingxingguan on September 25, 1937, when forces from the Eighth Route Army coordinated with local troops and helped to ambush and slaughter part of the Japanese Imperial Army's Fifth Division.[67]

The initial years of the war saw significant expansion of the Communist Party and its allied forces. Between 1937 and 1941 the number of members rose from some 40,000 to 763,447, and from a total force of some 92,000 at the start, the combined Eighth Route Army and New Fourth Army rose to some 440,000 troops over the same period.[68] Within the Communist base areas, there were also local militias, many of whose recruits divided their time between normal agricultural activity and military service, reducing the fear (prevalent in the Nationalist areas) of young men being recruited to the army and leaving the family without a breadwinner. Rather than the Nationalist policy of trying (not always successfully) to redistribute grain to military families, the Communists sought to lessen the distance between military service and everyday rural life. In addition, until 1940, the Nationalists subsidized the economy of SGN with an injection of some C$600,000 (then US$180,000) per month, providing valuable income for a desperately impoverished region. (Following the termination of Nationalist financial support, Stalin authorized a payment in 1940 to the CCP of some US $300,000.)[69]

The Communists wanted mass mobilization and were significantly more enthusiastic about popular participation in political activity than the Nationalists. But just like their rivals, the CCP did not wish to surrender the right to ultimate power. Their vision of democracy did mean widening political participation, but it was never liberal or fully pluralist. In their zone of control, the Nationalists had sought to broaden political involvement via the National Political Consultative Council, which allowed participation from other parties while retaining ultimate control of government for the Nationalists.[70] The Communists also sponsored wider participation in local assemblies while ensuring that the party made the real decisions. To criticize these systems (as observers did) as empty and lacking in real political power misses some of the point. They were not designed to measure up against pluralist models of liberal democracy, but rather against premodern systems in which imperial subjects had no inherent citizen rights to participation in government at all. Yet these ideological systems were also a sign of how reluctant the dominant parties were to share real power.

Yan'an, like Chongqing, became an idea as much as it was a physical place, and both cities stood in contrast with occupied China. Chongqing became symbolic of a new compact between state and society, namely that in a newly forged China the state should demand much more of its population as it faced a test that could destroy the nation, and that the citizenry should expect much more in return from those who governed them. The underlying compact in Yan'an was similar, but raised to an even greater level, with revolution rather than reform at the heart of the Communist project. Russia's revolution in 1917 had also taken place in the middle of an international war, but the methods that Mao and his party used were very different from the top-down Bolshevik seizure of power.

Mao made it clear that the primary task was to rally around the cause of the united front against Japan, and that class warfare would take a secondary place for the time being. Instead, the Communists took their time to develop genuine instruments of mass mobilization.

Not everyone was pleased with the growing status of the Communists in wartime China. Chiang, of course, was deeply distrustful of their intentions. So also was his colleague and rival Wang Jingwei.

Chapter 11

FLIGHT INTO THE UNKNOWN

O N NOVEMBER 26, 1938, Zhou Fohai and his aide Mei Siping were among a small number of Nationalist officials called to a secret meeting at the house of Wang Jingwei in Chongqing. Mei had just returned from Shanghai. Had Chiang Kai-shek known about this, Mei would have been instantly arrested, for he had spent the past few days in detailed, fevered conversation with senior Japanese military figures. Their demand was simple: Wang Jingwei should defect and establish a rival government to Chiang's in Japanese-occupied eastern China. A draft agreement had been signed by both sides, and a declaration had been prepared for Japanese premier Prince Konoye to announce the birth of the new government. But it would be cataclysmic for Wang, with his long revolutionary history, to make such an irreversible move, however deep his resentment against Chiang and his anxieties over China's fate.

Wang could not make up his mind. After the meeting, he looked disconsolate. Zhou Fohai was furious at Wang's indecision. "At home," he wrote, "we discussed Wang Jingwei's character. He has no definite ideas, and it's easy to change his mind. That's why he's failed these last ten years. But on this matter, although he will go back and forth, he will eventually carry out the plan." Zhou's judgment was perhaps a little harsh. Wang had, after all, risked execution for the revolutionary cause in his younger days; now they were asking him, a senior minister in the Chongqing government, to risk his life again, for there was no doubt that Chiang and the Communists would regard a defection as treason.

The next day Wang was still undecided, but Zhou was more forgiving. He reflected a little later that though Wang was hesitant and lacked self-control, he was also amenable to advice. "This is a big matter . . . I don't blame him for needing to think about all the options," Zhou wrote. "Even I've had to do the same."[1] Within a few days Wang seemed to have been won over. However, to put the defection into action was not an easy task. The principal actors needed to leave Chongqing, where the agents of Chiang's security chief, Dai Li, kept an eye out for suspicious behavior. So Wang would have to go to the Sichuanese capital, Chengdu, and Zhou

Fohai would go on ahead to the southwestern city of Kunming. Kunming was in Yunnan province, under the control of the militarist leader Long Yun. Long Yun, who was an ethnic Yi (Lolo), not a Han Chinese, was one of those provincial commanders who had a turbulent relationship with Chiang. While he recognized the authority of the Nationalist government in theory, he regularly welcomed dissidents who found Chongqing's atmosphere too oppressive. Yunnan was also close to the border with Indochina, part of the French Empire.

In common with Chiang Kai-shek, and, in his later years, Mao, Wang had a strong wife. While he was indecisive, she, Chen Bijun, was anything but, and she may have helped tip the balance. "Madame Wang was an outstanding woman," recalled Gao Zongwu, the head of the Asia Bureau of the Foreign Ministry, who would become close to Wang:

> and her influence on Wang Jingwei was very strong. Her aggressive and strong attitude was a compensation for the femininity and good looks and gentle movement of Wang Jingwei . . . Those who offended her would never get to see Wang Jingwei again; this was her greatest power.[2]

Gao also claimed that it was Chen Bijun's strong will that had captured for her the handsome Wang as a husband, rather than her looks. "She always resented Wang Jingwei's youthful appearance," Gao claimed, "because it made people think she was his mother." This ungracious comment runs in a long line of asides in Chinese history about strong and frightening women who sit behind the throne. In fact, Chen had many qualities that had no doubt impressed Wang, not least her own revolutionary commitment, as well as her immense courage and fierce loyalty to her husband. One factor that may well have weighed on Wang's mind when deciding whether to leave Chongqing was Chen's increasing conviction that Chiang was trying to assassinate him.[3]

The atmosphere among the defectors now became feverish as they made preparations to leave. At every moment it seemed that Chiang, who was away from his capital, might find out what they were doing. "I've heard that Chiang will be coming back before the 10th," Zhou wrote on December 1. "I have an inexplicable feeling, like a schoolboy who hears that the teacher is coming." And now Wang began to waver again, his anxiety manifesting itself in a stream of telephone calls. One day he was furious about a public statement issued by the Weixin government (the client government set up by the Japanese in north China), which seemed to claim sovereignty over all of China; another day he read reports in the Hong Kong and Shanghai newspapers (that is, those outside Nationalist control) attacking him, and wanted to know how to respond.[4] Zhou Fohai became increasingly worried that, though the defectors had placed their hopes on Wang, they could not depend on him.

On December 5 Zhou boarded a flight to Kunming. As far as the officials who saw him off at the airport were concerned, it was just a routine business trip. For Zhou, however, it was the start of his journey into the political unknown:

> We took off at 10:45 a.m. Farewell, Chongqing! The survival or destruction of the country, and my own success or failure, all depend on the success of this trip! . . . At the moment that the plane left the ground, was that the ending of my political life?[5]

Once in Kunming, chance encounters left Zhou feeling jumpy. "Today I heard people speaking the Chongqing dialect," he wrote. "I miss Chongqing. I'm not happy and I miss the past. This is a shortcoming in my psychology." His absence from home now set him thinking about his past life and in particular a lover long since gone. "I miss my dead friend, Man Qiu," he wrote disconsolately. "Even writing the words 'dead friend' is very painful."

Then news from Chongqing threw him into despair. Wang had canceled his departure. Chiang was back in town, and fearing that he would get wind of the plot, Wang was refusing to move. Mei Siping, now in Hong Kong, had to scramble to delay the announcement in Shanghai that would declare the opening of negotiations between Wang and the Japanese. Zhou could not sleep. "I worried worse than ever before in my life," he wrote. Should he go back to Chongqing and wait for another opportunity? After all, very few people knew that his visit to Kunming was anything other than routine.[6] Perhaps he could still change his mind, with nobody the wiser?

But Zhou decided that he could not return to Chongqing. If he went back to the capital now, he would only be delaying the decision for a few more days, and worse still, he might not be able to leave again. "If heaven does not let China die," he wrote, "then Mr. Wang *will* be able to leave Chongqing."

Zhou's insomnia continued. Away from Chongqing, he could not get to the mercurial Wang to persuade him to change his mind. And Wang seemed to be shrinking away from the decision. On December 17, Chen Chunpu, a relative of Wang's wife Chen Bijun, told Zhou that Wang had canceled his tickets to Hanoi. "I don't know what to do," Zhou wrote; "I saw five visitors, made a big effort, but inside I was really depressed." Zhou now reversed position: perhaps it made more sense to return to Chong-qing, observe the situation, and wait for a better opportunity. "My feeling was 80 percent to head back to Chongqing," he reflected, and "20 percent to head on to Hong Kong."[7] He still feared that Chiang might find out about the plot; if he did, Zhou could expect to be arrested immediately.

On December 18 Zhou went out into the streets and saw bands playing on the streets and policemen keeping guard. Clearly a major leader had arrived in town, but who? If it was Chiang, then Zhou's defection was over before it had begun. But if Wang had reached Kunming, the plan was finally under way.

After the fall of Wuhan, Chiang Kai-shek had made it clear that the gov-ernment had no intention of surrender, declaring that "this is a national and revolutionary war."[8] Chiang had never ceased to believe that the war of resistance was part of a decades-long attempt to fulfill Sun Yat-sen's mission of establishing a stable and legitimate republic. Over his career, Chiang had seen success interwoven with retreat, and it was quite plau-sible that the war against Japan was merely the latest of many setbacks. He also believed that Wuhan, which had been defended at the cost of so much blood, was no longer essential to his strategy. New routes to supply Free China from the northwest and northeast were being established, and the Nationalists were now defending several crucial lines. "We've devel-oped confidence over the last five months of fighting the enemy," Chiang declared — that is, since Taierzhuang.[9]

But Chiang was still facing huge challenges. By late 1938 there was still no likelihood of significant international intervention in China. The CCP continued to maintain control in parts of northern and central China, but the Nationalists knew that they would be forced to rely on their own resources to avoid defeat. Chiang's old refuge of Guling was no longer available to him, but he used the mountain retreat at Nanyue in Hunan province to call together senior officers and lecture them on the failings of their tactics so far. The first Nanyue military conference opened on November 25, 1938. Chiang delved into China's history, both ancient and recent, to inspire his listeners. First he cited the classic of Chinese military strategy, Sunzi's *The Art of War*. "If the enemy comes to us, we can take advantage of him," Chiang quoted. "If he does not, then we can attack him." Chiang declared that the Japanese, pulled in all the way along the Yangtze, were exactly where the Nationalists wanted them. Just a few weeks before, on October 12, the Japanese had landed at Bias Bay (also known as Daya Bay) off the coast of Guangdong province in southern China, and within ten days had captured the great southern port of Guangzhou (Canton).[10] Yet even this shocking loss was now spun as part of an overall strategic success. "Wait for the enemy," Sunzi had counseled, "and it will be easy to capture the location you want." The first stage of the war was over. Now it was time for the second, defensive stage, to begin.[11]

Chiang was well aware that this argument might seem desperate rather than logical. So he drew on a more recent historical parallel to make his point. Some seventy years earlier, the Taiping rebels had conquered much of central China. Zeng Guofan, the Qing official tasked with putting a stop to the uprising, had been defeated by the rebel troops and seriously considered taking his own life. But he was talked out of it, and instead studied the reasons for his defeat. He succeeded in reforming the Xiang (Hunan) army, and then won major victories at Wuhan, Changsha, and elsewhere, finally crushing the rebels. The parallels were clear.

But the path to a reformed military — and nation — would not be simple, and Chiang made his dissatisfaction clear to the assembled officers. He was swift to condemn the Japanese, saying that they had lost the special virtue that "people of the East" ought to have, and noting that "arrogant soldiers will always be defeated." However, the Nationalist army would also have to improve its record significantly. Over and over again, Chiang declared, the army had behaved in ways that undermined organization. Soldiers should collect the bodies of their dead comrades from the battlefield and have them buried in proper, marked graves. Wounded soldiers should be given better medical treatment; Chiang pointed out that there were horrific scenes all over the country of soldiers being left by their commanders to beg or steal to support themselves. In general, the army ought to "blend seamlessly" with the population, but in practice, in many areas, when the army arrived, the locals moved away, concerned that they might be harassed or exploited.

The fault did not lie just with the ordinary soldier, but also with officers who were too concerned with their own positions and not enough with the task at hand. When soldiers deserted, "lazy" officers refused to catch them. Officers contaminated intelligence reports by exaggerating their own achievements, and communications between the different armies often failed. Too much confidential information was leaked, and not enough strong intelligence about the enemy was being gathered. Senior officers were using very limited tactics, seeking to defend just "one line" on the battlefield instead of being more flexible about deploying their troops.[12]

Chiang also acknowledged his own share of the blame. On the last day of the conference, November 28, he declared that the loss of Nanjing had been "the greatest shame of his life." He took responsibility for the loss of Shanghai, Wuhan, and Madang, and also admitted that he should have destroyed the airfields and bunkers at Wuhan. By sparing them, he had left a base for the Japanese to bomb Chongqing. Yet even so, he chose his words carefully, blaming the loss of Guangzhou and Madang on his having chosen "bad subordinates."[13]

The conference laid down major reforms that were supposed to transform the Chinese armies into powerful fighting forces. These included the centralization of the recruitment bureaucracy, a cut in the overall numbers of troops and of the expenses to support them, and a centrally directed training program, with a third of the forces brought away from the battle areas into the safer heart of Free China for retraining at any one time. The whole program, of course, was also another way to reduce the power of individual commanders and subordinate them to national control.[14] Chiang ended his remarks with a reminder about the importance of discipline. "The key point of the war," he said, in language remarkably reminiscent of Mao Zedong's, "is whether we can master the masses."[15]

By Chiang Kai-shek's side in Chongqing was his old rival Wang Jingwei. As Wang took up his posts as head of the National Defense Council and the National Political Consultative Council, he might have reflected on how dramatically his revolutionary career had changed. Once he had appeared the clear heir apparent to Sun Yat-sen. Now he found himself in southwestern exile, facing an enemy apparently immune to any resistance that China could offer. He was also subordinate to Chiang, the pretender who occupied what Wang considered his rightful place as leader of the National Revolution, and who had now lost large parts of China's most ancient heartland to the Japanese. To Wang, Chiang's closest enemy, the message of resistance seemed increasingly hollow. "Wang was very unhappy about being vice chairman," recalled the diplomat Gao Zongwu. "He thought he was better qualified than anyone else to be party chair."[16]

Wang did not leave behind detailed personal writings, in contrast to Chiang's diaries or Mao's extensive notes and lectures, and we have come to understand him in later years through the eyes of others, such as Zhou Fohai.[17] When war broke out in 1937, Zhou was deputy director of propaganda for the government.[18] Even in the opening weeks and months of the war, Zhou had harbored doubts. He joined other political and intellectual figures who called themselves a "Low-Key Club" *(Didiao julebu)*, the name indicating a desire to discreetly keep open the possibility of a negotiated peace with Japan. Also in the group was Tao Xisheng, a former professor who was close to Wang Jingwei and now served on several key committees within the government. It was through these "low-key" activities that Zhou first became close to Wang.[19]

Crucial in the move toward a negotiated peace was Gao Zongwu, the Asian Bureau chief in the Foreign Ministry. Although a young man (only thirty when war broke out), Gao had shown consummate political skills in the highly factional politics of the Nanjing decade. He too had studied in Japan, at Kyushu Imperial University, and his writings on Sino-Japanese relations had brought him to the attention of Wang Jingwei, then foreign minister. Even after Wang temporarily left the government in 1935, Gao was tactical enough to hold onto his own position.

In August 1937, hiding in a shelter from the aerial bombing of Nanjing, Zhou and his friends began to discuss an end to the war. "In three months," Zhou wrote with some hope in mid-August, "they should be able to start talking about peace." The "Low-Key Club" had no doubt that a long war of resistance would be disastrous for China. "China's national strength is not sufficient," wrote Zhou, "so the war should end at the right point."[20] Many of them had visited Japan in their younger days, and felt they knew the country. Years of conflict with a highly uncertain outcome would be worse than a swiftly negotiated peace in which China might be able to make at least some of its demands heard. Gao Zongwu and his friends made sure that Wang and Chiang knew of any attempts to contact Japan.[21] Part of Wang's role in government was to consider a mediated end to the war, and Chiang was kept fully informed of these efforts.[22]

Chiang was reluctant to be too open to Japan. In August 1937 he rejected the idea of a discussion between Gao Zongwu and Japanese ambassador Kawagoe Shigeru because Gao was a diplomat, and a meeting would therefore give too formal a tone to the discussions. However, the "Low-Key Club" picked up signals that Chiang was not imposing an absolute veto on the idea. After a talk with Wang Jingwei, Tao Xisheng reported that Chiang had indicated he might be willing to allow some talks, but that they would have to be very discreet because he was worried about leaks from the Japanese side. Wang's friends sought to keep his spirits up. "We persuaded Wang not to lose heart," Zhou wrote. "Chiang has to stay tough in public," but perhaps in private, he could allow more flexibility. Wang told Tao Xisheng in mid-September that he thought they should cease fighting and negotiate via the British and the Americans; he claimed that Chiang had agreed, but that he feared the price would be too high.[23]

During early 1938, as eastern China stood in danger of collapse, the low-key activities had become more prominent. Gao Zongwu had resigned his official position so that he could undertake a new role as an envoy shuttling between Shanghai and Hong Kong, locations where unofficial conversations between the Chinese and Japanese sides could still go on. Gao also returned several times to Wuhan in the spring of 1938 to keep Zhou Fohai informed about the progress of his discussions. Gao and his colleagues met various mid-level Japanese officers and business figures, many of whom had spent time in China and felt great distress that war had broken out between the two countries. In early July 1938, Gao accepted an invitation to Tokyo and spent some weeks there discussing the possibility of peace with Inukai Ken, Matsumoto Shigeharu, and other bureaucrats and journalists who formed an informal "Breakfast Club" that gave advice to Prime Minister Konoye.[24] This was a risky move on Gao's part, as any implication that his presence there was officially approved would have damaged the Chinese resistance effort at a time when Chiang was trying desperately to defend Wuhan. In the end Gao was treated "royally" by his hosts, but not offered any specific concessions. At some point during the discussions, the focus moved from persuading Chiang Kai-shek to come to an agreement with Japan to the possibility of bringing over his official deputy, Wang Jingwei.[25] Back in Wuhan, reactions to Gao's unauthorized visit varied from annoyance to rage; both Wang and Chiang condemned it.[26] (Some scholars, however, maintain that Gao did approach the Japanese under orders from Chiang.)[27]

Wuhan fell on October 25, 1938. Zhou Fohai had a lucky escape; he had made his final journey to Chongqing on October 24, but had originally been scheduled to fly out one day later. Now Zhou had to think hard about what path China should take. Chiang and the CCP were united publicly in support of the "long war," in which they would wear down the enemy while waiting for the conflict to widen internationally. In his first days in the blistering summer heat of Chongqing, Zhou spent long evenings discussing the old days in Nanjing with friends, as well as discussing the war with Wang Jingwei. Zhou's disillusionment with resistance grew. He was disgusted by the destruction of his hometown of Changsha. "I've heard that we ourselves burned Changsha," he wrote, referring to Chiang's directions that the city should be set on fire to prevent it falling to the enemy. "Before the enemy even got there, we burned our own land. This is really like treating our own people as the enemy—terrible behavior—it's like destroying the fish to save the water, or driving away the birds to save the bush!" Zhou would have known that thousands must have died when the city was set on fire. Nor did Zhou see the political system as likely to come to the rescue. "I never see any calm or detailed discussion," he said of the National Defense Council meetings. "They just pass the regulations silently. No wonder decisions can't be carried out well." He singled out Chiang's brother-in-law, premier H. H. Kung, as someone who talked "nonsense."[28]

Zhou's crisis of conscience is laid out clearly in his diary for the end of October 1938, just days after the fall of Wuhan. "Do heroes make their own circumstances?" he asked:

> Or do circumstances make heroes? If the latter, then we can change the situation, save the country from destruction, but this depends on our future efforts. The future of the nation is beyond our prediction.[29]

On November 3, Prime Minister Konoye spoke on the radio, announcing his intention of creating a "New Order" in Asia, in which Japan and China would (supposedly) have equal status and would fight together against the real menace, communism. Although the statement did not directly reverse January's declaration that Japan would no longer deal with the National Government, Konoye's statement did propose that a Nationalist Party with different "personnel" might well meet with more favor in Tokyo. The message was enough to pique Wang Jingwei's interest, and he sent another member of the Low-Key Club to investigate.

It was thus at Wang's suggestion that Mei Siping traveled to Shanghai in the autumn of 1938. Between November 12 and 20, Mei discussed the terms of a peace agreement with Lieutenant Colonel Imai Takeo, the Japanese Army representative who had previously talked to Gao Zongwu. Also present were Gao, and on the Japanese side, Colonels Kagesa Sadaaki and Inukai Ken. The talks took place in a hastily renovated mansion, the Zhongguangtang, in the Hongkou district of Shanghai. The negotiators argued over several key issues. Japan wanted the recognition of Manchukuo, but the Chinese were reluctant, knowing that it would seem like a clear abandonment of Chinese sovereignty. Both sides were able to agree that the two countries should be allowed joint economic exploitation of Chinese territory, although the Japanese demand for "compensation" for losses suffered during the fighting was harder for the Chinese to swallow. Japan was also prepared to end its extraterritorial rights, while still holding onto its concession areas. The Chinese side's biggest demand, and the one on which their entire risky venture was posited, was an agreement that the Japanese would end their military occupation of China. The initial demand for an immediate end to the occupation was rejected, but the eventual agreement did contain a specific timeline: no more than two years to the end of the occupation, after the "restoration of peace and order." The discussions were also based on two important assumptions: that Wang Jingwei would defect to head a new government, and that the regime would start its life not in the zone of China occupied by the Japanese but in unoccupied parts of Yunnan and Sichuan in the southwest, and would then extend its authority in that region. The negotiators assumed that Chiang had so many enemies and rivals that the establishment of a rival regime, under a credible leader, and committed to peace, would be very attractive. Militarists such as Long Yun of Yunnan and Liu Wenhui of Sichuan were high on the list of "possible" defectors, along with the large armies that they controlled.[30]

This was the deal that Mei Siping brought to Wang's house on November 26. Now, less than a month later, Zhou sat in Kunming, sleepless and terrified, waiting for news. Who had arrived in the city on December 18?

The answer came: "It's Wang Jingwei." "I was very happy," wrote a relieved Zhou. After the dithering and hesitations, Wang had at least taken the first step. But the plotters were balanced on a knife edge: there was still a great deal that could go wrong. Once they took the next step and defected by crossing the border into Indochina, there would be no going back.

On December 19 Zhou heard that they would be able to hire an aircraft to take them to Hanoi. As ever, the plotters were nervous, trying to decide whether to travel by air or road. "In twenty minutes, we changed our minds seven or eight times . . . but finally decided to take the plane." They made their way to the airport. "At 3:15 p.m., we flew." As he left Chinese soil behind, Zhou's thoughts were not on political matters. "I missed my mother very much," he wrote. "I fear it'll be hard ever to see her again. I wept for her."[31]

To the ends of their lives, Zhou and the man he served, Wang Jingwei, saw themselves as the truest patriots. Faced with the prospect of the physical destruction of China by the Japanese assault, or else the establishment of a Communist China under Soviet control, Wang's group considered the negotiation of a just peace as the only realistic solution to the crisis of war. They were fueled by a genuine ideological enthusiasm that made them keener on a pan-Asianist future than on an alliance with Britain or America, powers whose imperialist behavior in China hardly made them preferable to the Japanese.

Wang was not, however, "pro-Japanese" in the sense of being a fervent collaborator who admired the Japanese way of life and denigrated his own. This would have been a strange position for someone whose early life had been so dedicated to the nationalist revolutionary cause. Wang could understand some Japanese, but he did not speak it or read it; "I had to translate for him when he was foreign minister," recalled Gao Zongwu. Gao also suggested that another colonial power might have had more influence on Wang. Before the fall of Wuhan, he had talked to Henri Cosme, the French ambassador. Cosme had advised the Nationalists to negotiate with Japan; after all, he pointed out, China was even weaker than France after it had lost the war with Prussia in 1870. Then, the French had wanted revenge, but it had neither the diplomatic nor military influence to achieve it.[32] Cosme's point was clear. It had taken more than four decades, but eventually, in 1918, France had vanquished the old enemy. Similarly, China might have to wait to defeat Japan; in the meantime, the Chinese should be realistic about their chances. In fact, Cosme's words would have more significance for himself than he knew at the time; after the Fall of France in June 1940, he was appointed as the Vichy regime's ambassador to Tokyo.

Wang Jingwei spent the flight to Hanoi in a state of intense anxiety. "He looked very worried that Chiang Kaishek might have found out his plans," Gao recalled, "and might send a plane to stop him and force him to land in Chongqing." Wang even issued emergency instructions to his traveling companions. "We're heading south," he said, "and the sun is on our right. If you start to see any shadows [i.e., if you sense the aircraft turning back], jump in the cockpit and force the pilot to go in the right direction."[33] But the precaution was not necessary. Wang's party landed safely in Hanoi at 5:30 p.m. on December 19.

The next day they moved to a small seaside resort some 100 kilometers distant, giving the defectors a little more time and space to breathe. Now that they had made the move, Zhou's mood changed. "Facing the big sea," he said, "I suddenly felt elated." He went on: "The ocean is wide and the sky is empty. When we were in Chongqing just fifteen days ago, we couldn't have imagined this." The group had fresh seafood for lunch and began to discuss everything that a new government would need: a military, a diplomatic service, and, of course, funds. Zhou, Chen Chunpu, and Tao Xisheng marked their arrival in a less than statesmanlike way. That evening they drank strong Chinese liquor and visited a Vietnamese brothel. Even that visit failed to comfort a maudlin Zhou: "An older prostitute sang us poems about the moon, birds, and lonely wives. I felt homesick for my native land."[34]

The last few days of the year were spent in a mixture of plotting and traveling. Indochina was only a way station to the next destination, Hong Kong. On the journey Zhou declared that of all the defectors, Chiang Kaishek would be angriest at him. After all, Wang had never been Chiang's friend, but Zhou had been close to Chiang, and his defection would be regarded as a more personal betrayal. Zhou drafted a letter to Chiang (and to his secretary Chen Bulei) explaining the reasons for his action. "I know they won't forgive me," Zhou wrote in his diary, "but I have to do it." Meanwhile, Wang was writing the public statement he would give to explain his decision to defect. In discussions, Zhou was at pains to stress two particular points. First, Japan would have to abandon its "traditional" thoughts of invading and humiliating China, and second, Japan would acknowledge that the War of Resistance (which Wang had, after all, voted for in committee) had been to guarantee the "independence and survival of the nation," and that if this were achieved peacefully (that is, through negotiation with Japan), then China would have "achieved the goals of the War." Wang was keen to make sure that any agreement would portray him as the patriotic victor in a righteous war.[35]

Some informal signals emerged from Chongqing, where officials were trying to keep the political temperature down after Wang's momentous decision. Chiang encouraged Guo Taiqi (Quo Tai-chi), the Chinese ambassador to Britain, to send a message to Wang asking him to come to Europe; Guo would even abandon his post and dedicate himself to looking after Wang. Zhou, in turn, wrote to Chen Bulei, arguing the move was not "anti-Chiang Kai-shek, but about advocating peace." He asked Chen to persuade Chiang not to attack Wang in the press, nor to have him assassinated. In the very first days after the defection, Chiang did order the press to be discreet about Wang's departure, claiming that the latter had gone to Hanoi for "medical treatment" and saying that if Wang had views that he wished to have heard, he should return to Chongqing to discuss them.[36] On December 21, Long Yun confirmed to Chiang that Wang's meeting in Hanoi was with the Japanese. Chiang was perplexed:

> I was told Mr Wang has secretly flown to Kunming. I don't understand how, at this moment when our country is faced with unprecedented danger, he disregarded all these considerations, and made this excuse of being unwilling to collaborate with the Communists, and left without letting anyone know. I felt extremely sorrowful. I just hope he will come to his senses and turn back.[37]

But all this was to little avail. On December 22 Konoye gave a hastily arranged press conference in Tokyo and announced a vague commitment to join China in friendship, economic cooperation, and anti-communism.[38] Chiang issued a public rebuttal, declaring that the "new order" that the Japanese proposed was "a term for . . . the enslavement of China as the means whereby Japan may dominate the Pacific and proceed to dismember other states of the world."[39] On December 31 a Hong Kong newspaper published a telegram from Wang Jingwei, confirming the rumors that had been swirling for days: Wang said that Konoye's statement created new terms to discuss peace. Any settlement would require that the Communists would have to abandon their separate organization, but also that Japan would have to make a specific commitment to withdraw its army from Chinese territory.[40]

"Every newspaper is attacking Wang," Zhou noted. "Considering the present situation, this is to be expected."[41] The defectors had made a huge sacrifice, risking accusations of treachery to come over and negotiate with the enemy. Now surely, they felt, they would be given the reward they deserved: the legitimate government of an independent China.

All that would be to come. On the last day of 1938 Zhou recorded that "Xisheng and I sat around on New Year's Eve doing nothing. That's how we spent the last part of the year." As it turned out, Wang, Zhou, and the Low-Key Club would be sitting around, doing nothing, for a very long time indeed.

Chapter 12

THE ROAD TO PEARL HARBOR

T HE EASTERN PROVINCE OF Anhui is usually cold and can become very wet at the height of winter. The weather was just one of
the problems besetting Xiang Ying, commander of the section of
the Communist New Fourth Army stationed in the province in December 1940. Just a few weeks before, Chiang Kai-shek had sent out orders
that the Communist forces in Anhui must retreat north of the Yangtze
River, out of the zone of Nationalist control patrolled by General Gu
Zhutong. He made it clear to Gu that if the Communists did not move,
then he should force them to do so.

Xiang Ying assumed that the evacuation would take place in cooperation with the Nationalist troops. But instead a telegram arrived with dis-
appointing news from party headquarters in Yan'an, where Mao and the
overall Red Army commander Zhu De were located:

> You should not have any further false hopes about the Nationalists.
> Do not rely on them to help you with anything . . . If you end up being
> attacked by the Nationalists on one side and the Japanese on the other
> side, it will be extremely dangerous for you.[1]

Only a week later Xiang Ying would find out just how dangerous his position was. For in the two years from 1939 to 1941 the conflict had become
not only a war of resistance against Japan and its Chinese collaborators,
but also a duel between the Nationalists and the Communists. Alliances
shifted against the backdrop of an international situation that also pitted
former friends against each other, and created strange partnerships that
nobody could have foreseen.

In the first two years of the war, the National Government had managed to survive against the odds. Its own efforts to cope with inadequate
armies, refugee flight, and aerial bombing had contributed significantly
to that survival, but the Nationalists had also benefited from fortunate
circumstances. The Communists had generally stuck by the terms of the
United Front and cooperated with the Nationalists — at the very least, by
not confronting the government outright. The Soviets had continued to

support Chongqing, and the European powers, while still neutral, provided sympathy and some tacit support for Chiang's regime, allowing it to stay supplied even in its southwestern exile. Japan had not succeeded in bringing on board collaborators who would pose a threat to the Chinese or be taken seriously by the outside world. Even the weather had been helpful: harvests in Free China in the first summers of the war had been remarkably abundant, easing somewhat the government's inability to import food as normal. By the end of 1940, every one of these factors would change, and in every case to the disadvantage of the Nationalists.

In September 1939 the Japanese Imperial Army, its operations now unified under the China Expeditionary Command, had sent 100,000 troops to take the central Chinese city of Changsha, which had already suffered grievously after the retreat from Wuhan in October 1938, when Chiang had ordered that Changsha be burned. If the Japanese could capture the city, then they would hold Hunan, one of the great breadbasket provinces of central China. From there, the way to Sichuan in the west would lie open, and they could hope to defeat Chiang's regime in Chongqing once and for all. But the Japanese assault on Changsha failed. The Cantonese general Xue Yue defended the city brilliantly, using a combination of formal field warfare along with guerrilla tactics to lure the Japanese into ambushes and prevent them from resupplying themselves. Changsha remained in Chinese hands.[2]

The Nationalist military now seized the initiative with a series of offensives across the whole country, bringing together eighty divisions of troops. In a series of coordinated attacks, the army was to strike out and recapture huge swathes of territory, from Yan Xishan's former area of control in Shanxi province in north-central China to Guangxi in the southwest.

But almost nothing went according to plan. Chiang's supposed ally, the militarist Yan Xishan, carved out his own deal with the Japanese for control of parts of Shanxi and withdrew from the campaign. And in the south, the Japanese surprised Chiang by launching an invasion of the southwestern province of Guangxi, capturing the capital city of Nanning on November 23, 1939, and cutting off the route to the sea. Instead of being able to deploy troops aggressively to retake captured territory, the Nationalists found themselves on the defensive once more. Two months of fierce fighting finally repelled the Japanese advance, but the momentum for the Nationalists' Winter Offensive had been utterly lost. Things worsened in the spring of 1940. In May the city of Yichang in Hubei province fell to a new Japanese advance. Yichang had been the transit point from Sichuan to the other parts of the country, and its loss meant that Chiang's regime was even more isolated. Chongqing now also became vulnerable to a new weapon, Japan's Mitsubishi Zero fighter aircraft, one of the most advanced in the world. In the summer of 1940 the Zero managed to knock out all of the aircraft that protected Chongqing from the sky, leaving the city even more vulnerable to air raids.[3] As had happened so often before, an initially successful Nationalist assault had turned into a disaster.

Chiang's troubles were made even worse by events some eight thousand kilometers away in Europe. In the late summer of 1939 two events changed the face of the conflict: the expected outbreak of war between Germany and Britain along with France, and the unexpected outbreak of peace between Germany and its ideological foe the USSR. The latter was marked by the announcement on August 23, 1939, of the signing of a nonaggression pact between Moscow and Berlin, perhaps the most astounding ideological reversal of the twentieth century. A week later, on September 1, Nazi Germany's troops invaded Poland, and war with Britain and France followed two days later. At a stroke, the attention of the European powers was concentrated on their own fight for survival. The war in East Asia, already a secondary concern for them, now became a minor matter indeed.[4]

Chiang wanted to create a concert of allies who would help defend China against Japanese incursion. He was stymied not only by the reluctance of neutral powers to come to China's aid, but by the speed with which alliances changed in the early years of the Second World War. Chiang had never been keen to see a general European war, rightly believing that it would distract attention even further from China. Nonetheless, he could see opportunities for new alliances, now that the battle lines had been drawn between the imperialist democracies and fascism. In this respect, the new warmth between Berlin and Moscow was a disaster for him. Chiang had been desperate to involve the USSR in the fight against Japan. Now the Soviets were effectively allied with the Nazis, who in turn were allies of Tokyo.

The post-Versailles world had made the Chinese deeply angry. (The iconic May Fourth demonstrations of 1919, after all, had been a direct response to the settlement at the Paris Peace Conference.) But at least that world had familiar points of reference, in particular the power of the two major European empires, along with the US. Now the empires were crumbling and it was unclear what the new geostrategic balance would be. For all that Chiang or anyone else knew, Germany would be the great new European power. The first years of the European war were a bewildering period of diplomatic cross-dressing.

The Nationalist government had earlier enjoyed a brief dalliance with Nazi Germany. Hitler's regime did in fact continue to supply Chiang's government with munitions in the early months of its war with Japan.[5] The Anti-Comintern Pact signed in 1936 had, in theory, bound together Germany, Italy, and Japan as the Axis, but they were always too mistrustful of one another to create a genuine alliance. Chiang found it useful to hint to the Western powers that he might be forced into a partnership with Germany, a particularly alarming prospect for the USSR, which had enemies both to the west and the east. But the contradictions in German policy toward East Asia finally became too great, and in April 1938 Germany bowed to Japanese demands and ceased to support China.

Britain was of little assistance. In May 1937 Neville Chamberlain became prime minister of a Conservative-dominated National Government, and found himself swiftly consumed by the problems of peace in Europe. If Czechoslovakia was for him a "far-off country of which we know nothing," the fate of China was even more obscure for many (if not all) decision makers in London. The Nationalists' efforts to gain US support were more effective. At the Nine-Power Conference held in Brussels in November 1937, the Chinese delegation had been unable to convince the United States to impose sanctions and confront Japan. By mid-1938, however, American attitudes had begun to change. As Japan moved further southward into China, it became increasingly clear that the occupied country would be closed to outside trade. In December 1938, US treasury secretary Henry Morgenthau facilitated a private loan of $25 million to China, to be repaid in kind with supplies of tung oil (a varnishing product).[6]

Chiang also clung to the possibility of an even more unlikely alliance. He had become a fanatical anti-Communist during the 1920s, but in the first years of the fight against Japan his greatest hope still lay in the entry of the Soviet Union into the war. Soviet advisers and pilots had assisted the Chinese effort in 1937–1939, yet the USSR did not actually declare war on Japan. With Japanese aggression in northern Asia escalating, though, the Soviets might be forced into the conflict.

Then, as so often happened whenever Chiang tried to master the trajectory of the war, events outside China took a turn that fundamentally changed the nature of the struggle. While Western attention focused on the darkening situation in Europe, a battle that would shape the conflict in East Asia took place on the borders of Outer Mongolia, Manchukuo, and the eastern part of the Soviet Union. Through much of 1938 and early 1939 one faction of the Japanese Imperial Army had attempted to pressure the Soviets on their eastern border. It appeared that the USSR might be an easy target; Stalin's paranoid purges meant that many of the Red Army's best officers had been executed or sent to Siberia. In May 1939 a dispute flared up near the village of Nomonhan between troops stationed in the Soviet client state of Mongolia and Japanese troops from Manchukuo. Within days both sides had built up their forces, with nearly 60,000 Soviet troops facing nearly 40,000 troops of the Kwantung Army. For the next four months, until mid-September, the two powers fought an epic battle that ended with Japan's resounding defeat and cemented the reputation of General Georgi Zhukov, later one of Stalin's most decorated generals during the Second World War. The despised Soviet Army had fought fiercely, and not only was a cease-fire declared, but the two sides also signed a nonaggression pact, ending Chiang's hopes of a Chinese-Soviet alliance.[7]

The crowning blow came in the aftermath of events in the frozen north of Europe. In the Winter War of 1939–1940 the Soviets invaded Finland, prompting Britain and France to sponsor a motion expelling the USSR from the League of Nations. At the time, China was a member of the League Council, and it refused to exercise its power of veto on the motion.[8] The Soviets were furious at Chiang's failure to prevent their expulsion, and for the rest of China's war with Japan the relationship between Chiang and Stalin would remain deeply mistrustful. China would have to fight Japan without further major Soviet assistance.

While Chiang struggled to set a diplomatic agenda in an unpredictable world, Wang Jingwei's plans stagnated. The midlevel Japanese officers and businessmen to whom Mei Siping and Gao Zongwu had spoken in Shanghai turned out not to have been speaking for the whole of the

Tokyo regime. In fact, they represented a rather small group, genuinely sympathetic to China and desirous of a peace that would not utterly humiliate their great neighbor. But Premier Konoye was far less convinced that working with Wang would bring about the result Tokyo wanted. Although Konoye indicated in his public statement of December 22, 1938, that he was prepared to reopen discussions with the Chinese side, he also made it clear that the withdrawal of Japanese troops from China within two years (a key piece of the deal offered to Wang in Shanghai) was off the table.

The Chongqing government, meanwhile, decided to treat Wang's defection in tones more sober than shrill. On January 1, 1939, Wang was dismissed from his public positions and expelled from the Nationalist Party. But orders were not yet issued for his arrest. Wang's group suffered a further setback on January 5 when Konoye's government resigned. His successor, Baron Hiranuma Kiichiro, was also cautious when it came to embracing the Low-Key Club, as were senior figures in the Japanese military. However, in May 1939 Wang started to press for an invitation to Tokyo.

The trip to Tokyo, in early June, was a disaster. On June 6 five major Japanese ministers held a meeting in Wang's absence, in which they made it clear that a regime run by him would only be one part of a wider patchwork of Japanese client regimes in China; Wang's dream of reuniting China under his rule was dead before he had arrived. In addition, Japanese demands on China would be harsh, including economic and military dominance across all of China's territory. The only senior minister who was willing even to make a show of discussing terms was Itagaki Seishirô, the minister of war. Yet Itagaki made it clear that he would not support the dissolution of the rival client governments, particularly the "Reformed" government that had its capital at Beiping and controlled much of north China. Japan had won control of north China in war and was not going to give it up lightly.[9]

Wang won concessions on only one issue. The Japanese wanted the symbol of his new regime to be the flag with five colored bars that had been used in the early years of the republic (and was used by the collaborator Wang Kemin's "Provisional" government in north China, which Wang Jingwei despised). Wang was adamant; the correct flag for his regime would be the flag of the Nationalist government, as endorsed by Sun Yat-sen: a white twelve-pointed star on a blue background, and a red field. After all, Wang considered his regime the continuation of the true Nationalist government, now that Chiang had betrayed the cause by allying with the Communists. Adoption of the flag would fulfil Wang's dream that he had nurtured for thirteen years, since Chiang Kai-shek had maneuvered him out of power during the Northern Expedition, namely, finally to complete the revolutionary destiny of Sun Yat-sen. The Japanese objected, ostensibly on the grounds that if the troops of Wang and Chiang ever came into conflict, then it would be impossible to tell them apart, as they would be wearing the same insignias. Wang would not budge. Finally, the Japanese agreed, as long as a yellow pennant reading "peace, reconstruction, anticommunism" *(heping, jianguo, fangong)* was added to the flag. Wang had scored a tiny victory, but not an insignificant one. The vast majority of the Japanese leadership despised Chinese nationalism, thinking of it as an alien transplant that had ruined the prospect of a pan-Asian brotherhood (in which Japan, of course, would take the leading role). For Wang to insist that the most potently symbolic flag of Chinese revolutionary nationalism should fly above his regime's buildings was a small success in the midst of a collaboration that already looked threadbare.[10]

Attempts by Wang, now back in Shanghai, to establish dominance over Wang Kemin's "Provisional" government and the other rival "Reformed" government under Liang Hongzhi, based in Nanjing, ended with all three leaders unwilling to work with the others. Japan's defeat at Nomonhan in the summer of 1939 did make Wang Jingwei more attractive in the eyes of the power brokers in Tokyo, as it became clearer that their armies might not defeat Chiang as easily as they had hoped. But they remained inflexible. Over two long months in November and December 1939, Colonels Kagesa Sadaaki and Inukai Ken of the Japanese Army and other Japanese negotiators sat with Wang's advisers, including Mei Siping, Zhou Fohai, and Tao Xisheng. (Wang himself did not take part directly in the discussions.) Kagesa, despite his sympathy for the Chinese side, was the channel for harsh and uncompromising demands from hard-liners in the Japanese Army. Japanese troops and "advisers" were to be stationed all over China, undermining Wang's argument that his government would restore the Nationalists to sovereignty. New concessions were made in key industries such as coal and ore mining, and the Japanese Navy was to be given control over Hainan island in the south. In spite of Wang's dreams of reunification, north China was to be kept separate, and Shanghai was also to be given special status (that is, with special privileges for the Japanese). The terms were almost entirely one-sided, and the signing of the agreement on December 30, 1939, was a gloomy affair.[11] Still, the negotiations had established that there would be a "reorganized" Nationalist government, led by Wang Jingwei, with its capital at Nanjing.

By now, Gao Zongwu was having serious doubts about the whole enterprise. Following the drafting of the secret treaty, he was asked to help translate it into Chinese. Wang was understandably paranoid about security, and insisted that the translation be done at his home in Shanghai. However, Gao was determined to obtain a copy. He finally found an opportunity when he was escorting a visiting Japanese politician from Wang's house, whereupon Gao slipped the translation into his own pocket. He then telephoned Wang and said that he had taken it by mistake. But before returning it, he took the document home and photographed it.[12] On New Year's Day 1940, Zhou Fohai talked to Gao Zongwu at length about the progress of their mission so far. "The two of us swore to work hard," Zhou recalled, "and to forgive each other," although he did not know why Gao was asking for forgiveness. But three days later, on January 4, Zhou recorded rumors that Gao, along with Tao Xisheng, had disappeared, probably to Hong Kong. "Now I understand what he meant on New Year's Day," reflected Zhou ruefully, realizing at last what Gao had had in mind.

Gao Zongwu and Tao Xisheng interpreted Japan's two-faced behavior at the negotiations in the last weeks of 1939 as a sign that collaboration with Japan would not be a genuine partnership, but deeply exploitative. The two defectors were spirited away from Shanghai by the mobster and power broker Du Yuesheng ("Big-ears Du") and reappeared in Chongqing in a monumental propaganda coup for the National Government. Gao and Tao announced in a statement in Hong Kong just how crushing Japan's demands were and called upon Wang to end negotiations and "restrain the horse from falling over the precipice."[13] Gao was then given permission to emigrate to the United States, and Tao rejoined Chiang's staff and became one of his top propagandists. (Both lived on to a peaceful old age.)

The Japanese wanted to keep their options open by holding Wang in reserve, while hoping they still might tempt the real prize, Chiang Kai-shek, to their side. For instance, the Japanese declared that they did not want to send an ambassador to Wang's prospective new government in

Nanjing (which would imply full diplomatic recognition), but instead would send a "special envoy." "I consider that our central government *is* the national government," fumed Zhou Fohai. "There is no 'recognition problem.'" In conversation with a Japanese official, he said: "If the new national government has no significance, then what is the point of organizing it? You want to keep a space open for negotiating with Chongqing. We don't oppose the Japanese talking to Chongqing, but if you won't recognize the new government, then we prefer not to organize one."[14]

Zhou had a somewhat inflated view of his contributions to the prospective new government in Nanjing. On January 26 he wrote in his diary that he, not Wang, had chosen the key ministers: "Ten minutes with my pen will produce the National Government," he joked.[15] But it was not just ministries that Zhou organized; he also took charge of muscle. Wang's great deficiency as a power broker was his lack of military support. It had been his downfall during the Northern Expedition, and a decade later it was now hampering his chances of being taken seriously by Japan. This lack also placed him and his followers in grave personal danger from assassination squads organized by Chiang's security chief, Dai Li. Zhou had little choice but to turn to two of Dai Li's former employees, thugs named Ding Mocun and Li Shiqun, who ran an enforcement squad from a mansion at 76 Jessfield Road in the part of Shanghai known as the "Badlands."[16] With this dubious backing, Wang's regime lost much of its already limited prestige before it had even formally been constituted.

As winter turned to spring, Zhou was torn between aspiration and venality. He still harbored hopes of reconciliation with the government in Chongqing, optimistically sending a message to Chiang Kai-shek via an American intermediary to say that even the establishment of a new government at Nanjing should not stop discussions between Japan and the Nationalists. Late in March he found himself close to quarreling with Wang Jingwei and his wife Chen Bijun over financial subsidies for their native province of Guangdong. Behind the squabbling lurked the fear that the Japanese, who were clearly hedging their bets, might seek to halt the new administration in its tracks.

But despite the obstacles, Wang finally got his new government in Nanjing. On March 30, 1940, Wang Jingwei's *huandu* — the "return to the capital" — officially came into being. The regime's newspaper, the *Zhonghua ribao (China Daily),* was filled with fulsome praise for the government of "Chairman Wang," positioned not as a new regime but rather as a restoration of the true Nationalist Party to its rightful capital at Nanjing. The cartoons that filled the middle pages were pure propaganda: pictures of Wang as a superhuman giant radiating light toward a group of children representing the Chinese people.[17]

Zhou Fohai recalled the ceremony in his diary with his usual touch of egomania. "My idea has come to reality," he declared. "This is the happiest thing that has happened in my life." He went on: "The National Government has returned to the capital, the national flag is fluttering in the city, and the whole thing was started up by me. After this, the movement will take *me* as its center . . . my whole life has not been in vain."[18] Zhou spoiled the moment by going on to drink too much after the ceremony and giving himself a stomachache. Wang Jingwei was in a less celebratory mood. One witness to the ceremony declared that he "stood there as if in a daze . . . tears copiously flowing down his face."[19] The motive behind his defection, his vision of an equal collaboration with the Japanese, now looked very hollow.

In February 1940, Frank Lockhart, counselor at the US Embassy, filed a report to Washington on behalf of Ambassador Nelson Johnson, summarizing the war situation in the year just gone by:

> There were no indications that Chinese determination to continue resistance had lessened, despite the uncertainties in the international situation, friction in the "United Front," and the severe strain of war on the national economy. General Chiang Kai-shek retained the confidence of the nation and his influence was effective in settling the difficulties which arose between various factions in the government . . . One important factor in maintaining and increasing Chinese determination to resist was the ruthless Japanese bombing of civilian populations, the most murderous instance of which occurred in Chungking in May.[20]

Had he known of this positive assessment, Chiang Kai-shek would have valued it. China's situation was precarious by the spring of 1940. In March high-level Japanese negotiators tried to secure an agreement with Chiang in Chongqing, while Wang Jingwei was attempting to formalize his own Nationalist government in Nanjing. This strategy, known in Chinese as the Tong Operation, and in Japanese as Operation Kiri, led to talks in Hong Kong between March 7 and 10, 1940. The Nationalists were in a perilous military position: the United States remained neutral, and

Europe was in turmoil. In fact, during that spring, as the fall of France looked imminent, the British government similarly put out very discreet feelers to test the possibility of a negotiated peace with Germany. For China, there was no possibility of Western assistance. The Japanese saw it as a propitious moment to persuade Chiang to concede.[21] Now, at a time of great danger for his government, Chiang opened the door to negotiations just a crack.

As a result, the Japanese continued to stall on recognition of the new government of Wang Jingwei. Throughout the summer and autumn of 1940, Japan remained ambivalent about the defector. Senior Japanese figures such as Count Arima Yoriyasu of the Privy Council declared that Wang's behavior proved his dishonesty, and Foreign Minister Matsuoka Yôsuke declared his continuing interest in an agreement with Chongqing.[22] Zhou Fohai summed up the frustration of the defectors, who felt that they had made a supreme patriotic sacrifice: "Chongqing sees us as collaborators, we see ourselves as heroes. We think only peace can save the country—that's why we think of ourselves as heroes. If we end up classed as heroes, then China and Japan will be at peace. If we end up classed as collaborators, then China and Japan will never be at peace."[23]

Senior Japanese military figures met with a Chinese intelligence agent posing as the younger brother of Chiang's brother-in-law T. V. Soong. The talks foundered on issues of principle: Japan wanted to station troops in north China and gain formal recognition of Manchukuo, which Chiang absolutely refused. Japan responded by turning up the temperature. In June the Imperial Army captured the major city of Yichang in Hubei province. With Chongqing under continued pressure, talks resumed from June 4 to 6, in Macau.[24] In these talks the Japanese pressed for recognition of Manchukuo, and the placement of Japanese troops in north China, while the Chinese side continued to play for time, arguing that Tokyo's final position was still not clear.

The Japanese also exploited the weakness of China's potential European allies. Chiang's government desperately needed supplies sent along the railway from the Indochinese port of Haiphong to Kunming in Yunnan province, nearly one thousand kilometers to the northwest. In January 1940, as Paris prepared itself for a German invasion, Japanese diplomats had sent messages to their French counterparts demanding that the colony's railway be shut down. The Japanese repeatedly bombed the railway, and when the French ambassador in Tokyo protested, Matsuoka

Yôsuke, the foreign minister, replied that "the Japanese Government intended to continue bombarding the French railroad from Indochina until the French should stop sending supplies to Chiang Kai-shek."[25] France fell in June 1940, and like most of its colonies, Indochina came under the control of the collaborationist Vichy regime. As this new government was supposed to be neutral, it continued to allow supplies to be sent to Free China via the railway. Throughout the summer of 1940, the Japanese put the Vichy colonial authorities under pressure to close the railway, but the French refused to do so, although they agreed in August that a limited number of Japanese troops (no more than 6,000) could be stationed within Indochina. But the Japanese were not in the mood to compromise. On September 22 Japanese troops under Lieutenant General Nakamura Akihito invaded Indochina. The fighting ended within a few days when Indochina capitulated, but Japanese troops remained in the colony until the end of the war, severing the Nationalist government from the vital railway line.

In July 1940, while the Battle of Britain raged over the skies of the south of England, the Japanese government demanded that London close the Burma Road, linking the British colony to the border with China. This would cut off supplies of war materiel that were being shipped to Rangoon and then transported onward via the Burma Road into Nationalist China. Churchill's government had seen France fall in June and feared that Britain was in danger of imminent invasion. Unable to contemplate opening up a new front for conflict in Asia, they closed the road. In less than a year, all of Free China's supply routes from the south coast, from Indochina, and from Burma had been cut off (although the latter did reopen in October 1940). Better strategy by the Nationalists might have helped keep the sea routes open for a while longer. But the land routes were lost because of the policies of the British government and Vichy France, over which Chiang Kai-shek had no control. The Nationalists were clearly vulnerable.

Chiang continued to show determination mixed with guile. Having agreed to talk to the Japanese in August 1940, he suddenly canceled the meeting on the pretext that the Japanese had not revoked their *aite ni sezu,* the declaration of refusal to deal with the National Government. The Nationalists had achieved an important overall goal by casting doubt on Japan's commitment to the Wang regime in Nanjing.[26] To the Chinese, it seemed obvious that the Japanese wished to use anti-communism as an excuse to station Japanese troops in China on a long-term basis. Chiang's strategy of hinting at talks with Japan without ever holding any official meetings offered two main benefits. It made Japan hold on until well into 1940 before finally allowing Wang Jingwei to set up a government in Nanjing, and it sent the Western powers the message that if they did not grant further assistance to Chongqing, Chiang would be forced to seek some sort of agreement with the enemy. On November 30, Wang Jingwei's government was officially recognized by Tokyo. On the same day the US government announced a loan arrangement of US$100 million to Free China, as well as the dispatch of fifty military aircraft.[27]

Chiang's actions did not suggest a genuine willingness to negotiate with the Japanese for a harsh peace settlement. He made it very clear that he would continue to resist Japan, even in the darkest days of 1940, when China, like Britain, came closest to collapse. He gave the impression of dancing close to the edge of cooperation with Japan, but never took steps that would send him directly over the precipice. The threat of a Japanese takeover of China frightened the Allied powers, and Chiang knew he desperately needed to draw them in. For not only were his armies and regime on the brink of disaster, with little prospect of external assistance. A new threat now emerged from within his own alliance.

Beginning in early 1939, the Nationalists started to take measures to restrict the growth of the CCP. The year marked the beginning of the terror raids on Chongqing that would do so much to undermine the National Government's position, and as the bombs fell, Chiang and his colleagues became alarmed by the growing strength of their rivals to the northeast, based in Yan'an. Chiang ordered new political and economic measures against Mao's heartland. In particular, he sought to regain control of parts of Hebei, Shanxi, Henan, and Shandong that the CCP had come to think of as its own areas of control. The Nationalists imposed a blockade of some 400,000 troops around the SGN base to the south and the west. The campaign aimed to box the Communists in, rather than to invade their territory, but it was a clear sign that relations between the two sides were beginning to break down.

However, the conflict remained a strange, shadowy one. Neither side could afford to let its own public, let alone the international community, think that the United Front had failed. When clashes broke out between Nationalist and Communist troops at the borders of the SGN region, the

CCP claimed that the fighting had initiated solely at the local level and did not reflect any wider abandonment of the United Front. Chiang could hardly disagree openly.

Yet Mao also wanted to hint at the risk that the Nationalists ran by seeking to suppress the Communists. In a July 1939 speech on long-term cooperation between the two parties, Mao made a pointed comment about past Nationalist attempts to restrict the growth of the CCP, speaking out to the "diehard elements" in the Nationalist Party who sought to crush the Communists:

> You insisted on "suppressing" us, but what is most curious is that the more we were "suppressed" the more numerous we became. Our party used to be only as big as a little finger, but thanks to the "Encirclement and Suppression" campaigns it grew enormously and became as big as a thumb . . . The entire Red Army was forged by fighting you, and all the Red Army's guns were given by you, so I invite my friends to consider it: To fight or not to fight? We, too, have thought about it; let's everyone make peace![28]

The two sides felt ambivalent toward each other even as relations soured. Chiang had always been wary of Mao, but he had a rather more positive view of Zhou Enlai, and the respect was mutual. In August 1939 Zhou wrote a report for the Politburo of the CCP in which he argued that both parties needed to rein in their more extreme and backward-looking members. Shortly afterward, when Zhou fractured his arm, Chiang sent his personal plane to Yan'an to fly Zhou and his wife to Xinjiang, for transport on to Moscow for treatment.[29]

Nonetheless, the Nationalist blockade continued, with disastrous effects on the economy of the Communist base area. Then, in early 1940, Chiang terminated the financial subsidy from the Nationalists. Making matters worse, after very good harvests during the first two years of the war, the yields in 1939 and 1940 were much poorer. The bad harvests also created problems for the Nationalists, as the food price index in Chongqing rose by nearly 1,400 percent in 1940–1941.[30] But prices rose in the isolated and impoverished SGN area: in 1941 one needed 2,200 yuan to buy what would have cost 500 yuan in 1940.[31] The CCP now had a much larger population to deal with, and severely reduced resources. The solution they turned to was a radical form of economic self-sufficiency. "Production campaigns" were launched which over the next few years would greatly increase the amount of land that fell under cultivation, as well as boosting the production of cotton, rearing of livestock, weaving of cloth, and extraction of products including salt, coal, and even some oil and gas.[32] This idea would prove psychologically powerful, as the inward economic turn created a new distrust between the Nationalists and Communists, which would resonate throughout the rest of the war, and for years afterward.

By the summer of 1940 the two major Communist armies dominated much of north and central China. In August of that year, the Eighth Route Army under the command of Peng Dehuai launched the only major conventional military offensive by a Communist army during the war: the Battle of the Hundred Regiments. Some 40,000 troops (in 22 regiments, although more troops joined in until the total number of regiments was 104) launched an all-out assault on railway lines, roads, bridges, and other elements of the infrastructure necessary for Japanese control in north China. The fighting continued until October, and invited a massive and brutal Japanese counterassault.[33]

Meanwhile, the New Fourth Army penetrated south of the Yellow River, and just to the north of the Yangtze River, into areas previously dominated by the Nationalists. The Subei region, and the Anhui province to the north and west of Shanghai, became a Communist stronghold under the senior New Fourth Army commander Xiang Ying. In July the Central Military Commission proposed that the Communist troops should concentrate north of the former path of the Yellow River (which had changed after the breaching of the dikes in June 1938). Relations between Xiang Ying and his Nationalist counterparts, Generals Gu Zhutong and Shangguan Yunxiang, had been friendly enough, but now positions hardened. On the Communist side Zhou Enlai may have supported the plan, but Mao appears to have strongly rejected it.

On October 19, He Yingqin, chief of the General Staff under Chiang Kai-shek, told Zhu De, commander of the Eighth Route Army, that all Communist troops must be moved, including any troops which had previously been authorized to take positions south of the Yangtze. On December 9 Chiang gave his orders: by December 31 he wanted all New Fourth Army troops to be north of the Yangtze, and by January 31 all New Fourth Army and Eighth Route Army troops must be north of the

Yellow River. He made his views clear in a confidential message to Gu Zhutong. If the deadline was breached, "then you must take care of this matter; no more tolerance."[34] Xiang Ying received ambiguous commands from Mao, telling him at one moment to move his troops north, but at others, to take a roundabout route suggesting something less than urgency.[35] Mao himself may not have been sure what he wanted to achieve, half hoping and half fearing to provoke an incident with the Nationalists.[36] Then, on December 26 , he sent a furious message to Xiang Ying, warning him not to trust the Nationalists. Mao was already beginning to shift the blame. Despite his own vacillations, if a calamity happened to the New Fourth Army in Anhui, he wanted the local commander, not himself in Yan'an, to take the blame.[37]

On January 4, 1941, troops of the New Fourth Army began to move south, not north. The Communists argued that this was necessary to avoid marching through the areas controlled by Japanese troops. The Nationalists suspected that it was, instead, a move to expand CCP areas of control. Shortly afterward, clashes began between the two sides.

Dong Nancai was one of the New Fourth Army officers on the move, serving under Xiang Ying's deputy (and rival), Ye Ting. Dong recalled that the move happened in deep winter, and that conditions were cloudy and very cold. At various points the troops rigged up temporary bridges to cross water, although sometimes "because the people were too many, the speed was too slow, burdens too heavy, there were some comrades who fell in the water, and had to brave the cold to swim across the river."[38] Over the next two days the army came up against Nationalist troops, with no quarter given on either side: "even [our] cooks took their kitchen knives," such was the ferocity of the battle, although the Communists emerged victorious. As they went on, the troops had to negotiate between sudden, deadly skirmishes with the enemy, and dangers from the surrounding environment: some men fell to their deaths from the steep mountain ledges.[39]

During these encounters the overall commander, Xiang Ying, disappeared; it is not clear whether he was struck by terror and deserted his post, or whether he was trying to find another way to strike back against the attacking Nationalists.[40] Then he suddenly reappeared, telling party headquarters on January 10, "The day before yesterday, we tried to break out of the circle, but we were prevented, and were surrounded . . . there was a huge possibility that we would be eliminated . . . I planned to take a small number of troops, and find a sideways path out." He admitted, "This action of mine was really terrible. I await punishment." The party's headquarters was not slow to reply, calling him a "coward" and a "waverer."[41] Yet even Xiang's return could not compensate for the overwhelming strength of the Nationalist forces. Gu Zhutong's attack led to the death or capture of 9,000 of Xiang's troops.[42] Xiang Ying himself was murdered on March 14.

But the Nationalist military victory turned into a public relations firestorm. The immediate response from most outside observers was not that Communist troops had refused to obey orders, but rather that Chiang had treacherously turned on his allies in the hopes of defeating his domestic enemies, while ignoring the Japanese. On January 15 Mao sent a message to Zhou Enlai and Ye Jianying declaring that "all of Chiang's talk about virtue and morality is a pack of lies and should under no circumstances be trusted."[43] Public opinion, both domestic and international, came down firmly against Chiang's act. *Time* magazine observed:

> This was a victory for the Whampoa . . . clique of Chinese generals who hate & fear the Communists and are jealous of the publicity given to the Fourth and Eighth Route Armies. But it was no victory for China. What has kept the Communists fighting for Chiang is the fact that they fear Japan more than they fear Chiang. If Japan (or Russia) could convince the Communists that they have less to fear from Japan (or Russia) than from Chiang, China's jig would be up.[44]

Chiang knew that he could not afford to drive the Communists to turn their fire on him rather than the Japanese. He abandoned plans to push Communist forces north of the Yangtze, and made no serious attempt to do so for the rest of the war years. Meanwhile, the Red Army knew that it could develop without worrying about suppression by Chiang.

Mao's indecision had made him, in part, responsible for Xiang Ying's inability to stage a successful retreat, and the former must surely accept some of the blame for the clash. Nevertheless, the battle was a victory for Mao in the struggle to control his own party. Xiang Ying had been a rival, with his own autonomous area of control. Now, his defeat and death bound the future of the CCP even more tightly to Mao's actions in Yan'an.[45] Overall, the "New Fourth Army Incident," as it became known, which had seemed such a disaster for the Communists, was to prove a major turning point in the upward rise of the fortunes of the CCP — and of Mao.

In fact, the resolution of the "New Fourth Army Incident" marked the conclusion to one of the most important years in the history of Chinese politics. The internal struggle of ideas going on during 1940 was evident to informed observers at the time. Early in 1941, US ambassador Nelson Johnson sent a detailed assessment of the political situation to Washington, in response to another report forwarded to the US by Major Evans Carlson, an American military officer who had undertaken an extensive tour of the Chinese interior. The difference between the two messages illustrated the growing rift in American opinion about the politics of China. Carlson, and his traveling companion, the New Zealander Rewi Alley, were increasingly sympathetic to the Communists, having traveled in their areas of control in 1938 and being impressed by their discipline. Carlson characterized the Nationalists as moving toward "fascism" and demanded that in return for funding from the US, Chiang's government should be forced to institute more "democratic" structures.[46]

Johnson disagreed strongly. The Nationalists wished to retain power, which was "only normal and natural," but during the war years they had established the National Political Consultative Council, a body on which various parties including the Communists were represented. He also pointed out that the CCP were able to publish their own newspaper in Chongqing in a way that would not have been possible before the war. One might have expected the Nationalists to use the excuse of war "to extinguish . . . all political opposition," but instead they had preferred to "muddle along." Johnson also felt that the influence of the various cliques within the Nationalist Party had been exaggerated. Chiang Kai-shek, in contrast, had "grown in stature, as he has come to be recognized as the symbol of united resistance to Japanese encroachment"; in the end "it is he who makes the final decisions." Johnson did agree with Carlson's assessment that Chiang's government was reluctant to sponsor a mass popular movement driven by anything beyond a widespread sense of anti-Japanese anger, although he did note that the Nationalists had undertaken cooperative movements and county-level reforms. But Johnson did not agree that American assistance to China should be predicated on wholesale political reform by the Nationalists. Chiang was determined to fight the Japanese, and the US should support him in that endeavor. In a remarkably prescient comment, Johnson observed:

> It is my view that since the fall of the Manchu dynasty and the collapse of the traditional Chinese concept of government the Chinese people have been feeling their way along toward a new evolving form of government. A definitive form of government has not yet been established and may not be established for decades; it may or may not be in the form of a democracy, but it will be a type of government that will be adapted to the needs of China and its people.[47]

Johnson's comment was astute and one that has resonances even in contemporary China, ruled by a party Communist in name but hardly at all in policy. Once again, the discord stemmed from the different claims to ownership of the legacy of Sun Yat-sen. The year 1939 saw a growing centralization of power in the person of Chiang Kai-shek, as he took up the title of "director-general" of the party, giving him an equivalent status to Sun Yat-sen. Sun's philosophy of the "Three People's Principles" of nationalism, democracy, and livelihood for the people (*minzu, minquan, minsheng*) had been only patchily implemented at best in the ten years that the Nationalists had ruled at Nanjing, but at least some intention to act upon them was visible during the war.

However, Mao used the occasion of one of his most important speeches to seize Sun's legacy for the Communists. As relations with the Nationalists worsened in 1939, Mao's previously more conciliatory language began to change. On January 9, 1940, he gave a speech, published as a longer article shortly afterward. Its title, "On New Democracy," showed a change in political terminology. Unlike the term *minquan*, which Sun had used to define democracy, and which translated more as "popular rights" (that is, something which government might bestow upon a citizenry), Mao used the term *minzhu*, whose elements implied instead "popular rule," with the implication of direct control.

Chiang's advocacy of the Principles, he argued, was little more than an attempt to preserve the economic status quo and downgrade the importance of communism. Mao proposed a "New Three People's Principles," espousing a Communist program much more openly. Requirements included an alliance with the USSR, to be given priority over unity with the imperialist powers; cooperation with the Communist Party; and assistance to the peasants and workers. Yet although these principles were explicitly proposed in opposition to the Nationalists, Mao took care to confirm that they were "a development of the old Three People's Principles, a great contribution of Mr. Sun Yat-sen."[48]

Wang Jingwei's regime in Nanjing was the third government simultaneously to take the ideas of Sun Yat-sen and find within them the threads of a different policy. For Wang, it was Sun's attachment to pan-Asianism that was most critical, since it provided the basis for an argument that collaboration with Japan was in fact a version of the nationalist project that Sun had pursued. Wang's regime also launched a campaign of public mobilization called the New Citizen Movement (Xin guomin yundong), which claimed to incorporate the civic elements of Sun's program. It was also an echo of the New Life program of moral exhortation launched by Chiang's regime in 1934 to rejuvenate the country, and which was now being used to define wartime relief and rehabilitation programs.[49]

However, none of the three principal actors was seeking to establish what the West, and particularly the United States, would regard as a democracy: a liberal, multiparty regime with significant civil liberties. Both Chiang and Mao spoke in terms of "democracy," but their understanding of the term meant something more like mass participation in politics under the direction of a dominant party. They were not unusual in this. Many of their counterparts in anti-Western struggle, such as the Indian nationalist Subhas Chandra Bose and the Burmese Ba Maw, were progressive and secular in their aims, but like the Chinese leaders, were not necessarily pluralist. Across the region, the Indian nationalists Nehru and Gandhi were exceptional in their adherence to a model of wide-ranging democracy.

Wang Jingwei's government in Nanjing paid tribute to Sun Yat-sen for its ideology, and among its most active programs was the New Citizen Movement, a lightly disguised adaptation of Chiang's New Life campaign. The government invested heavily in propaganda, such as posters and articles celebrating Wang's return to Nanjing (and in one case, contrasting a picture of Chiang Kai-shek with his face crossed out), and instructions for the formation of youth groups, complete with illustrations of uniforms.[50] In the countryside, it moved swiftly ahead with a program endorsed by Japan and euphemistically termed "village clearance" (qingxiang). Masterminded by the regime's security chief, Li Shiqun, the strat-

egy aimed to root out any resistance from supporters of the Nationalists or Communists who might be hiding in the countryside. The policy
had its successes: all the governments that collaborated with the Japanese
used a fairly standard template of terror and intimidation along with a
certain amount of relief and rehabilitation to imply that those who cooperated could be assured of the necessities of daily life.[51] One Communist
New Fourth Army document from 1941 noted that in certain counties
in Jiangsu province, "the enemy and their puppets have shipped a lot of
rice between harvests . . . the people are finding it very difficult to obtain
ordinary goods, so the Japanese and the puppets have set up cooperative
stores, selling goods at less than the market price."[52]

Yet the cooperative stores were the benevolent face of a far more violent strategy against resistance, in which the Japanese hoped that their
Chinese collaborators would do a great deal of the work for them. Jiang
Weiqing served as a brigade commander with the beleaguered Communist New Fourth Army in the spring of 1941. He had only 4,000 or so
troops to face around 100,000 collaborationist Chinese troops and police
(supplemented by some 3,000 or so Japanese) serving the Wang regime
in the areas around Suzhou, Changshou, and Taicang. Jiang recalled the
techniques used to prevent Communist infiltration. Along the highways,
there might be a checkpoint every *li* (around one third of a mile); the
roads themselves were edged with a bamboo barrier, and every mile or
so there would be a watchtower. On the road, motorized troops would
roar past, and motorboats would patrol the river. Troops would be sent at
dawn to track down anyone hiding in the fields, using dogs and big bamboo sticks that could part the stalks of the crops, "like combing your hair."
Anyone they found would be chased on horseback or sometimes bicycle;
at night, portable searchlights could aid the chase.[53]

Jiang and his small band of troops had to adapt. For some forty days
they hid at the side or in the rear of the most carefully monitored areas,
wearing plain clothes and sticking to groups of two or three. "When the
enemy settled down," Jiang recalled, "we would suddenly attack them
from all sides. We'd kill the sentry and the horses, set their weapons store
on fire, and then throw a bomb into their sleeping quarters." Another
favored technique was to sneak into a watchtower in the dark, start firing,
and hope that the defenders would fire back at each other in the confusion.[54] These techniques were not going to bring the Japanese to their
knees. But they showed how guerrilla tactics could prevent the new order

under Wang from becoming stable, and were a reminder that not every-one had agreed to surrender. Of course, for local farmers, the presence of Communist (or Nationalist) guerrillas was not necessarily a welcome one; resistance fighters in the locality could lead to horrific reprisals from the Japanese and their allies.

The disastrous year 1940 seemed to cast doubt on the idea that there might be any future for China outside the Japanese Empire. As 1941 ground on, yet another horrific event shocked the weary wartime capital. On June 5 Chongqing was subjected to some five hours of bombing, send-ing the population rushing into the air-raid shelters. In one particular tunnel in the Shibati district conditions were even less salubrious than usual. The large shelter should have had electric lighting and fans, but the electric generators had never been connected. Conditions inside were dark and stifling. About 10:00 p.m. people had started to emerge from the tunnel, when rumors began to spread that the Japanese were coming back with poison-gas bombs. The air-raid wardens began to force people back into the shelter, even though some were still coming out. People fell on top of one another, then panicked because they were suffocating. In the next few hours hundreds died, trapped underground in the darkness. The exact figure was never known: the official version said 461, although a police report of the time put the number much higher, at 1,527. What the rescuers did remember clearly were the agonized expressions of the dead: people entwined in each other's arms as they lost consciousness, clothing in strips because desperate people had torn away at each other's garments, and corpses covered in sweat so copious that it appeared that the bodies had been soaked in water. One survivor, Tang Zhengchang, recalled a hand grabbing him from a pile of corpses, moaning "Sir, please help me . . ." The hand had held Tang's shorts so tightly that they pulled them down; Tang jumped out of them and fled the tunnel, naked from the waist down.[55] Official reports of the disaster were toned down. But the event added yet more gloom to the city's mood.

Nonetheless, events far away would provide a sliver of hope for the National Government. Late in 1940, Franklin D. Roosevelt had been re-elected as president of the United States. "I am not going to send your boys into any foreign wars," he had declared in his contest against Repub-lican nominee Wendell Willkie. Yet Roosevelt and his secretary of state, Cordell Hull, were both aware that the Nazi domination of Europe had laid down a profound challenge to American influence there. And with

China's "Open Door" to trade closed off under Japanese occupation, it was becoming clear that simple neutrality might no longer be an option.

In a 1941 report on China's domestic and international politics, US ambassador Nelson Johnson observed that during the great German sweep through Europe in the middle of 1940, the Chinese had been anxious about Allied commitment to their cause. However, Britain's refusal to surrender, along with continuing Soviet goodwill, had encouraged the Chinese public, which now looked to the US and Britain for support, and felt that "victory" was "virtually theirs."[56]

Then on June 22, 1941, the world woke up to the news that some 3 million German troops were on the move into the Soviet Union. Operation Barbarossa, Hitler's invasion of the USSR, was a stunning reversal of the previous two years of nonaggression between the two major European dictatorships. The war in Europe was utterly transformed. Less obviously, so was the war in Asia. Thanks to intelligence leaks, Chiang Kai-shek had already become aware that conflict between Germany and the USSR was likely. Following the signing of a treaty of neutrality between the USSR and Japan on April 13, 1941, Chiang predicted that the US would be drawn into the war in Asia, and even that Japan might later change its mind and attack the USSR. In that event, China would play a crucial role as the key Asian ally of both Washington and Moscow.[57] The German invasion had taken Stalin by surprise (largely because he had failed to heed increasingly shrill warnings from senior colleagues who were receiving intelligence from well-placed spies in Germany), and the Comintern, seeking to shore up its alliances, now demanded that the Chinese Communists cooperate further with the Nationalists.[58] The Central Committee of the CCP responded on June 23, 1941, with a declaration that it would "persevere in the Anti-Japanese United Front, persevere in [Nationalist]-Communist cooperation," as well as allying itself with the British, the Americans, and others who opposed the "fascist rulers" of the Axis powers.[59]

In Chongqing and Yan'an the German attack on the USSR was seen as a positive sign that the war might be turning against Japan. In Nanjing it was seen differently. On June 22 Zhou Fohai recorded in his diary that, though the outcome of the war "cannot be predicted," the members of the Nanjing government "all believe Germany will win and will take Moscow within two months." Zhou guessed that the Japanese could not reconcile their treaty of neutrality with the USSR and their membership of the Anti-Comintern Pact, which was supposed to bind the Axis powers together against Soviet expansionism. However, because the Germans had attacked first, Zhou noted, Japan was not obliged to assist them.[60] Zhou also saw developments through one lens that he had never abandoned in his own mind: that of a Chinese nationalist. "If Chongqing joins the Allies and they win," he noted, "then this is good for China." If they lost, then it would be a disaster for Chiang Kai-shek; but because Wang Jingwei had formed a government in Nanjing in collaboration with Japan, China had "a foot in both boats."[61]

The summer of 1941 marked a decisive shift in the geopolitics of the war. Up to that point, the conflicts in China and in Europe had been self-contained (if desperate) struggles on the Eurasian landmass. But Germany's invasion of Russia now confronted Japan with the choice of whether or not to enter the war against the USSR as well. The debate in Tokyo did not last long. Although some in the government, including Foreign Minister Matsuoka, advocated striking against the USSR before heading south, the Kwantung Army and the Navy both advised against assisting Germany, at least until it had succeeded in drawing significant numbers of Soviet troops away from Siberia to the European front. Konoye, now prime minister again, agreed.[62] Having dismissed the idea of attacking the USSR, Japan's leaders turned their attention instead to another great power: the United States. The inability of the Japanese to achieve further traction in China led to calls for a wider expansion of their influence in the region, in particular Southeast Asia, with its rich supply of oil, rubber, and other materials that were essential to the war effort. From 1940 onward, demands such as the closing of the Burma Road had made it evident that Tokyo was following a more assertive policy in Asia. Despite their inability to subdue China, Japanese leaders were making the decision to raise the stakes yet further.

Japanese politics had become increasingly dominated by the inability to end the China war. As early as 1938, military spending was taking up some 70 percent of Japan's budget, and, in the same year, a National Mobilization Bill gave the government "total war control" over the *zaibatsu* (Japan's big industrial combines). By 1940, the New Order was making itself felt in all aspects of Japanese life, with campaigns against extravagant consumption becoming prominent. In February 1940, one Japanese parliamentarian was expelled from the Diet for daring to speak out against the "holy war" that Japan was fighting in China.[63] In this atmosphere, the possibility of backing down from Japan's imperial ambitions became ever more remote.

The Roosevelt administration was increasingly concerned by these developments. Although still neutral, under the terms of its Lend-Lease program the US was providing significant assistance to Britain and the USSR in their efforts to resist Germany. Now the administration increased the amount of aid available to China also. On February 10 Roosevelt's representative Lauchlin Currie visited Chongqing to let Chiang Kai-shek know that the US would soon deliver $45 million worth of military equipment.[64] General John Magruder, the head of a small group designated as AMMISCA (the American Military Mission in China), had been sent to Chongqing in September 1941 (a few months before Pearl Harbor) as part of the discreet preparation for possible Chinese entry into an alliance against Japan.[65] The China branch of the OSS (Office of Strategic Services, predecessor to the CIA) was headed by General William ("Wild Bill") Donovan, who had been sent out by Roosevelt to China in early 1941.[66]

The Americans made repeated attempts to dissuade Japan from a push southward into Southeast Asia, but the two sides reached ever higher levels of confrontation. The Japanese occupied the southern part of French Indochina, and in response, in July 1941, the US imposed an embargo on oil sales to Japan. Konoye, now unable to resist the increasing pressure for war from the army and navy, resigned on October 16, and was replaced as premier by General Tōjō Hideki. Tokyo hastened preparations for war with the Western powers.[67] Among the targets would be Singapore, Hong Kong, Malaya, the Netherlands East Indies, and the Philippines.

Over the autumn of 1941, ever more desperate talks took place between the United States and Japan. The United States was insistent that Japan must withdraw its forces from China; Japan was equally adamant that it would not do so. While civilian and military factions argued about how fast they should move toward war, there was little doubt in the minds of leaders in Tokyo that conflict was coming. At the imperial conference on November 5, it was formally agreed that if there were no satisfactory diplomatic solution by December 1, war would follow shortly afterward. Negotiations in Washington between Ambassador Nomura Kichisaburō and diplomat Kurusu Saburō and Secretary of State Cordell Hull got nowhere. On November 26, a note from Hull was handed to the Japanese representatives, reiterating the American insistence that Japan must leave China and Indochina. On December 1, the imperial conference made the decision to go to war; the next day, the date was set for the attack to take place on December 8 (December 7, US time).

In the early morning of December 7, 1941, the US Pacific Fleet was anchored at Pearl Harbor in Hawaii. Two waves of Japanese bomber aircraft, launched from six aircraft carriers, attacked the vessels and their sleeping crews, destroying the battleship *Arizona* outright and damaging seventeen others, as well as most of the military aircraft parked nearby. Some 2,400 Americans died, and another 1,100 were wounded. Within a day Japanese invasion forces had attacked Siam (then an independent state), Malaya, and the Philippines.

Chiang Kai-shek heard the news at one o'clock in the morning and immediately dictated a letter of support to President Roosevelt, pledging commitment to a new "common battle."[68] The news reached Zhou Fohai in Shanghai as well. On December 8 (across the international date line from Hawaii) he had heard the sounds of firing as the Japanese took over the rest of the city, and then received reports that Japan had declared war on the Western powers. "I heard they'd bombed Honolulu, Manila, Singapore, and Hong Kong," he wrote. He also observed mournfully: "From now on, the Pacific becomes a killing ground."[69]

PART IV

THE POISONED
ALLIANCE

Chapter 13

DESTINATION BURMA

SINCE THAT TERRIBLE DAY in December 1941, they had been captives. Spring had come to Guangdong province, but the new season left missionary doctor Velva V. Brown and her American colleagues still in limbo, trapped in the city of Shantou (Swatow), on the south coast of China.

Brown had been stationed in China since 1923. The outbreak of war in 1937 had affected Shantou, particularly when Japanese bombs hit the city, but after the initial shock the majority of Americans stayed on. "Business as usual is our motto," declared Brown to her family at home, as she struggled to keep the hospital going in the face of invasion and upheaval.[1] But four years later, as the autumn of 1941 drew on, it became evident to all Americans in China that their protected status might not last. The American Baptist Foreign Mission Society sent out a cablegram on November 15 declaring "in view of increasingly critical developments we advise and urge that all women of mission, all men who are near retiring age or not in good health should return to United States . . . by first available passage."[2]

On December 7 in China (December 6 in the United States) Brown and other missionaries huddled around the radio in the mission house, waiting for news from the last-ditch talks in Washington, DC, between Cordell Hull and the Japanese representatives, Ambassador Nomura Kichisaburô and special envoy Kurusu Saburô. (In Washington, Cordell Hull had little hope that peace could be negotiated, but wanted to seize the "one chance out of a hundred" that the two sides could avoid war. Hull reported that after a final, almost silent visit to his office, the two Japanese envoys "turned without a word and walked out, their heads down.")[3] Then, at 4:00 p.m. the next day, the Mission sent a message speaking of "the staggering news of the Japanese attack on Hawaii."[4] Their missionaries were caught behind what had suddenly become enemy lines. At home, President Roosevelt condemned the attack as a "date which will live in infamy." "Next morning word came to us that war had been declared,"

Brown wrote.[5] Later that day, Japanese military police began the process of rounding up foreigners.

Until December 8, 1941, the war in China had been a distant concern for the Americans and the British, distracted at home by the Depression and then the war in Europe. For the many Westerners who remained in China after 1937, the war was an everyday reality, but their protected status as foreign neutrals always gave them some measure of distance as well as protection, particularly for those who remained in the zones controlled by the Japanese. Now, though, they were enemy aliens. All across eastern China, Americans and Britons were rounded up and interned. The International Settlement of Shanghai, for so long an oasis of neutrality in the midst of a war-torn city, was now reunified under Japanese control. In that city thousands of foreigners with Allied nationality were sent to holding camps. For some, this harsh environment would be home until the end of the war, if they survived at all. An eleven-year-old British boy, Jim Ballard, would become a teenager in Longhua, a holding camp of some 2,000 people; as the novelist J. G. Ballard, forty years later he would tell a semi-autobiographical version of his story in *Empire of the Sun,* detailing the hunger, cold, and disease which were the everyday fate of Longhua's residents. While they could not know what had happened to their fellow Westerners in Shanghai, Velva Brown and her friends in Shantou were rightly nervous of what might become of them. The Japanese did not treat the missionaries too harshly, but the period of waiting stretched for weeks, then months, during which the balance of power in Asia changed with frightening speed.

The prisoners had plenty of time to reflect. For decades Americans had set off in thousands to China. Many came, like Velva Brown, as doctors, missionaries, and teachers. The novelist Pearl Buck lived for years through China's revolution and journey toward modernization, and became one of the best-known interpreters of China to an American audience. Henry Luce was born in China, the son of missionary parents. As owner of *Time,* America's most influential newsmagazine, his strong partisanship toward Chiang Kai-shek meant a powerful boost in the US for the Chinese wartime effort. Yet despite the many advantages that it had brought to China, the American presence was ultimately an imperial one, just as much as the British or French. Americans had also been prominent in the opium trade and enjoyed privileges of legal immunity in China. At 7:48 a.m. on December 7, 1941, with the destruction of US naval vessels in a Hawaiian harbor, that world disappeared.

News finally came for Brown and her friends on April 4. They were lucky. They would be evacuated as part of a wider US-Japanese exchange, which would also cover prominent figures such as Ambassador Nomura in Washington and the US ambassador in Tokyo, Joseph Grew. "One of the most heart-breaking things about leaving," wrote Brown, "was the dismissing of my staff, and especially old servants, many of whom had been with us for fifteen or twenty years." The mission staff were told to pack their belongings in no more than three suitcases. While the old order prepared to leave, the new order rolled in; as the Americans packed their bags, Japanese and Taiwanese picnickers came "sightseeing" to decide "which house they might want to live in."[6] For a century the Americans had been part of an imperial presence in China that had sometimes been benevolent, sometimes violent, but always under the ultimate control of the West. Now a new empire had come to take its place.

The journey home was awkward. Among the company were the American and British consuls who had been based in Shantou, along with merchants and missionaries, but there was no concession to status: all were given "bed-sized strips of Chinese matting which we spread side by side . . . on the iron floor of the hold," Velva Brown wrote.[7] Most of the travelers had to scramble to make the padding comfortable on the hard overlapping metal plates. It was nothing like the appalling journeys that the Chinese refugees had to make in 1937 as they fled the Japanese advance. But it must have felt humiliating, and very final.

Thousands of miles away, in Washington, DC, a newly promoted lieutenant general in the US Army was about to receive orders that would start a very different American relationship with China. That encounter would last only four years, but the aftermath of his tenure would shape Chinese-American relations for more than half a century. Chiang Kai-shek would gain what he had craved for so long: a seat at the top table of global decision-making, with China treated, at least in name, as an equal partner. Within a few weeks of Pearl Harbor, Chiang would show his value to the new alliance by setting an example to other Asian leaders who, like him, could boast anti-imperialist credentials. Chiang would visit India and speak to the leaders of their independence struggle as an ally and friend, a fellow non-European. Then he would join the Allies in their first joint campaign, not in China, but in the jungles of neighboring Burma. Yet the price he would pay for China's entry, at long last, into the alliance, would be a heavy one. Chiang desperately needed his new partners, but accepting this alliance would unleash forces that would threaten the very basis of his rule. The complexities of that bargain would be most visible in the four-year duel between Chiang and that American general: Joseph Warren Stilwell.

From the very earliest days, it was clear that the new Allies were wary of one another. The rhetoric was highly positive, of course. On New Year's Day of 1942, Chiang spoke to the nation about the new reality. He declared that the Allies were striving to protect civilization in the face of Axis barbarity. China's hope, during its years of desperate resistance, had been that another great power would enter the conflict on its side. Now there were two, the United States and the British Empire. Chiang also knew that he must use this opportunity to correct the wrongs that had been done to China over the past century, not just by Japan, but by the very countries that had now come to China's aid. The aim was not just complete victory in the War of Resistance but also to use Sun Yat-sen's Three People's Principles, to "guarantee our nation's eternal independence and survival."[8]

Chiang was diplomatic as he set down his goals in public. In his diary he was more frank and ambivalent about the new alliance. As he reflected on the month of December 1941, Chiang recorded details of the conversation that his ambassador to the US, the scholar (and former strong critic of the Nationalists), Hu Shi, had had with Roosevelt: the president had asked that China should show sympathy, but not celebrate noisily (presumably the American leader was still nervous about how the new alliance would go down at home and might not relish his voters seeing overly jubilant crowds in Chongqing). Of course the Chinese would not celebrate, Chiang wrote. Even this request showed "the contempt that the Americans and British hold for us. Even Roosevelt can't get out of these old attitudes. Such a pity."[9] Just three weeks after Pearl Harbor, as it became clear that China would have to bow to US and British priorities when it came to providing military supplies, Chiang wrote (at the first Three-Power conference) that China had been "shamed" by the way that she was treated by the Americans and the British.[10]

Although Roosevelt had disappointed Chiang, it was the other ally, the British, who bore the brunt of his criticism. "The British don't take us seriously," Chiang wrote, adding, "The next generation should understand the difficulty of building the country up from its past shame." It was not just Japan that he considered to be the source of China's troubles, and he had no intention of forgetting Britain's long record of imperialism in China. On December 15, just a week after Pearl Harbor, Chiang noted:

> I can't describe how humble the attitude of the British ambassador [Sir Archibald Clark Kerr] and his military attaché was . . . But their greed, and their search for a small profit while avoiding the big questions is the same as ever. This is the real character of the British; I wouldn't have imagined this in normal times of this bold Saxon race.[11]

Two days later, he added, with honest ambiguity: "I despise them, but I also respect them."[12] Chiang also laid down the list of demands to the British that he would make in exchange for participation in the war: the return of Kowloon in Hong Kong, the return of control over Tibet (where the British exercised influence), as well as the return of Outer Mongolia and Xinjiang from Soviet control (the region, under warlord Sheng Shicai, was at that point essentially a satellite of the USSR), and the recognition of Manchuria as China's sovereign territory.[13] The British also noted the change in Chinese attitude; their British military attaché in Chongqing declared that the Chinese had "reached a pitch of arrogance and conceit that is unbelievable."[14]

Informed American observers also became more wary about the regime they were supporting. Three years earlier, Ambassador Nelson Johnson had declared his confidence that the Nationalists were sincere in their war efforts and permitted a more pluralistic political culture than might have been expected. Now, Johnson's successor Clarence Gauss, who took on the post in 1941, sounded a more cautious note. When Secretary of State Cordell Hull asked whether there was any danger that China might abandon the war, Gauss dismissed that particular fear, but noted that "the Party has for years given lip service to reform and improvement but little of tangible character has been accomplished."[15]

The problem was that the Chinese and the Westerners looked at China's role through almost entirely different lenses. To the Western Allies, China was a supplicant, a battered nation on its knees, waiting for the

Americans and British to save it from certain destruction at the hands of the Japanese. In Chiang's view and that of many Chinese, their country was the first and most consistent foe of Axis aggression. Despite numerous opportunities to withdraw from the conflict, China had fought on when the prospects of outside assistance seemed hopeless, and it now deserved to be treated as an equal power. The United States maintained a more openly friendly attitude toward its Chinese allies than did the British, too many of whom veered between affable detachment and contempt, although some were sympathetic. Yet Chinese requests for a presence on the joint Allied boards and committees, or for a joint ABCD (American-British-Chinese-Dutch) military staff based in Chongqing, were not taken up.[16] This was in part because of justified fears that the Chinese headquarters would leak intelligence, but overall neither the British nor the Americans treated Chiang as a true equal, nor China as a theater of primary significance. (In contrast, the Soviet Union was hardly an entirely trustworthy ally either for the US or Britain, but its bargaining power and importance meant that they were obliged to treat it as a full strategic and intelligence partner on most key issues.) The Western Allies were at odds about the best way to prosecute the war, and within the US military leadership there were calls from the Navy for the Pacific, not Europe, to be the first priority. General George C. Marshall, chief of staff of the United States Army, weighed all the options, but ultimately favored a Europe First strategy.[17] Both sides' views contained elements of self-deception: the British and Americans wished to give the impression that China was a serious ally without actually putting much effort into the relationship, while Chiang overestimated what he was worth to the Western Allies.

But Chiang's view was hardly irrational. The US knew that if China fell, then the more than 600,000 Japanese troops held down there by Nationalist and Communist forces could be redeployed to the Pacific Theater. Therefore, at the very least it became imperative to "keep China in the war."[18] In January 1942 Chiang requested a loan of $500 million from the United States. Gauss and the US treasury secretary were wary of the request, justifiably fearing that significant portions would be skimmed off the top by corrupt elements in the government.[19] But American censoriousness about Chiang's demands distracted attention from the fact that, compared to the rest of the Allied war effort, the amounts being assigned to China were very small. (In 1941 and 1942 the total proportion of US Lend-Lease aid to China was around 1.5 percent of the total, dropping to 0.5 percent in 1943 and 1944, and would rise to 4 percent only in 1945.)[20] Despite the misgivings of American officials, the loan was passed by the House of Representatives on February 3, 1942.

Yet if they had cared to notice, the spring of 1942 showed Chiang's critics how useful he could be. Chiang had authority in at least one area where his Western counterparts were compromised: his unwavering anti-imperialism. This would become particularly important as the newly begun war in Asia threatened the prize possession of the British Empire, the subcontinent of India. Axis planners had expressed covetous and ambitious plans to create a pincer that would attack from the Middle East and East Asia, capturing the Indian Empire with its manpower and rich resources. It was vital that no such plan ever came to fruition, but there was genuine fear that the turbulent state of domestic Indian politics might make it more likely.

India's capital was indeed at war, but New Delhi looked very different from the rubble-strewn, jerry-built temporary capital at Chongqing. Three decades before, Sir Edwin Lutyens had created a gleaming new city in white marble that was supposed to be fit for a raj and that would last many centuries. Yet even as it was erected, the British had had to engage with a growing Indian independence movement pressing for swift political change. Winston Churchill had been one of the most diehard opponents of handing over power to the Indians, but his views looked old-fashioned by the 1930s and helped to isolate him within his own Conservative Party. During that decade, although the British viceroy remained supreme, significant amounts of executive power had been handed over to elected constitutional assemblies of Indians. Yet in 1939 the viceroy, Lord Linlithgow, had committed India to the war effort against Germany without consulting the leaders of the Indian National Congress, the major secular pro-independence movement in India. Jawaharlal Nehru and Mahatma Gandhi, along with the movement's other prominent leaders, were furious. Like Churchill, Linlithgow was an opponent of swift transfer of power to the Indians, and this gesture seemed a calculated snub. Most of the Indian National Congress leaders had declared their support for the struggle against fascism (the major exception being the former Congress Party president Subhas Chandra

Bose, who left India for Germany in January 1941 and ultimately led the Japanese-sponsored Indian National Army). By early 1942, however, Nehru and Gandhi were increasingly concerned that Indian political and military backing for the British cause was not being translated into a concrete timetable for independence. Relations between the British and Congress became fraught, particularly after the outbreak of war in Asia in December 1941.[21]

The connection with India was of vital importance to the survival of Chiang's government. One of the consequences of war between Japan and the British Empire was that the Burma Road might well close. Chiang had had a foretaste of what this meant when Churchill's government had shut it for three months under Japanese pressure in the summer of 1940, but at the end of that year it was still supplying China with some 20,000 tons of goods per month.[22] With the loss of those supplies, the airlift of material over the Burma "Hump" from India became ever more important, and Chiang was increasingly concerned that the British hold on India should not be weakened before Japan had been defeated. Chiang proposed a visit to India to meet the Congress leaders. The idea outraged Churchill, but it was eventually arranged thanks to the intervention of Sir Archibald Clark Kerr, the British ambassador in Chongqing.

Chiang had not been overseas since his visit to the Soviet Union as a young officer, nearly twenty years previously. When he arrived in the Indian capital, it was the center of a massive effort by the British Empire to use its largest colony as a bulwark against a Japanese invasion. The size of the Indian Army had been increased tenfold. Yet the city was also tense; the ineptness of the British authorities' declaration of war on India's behalf still made the political atmosphere explosive.[23]

In Delhi, on February 11, 1942, Chiang met Nehru, as well as Maulana Azad, the chair of the Congress and one of the Muslim leaders opposed to the separation of the country into the two states of India and Pakistan, as Mohammad Ali Jinnah's Muslim League advocated. Chiang felt that he and Nehru had hit it off, which is unsurprising. Nehru had visited China in 1939 and had several positive meetings with Chiang. Although Nehru's background and temperament made him a democrat in a way that was never natural for Chiang, the two leaders were both secular and inclined to find pragmatic compromises even while holding fast to their anti-imperialist goals. Nonetheless, Chiang took advantage of his senior status to lecture the Indians. "Based on my revolutionary experience," Chiang recorded, he told the two pro-independence leaders that they "should *not* make mistakes in procedures or strategy." Chiang had sympathy for the Indian nationalist cause, and no love for Churchill or the British. But he was concerned that Gandhi and Nehru's opposition to the British presence in India might weaken the Allied war effort. (In fact, Nehru and Gandhi had different positions: Nehru advocated resistance to Japan, but autonomously from the British effort, whereas Gandhi took a much stronger position of nonviolent resistance.)[24] "The extreme nature of their attitude surprises me," Chiang wrote. He was much less enthusiastic about Jinnah, whom he also met, calling him "dishonest" and writing that "the British make use of people like this — but it's not true that Hindus and Muslims can't get on," and suggesting that "truly patriotic Muslims" should stick to Gandhi and the Congress.[25] Chiang was leader of a country that had been splitting itself into fragments for much of the twentieth century; no wonder he looked coolly on an Indian politician who advocated separatism.

The visit soon ran into a diplomatic storm. Churchill was adamant that Chiang, a national leader, should not visit Gandhi at his home at Wardha, near Bombay, as if the latter were a dignitary in his own right. Instead, Gandhi should make his way to New Delhi. Chiang was furious. Chiang received repeated late-night messages from the British authorities ordering him not to visit Gandhi. He refused to reply.

At midnight on February 15, Chiang received a message from Gandhi himself, which moved him deeply. "To lose one's country is a painful loss of freedom," reflected Chiang. "I summoned Ambassador Clark Kerr and told him that before I leave India, I have to meet Gandhi."[26] Eventually, it was agreed that Chiang and Gandhi should meet at Santiniketan, the university near Calcutta founded by the Nobel laureate poet and polymath Rabindranath Tagore.

On February 18 Chiang and Gandhi talked for some five hours, with Song Meiling interpreting. Gandhi told Chiang that he was sympathetic to the War of Resistance, and he would not obstruct British assistance to China. However, Chiang also tried to float the idea of mutual cooperation — in other words, supporting a more active Indian role in the war. Gandhi did not reply directly, but stated that Chiang "should not force him to change his principles," and then used his long-favored technique of ending an awkward conversation by turning to his spinning wheel, on which he made plain *khadi* cloth. The next day Chiang wrote of his frustration:

After meeting Gandhi yesterday, I'm disappointed. My expectations were too great, but perhaps the pain of being ruled by the British has hardened his heart . . . he knows and loves only India, and doesn't care about other places and people . . . Traditional Indian philosophy has made him this way. He only knows how to endure pain, and has no zeal — this is not the spirit of a revolutionary leader. I judge that the Indian revolution will not easily succeed.[27]

Gandhi also realized that the two had reached an impasse. "I would not say that I learnt anything," he wrote to his colleague Vallabhai Patel, "and there was nothing that we could teach him."[28] Song Meiling later told Nehru that she was pessimistic that Gandhi's approach would bring about Indian freedom, greatly upsetting the Congress leader. Chiang's assessment of Gandhi was not fair: he was an internationalist whose lifelong struggle had started in South Africa, not India, and his distinctive nonviolent philosophy of resistance owed much to thinkers such as Tolstoy as well as to traditional Indian thought. But Chiang was right to see a fundamental disconnect between their aims. Gandhi's principles of nonviolence made little sense to a leader shaped by the warlord conflicts of the 1920s and 1930s, and while Chiang did not live a personally extravagant lifestyle, the extreme simplicity that Gandhi advocated was a long way from Song Meiling's opulent tastes.

In his parting speech on February 21, 1942, the last day of his visit in India and broadcast from Calcutta by Song Meiling in English, Chiang's words were bold. He reminded his listeners about the Nanjing massacre, implying that they should not place their anti-imperialist hopes in the Japanese, and warning that if the Allies lost, then "world civilization may be set back over a hundred years." But he also made an explicit link between China's freedom and that of India, and warned the British that they should give real power to India ahead of demands from Indians themselves.[29] (Churchill once again was furious, of course.)

In his diary Chiang reflected on the two dynamics that had shaped his visit to India. "In my farewell statement," he wrote, "I completely supported the liberation of India. The British may not understand this, but I deeply believe it may be of advantage to Britain." He noted that Nehru had complained of the contradictions in Chiang's attitude to India, supporting independence but also requesting that it throw its lot in with the British war effort; Chiang had replied that all politics was confusing, and if it were clearer then it would be "philosophy, not politics." After all, in February 1942, the war in Asia was in its very earliest months. The Burma campaign was about to start, and Chiang could not know (any more than could Churchill or Roosevelt) whether India might fall to the Japanese. It was entirely in Chiang's interests that the country's most prestigious pro-independence figures should wholly endorse the war against Japan rather than merely giving it tacit assent. But Chiang's visit to India also strengthened his view that the war was an opportunity to create a new, anti-imperialist united Asia. "Revolutionary opportunities are hard to find and easy to lose," he chided Nehru at the final lunch they held on February 21. "This is India's *only* good revolutionary opportunity. If we lose it, we won't get it again." Nehru was silent, "but seemed to understand."[30] Chiang followed up in March with another speech in which he once again urged the Indian leaders to back the Allies. He also stressed to the British that India was already supplying more soldiers than any country except China, and that a promise of swift independence would energize the country yet further.[31]

Anti-imperialist solidarity had its limits. A mission to India by the leftist British politician Sir Stafford Cripps in April 1942 failed to achieve any accommodation between the colonial authorities and Congress. Just a few months later, in August 1942, Nehru and Gandhi began the Quit India movement, which demanded swift independence from the British and led to the arrest of the top Congress leadership and around 100,000 other activists. Some 2.5 million Indian troops did fight for the Allies during the war, although without the explicit support of Congress.

Nonetheless, Chiang's gesture in visiting India was important. In an era when non-Western people around the world were seeking freedom, it was still a rarity for leaders of independence movements to be visited by the head of a sovereign non-European nation. No other Allied leader could have met Nehru or Gandhi with the same credibility. Chiang was privately disappointed that he had been unable to persuade the Congress leaders to back the war effort fully. In this, his agenda was no different from that of Churchill or Roosevelt, although the British leader, at least, failed to realize or acknowledge that. Had the British authorities backed Chiang more fully, the result might have been different. Above all, however, the visit marked China's first wartime gesture as a great power, a sovereign actor in international relations.

• • •

On January 14, 1942, the United States secretary of war, Henry L. Stimson, dined in Washington, DC, with a single guest: General Joseph Stilwell. The subject of their conversation was China. Stimson "thinks the Chinese will accept an American commander," Stilwell wrote in his diary, adding that Stimson had said, "More and more, the finger of destiny is pointing at you."[32]

While Marshall had decided to concentrate forces on Europe, he recognized that it was still important to show the Americans were fighting in Asia; after all, the provocation had come from Japan, not Germany. Yet he did not want to assign US ground troops to China. The solution seemed to be to persuade Chiang to allow an American chief of staff for the Chinese armies, which would show that the Americans stood side by side with the Chinese, but did not require the assignment of significant troop numbers. Stilwell was Marshall's choice to take the role.

Stilwell had taught at West Point, where his cutting remarks had led to him being nicknamed "Vinegar Joe," a moniker in which he took great pride. Between the wars he undertook several tours of duty in China, becoming proficient in Chinese and including a period as US military attaché from 1935 to 1939, during which he had witnessed the outbreak of the Sino-Japanese War. His reports show one constant theme: puzzlement and anger that the Chinese military preferred to retreat rather than to hold territory. When asked on one occasion when the Chinese might choose to fight back, he replied, "Not until they lose their inherent distaste for offensive combat."[33] The Chinese military officers, he believed, simply did not have the skills needed for modern warfare. The ordinary fighting man, on the other hand, had the fortitude to conquer — as long as he was led by a commander who knew how to use him. Stilwell had no previous direct experience of generalship, but he had a powerful friend in George C. Marshall. Stilwell believed that as long as he was given genuine "COMMAND" (as he put in his diary) over Chinese forces, then he could use them effectively against Japan.[34] Yet on February 6, 1942, Marshall sent a message to General John Magruder, the head of the American military mission in Chongqing, that made Stilwell's role clear: "American forces in China and Burma will operate under Stilwell's direction . . . but General Stilwell himself will always be under the command of the Generalissimo."[35] The gap between the official understanding of Stilwell's role and Stilwell's sense of his own position would soon come to assume crucial importance.

The official entry of the United States into the Second World War had turned Chongqing into a very different city after December 1941. Although American troops were not sent to fight in China, an influx of American bureaucrats and military personnel was now a constant part of everyday existence. Sometimes the influence could lead to odd results; one report claimed that a local student had been reprimanded for starting to speak her native Chinese in an American accent. "Young lady," scolded her teacher after she tried out her new voice in class, "remember I am your professor, not your boyfriend."[36] Other aspects of the American presence were visible as well as audible. Graham Peck spent the war years in China working for the US Office of War Information. His job was to spread positive propaganda about the war effort and China's new American allies. In his compelling memoir of his assignment to Chongqing, Peck described the arrival of a heartening new presence in the war-weary city. With a "thick powerful roar, smooth as the tearing of heavy silk," he recalled, there appeared "American P-40 fighter planes with the grinning sharks' faces of the 'Flying Tigers' painted on their snouts." For half an hour the P-40s performed to their audience, dipping up and down in the air, "like a school of happy flying fish," and in response they heard "the noise of half a million people shouting together to the sky," the population of Chongqing overjoyed at the presence of their new, technologically superior allies.[37]

Having been in Chongqing since 1937, General Claire Chennault was delighted that the US and China were now officially allies. The Flying Tigers (AVG) that he commanded were augmented with a hundred P-40 aircraft that had been promised before Pearl Harbor, and were delivered in late 1941, mostly before that attack.[38] (In 1942 the AVG would be officially redesignated as part of the 14th US Air Force, and would become the only Americans to see active combat service in China itself.) Yet the arrival of Stilwell spelled trouble for the American flier. Chennault was convinced that airpower held the key to a swift victory over the Japanese within China. Stilwell, in contrast, believed in the power of well-trained ground troops. The stage was set for a confrontation that would make the complex relationship between the US and China still more tense.

Chiang Kai-shek's great hope was that the US might supply American ground combat troops to fight in China. However, this was never seriously considered by the Allied commanders. The official US Army historians stated clearly that:

there were no U.S. ground combat units, for the U.S. effort in China had always been intended by the War Department to help the Chinese defend themselves, to which end the War Department and the Joint Chiefs had been willing to give advice plus technical and air support. Moreover, since every American flown into China meant that .62 of a ton of supplies had to be flown to China every month for his support, Stilwell had kept the number of U.S. ground force and service personnel in China to a minimum, hence there were few indeed in that category.[39]

Stilwell's chance to put Chinese troops into action would come very soon indeed. One of the first decisions made by the Allied commanders was to repel Japanese advances not in China but in Burma. Even before Pearl Harbor, the British and the Chinese had concerns that Burma, which lay between China and Britain's Indian Empire, was vulnerable to Japanese attack, and that the fall of Burma could allow the Japanese to take northeast India, Calcutta, and make the whole of eastern India vulnerable. The Burma Road had been supplying some 20,000 tons a month of supplies, to which the only alternative was to fly much smaller amounts across the Hump from India to China. However, the Japanese threat to Burma was not considered a major one, and only around 12,000 troops were stationed there.[40]

Then, in February 1942, the Japanese launched their assault on Burma. They had not previously considered the British colony a priority target, but the events of the previous month had inspired them. After Pearl Harbor, in quick succession they had conquered Hong Kong and the Philippines. It suddenly seemed that the mighty British Army was not such a formidable foe, and Burma now looked a more attractive target. It offered the twin temptations of cutting off the Nationalists from supply via the Burma Road, and making the eastern flank of British India vulnerable. On February 9 the Japanese 15th Army moved to take the capital, Rangoon, and then drive north toward Toungoo and Mandalay.

In response, Chiang offered up the Fifth and Sixth Armies to defend Toungoo, in central Burma, to provide relief for the British defense of Rangoon, but this gesture was rejected by Archibald Wavell, British commander in chief for India and supreme commander, Far East. Wavell's justification was in part logistical, but also owed a great deal to imperial pride. He wrote to Churchill that it was "obviously better" that Burma should be defended by British troops rather than Chinese, although in this case Churchill disagreed with Wavell's decision.[41] Stilwell, still in Washington, wrote contemptuously that Wavell "didn't want the dirty Chinese in Burma."[42] (Something similar had happened during the Great War, when the Chinese offer of combat troops to the Allies in Europe had been accepted by the French but was turned down by the British.)[43] Yet in Southeast Asia the British position was becoming even more precarious. Singapore, the premier military harbor in the region, fell to the Japanese on February 15 in one of the greatest disasters for the British Empire during the whole of the Second World War.

The British, under General Harold Alexander, were unable to defend Rangoon, and withdrew. The Japanese captured the city on March 8 and immediately made plans to strike north, to Toungoo. Despite the mutual distrust between Alexander and Chiang, the British and Chinese were united in the conviction that the best strategy was now retreat. Alexander's concern was to bring the Empire troops back for the defense of India while using Chinese troops as a buffer. Chiang advocated the defense of Mandalay, in central Burma, but demanded that the British provide more active assistance before Chinese troops were sent to protect the city. Both sides had given up southern Burma as lost.[44]

Not so Stilwell. He arrived in Chongqing via India in early March 1942, having been named Chiang's chief of staff. After his first formal meeting with the generalissimo, Stilwell noted approvingly that "he seems willing to fight and is fed up with the British retreat and lethargy."[45] Chiang's initial reaction to Stilwell's appointment was also favorable. But he made it clear that he was commander in chief for the China Theater, and that he expected Stilwell to follow orders. Chiang was content to allow the Americans the gesture of appointing Stilwell to show the closeness between the US and China, but he had no intention of actually ceding command to a Westerner.

On March 9 and 10, Stilwell held meetings with Chiang on the strategy for Burma. Chiang advocated a cautious approach: Chinese troops should be sent into the north of Burma to defend the border with Yunnan province (ruled over by the ethnic Yi militarist Long Yun). Chiang believed that there was a chance of defending Mandalay, and wanted Stilwell to pressure the British into supporting a Chinese defense of the city. Stilwell instead spoke out in favor of an offensive strategy, arguing that a push against the Japanese from Toungoo would ensure a great victory. "Rangoon is the vital point," he noted in his diary on March 9, 1942. "Without it, supply stops." He added: "I have a hunch the Japs are weak."[46] As no US forces would take part in the campaign, Stilwell would be conducting it with Chinese troops, in particular the Fifth and Sixth Armies, among the best that China had left.

Like Chiang, Stilwell was convinced that China would be valuable as an active participant in the world war. He genuinely believed that Japan should be opposed on the Chinese mainland. Some of his more senior commanders did not agree. In a memorandum to the British and American combined chiefs of staff, Marshall was frank in his assessment of Stilwell's appointment: "Because the Pacific is a secondary theater," he noted, "we must depend on the Chinese to contain increasingly more Japanese divisions than at present."[47] By advocating an offensive strategy, therefore, Stilwell was going against Marshall's advice.

Such risky tactics could have their uses: a decade later, the daring amphibious attack by General Douglas MacArthur at Inchon in Korea would help to turn that war against the insurgent Communist forces. But MacArthur was a great deal more experienced, and had far greater resources, than Stilwell in 1942. Chiang opposed Stilwell's idea, pointing out that there was insufficient air cover or tank support for the Allies in Burma, and that if the Fifth and Sixth Armies were lost, then the defense of southwestern China would become even harder. He reiterated that Stilwell did retain command of the troops, but asked that he wait for Chiang to decide the right moment for an offensive after the Chinese forces had built up their strength near Mandalay.

At first, Stilwell maintained a degree of self-awareness about his position as an American commander of Chinese troops. "I am amazed the way the Chinese accept me," he noted.[48] He was less inclined to seek acceptance from the British, referred to as "Limeys" throughout his diaries, and mocked Major General Lancelot Dennys, the British military attaché in China, for wanting the Chinese to "rush in and save the British empire."[49] But his conviction that he could understand the Chinese and ignore the British awakened within him a recklessness that would not take long to show itself.

After their initial, brief warmth, Stilwell and Chiang clashed over and over again. Stilwell had started referring to Chiang in his diaries as "the Peanut," and the nickname was clearly not meant to be affectionate. Chiang's desire for a defensive strategy on the border with Burma led to a mocking response from Stilwell. "In a month, *if nothing* happens, maybe we can take the offensive. He wants to be sure it will be easy," scoffed Stilwell in his diary. "Again told me Fifth and Sixth must not be defeated, so I told him to send someone else who could guarantee that, because I couldn't."[50] Stilwell interpreted Chiang's objections as excessive caution, or even cowardice. Yet it was hardly surprising that the leader of a country with its back against the wall might have doubts about a bold strategy — proposed by a foreign general with no command experience — which threatened to destroy two of his best remaining armies. However, Chiang did not wish to create a rift with his newly appointed chief of staff, so with misgivings he allowed Stilwell to implement his strategy.

On March 21 Stilwell returned to Burma. Toungoo was now under attack, and without fully discussing his plan with either the Chinese or the British, Stilwell ordered the Nationalist troops of the 55th and 22nd Divisions under his command to hurry south to launch a counteroffensive against the Japanese at Pyinmana and Pyawnbwe.[51] In a letter home to his wife, Stilwell seemed to acknowledge that this was a risky move. "The Jap air raids on Magwe about cleaned out our meager support, and now we'll be taking it on the nose for some time with no answer available." He continued, "However, the Chinese have had a lot of that, and I believe, can take more of that without cracking."[52]

The test of Stilwell's assessment would come soon enough. The next day, March 25, the Japanese surrounded Toungoo. Stilwell refused to give the order that would have allowed the 200th Division trapped there to retreat. He believed himself to be standing firm while everyone else was hysterical. "Chiang K'ai-shek and his changeable mind had me worried," Stilwell noted, adding that the lesson was "always be slow to *put an unacceptable plan into action*." (Chiang's desire to retreat was the "unacceptable" idea.) Du Yuming, the general commanding the Fifth Army, was having one of "his depressed fits and everything was wrong . . . Christ, he's terrible when he's like that." And "riot among British soldiers at Yenangyaung. *British destroying the oil fields.* Good GOD. What are we fighting for?"[53] Stilwell's certainty of his own correctness might have been more understandable if his strategy was working. It was not. "I know that I've sacrificed a great deal for nothing, for the sake of this plan of the Americans and British," Chiang wrote despairingly in his diary. "But now I do have to stick it out to the end."[54] As the Japanese moved ever closer to the town, Chiang finally got a message through allowing the divisional commander to withdraw on March 30. This gave Stilwell fuel to accuse Chiang of attempting to interfere and second-guess his command. At noon the next day, Stilwell boarded a plane, and by two o'clock the following morning he was back in Chongqing. That morning was April 1. Stilwell wrote: "Am I the April Fool? From 3/19 to 4/1 in Burma, struggling with the Chinese, the British, my own people, the supply, the medical service, etc., etc. Incidentally, with the Japs." Stilwell's self-pitying tone brought him far closer than he would have cared to acknowledge to his adversary Chiang, who had written early on in the war that "nobody understands me but my wife." Chiang's diary did, in places, show self-doubt. There was little of that in Stilwell's evaluation of the Toungoo debacle: "Through stupidity, fear, and the defensive attitude we have lost a grand chance to slap the Japs back at Toungoo. The basic reason is Chiang K'ai-shek's meddling." He also described Chinese politics and military strategy as "twisting, indirect, and undercover."

Stilwell was not a fool, April or otherwise. But he showed characteristics that suggested severe limitations on his skills as a military commander. He had a particular way of viewing the world, and anything that ran counter to the assumptions that shaped that view was dismissed as irrelevant, or worse, maliciously intended to undermine him.

At midday Stilwell went to Chiang and "threw the raw meat on the floor," demanding to be relieved of his command. "I have to tell Chiang K'ai-shek with a straight face that his subordinates are not carrying out his orders, when in all probability they are doing just what he tells them." He did observe that it must have been difficult for the Chinese to hand the command of their armies to a "goddam foreigner . . . in whom they can't have much confidence." But the next line of the diary found Stilwell in a less circumspect frame of mind: "The worst has happened in the press. Before I have a chance to get my feet on the ground, a flood of crap is released, to justify which I would have to be in Rangoon within a week. What a sucker I'll look like if the Japs run me out of Burma."[55] Stilwell would be portrayed by his allies in the press as a driven and selfless man determined to fight the war "wholeheartedly, democratically, with no tolerance for corruption, duplicity, or the niceties of diplomatic small talk," in the words of Theodore White.[56] In fact, Stilwell may have been more image-conscious than any other commander at his level, perhaps more so since his lack of command experience was now compounded by failure in Burma.

Chiang was caught in a dilemma. It was true that he had ordered the divisional commander at Toungoo to retreat, thereby probably saving his life and that of his troops, as Stilwell had shown no intention of retreating in the face of overwhelming Japanese opposition. Chiang regarded Stilwell as a rash decision maker, too eager to risk the best Chinese troops left. (That same week, Chiang cast doubt on Stilwell's assurance that he could have a new airfield built within thirteen days. "He's been deceived by the British," Chiang wrote, "and now he's cheating me.")[57] However, he had waited well over four years to gain the United States as an ally. He could not afford a full-scale conflict with the senior American commander in the China Theater after less than four months. Chiang consulted his wife Song Meiling, who stressed the importance of appeasing Stilwell. (Stilwell had more time for her, calling her "direct, forceful, energetic, loves power . . . Great influence on Chiang K'ai-shek mostly along the right lines, too.")[58] Chiang invited Stilwell to Huangshan, the villa outside Chongqing which provided a retreat from the dusty and noisy city, as well as relative safety from air raids. He announced that General Luo Zhuoying would be sent back to Burma with Stilwell and would be responsible for transmitting his orders to the Chinese commanders lower down. In addition, Chiang himself would accompany them back to make it clear that he personally endorsed Stilwell's authority over the troops. "This is a major victory for me," Stilwell wrote, adding, "When you consider their history and experience with foreigners, this is really a handsome gesture that Chiang K'ai-shek is making."[59] The party flew down to Maymyo in central Burma, including not only Chiang and Song Meiling, but also the writer Clare Boothe Luce, wife of the publisher of *Time* magazine. There, in public, Chinese officers were instructed that Stilwell's orders be obeyed without question.

In Burma the situation was now critical. Stilwell wanted to make a stand with the Chinese Fifth Army at the town of Pyinmana in central Burma, in the hope of drawing the Japanese into a trap. But the plan quickly fell apart. The British troops were reluctant to protect the Chinese troops on their right flank, fearing that they would be surrounded. On April 18 troops under the British major general William Slim (promoted to lieutenant general during the campaign) were in danger of being surrounded by the Japanese in the oil-rich area around Yenangyaung, west of Pyinmana, forcing Stilwell to divert Chinese troops to relieve them.[60] "Wild tales of the Jap tank division at Loikaw," wrote Stilwell on April 20. "Aiming at Lashio? Jesus. This may screw us completely."[61]

The Allied hope of thrusting south hastily gave way to a desperate attempt to withdraw before the Japanese destroyed the Allies' best troops in the region. However, the retreat was hampered by the unwillingness of the British, the Chinese, and Stilwell to trust one another's motives or judgments. Meanwhile, the Japanese army struck hard at Lashio in eastern Burma, as Stilwell had feared, seizing it on April 29. Now there was a real danger that significant numbers of Allied troops would be trapped in Burma, unable to break through Japanese lines. "Imminent danger of disintegration and collapse," Stilwell wrote.[62]

A new battle of wills began between Stilwell and Chiang. Stilwell ordered Du Yuming to lead his Fifth Army troops not back to China, but to India. Chiang was aghast when he heard the news that his chief of staff had ordered a substantial part of his army into another country, and wondered whether Stilwell had lost his resolve because his proposed attack in Burma had gone so wrong.[63] Chiang reversed the order and instead commanded Du to bring his troops to the northern Burmese town of Myitkyina. Chiang then received the news that Stilwell was leaving Burma for India, along with his closest staff. Once again, Chiang could not believe that Stilwell would abandon the troops supposedly under his control.[64] "One doesn't expect this of one's military adviser," he wrote, horrified. "Could it be that because of the battle, his nerves have given way?"[65]

Stilwell was determined to leave. On May he set out with a party of some eighty people, including American, Chinese, and British soldiers, Indian engineers, and Burmese nurses. Stilwell led this unlikely group on a terrifying journey through a jungle where disease and snakebite were as much a threat as the enemy. "Limeys' feet all shot," he recorded on May 8. "Our people tired . . . Chattering monkeys in the jungle. Bombers over . . . Hot camp. Insects." They finally made contact with civilization again on May 20, when they arrived at Imphal in northeast India, to be met by an "old fool" of a provincial administrator.[66]

Never one to miss an opportunity for good press, Stilwell made an official statement in New Delhi on May 25. "I claim we got a hell of a beating," he declared. "We got run out of Burma and it is as humiliating as hell. I think we ought to find out what caused it, go back, and retake it." In a letter to his wife he was franker about assigning blame, and what he intended to do about it. "I'll be going back to report to the G-mo [Chiang] and I sure have an earful for him. He's going to hear stuff he never heard before and it's going to be interesting to see how he takes it."[67]

In fact, Chiang had already determined that he must from now on sign off on Stilwell's orders, although he did not tell Stilwell this.[68] "Now I know that the alliance is just empty words," Chiang wrote, "and I don't exclude America from this."[69]

Remarkably, Stilwell's group had made it out of the jungle without any deaths. The troops he had commanded, and had left behind in Burma, fared less well. Luo Gu was one of the soldiers who served in the Fifth Army under General Du Yuming. They fought fiercely against the Japanese, even capturing a couple of elephants. But at the start of May, as communications broke down, they attempted to march northwest, to Mandalay. "The jungle covered everything for miles," Luo recalled, "leaving us deadly thirsty." Soon they got lost. As they waded around in rice paddies, insects attacked them from all sides, and a massive thunderstorm soaked them to the skin. Days turned into weeks, and conditions worsened further. The soldiers destroyed their weapons, as they no longer had the strength to carry them and they did not want them captured by the Japanese. A month after they had started out, Luo recorded, "the soldiers are all in rags and look very gaunt. Everyone is carrying a bag of rice, a water-can, a diesel tin, and in the other hand, a walking-stick." The soldiers' difficulty in walking was compounded by their diet. "Because we haven't had any oil for a month," complained Luo, "my stools are very hard and my anus has split. When can we get hold of a drop of oil?" And everywhere they traveled, they found corpses scattered. The company cook was one who went missing; the remains of his body were found half eaten, presumably by one of the many tigers that stalked the jungle. By the middle of June the soldiers were starving, digging up roots to try and survive; meanwhile the monsoon rains poured down every day. Even when supplies were dropped in the area from the air, tragedy struck, as some soldiers were hit and killed by the falling boxes. More then died from eating too fast after a period of long deprivation. Only at the start of August did Luo and his companions finally reach India.[70]

Most of the Chinese troops of the 38th Division under General Sun Liren did make it to India, although the numbers were lowered by Japanese attacks as well as disease. Parts of the Fifth Army had to make their way north to Myitkyina in Burma, under constant aerial attack from the Japanese. The 96th and 200th Divisions did, somehow, make their way back to China as coherent units. Much of the Sixth Army was not so fortunate, wiped out by the Japanese assault. The Japanese were on China's doorstep, driving into Yunnan. But now Chiang sent in troops — along with Chennault's Flying Tigers — to drive them back.[71] The Japanese did not need to thrust into China at this point. They had achieved their main aim of cutting off supplies to Chongqing via the Burma Road. With no reliable access to land or sea supplies, the National Government was now perilously close to being completely isolated.

Did Stilwell's failed strategy in Burma destroy a key defense for the Nationalist government? The alternative, a retreat to north Burma — advocated both by the National Government and by the British — might still have seen the region overrun by the Japanese and the loss of the Burma Road. But Stilwell's highly risky gamble was much more likely to fail than succeed. It led to the death or injury of some 25,000 Chinese troops along with over 10,000 British and Indian troops (with only 4,500 Japanese casualties).[72] Retreat might have meant that more of the Fifth and Sixth Armies were saved for the defense of China. Whatever the alternative, the reality was that by the spring of 1942 there was no further possibility of Nationalist China being supplied through Burma. The political and financial consequences of Stilwell's choice would rebound on Chiang's government for years to come. The ending of the Burma supply route also put another opportunity in Stilwell's hands. Some 45,000 tons of Lend-Lease supplies intended for China were now instead assigned to the Nationalist armies that had made it to India.[73] Throughout the war Stilwell would retain control over the Lend-Lease assigned to China, diverting much of it to projects which he favored, and exacerbating tensions that would corrode the alliance with the Nationalists.

The Burma debacle also set the tone, only a few months into the global war, for a shared Western understanding of the Chinese war effort. Western officers (primarily Americans, and Stilwell above all) were seen as making an ever more futile effort to motivate China to fight — against the wishes of a corrupt and unwilling leader, Chiang Kai-shek. Chiang understood this very well. Stilwell's reports on the Chinese military are "contemptuous and blacken our name," wrote Chiang. "They are lukewarm about helping us. Thinking about this angers and pains me."[74]

Chiang's troops in Burma had done little to raise China's military prestige — although, with the British in retreat all around the region, it was not as if China's performance was exceptionally poor in comparison. The Allies blamed Chiang for putting China's interests first, but it is hardly surprising that he wished to do exactly that. They also blamed him for not acting as if he commanded a strong and disciplined army of the British or American type, even while they labeled him insignificant precisely because his regime was weak. The circumstances that made the Nationalist armies so weak — in particular the four years of sustained warfare — were not understood as justification for extra assistance to Chiang, but instead were treated as a kind of failing.

As the Burma campaign ground on, another incident took place which showed the low status that China held in the minds of the Western Allies. On April 18, 1942, sixteen B-25 bombers took off from the aircraft carrier USS *Hornet* and raided military and industrial targets in cities including Tokyo, Osaka, and Nagoya. They did relatively little damage, but the raids showed that Japan was now vulnerable to attack from the air. The sortie became known as the "Doolittle Raids," after their commander, Lieutenant Colonel James Doolittle. The news of the attack was a huge propaganda boost for the American war effort. But it appalled Chiang. On their return the fighters were supposed to land at airfields in the Nationalist-held parts of Zhejiang, in eastern China. In fact, none of them did so; they all crash-landed at various points in eastern China, bar one that landed in Vladivostok on the Russian coast and was then interned for a year. However, the Japanese reacted with fury. They attacked and destroyed all the airfields in Zhejiang which Chennault had built up, and committed atrocities against the local population in the surrounding areas. What went down very well with the American public had a hugely negative effect on the Chinese war effort.[75]

Over the next year, the presence of American fliers would continue to cause tension between the two sides. One US military attaché wrote with some dissatisfaction that his Chinese counterpart had said that "the Chinese are beginning to hate the Americans" because of the air-raid warnings that had to be called whenever American planes flew overhead. (Until the approaching planes arrived, villagers would not know whether they were friendly or not, and village headmen frequently found themselves having to scatter the local population in case they were bombed, disrupting everyday life.) Chennault had replied that he could only warn them "when the Chinese proved to him that there was not one single Japanese spy in unoccupied China," which was clearly impossible.[76] The Americans were justifiably worried that letting the Chinese side know when the raids were taking place would expose their pilots to terrible danger if the enemy got hold of the information. But refusal by the Americans to take senior Chinese officers into their confidence inevitably highlighted the inequity between the two sides.

Additionally, Chiang Kai-shek's regime was being undermined from within. And the culprit was neither a rogue general nor an uncertain ally, but disastrous natural and social forces that would set him at odds with his own people.

Chapter 14

HUNGER IN HENAN

THE JOURNALIST LI SHU visited Henan province in central China in February 1943. The region has a particularly important place in Chinese history, for the Yellow River that flows through it nurtured China's earliest civilizations, and cities such as Luoyang and Zhengzhou have histories reaching back thousands of years. The fertile soil of the region produced grain that fed millions of Chinese every year, and its huge population had swelled the ranks of China's military for the past five years of the war. In 1938 there had been dreadful suffering in parts of the province when Chiang Kai-shek had ordered the dikes destroyed to prevent the Japanese advance. Now rumors were spreading about a terrible famine that was devastating the population. Official censorship made the story obscure and difficult to verify, and Li wanted to find out more about conditions on the ground in the province.

"As I was traveling from Yinjingpu to Yanshi," Li Shu wrote, "I saw three corpses by the side of the road. One of them was an old white-haired man, and someone had stripped off all his clothes. His face was down in a field of grain."[1] Li Shu traveled further into the interior. At one point he asked an old man why so many people had gathered at the banks of the Luo River. The answer came that they were gathering up bird excrement. (At one time, geese must have been plentiful nearby.) They would then rinse off the feces and release the precious morsels that lay embedded in them: undigested, edible grains of wheat.[2] However horrible this story was, it was not the worst experience that Henan's people would endure in that spring of hunger.

As China's role in global politics suddenly expanded, the situation at home began to change too. After Pearl Harbor, Chiang's time was filled with ever more negotiations with Stilwell, Roosevelt, Wavell, and Churchill. The Burma debacle showed how far those alliances had yet to go to become genuine partnerships. Meanwhile, Chiang's eyes were not always fixed on the rapidly changing situation much closer to home. In China's provinces, far from the influence of the capital, the hastily implemented system of bureaucracy, relief provision, and military administration was vulnerable to pressure — not only from the ever-present Japanese threat, but also from the growing social tensions within Chinese society as the government and its allies asked the people to endure more and more despite dwindling resources.

Although China had gained its longed-for alliance with the Western powers, there were also multiple signs that all was not well with the wartime state. Graham Peck's job for the US government agency the Office of War Information (OWI) was to accentuate the positive about the American alliance with Chiang, but he swiftly became convinced that the immediate response had been "cynical gaiety . . . and the Kuomintang's [Nationalists'] growing alienation from reality."[3] The new determination in Chongqing could not hide the fact that the Nationalist grip on power outside the southwest of the country was becoming very precarious.

One person who could give Chiang firsthand information about the degeneration of Nationalist rule was his son Chiang Ching-kuo (Jiang Jingguo). The relationship between the two had always been a somewhat distant one. Ching-kuo had gone to the USSR in 1927, and remained there for a decade, marrying his Belarussian wife Faina in 1935. He returned to China in 1937 and was placed in charge of a prefecture named Ganzhou, in the impoverished Jiangxi province. While he was there, he kept a diary in which he recorded numerous instance of how far the Nationalist attempts to modernize and centralize had penetrated (or failed to penetrate) the more remote provinces.

In June 1940, early in his stay at Ganzhou, Ching-kuo visited a shabby local primary school, one of whose "students" was actually a thirty-year-old draft dodger. Ching-kuo fired questions at the students, but got no answer to his query "Where is the national government?" (The question "Where is Wang Jingwei?" received the answer "In Japan," but when he asked "And where is Japan?" a long pause ensued, with one student finally replying "It's in Japanese imperialism.") Other institutions were equally depressing. A hospital had nothing but rice porridge to offer its patients. In one messy county office, the already dreary atmosphere was not enhanced by the discovery of a large pot full of urine that had been left there. Ching-kuo discovered that the county magistrate was using a pile of household registration forms as a pillow; when asked why he had no blanket, the magistrate replied that it was locked up in case someone stole it.[4] Ching-kuo remained in Ganzhou throughout the war, and the area became well known for the social reforms that he was able to implement there. But even after a couple of years in the area, Ching-kuo was still struck by the desperate poverty of the locals, whether it was a sixty-six-year-old woman who complained that in the three years that she had been using it, the local soup kitchen never gave her enough rice, or the humble house in which he noted a "strong stench"; this was because the owner had to work by collecting dog excrement, which he stored ("in twelve jars and three toilets") before weighing it out and selling it.[5] National unification was a concept that had little meaning in places as remote as this.

To create the new China he wanted, Chiang had to defeat Japan, and to do that he needed a military alliance. Finally, he had been able to form one after Pearl Harbor. Yet the immediate consequence of that alliance was that Chiang's regime was now even more cut off from supplies from the outside world. And since supplying the Army was essential to maintaining China's resistance against the Japanese, this made it yet harder to keep both society and the economy stable.

Arthur Young also saw the effects of the new alliance, both as a chronicler of China's wartime finances and a participant in controlling them. He had worked for the US State Department as an economic adviser, and was then invited in 1929 to become financial adviser to Chiang's government. When the war broke out, he remained in China and became a trusted figure as the country's nightmare deepened. As early as September 11, 1937, Young had suggested "new taxes in kind . . . payable in foodstuffs needed by the military forces." The policy seemed less urgent in the early days of the war, when harvests were abundant. But the poor harvest of 1940 prompted the Executive Yuan (a major Cabinet-level body of the government) to adopt a resolution that the land tax should be collected in kind — that is, in grain — rather than cash, a policy supported by Laughlin Currie, Roosevelt's special representative in China. On July 1, 1941, collection in kind began, followed soon after by new rules allowing the compulsory purchase of both rice and wheat.[6] (In the northern provinces such as Henan, Shanxi, and Shaanxi, wheat was the staple grain; in the southern provinces, including Yunnan and Guangxi, it was rice. Sichuan supplied both.)[7]

The policy was not irrational. The armies were diseased, poorly motivated, and hungry, and, without significant grain supplies coming from British India, grain requisitioning was essential. Otherwise, the large Nationalist standing army could not have existed at all. General Stilwell complained that China was doing little fighting against Japan in China, but this complaint was misleading for several reasons. The Allied strategy was focused on the European and Pacific Theaters. To open up a full-scale campaign in China itself would have stretched resources well beyond even the capacities of the US and the British Empire. The only thing preventing Japan from advancing further into central China was the very existence of the Nationalist armies. A decision by the National Government not to defend its territory might well have led to a successful Japanese invasion in 1942 or 1943.

Nevertheless, the policy of grain requisitioning did real damage to an already vulnerable economy. When Wang Jingwei's government was established in Nanjing in March 1940, his Japanese sponsors issued a new currency and used terror tactics to force the population to accept it. The Nationalist-linked Bank of China became a particular target. On March 24, 1940, a bomb went off at the bank's branch in the French Concession of Shanghai, killing seventy people; there were numerous other incidents of arrests and intimidation of bank employees in the following months.[8] People who still had Nationalist *fabi* currency had to find ways to use it in the areas still controlled by the Nationalists, leading to a sudden influx of banknotes there.[9] To make matters worse, this happened just at the moment when food was becoming scarcer, as the supply routes to Free China were being cut off one by one. Inflation became rife.

The grain-tax policy did reduce inflation, because the army no longer had to purchase so much food on the open market. From 1942 onward the Chongqing government was able to collect some 60 million *shidan* (one *shidan* is around 50 kilograms) of grain per year. However, the burden now fell heavily on the most fertile provinces under the control of the National Government, particularly Sichuan. The policy also provided multiple opportunities for corruption and speculation.[10] Above all, the new system shifted an even greater responsibility for the war effort to the countryside. From the earliest days of the war, the rural areas had borne a heavy burden as targets for conscription, but farmers had not suffered major food shortages; good harvests and no land tax in kind meant that they had been able to supply themselves when necessary. Suddenly, the burden of feeding the armies fell directly on the peasants. In Henan, a traditionally fertile province on the frontline of control between the Nationalists and the Japanese, this would become terrifyingly clear in the summer of 1942.

In the first years of the war, harvests had been particularly good. But the rice harvest of southern China dropped from 753.3 million *shidan* in 1939 to 618.9 million in 1940, and in fact would never again reach the heights that it had attained in the first three years of the war. The wheat harvest in the north, which had hit 201.1 million *shidan* in 1940, dropped to 165.1 million in 1941.[11] Variable harvests had been known before. But the combination of a poor harvest with other wartime constraints was deadly.

Zhang Zonglu was one of those who saw the result. In 1942 Zhang was head of Henan's construction ministry. He was one of the new generation of foreign-educated technocratic Chinese on whom the Nationalist government had pinned its hopes for development during the Nanjing decade, and had graduated from the University of Missouri and Columbia University. His career advanced rapidly and he served a term as the president of Henan University. But his international education and experience in the Nationalist hierarchy had done little to prepare him for the trials that his province would face in wartime.

Zhang later reflected that a variety of factors had come together early in that year to produce terrible results. Much of the province had been invaded and occupied by the Japanese during the Battle of Southern Henan in early 1941.[12] In the spring of 1942 there had been no rain, and the harvest that season produced only some 10 to 20 percent of the normal yield. "After the harvest, people were very uneasy and panicked, so they hoped for the autumn harvest," recalled Zhang. "But there was no rain all summer, and the early autumn crop all died." Even places that could escape the drought because they had wells were not immune, because "locusts came and ate everything."[13]

The problem was not lack of food, but the lack of a system to bring the food where it was needed. There was grain in the neighboring provinces of Shaanxi and Hubei, but the authorities there refused to transport it to Henan. This was not pure selfishness. Now that the grain tax was being imposed in kind, huge amounts of grain were being levied or confiscated to feed the armies, and a provincial authority had no interest in selling its precious grain for increasingly worthless government currency. Chiang did announce a reduction of the grain quota for Henan, but in practice the head of the Henan grain administration collected even more than the quota demanded.[14] Venal officials were making a natural disaster into a man-made one as famine began to sweep across Henan.

In the summer of 1942 the Chongqing government sent out officials to see the situation in the countryside for themselves, and also to check that the grain tax was being collected. Zhang Zonglu was one of those sent out as an inspector. The head of Gongyang county, Zuo Zongnian, was in tears as he told Zhang that he could not manage to complete the grain collection. In Zheng county, county head Lu Yan told Zhang about a family named Li who gave their last grain to the tax collectors, then all killed themselves by jumping in the river. "Then he began to weep," Zhang added, "lost his voice, knelt down and knocked his head on the ground, and begged for exemption from the grain tax." The more Zhang saw, the worse it was:

> During our trip, starving people were digging up grass roots, taking leaves, and stripping bark from the trees. Going south from Zheng-zhou, an unceasing stream of refugees begging for food was so misery-inducing that you couldn't bear to look.[15]

These scenes took place very early in the famine, just after the main autumn harvest had failed. There was worse yet to come. As he journeyed on, Zhang saw desperation at every turn. Just outside Fangcheng, there was a market for people to sell themselves. Zhang saw a married couple whose only hope of survival was to sell off the wife. When they had to part, the wife called out, "My trousers are better than yours, you take mine." Hearing this, the husband cried out "I can't sell you — let's die together."

For many, the only other answer was flight:

> Wherever I went, there were refugees fleeing south, begging for food and those who couldn't move any more just dropped dead by the side of the road. You could exchange a child for a few steamed rolls. When I went to Luoyang, all around the station there were refugees, groan-ing and crying — hearing them was unbearable. If a train came, they would fight to get on it, hanging from the roof — they didn't care how dangerous it was. Those who couldn't get on the train . . . wept and sold their children — no matter what the price, they just handed them over. When the train went west, when it entered a tunnel, because the people on the roof were piled up, countless numbers of them were crushed against the roof of the tunnel, and fell down dead.[16]

The historian Liu Zhenyun's father was one of those who fled the fam-ine in 1942. Liu's uncle carried the children in baskets along the road, while Liu's father pushed a cart with all their possessions. But on arrival at Luoyang, as he exited a rice kitchen run by Catholic nuns, Liu's father was seized for the army. Liu's parents had no idea what had happened to him after that: "They thought I'd been kidnapped. The next time I saw them was several years later." His parents then joined the hundreds riding on train roofs. A cousin made it too, but Liu's little sister did not. She was never seen again.[17]

Zhang Zonglu mentioned that he had heard that villages beyond his tour of inspection had become so desperate that people had turned to cannibalism. Li Shu also encountered a man who had been imprisoned for eating and trafficking in human flesh.[18] These acts were rarely reported, so great was the taboo on this ultimate transgression, and accounts may have been exaggerated in some cases. Yet over time evidence did emerge of the lengths that people went to during the famine. Early in China's Cultural Revolution of the 1960s, during the interrogation of three locals in Duanzhang, a small village in Henan province, a man named Wang Jiu, described as short and with protruding eyes, confessed to an act that had taken place in the winter of 1942, "during the great famine disaster." An old refugee who had turned to beggary lived in a broken-down house at the east end of the village. Wang Jiu, with two friends, killed the old man, cooked his flesh, and ate it. They then started to lure travelers in and killed and ate them one by one. Then they committed an act that surpassed even their previous crimes. A woman aged over forty, who had a little girl with her aged seven or eight, was staying overnight at Wang's house. With no other travelers to be found, Wang and his friends strangled the woman and her daughter. Wang had to be questioned repeatedly before he would describe how the victims had been eaten. Eventually he confessed: the others had eviscerated and eaten the mother; Wang himself took the girl home and ate her.[19] The war was destroying the very fabric of humanity.

Over and over again incompetence and corruption were revealed as the prime causes of the famine. Li Shu exposed the case of an official who had been in charge of the granary in Shijiudian village in Runan county. The county had a grain storage system that was supposed to operate in times of famine, and the stores had not been touched since the outbreak of war in 1937. Now, in a time of need, the granary was opened, as it was supposed to have sufficient resources to support some 15,000 people. But local officials had never actually stored the grain, instead using it to make private deals.[20] Restaurants did still operate in cities within the famine zone, including in Luoyang and Zhengzhou, but only those with money could afford them.

The major newspaper *Da gongbao* had sent correspondents to cover the famine. It published a report in February 1943 which gave frank details of the disaster, and led to the paper being banned from publication for three days.[21] Fewer constraints operated on Theodore White, although his reports from China were toned down by order of Henry Luce, owner of *Time* magazine, who wanted to maintain the good image that Chiang Kai-shek enjoyed in the United States. However, the anger in White's report of March 22, 1943, blazed through even the editing at *Time*. All of the horrors noted by Chinese observers were seen by White too: "dogs eating human bodies by the roads, peasants seeking dead human flesh under the cover of darkness, endless deserted villages, beggars swarming at every city gate, babies abandoned to cry and die on every highway." Among the sights White saw were of a refugee whose leg had been cut off by a train; crowds of supplicants begging foreign missionaries for food; and a woman on trial for eating her baby, who gave as her defense the claim that the child had died first. White reported the conjunction of events that had caused the famine: the demand for grain to feed the armies and civilian officials, along with the delay in supplying food to the famine areas, exacerbated by the appalling state of the roads that made it even harder to provide the grain needed. White was not permitted to make direct criticisms of Chiang, but he made his view clear. "Most terrible of all is the knowledge that the famine might have been averted," he wrote. In the final words of his dispatch, he described the feast that local officials had offered him at the end of his two-week journey, with delicacies including chicken, beef, water chestnut, bean curd, and "three cakes with sugar frosting."[22]

White's disputes with Luce ultimately led him to resign from *Time*. In the book he published after the end of the war, *Thunder out of China*, White could make his indictment of Chiang clear. White described the horror that famine had wrought in one of his most memorable images: "A girl no more than seventeen, slim and pretty, lay upon the damp earth, her lips blue with death." White again recounted his journey through Henan, complete with callous officials and starving peasants, and concluded, "We knew that there was a fury, as cold and relentless as death itself, in the bosom of the peasants of Honan [Henan]."[23] At the time he published this, he knew what he could not have known for certain in 1943: that within a year the peasants would have their revenge on the state that had extorted so much from them, and whose negligence had led to the deaths of some 4 million people.

One official above all seemed to take little account of the unfolding catastrophe. People said at the time that there were four disasters, recalled Zhang Zonglu: "flood, drought, locusts, and Tang Enbo." General Tang Enbo, who had played such an important role at the Battle of Taierzhuang in April 1938, was still a close ally of Chiang Kai-shek. Concerned about a possible Japanese advance, at the height of the famine Tang compelled several hundred thousand peasants to work on building roads. The peasants were assured that their labor would be taken into account as part of their tax burden (a throwback to the *corvée* system of labor that had existed even under China's very earliest empires). Zhang declared that few believed those promises, accusing Tang of building roads for his own convenience rather than as military priorities. Tang's officials also became known for their illegal, often violent, means of recruiting soldiers.[24]

"I heard that the Henan famine was serious," Chiang wrote in his diary in April 1943, "and that the officials were ignorant of it." A week later he showed more alarm: "In the Henan famine area, people are starving, dogs and animals are eating corpses. It's unbearable to hear about this dreadful situation." He added that if the war dragged on more than a year, then China might not be able to sustain the situation much longer.[25] Yet Chiang took only limited, inadequate measures. His diary reveals how stretched he was by the spring of 1943. "I really have been feeling dizzy . . . The economy is weak, the military and political situation is depressing, and the worst time is now. During the six years of the War of Resistance, my strength has been exhausted and my mind has been dulled." A few days later he observed: "Our social reality is covered in scars. We are exhausted after six years of the War of Resistance."[26] The toxic mixture of dubious internal allies, a stretched economy, and the conflict with Stilwell was distracting Chiang from the unfolding disaster in Henan.

Chiang's sympathy for the victims of the famine, at least in the abstract, was not in doubt. However, the ramshackle system which held Nationalist China together was now under intolerable strain. In Chongqing and in Sichuan province the structures of the modern warfare state had been established, and continued to operate, albeit in the most stretched of circumstances. A combination of revenue (much of it from foreign donors), fear of international criticism, and a genuine sense among at least some of the elites (such as the American-trained technocrats Weng Wenhao and Jiang Tingfu) that the war should be the occasion for a rebirth of the Chinese Nationalist revolution, meant that developments in and around Chongqing remained relatively stable. But the further east one traveled from Chongqing, the harder it became to believe that the Nationalist state had real authority beyond words on paper or devalued banknotes. The delicate balance of power that underpinned the state prevented cooperation across boundaries. Refugee relief programs in Sichuan were inadequate, but at least they were under development. In Henan, an area where control had passed back and forth between the Nationalists and the Japanese, with the Communists always present in the rear, the relief programs lacked substance. In Zhejiang, where the lines of control were even more blurred, refugee relief existed more in name than in reality.[27]

Chiang's regime must be held responsible for the famine in Henan. Actions directly attributable to the government, such as the switch to grain tax in kind, the failure to send grain rather than paper money to relieve the situation, and corruption, place the blame squarely at the feet of decision makers in Chongqing. However, Chiang's was not the only government to make the same errors. Just a few months later, from July to November 1943, another famine of approximately equal severity (around 3 million deaths) took place some 640 kilometers to the west, in Bengal province in India. Following a cyclone off the coast on October 16, 1942, the supply of rice, which had already become restricted after the loss of Burma, started to shrink — in part because of rumors of shortages, which encouraged hoarding — leading to the widespread inability to obtain and purchase food. By the middle of 1943 the haunting images from Theodore White's descriptions of Henan were echoed throughout the Bengali countryside. Unlike Nationalist China, British India was not under intense active assault (there were serious air raids over Calcutta, but nothing like the destruction wreaked on Chongqing), and although it was a colonial state, it was governed under a system that was supposed to draw its inspiration from parliamentary democracy. Yet just as with Da gongbao, the province's newspapers, including the Calcutta Statesman, were censored to prevent their reporting the famine. As with Chiang Kai-shek's government, there were plenty of accounts of incompetent officials lacking either initiative or energy, and concerned more with patronage than governance. As in China, grain was taken away from Bengal even while people were starving, because it was needed to feed troops overseas. The British War Cabinet refused to divert wartime shipping to send supplies to the starving. Leading politicians, including Churchill and the secretary of state for India, Leo Amery, displayed attitudes toward the Indian population ranging from detachment to outright hostility, the latter a product in part of the Quit India movement (which Chiang had tried to persuade Gandhi and Nehru against), but also of the prime minister's long-standing dislike of Indians.[28] But unlike the administration of British India, Chiang did not have the resources of a global empire behind him, or a subcontinent under his control and out of the line of fire.

The Henan famine was an example, albeit one of the most horrific, of a wider phenomenon: the unraveling of the Nationalist state after 1941 following China's entry into the global war. In retrospect, it is surprising that there were not even more famines during the war years, although the massive impoverishment of the countryside was a clear consequence of the conflict.[29] Two decades after the war, Arthur Young reflected, with some understatement, that "it was unfortunate that the National Government failed to deal more effectively with agricultural problems." He observed that when the Communists had come to power after 1949, they had immediately instituted a land tax, and also that once the Nationalists had moved to Taiwan in 1949, they managed to institute a land-reform policy that did indeed draw revenue successfully from the agricultural sector. Young acknowledged that part of the reason for the failure in wartime arose from tensions between classes, since landlords strongly opposed the idea of their fields being taxed. The other reason was the government's "urgent problems of survival."[30]

The Henan famine showed that the consequences of the financial squeeze on the Nationalists were something like a Greek tragedy: individuals could have behaved differently, but overall the result was inescapable. (In contrast, the Chinese famine during the Great Leap Forward under Mao in 1958–1962 could have been ended by a top-level policy change, and eventually was.)[31] Corruption, carelessness, and callousness all played their part. But in the end there was no obviously better choice that Chiang could have made. Young acknowledged this, writing that the sight of speculation and hoarding caused "local people to have an adverse attitude to the National Government. Thus, it helped to soften up the country for the communists." Yet he maintained that "as a fiscal measure, it [the grain tax] was an indispensable means of covering war costs, and an item to the government's credit."³² The continuing resistance of the National Government may well have been dependent on the grain tax. But those who paid the price were the peasants Theodore White saw dying in the fields of Henan.

As the war situation worsened, so did the economy. The introduction of the grain tax in kind in 1942 had worsened the situation for the peasants, but had at least succeeded in lessening the effects of inflation on food prices for the army. However, inflation soon began to take hold again. Part of the cause was the Japanese-influenced dilution of the currency, and Arthur Young, whose sympathies were entirely with Nationalist China, fully acknowledged a variety of other reasons, including scarcity of goods, the refugee crisis, and the reduction in the labor force because of recruitment to the armies. Yet overall, his judgment was that "China's wartime inflation was caused chiefly by monetary excesses."³³ When Chiang's government found itself in difficulty, it turned to the printing press to produce more banknotes. Between mid-1941 and late 1944 prices rose by 10 percent or more per month.³⁴ In February 1940 a *shijin* (approximately half a kilogram) of rice in Chongqing had cost 2 yuan; by December (during the year when the Burma Road had been closed over the summer) it was 18.35, and by the start of 1942, just after Pearl Harbor, it stood close to 40, a twentyfold increase in just two years. In the last year of the war, prices would rise even faster.

During the war years China did not quite experience the kind of massive hyperinflation that marked the Weimar Republic in Germany or Hungary in the interwar period, something that Young noted was "to China's credit." (It was during the Civil War of 1946–1949 that prices would finally run out of control.) But the rise in prices had a tangible effect on the already miserable living standards of many groups whose support the government needed to survive, and made the difference between the haves and the have-nots starker. The very rich, who could convert their holdings into foreign currency and send it abroad, did so. (In Young's estimation, some $300 million left China in this way during the war.) Senior army officers could use their status to reward themselves financially, as their units' pay was delivered in a lump sum for them to distribute. But the inevitable result was that junior officers and privates found their allotted pay reduced, and that its purchasing power shrank month by month. The grain tax might mean that rice was provided for them, albeit in grudging quantities, but they still had to buy meat, vegetables, toiletries, and clothes. By June 1944 the monthly cost of living for ordinary soldiers in Chengdu, one of Sichuan's major cities, was over eleven times their pay.[35] This meant that they had to turn to various desperate measures to cope.

Chongqing's press was heavily censored. But a saying of the time had it that the lack of newsstands was compensated for by the number of teashops and the stories that circulated within them. One story making the rounds illustrated the effects of the rocketing price index on people's everyday lives:

> In a certain agency in Chongqing there was a colonel who up to then had worked in the city, and had a wife and three children. His life was very tough! One day the agency sent him to a place outside the city to carry out an inspection, which would require a month. His home only had one quilt, and he did not have the money to add another one. The weather was cold, and if he took the quilt with him, then his family would freeze. So the only thing to do was not to go. "The duty of a soldier is to follow orders": the senior officer knew that he had deliberately opposed his order, and because the senior officer did not believe that one man could be so poor that he could only have one quilt, he cashiered him.[36]

The details of the story might have owed as much to mythmaking as fact, but there was no doubt that inflation seriously damaged the prestige of the army as a profession. Arthur Young reported tales of officers deserting because their low incomes made them look foolish. Another teahouse story told of an officer who was caught by a superior hauling water to make cash on the side. His commander told him to carry on, but "take off your lieutenant colonel's badge first."[37] The Nationalist armies were suffering from the rot that sets in when an army is left on the defensive for too long, unsure of its purpose and forced into endless waiting. These soldiers could not know that within a few months China would face the greatest enemy assault since the brutal summer of 1938.

While the army fell victim to inflation, and scarcity of goods and starvation reigned in the countryside, life in the cities also became pinched and wearying. Graham Peck noted that those with money and black-market connections could obtain luxuries including "expensive imported clothes, canned goods [and] liquor," but that "many wandering beggars from the country had begun camping in the official auto-dugouts [shelters] on the edge of town."[38] Chinese observers also recorded the depressing reality of everyday life for those on fixed salaries, without entrepreneurial connections. One notice in a university canteen attracted hollow laughter: "Don't try to eat enough to be full." Another, more intentionally dry wit noted:

> There are a lot of mice in Sichuan. There are a lot of sparrows too. If somebody could invent a trap for mice and sparrows, then the traps would be on sale everywhere. But Sichuan people couldn't catch sparrows. They didn't find out whether the flavor of sparrow was good enough to eat.[39]

The civil servants who kept Chongqing's government running also found themselves on the wrong side of the growing gap between those privileged few who could use connections and the black market to get hold of quality goods, and the vast majority who could not. Between the start of the war and the end of 1943 the income of teachers had risen only a fifth as much as the cost of living, and that of government officials only a tenth.[40] The middle class had once put its hopes in the Nationalists to bring about a modernized, stable China that would enable them to fulfill their aspirations. Inflation destroyed the savings of many of these Chinese. Arthur Young told the story of a family who had been saving a large amount each year for college fees; when their son reached the age of eighteen, "they took all the funds and bought him a cake."[41]

Young also paid particular attention to the disastrous effect that inflation and corruption had had on China's educated intellectuals, who became "disillusioned and antigovernment" and whose complaints were then suppressed.[42] One dissatisfied official described his home life in a sarcastic poem, griping that "the holes in the clothes on your body increase, so it's lucky that Sichuan doesn't get very cold," and that "the whole family is crowded in one small half of a room, all constantly crying out like birds."[43] The financial crisis also had a disastrous effect on the Nationalists' hopes of using the war to build a new, more integrated nation. From refugee relief to Du Zhongyuan's far-off visions of a highway and airline network for China, all plans were now hostage to the reality of limited funds and soaring inflation. By 1943, even when adjusted for inflation, the government was spending just 25 percent of what it had been in 1937 on military and civilian expenses.[44]

Resentment toward those who could avoid the financial crisis grew. While few accused Chiang Kai-shek himself of being extravagant, stories alleging his wife's profligacy abounded. American reporters on the ground, increasingly disillusioned with an ally whom they perceived as corrupt and unenthusiastic, used gossip about Song Meiling's behavior as a symbol of a wider malaise within the government. In one story, boxes being sent across the Burma Hump for Madame Chiang turned out to be full of clothes and trinkets. (The rumor was embellished as it spread; before long, it was said that the boxes had been stuffed with "ermine brassieres.")[45] H. H. Kung, the husband of Meiling's sister Ailing, was widely suspected to be the most corrupt man in China.

Naturally, many observers, including Americans such as Peck and White, threw the Nationalists' failures into starker relief by comparing them with Communist successes. Yet all was far from well in Yan'an. The Nationalists' subsidy to the region had ended in 1939, and the blockade that replaced it made the economic situation much more difficult. The bad harvests in 1940 and 1941 that caused the disastrous famine in Henan also affected the ShaanGanNing area. Because the Nationalist currency *(fabi)* was no longer freely available there, the Communists had to issue their own currency for local use, saving the hard-to-obtain Nationalist *fabi* to import goods that could not be produced locally. The result was massive inflation, higher even than in the Nationalist areas. By 1944 prices that had increased 755 times since 1937 in Chongqing had increased 5,647 times in Yan'an. The economy of Mao's base area was in danger of collapse.[46]

Mao's response was to stress the importance of self-sufficiency. If goods could not be imported or exported successfully, and there was a lack of convertible currency, then the region would have to supply itself. In December 1942 Mao published an important essay on the economic solution for the besieged region. His proposals were notably pragmatic. "We shall simply be resigning ourselves to extinction," Mao wrote, "unless we develop both the private and public sectors of the economy." Up to that point, there had been few taxes on much of the population of the region.

Now heavier taxation was essential, Mao admitted, but in exchange the party must actively support the development of handicrafts, agriculture, and commerce so that the farmers can "gain more than they give."[47]

The taxes were certainly heavy, and included major taxes in kind (grain, straw, and wool) on the peasants, as well as some taxes in cash. But the party took great care to avoid the mistakes that had caused such misery in the Nationalist areas. The poorest fifth of the peasantry were still exempted from taxes, although this further increased the burden on the middle-level peasants. For those paying grain taxes the amount levied shot up from less than 1 percent of the total crop in 1938 to 13.6 percent of the total in 1941. (It decreased somewhat in the following years.)[48] Mao contrasted this policy with one that made "endless demands on the people," stressing military and government priorities to the detriment of the wider population: "That is a Kuomintang [Nationalist] mode of thinking which we must never adopt."[49]

At a time when the famine in Henan was reaching its height because of the massive demands of the land tax in kind, this was an important point indeed. Peasants forced to pay the Communists much higher levies felt bitter, but they escaped the harrowing deprivations experienced in Henan, where villagers gave their last grain to the tax collectors and were left to starve. The Communist policy was exacting, but it was progressive. It was also effective: during the war years, production of grain in Yan'an increased by almost 40 percent; more than fourteen times as many bolts of cotton were woven by 1943 as compared to 1938; and there was active development of salt, coal, and even basic oil and gas.[50] Not that the Communists were above supplementing their income in more dubious ways: there is good evidence that they were also producing opium in the base area, strictly for export to the Nationalist and Japanese zones.[51]

The Communist policies in Yan'an saved the region from collapse and also showed that there was an alternative to the increasingly destructive cycle that was corroding the relationship between the Nationalist government and its people. Yet Mao did have one major advantage in stabilizing the region. While there were some 40,000 troops stationed in the Shaan-GanNing region that he controlled, his commitment to guerrilla warfare meant that he was not required to raise the large standing armies that the Nationalists needed in order to participate fully in the wartime alliance. One of the favorite accusations of Chiang's Western allies was that the Nationalists were unwilling to recruit enough troops to make a proper contribution to the war, and were hoping that the Westerners would win it for them. (This was at the heart of Graham Peck's indictment of the regime.) Yet these same observers, many of whom admired the Communists, did not acknowledge the crippling burden (in an already stretched economy) of having hundreds of thousands of economically unproductive soldiers on call. Nationalist China was, in a different way, as besieged as Yan'an. Yet the lower burden of military expenses meant that Mao could deploy his tax revenues in ways not open to the Nationalists.

As long as life in the Nationalist zone continued to become harsher and more unequal, the Communists provided hope and an obvious point of comparison. One newspaper advertisement that appeared in Kunming, in the southern part of the Nationalist zone, on December 28, 1943, pierced the core of the quiet anguish of the increasingly destitute middle class:

> To those who want to adopt a child: a couple working in an educational institution do not have the capacity to bring up a child and want to give up their own (to be born next spring) without conditions. Stable families who are able to nurture and educate a child but have not been able to have children, and are willing to adopt, please write to . . .[52]

In any country this would have been an act of desperation. In China, where having children to carry on one's ancestral line was (and is) so central to the culture, this was a sign that the experience of war had distorted life almost beyond recognition. The only hope was that the war might end before China itself collapsed. In that atmosphere of fear, uncertainty, and social breakdown, all of China's regimes, whether under Chiang, Mao, or Wang, would resort to new and terrible techniques to control their people.

Chapter 15

STATES OF TERROR

THE FIRST DAY OF February 1942 marked a turning point in the history of China's Communist Party. On that day, at the opening of the Party School in Yan'an, Mao addressed over a thousand party cadres and laid down a stinging critique. "There is something in the minds of a number of our comrades," he declared, "which strikes one as not quite right, not quite proper." Mao attacked a variety of "ill winds": in one case, he compared the verbose and jargon-ridden political writings of some activists to the "eight-legged essay," the stiff and formal exercise which candidates traditionally had to compose in the imperial examinations. Mao also took aim at the educated elites who had joined the revolution in Yan'an. "We all know that there are many intellectuals who fancy themselves very learned and assume airs of erudition," chided Mao. "Many so-called intellectuals are, relatively speaking, most ignorant and the workers and peasants sometimes know more than they do." Mao also warned against "sectarianism," declaring that party members who wanted "independence" were actually seeking "fame and position and want to be in the limelight." He reminded members that they were, after all, part of a Communist movement, and that the "Party not only needs democracy but needs centralization even more."[1]

The speech marked the formal opening of the Rectification Movement. The campaign's name in Chinese, *zhengdun zuofeng,* implied a "corrective wind." It would turn out to be a harsh blast indeed. It marked a thorough ideological shakeout for the party, portrayed, in the language of the time, as a chance to "rectify the Party's work style." It included intense devotion to the study of Mao's works, and a thoroughgoing, almost religious commitment to the goals of the Chinese Communist Party. Those who declined to take part could expect pressure: psychological at first, but then something less abstract and more sinister.

One witness to Mao's ideological whirlwind was Peter Vladimirov, who had been sent as Soviet adviser to the CCP in May 1942. Bewildered, Vladimirov wrote that "not only party members but even soldiers and civilians are now required to cram [Mao's] speeches," adding that "all that, in the conditions of arduous war and economic difficulties . . . looks ridiculous." In his view, the campaign was evidently meant to "cover up something very serious, something that Mao . . . needs very badly."[2]

But Vladimirov had missed the point. The Rectification campaign was not a screen for something else. It was central to Mao's mission of a thorough reinvention of Chinese society. And it was only the "arduous war" that allowed Mao to fulfill his goals so successfully. The war experience was crucial to the formation of the modernized Communist state, underpinned by terror in service of the revolution that Mao sought to build.

It was not only the Communists who used the heightened circumstances of war to remodel their states. So too did the Nationalist regimes of Chiang Kai-shek in Chongqing and Wang Jingwei in Nanjing. As the economic climate worsened, Chiang's government began to lose the precarious pluralism that had marked its earliest wartime phase. From the very start of the war, there had been light and darkness in the Nationalist program. One side of it was open and modernizing, symbolized by the plans to institute welfare relief, build technologically advanced facilities such as arsenals, and political participation from nonparty members. The other was darker and more inward-looking, harking back to Chiang's connections to the criminal underworld and the intrigue that had brought him to ultimate power in China. Wang Jingwei's state, of course, experienced a crisis of legitimacy from the start, and was defined by its need to justify its pro-Japanese stance during the war.

As China's physical isolation deepened and its military and economic crisis worsened after Pearl Harbor, the Nationalists tried to shore up their bureaucratic and social infrastructure. In turn, the Communists and the Nanjing regime tried to create rival states in response to the weakening of the government in Chongqing. The essential element of that infrastructure in all three governments — intricately linked to their functioning, but rarely mentioned — was state terror. Each regime had its supreme leader: Chiang, Wang, Mao. But behind each of them was a shadowy figure, in charge of a security apparatus empowered to enforce the will of the state through psychological pressure, and use torture on those who refused to obey. China's wartime existential crisis provided a perfect excuse for the rival, yet parallel, states to use similar techniques, from blackmail to bombing, to achieve their ends, and mute the criticisms of their opponents. If each of them paid tribute to Sun Yat-sen in public, they also each paid court to the thinking and techniques of Stalin in private.

There were three masters of these techniques. For Chiang, it was Dai Li, the man nicknamed "China's Himmler." For Wang, it was Li Shiqun, a burly and deceptively genial former street hoodlum. And for Mao, it was Kang Sheng, trained by one of the world's greatest experts in the abuse of human bodies and minds: the head of the Soviet NKVD, Nikolai Yezhov. The three of them would profoundly shape China's wartime regimes and fuel the zero-sum struggle for power. Dai Li's involvement with American intelligence would help create a fog of war that would lead to disastrous consequences for Allied operations in China. Li Shiqun's machinations would force Zhou Fohai, Wang Jingwei's most loyal follower, into yet another fateful personal decision with profound implications for the Chinese who served Japan. And Kang Sheng would create the structures that went on to shape the even greater terror that would one day define the People's Republic of China (PRC). These men were implacable enemies. The irony was that they were engaged in three different facets of exactly the same project: using the war to create a strong Chinese state, with modernization and terror as its *yang* and *yin*.

Since Chiang's earliest days as a revolutionary, Dai Li had been at his side. A young man from Zhejiang province on the make in the 1920s, Dai Li had become involved in the underworld intrigues of Shanghai Green Gang boss "Big-Ears" Du Yuesheng, a connection that had led to a close friendship with his fellow Zhejiang native, Chiang Kai-shek. At the Huangpu Academy, while the Northern Expedition was being planned, Dai Li had begun to spy on his Communist colleagues, and Chiang, after his victory in 1928, placed Dai Li in charge of the regime's military intelligence. From the earliest days, Dai Li was simultaneously mysterious and notorious, careful to prevent pictures of himself from being publicly disseminated. When the war broke out, Dai Li became even more central to Chiang's regime. He had a reputation among Chinese and foreigners alike not just for brutality but for all-out sadism. One tale of Dai Li's role in the purge of the Communists in Shanghai in 1927 held that he heated up locomotive fire boxes at a railway siding, then threw in tied-up prisoners, whose screams as they burned to death were drowned out by the whistling of the engines. John Keswick, head of the British Special Operations Executive in China, simply declared that Dai Li "would never hesitate to bump anybody off. A real blower-upper."[3]

As the war ground on, Dai Li concentrated his power in an organization known blandly as the Military Investigation and Statistics Bureau (MSB, or *Juntong* for short). In fact, the MSB was a personalized instrument of enforcement by means both legal and otherwise. Mere mention of the MSB and its headquarters at Wanglongmen in south Chongqing was enough to terrify most ordinary citizens in wartime Chongqing. The phrase "I'm with Wanglongmen" could open the door to everything from free train rides to gratis brothel visits. For anyone foolish enough to cross an MSB agent, or to voice a political opinion that was judged subversive, the punishment could be a visit to a jail where the alleged dissident would be left to the mercy of gangs. Torture and kidnapping were an ever-present threat. The atmosphere of menace was heightened by the knowledge that the city was infested with MSB informers, mostly low-lifes who survived on bringing in a few denunciations each year and were unscrupulous about methods or accuracy. Many of the agents themselves had been recruited in Wuhan from the gangs there and brought upriver to Chongqing.[4]

Dai Li's particular obsession, amply fueled by his master Chiang Kai-shek, was the Communists. The United Front agreement had permitted the CCP a bureau in the temporary Nationalist capital, at Hongyancun (Red Crag) in Chongqing's western suburbs, as well as the right to publish the *Xinhua ribao*, the Communist newspaper. But at all times, the MSB kept a close eye on Communist activities, with a Nationalist Party office located within the same complex of buildings at Hongyancun. The Communists nonetheless brought off some major coups under Dai Li's nose in Chongqing. A young woman named Zhang Luping managed to infiltrate Dai Li's telecommunications headquarters, allowing her group access to the traffic from hundreds of MSB radio stations. Highly placed agents inside the government included General Yan Baohang, a top military adviser to Chiang Kai-shek, who was able to leak details of the upcoming invasion, Operation Barbarossa, to Moscow (only to have it dismissed by Stalin as "Oriental nonsense" just days before Germany invaded the USSR).[5]

In general, though, Communist activity in Chongqing was limited: the city was simply too dominated by the Nationalists to be safe for the opposition. Instead, party members in Sichuan concentrated in Chengdu, or else went further afield: Guilin in Guangxi province was a major Communist center during most of the war. Freest of all in the southwest was Kunming, the capital of Yunnan. The warlord Long Yun, who ruled the province, maintained an uneasy relationship with Chiang's regime, and allowed large numbers of political dissidents of all types to gather in the city. Lianda, the Southwest United University, which was made up of a combination of some of China's greatest universities in exile (including Peking, Nankai, and Tsinghua), was a hotbed of radical thinking.[6]

Dai Li assumed a new importance to China's American allies after Pearl Harbor because of his role at the top of China's major intelligence organization. The Americans were already cooperating more closely with Chinese intelligence than were the British, thanks in part to an incident in June 1940 when Dai Li, transiting through the Kai Tak airport in Hong Kong, had been arrested by the colony's authorities and hustled off to the public jail for a night before being released in a diplomatic flurry the next morning. The incident added to the already strongly anti-British tone of the Chiang regime.[7] The US-China alliance now allowed cooperation between Dai Li and US rear admiral Milton Miles (known informally as "Mary," a joking reference to the silent-movie star Mary Miles Minter), under the banner of the Sino-American Cooperation Organization (SACO). SACO's name leaves a very sour taste in today's China, where it is associated with anti-Communist activities and the jailing and torture of political dissidents. At the time, it was one of the most powerful agencies in China, overseeing intelligence activities there, including those of the US Office of Strategic Services (OSS).

The American presence in China was complicated by the rivalry of generals Stilwell and Chennault. Stilwell was now thoroughly hostile to Chiang, whereas Chennault admired him and was even close to the Generalissimo and his wife Song Meiling. The Americans differed on tactics too: Chennault continued to insist that airpower would be crucial to a swift victory in China, whereas Stilwell remained sure that the war would only be won by long, hard campaigns on the ground.[8]

Now Milton Miles's arrival added yet another complication to a relationship already fraught with misunderstandings. The American intelligence agencies promptly launched a turf war with each other. The China branch of the OSS, headed by "Wild Bill" Donovan, had come to a temporary agreement with Miles and Dai Li that it would coordinate intelligence activities with them, but the agreement began to strain at

the edges as Donovan moved toward establishing his own separate operation in China.[9] In late 1942 Dai Li became ever more suspicious that
the OSS would become a front for senior American and British officers
who would bypass him when gathering intelligence in China. Dai Li also
found it unacceptable to have to cooperate with (or worse yet, report to)
Stilwell, whose poisonous relationship with Chiang was clear. Instead, an
intelligence operation in which Miles (and the US Navy) would be paramount rather than Stilwell (and the Army) was attractive.

Tensions came to the surface at a banquet that Dai Li held for Donovan on December 2, 1943. Donovan told Dai Li that if he would not cooperate with the OSS, then the OSS would proceed without him. Dai Li
threatened to kill any OSS agents who operated outside his command;
Donovan then shouted that he would kill Chinese generals in return. The
temperature cooled the next day when Chiang Kai-shek told Donovan
that the Americans must "remember that this is a sovereign country . . .
please conduct yourselves accordingly."[10] But the fundamental quarrel
had not been resolved. In the midst of the war against Japan, there was
a covert civil war between SACO and OSS in China, and the activities
of Dai Li and the Nationalists contributed to the mess, and even took
advantage of it. A large part of the dysfunction lay in the inability of the
American intelligence agencies to coordinate with each other and decide
what their policies in China actually were. The fog of American intelligence confusion in China thickened.[11] British intelligence, in the form of
the SOE (Special Operations Executive) and the SIS (Secret Intelligence
Service), had some successes in China, including making contact with
the Communists in north China, but overall, it was equally unable to
create a coordinated and effective structure. Indeed, Ambassador Gauss
would declare at one point that there were at least fifteen Allied intelligence organizations working in China, and that they were "completely
uncoordinated to the delight of the Chinese."[12] Within a year, the lack of
intelligence coordination would have grave consequences for the path of
the war.[13]

Meanwhile, Dai Li was able to expand his own empire of terror within
the Nationalist state. On April 15, 1943, US secretary of the navy Frank
Knox and Chinese foreign minister T. V. Soong formally signed the
SACO agreement. The English version declared that the organization was
"for the purpose of attacking a common enemy along the Chinese coast,

in occupied territories in China, and in other areas held by the Japanese." The Chinese version specified the formation of special forces and other squads that would carry out special operations behind enemy lines.[14] Miles and Dai Li would both use their joint command of SACO (technically, Dai as head and Miles as deputy) to carve out their own power bases: in Miles's case, solidifying the predominance of US Navy intelligence (the Naval Group China) over the OSS, and in Dai Li's, emphasizing his own power and autonomy within the Nationalist regime. Miles was also able to impress Dai Li with the technological innovations that he brought to China, everything from deadly toxins to exploding pancake flour.[15]

SACO's primary purpose was supposed to be the training of guerrilla forces to harass the Japanese behind enemy lines in tandem with a planned invasion of the Chinese coast by US troops. Although fewer than 27,000 trainees were officially put through SACO's training camps, some estimates put the number of troops at 40,000 or even higher. The training sessions were a mixture of the sinister and the farcical. The American instructors openly admitted that they could not tell one Chinese from another. (At one point, one suggested that the Chinese recruits should have numbers painted on their backs to differentiate them.) This suited Dai Li's purposes well, since he preferred that SACO's recruits serve him alone. His officers were forbidden to fraternize with the Americans on their compound (who made this easier by living in a separate, and much more luxurious house), and even other Nationalist Party organs were not permitted into the SACO training camps. Instead, the recruits were made to subscribe to a personality cult of Chiang Kai-shek, the great leader whose "eyes and ears" the officers were meant to be.[16]

The forbidden zone that housed SACO's activities was the hilly area of Geleshan, on the outskirts of Chongqing. This zone, some nine by seven kilometers in area, became the private fiefdom of Dai Li. Nobody was permitted to enter without a transit pass; those who wandered in by chance were captured, often tortured and killed. Not a single woman was allowed to enter, in case she was a honeytrap spy, nor could SACO agents marry while in the service. In the valleys between the hills lay Dai Li's training camps for MSB agents, housing for the American personnel, and in the smallest valley, the "Bai Mansion," a concentration camp where political prisoners were tortured to death. Chiang's regime now had its enforcers, and their training was bankrolled with American cash. Dai Li's "eyes and ears" would have to defend the fraying Nationalist state where Chiang's rhetoric and the creaky social-welfare system could not.

Chiang's regime was not the only one to create a wartime terror state. From the earliest days of its collaboration with the Japanese in 1938, Wang Jingwei's government in Nanjing had started to develop its own security organization.[17] Zhou Fohai had started the process shortly after Wang's defection from Hanoi, and had recruited two Shanghai gangsters named Li Shiqun and Ding Mocun as the face of his operation. The burly Li and the frail Ding had, like Zhou, begun their political lives in the Communist Party, but had quickly defected and become part of Dai Li's MSB. They developed a taste for thuggish violence and political brutality before defecting once again, this time to Wang's service early in 1939. The Japanese lieutenant colonel Haruke Keiin shivered at Ding's "cold manner and snake-like eyes," but was more cheered by Li's "bright and cheerful manner."[18]

Ding's appearance was a better indication of how the two men operated. Throughout 1939, as Wang Jingwei sought to negotiate terms with the Japanese, Zhou Fohai worked with Ding and Li to create a terror apparatus that would enable them to control Shanghai's political life. With the assistance of Lieutenant Colonel Haruke, Ding and Li held court at a large house at 76 Jessfield Road, in the area of Shanghai that was under no one clear authority and had become known as the "Badlands" because of the crime and terror that flourished there.[19] "Number 76" became a name that filled Shanghai's citizens with fear, just as "Wanglongmen" did for their counterparts in Chongqing. Political hostages were kept in a basement at "Number 76": if Dai Li's undercover men in Shanghai killed a pro-Wang public figure, a pro-Nationalist figure would be shot in retaliation.[20]

Li and Ding's operation carried on as Wang's regime was officially inaugurated in March 1940. Over the next three years, it became clear that their murderous and criminal efforts were working in the short term, giving them control over the streets, but weakening the legitimacy of Wang's state overall. By 1943, Wang Jingwei himself looked just a shadow of the man who had made that flight into the unknown in 1938. And one of his closest associates had lost confidence in him. "I feel Wang Jingwei is dominated by his wife, surrounded by his followers, and gradually losing all his status as a leader," grumbled Zhou Fohai early in the year.[21] Zhou's comment reflected a real split in the Wang government's top ministers. Chen Bijun, Wang's wife, had a coterie of relatives around her known as the "palace faction." Zhou, in contrast, was closer to Li Shiqun and Ding Mocun, but even here there were tensions; by early 1942 Zhou and Li were also fighting for dominance.[22] The division had become more acute in December 1941, just as war was breaking out between Japan and the West, when the Wang government's security service swooped down on key MSB agents of the Chongqing government who had been secretly working at the highest levels of Wang's regime, including Yang Xinghua, Zhou's own brother-in-law. This was potentially a disaster for Zhou. He stood firm against Li Shiqun's demand that the agents should be executed, and instead had them restored to government as part of his own faction.

Zhou was disturbed by more than just the turf wars. Three years after he had helped Wang Jingwei to defect, Zhou was becoming convinced that he had made the wrong decision. Now that the Chongqing government had two mighty Western nations on its side, there was little need for a collaborationist government to act as a bridge between Chiang and Tokyo. Dai Li used his MSB network, with its underground agents in Shanghai and Nanjing, to pile on the pressure from afar. He arranged for a letter to be delivered to Zhou with a verse reading "be aware of your mother in adversity in Chongqing; she leans against the gate hoping for her son to return." Zhou's sleep became troubled, as he saw visions of his mother in his nightmares. His thoughts even became suicidal.[23] By late 1942 Zhou had decided that he would again change allegiance.

Just as he had done when defecting in 1938, Zhou concealed his intentions from those closest to him. He showed no signs of his change of heart in public, but sent a message to Dai Li offering his "voluntary surrender." Dai Li was delighted to have such a senior catch, and began to make full use of Zhou as a ringer inside Wang's government. Zhou arranged for a powerful radio transmitter to be hidden in his residence on Yuyuan Road in Shanghai. (Astonishingly, Zhou was able to install the transmitter with the approval of sympathetic Japanese officers who were keen to monitor news from Chongqing.) Yet, as had happened during his previous attempts to negotiate with Chongqing, Zhou had little success in opening any direct conversations with his former friend Chiang Kai-shek. In March 1943 Zhou sent Wu Kaixian — an old associate of his from the Nationalist Party's "CC Clique" and by then a senior figure

in the underground Nationalist Party in Shanghai — to Chongqing with
proposals extending a peace offer to Chiang. There was no response.[24]
Zhou's secret contacts would have to be confined to Dai Li's shadowy empire. Any whisper of collaboration attached to Chiang himself could have
destroyed American confidence in the Nationalist regime.

In September 1943 Dai Li sent a new demand: Zhou must help to assassinate Li Shiqun, who was proving too effective a head of security for
Wang's regime. Far too many MSB agents were being uncovered and assassinated in the Wang regime's territories.[25] Li was the main obstacle
blocking Zhou's path to power, and Zhou must have felt sanguine enough
about the plot to set aside a million Chinese dollars to bankroll it. But
in the end it was the Japanese who acted. Fearful that Li was beginning
to overreach himself, an officer of the Military Police (Kempeitai) invited him to a dinner at the Broadway Mansions, an upmarket hotel near
Shanghai's waterfront, on September 9, 1943. Shortly after he had dined,
Li began to sweat, and then became racked with agonizing pain. Within
a day he was dead. The Japanese had laced his fish dish with a deadly
toxin.[26] Now Zhou's great rival was off the scene. Any possibility of a disciplined, rational system of intelligence that could strengthen Wang's regime had begun to fall apart in a nest of deadly personal rivalries.

While the secret services of the Chongqing and Nanjing regimes battled
with each other in the south and center of China, the Communists continued to discipline their population in the north. They did this in the
face of an initial setback. The Hundred Regiments Campaign of late
1940 had surprised the Japanese, as the Communists had undertaken
few formal military campaigns. In response, in the spring of 1941, the
Japanese launched a policy known as the "Three Alls" *(sankô):* orders to
Japan's North China Area Army (NCAA) to "kill all, burn all, loot all."
Over the next three years the 250,000 troops in the Communist bases
in north China were subjected to a wrenching assault by 150,000 men
of the NCAA assisted by 100,000 Chinese collaborator troops. Rather
than launching raids and then leaving, the Japanese army would destroy
whole villages, ruin local crops, and confiscate grain stores; then they
would return repeatedly to make sure that no resistance could spring up
again. Communist sources admitted that the population of the base areas
shrank from some 44 million to 25 million people, and there were large

numbers of desertions from the Communist armies.[27] The top priority for the Communists in most of the north was not active resistance, but sheer survival.[28] The exception was Mao's base area of ShaanGanNing.

The Japanese fury in north China made the continuing resistance of Yan'an yet more important, as well as giving Mao a significant advantage. While his area was relatively safe from either Nationalist or Japanese attack, many of the other Communist bases were effectively behind Japanese lines. Throughout the war, there had been two poles of resistance to Japan. Marine Corps officer Evans Carlson — who had reported on China to the US government after conducting an extensive tour of the country in the late 1930s — wrote that Chiang and Mao were the "twin stars" of China: their capital cities, Chongqing and Yan'an, symbolized the hopes of millions that China would triumph. But the years of war had worn away at Chongqing, whereas the power of Yan'an had grown. Policy was central to the rise of Yan'an — but as in Nanjing and Chongqing, so was terror.

No longer just first among equals, Mao saw his status continue to rise as "Mao Zedong Thought" became synonymous with ideological correctness in the base area. The study of Mao's thought became the basis on which party membership was decided. Of twenty-two important texts that would-be party members had to master (in a list issued in April 1942), eighteen were by Mao.[29]

But thought reform was buttressed by the work of Mao's security chief, Kang Sheng. As part of his training in the party's underground days, Kang had been sent to Moscow in 1936. Stalin's purges were then at their height, with the worst phase named the *Yezhovshchina* after Genrik Yezhov, the NKVD chief who headed it (and would eventually be consumed by it in 1938). Under NKVD training, Kang had set up an Office for the Elimination of Counterrevolutionaries in Moscow, and used it to send out execution orders against CCP members in China who were classed as "renegades" or "counterrevolutionaries." Many of them were guilty of nothing more than knowledge of embarrassing episodes from Kang's past such as his one-time cooperation with the Nationalists.[30] Kang Sheng rivaled Dai Li in sadism. But unlike Dai Li, who was fiercely devoted to Chiang Kaishek, Kang Sheng was more pragmatic in his relationship with the CCP leadership. He saw Mao's star rise in the 1930s and hitched himself to it.

Kang's moment would come with Mao's declaration of the Rectification in Yan'an in 1942. The immediate target was clear. Mao wanted to demonstrate his dominance over Wang Ming and the other Communist leaders who had spent time in Moscow (known as the "Twenty-eight Bolsheviks"). But there was a wider target too: the individualism and lack of discipline exhibited by so many of the party's prominent intellectuals. The romantic era of joining the underground and running off to Yan'an in protest against China's ills was over. Instead, party membership meant building a machine to rule China. Among the prominent intellectuals who took issue with Mao's declaration was Ding Ling, the writer whose frank short story "The Diary of Miss Sophie" had caused a literary sensation in 1920s Shanghai. After a long and dangerous journey, Ding Ling had arrived in Yan'an in January 1937, and she became one of the region's best-known literary figures. Her fiction combined revolutionary conviction with skepticism about the party's commitment to the ideal of women's emancipation, an issue that always seemed to take a backseat to class struggle in CCP rhetoric. Her short story "When I Was in Xia Village," published in 1941, had a highly ambiguous character at its center, a young woman named "Purity" who becomes a prostitute behind Japanese enemy lines as a cover for espionage. When she returns to her home village, her sexual history leads the locals to freeze her out for her "immoral" behavior. The story's power lay in its nuance and refusal to conform to black-and-white moral categories.[31]

After Mao's speech inaugurating the Rectification Movement, Ding Ling responded with an editorial, published in March 1942, entitled "Thoughts on March 8," the date of International Women's Day. In her essay she pointed out that even in the revolutionary atmosphere of Yan'an, women were judged differently from men. "Women cannot transcend their times," she pleaded. "They are not ideal, they are not made of steel . . . I wish that men, especially those in positions of power . . . would see women's shortcomings in the context of social reality."[32] Another young writer and translator, Wang Shiwei, wrote an essay entitled "Wild Lily" which also criticized smug attitudes in Yan'an and accused senior cadres of having lost their true revolutionary spirit.[33] Mao did not take long to react. In April, Ding Ling was fired from her position as literary editor of the Yan'an party newspaper, *Liberation Daily*.[34] Other refugee intellectuals would also discover that their reception in Yan'an had grown chilly. On May 2, three months after the Rectification Movement had been formally launched, over a hundred writers and artists gathered on wooden benches in the Yangjialing district of Yan'an. They were awaiting Mao, who was due to open that day's event: the Yan'an Forum on Art and Literature. Ever since they had arrived at Yan'an, leftist thinkers and writers found themselves torn between their loyalty to their hoped-for revolution and the party they admired, and their convictions that as artists they must be true to their own visions.

Mao's opening comments were punctured by the sound of gunfire from Nationalist positions nearby, but he made himself perfectly clear nonetheless: artistic vision must be subordinated to the needs of the war — and the revolution. In Yan'an the audience for literature and art consisted of "workers, peasants, soldiers, and revolutionary cadres," and it was time for artists to "learn the language of the masses" rather than indulge in "insipid" and "nondescript" works that favored self-indulgence over political robustness.[35] The three conferences that followed this introduction over the next few weeks marked a powerful change in the relationship between the Communist Party and the intellectuals who supported it. Speaker after speaker stood up to harangue, repent, and denounce. Hu Qiaomu, who would later become the chief propagandist for the party in the 1970s, declared that the great Chinese writer Lu Xun, who had died in 1936, should have accepted the formal leadership of the party (he had been a fellow traveler but never joined): that he had not been was "not to his credit." One literary writer, He Qifang — declaring "I urgently need to be reformed" — made a powerful self-criticism, a plea for forgiveness by the party. At the end of the Forum, on May 23, Mao came back to stress that this had been the beginning, not the end of the changes. "Intellectuals who want to serve the masses," he said, "must go through a process in which they and the masses come to know each other well." Mao added an ominous coda: "This process may, and certainly will, involve much pain and friction."[36]

Mao's words marked a severe change of mood in Yan'an. Not only was it much harder for people to enter the region, but it also became very difficult to leave.[37] The city was cut off from the outside world not only by enemy blockade, but also by a new hardness of the party line. An earlier atmosphere of openness and collective enterprise gave way to a much more all-or-nothing environment. Ideas of pluralism and "new democracy" were replaced by a turn toward party control.

Kang Sheng was the mastermind behind the "pain and friction" that underlay the Rectification process. He used a classic Soviet technique of accusing loyal party members of being Nationalist spies. Once they had confessed under torture, their confessions could then set off an avalanche of accusations and arrests. As the war worsened in 1943, and the Communist area became more isolated, Kang stepped up the speed and ferocity of the purges. When colleagues asked whether there could really be as many secret Nationalist agents in Yan'an as Kang's roundups seemed to indicate, he replied, "We can talk about that after their arrest. When they're locked up, we can interrogate them."[38] In public, he portrayed the movement as being for the good of the party and its members. "Why does the Communist Party take so many pains to rescue you?" he asked in a speech of July 1943. "Simply because it wants you to be Chinese, and not be cheated into serving the enemy." He made it clear that "leniency has a limit." When it came to those who refused to admit their guilt, "we must use stern methods to stamp them out."[39]

Psychological pressure was key to the campaign. One technique was literally to confine the accused within a circle and to refuse to let him or her exit until there was a confession. One victim recalled the process with terror more than half a century later. "Do you believe in the Party?" she was asked. She replied that she did. "Then if . . . we say you're a problem," came the reply, "you're a problem." She remembered that at the time, she felt as if she had wanted to jump off a cliff.[40] The intellectual Shi Bofu was imprisoned after accusations of spying. His wife Gao Luoying "confessed" that she had intended to murder the prominent party intellectual Zhou Yang. She suffocated herself and her three children to death in her cave home with carbon monoxide gas. "She'd cut herself off from the Party, and therefore from the people," Zhou Yang responded on hearing the news. "You can see how great her hatred for the Communist Party was, because she killed herself and her children."[41]

But "rectification" was by no means purely psychological. The movement involved physical punishment and often flat-out torture. A document from one of the educational institutions in Yan'an, the Lu Xun Art Institute, belied the school's cultured-sounding name, revealing that techniques there had included tying up and beating the ideologically recalcitrant. The Art Institute even maintained its own labor camp, which some inmates suggested was as bad as the ones run by the Nationalists. Wang Shiwei was one of those who fell victim as the party organized protests against him. First, posters appeared denouncing him. Then he was expelled from the party as a "Trotskyist" and finally detained incommunicado. He was eventually executed in 1947. Ding Ling was also heavily criticized, and was forced to recant the views expressed in her "Thoughts on March 8." She was exiled to two years' work in the countryside.[42]

When the Cultural Revolution broke out in 1966, many outside observers found the phenomenon of the Red Guards, who persecuted and tortured their class enemies, inexplicable. But a quarter century earlier the Rectification Movement had provided a clear blueprint. It marked the moment when Mao's China came into being. It was not immediately obvious because the outside world was hardly focused on what was happening in the blockaded northwest region where the Communists were based. Yet the signs of the state that would become the People's Republic of China less than a decade later were there. What had been a radical opposition party was now unmistakably a party of government, with millions of people under its rule. The "Yan'an Way" policies that balanced land reform and progressive taxation would be part of the early years of the PRC. So, too, would the terror tactics. Enemies of the people would be publicly humiliated, beaten, or killed by their new masters.

The years following Pearl Harbor saw a distinct and growing division in the choices of the major political actors. In the early years of the war, both the Nationalists and Communists had stressed the pluralist and cooperative parts of their program. This was a sensible move for parties that had to gain as much leverage as possible both with their own people and with the outside world. Nor was the language of pluralism simply a smoke screen for the creation of a dictatorship. Particularly before 1941, both the Nationalists and the Communists had made an effort to appeal to those outside their own parties. But both Chiang and Mao ultimately envisaged a modernized China in which only one party would have a dominant role, a goal not compatible with true pluralism. Neither the Nationalists nor the Communists believed that a modern state was the same thing as a liberal state. In fact, the reverse was true. Drawing inspiration from Lenin, both parties recognized and accepted the use of terror as part of the mechanism of control. The disaster of war, and the growing social crisis within China, began to chip away at the technocratic and tolerant side of both regimes and solidify the power of those elements who favored violence and coercion.

At the same time, each of the three regimes operating in wartime China had its own interpretation of what terror meant and how it should be implemented. For Li Shiqun and Ding Mocun, control of the streets and personal aggrandizement were much more of a priority than any ideological commitment. Dai Li's motive was less venal. While he loved power and was clearly a sadist, he was driven by a loyalty to Chiang Kai-shek, whom he regarded as the keystone preventing China's collapse. Yet Dai's desire to create a corps of agents who would act as the regime's terrifying but incorruptible eyes and ears was crippled by the dishonesty and violence that characterized so many in the MSB. The public saw the agents not as ideological stalwarts, but as weak men given power to exercise for their own benefit. The Communist terror of Kang Sheng was different. The purpose of Rectification was not to line anyone's pockets. Rather, it envisioned — and achieved — one clear aim: it would bring together radicalized ideology, wartime isolation, and fear to create a new system of political power. The war against Japan was giving birth to Mao's China.

Chapter 16

CONFERENCE AT CAIRO

O N FEBRUARY 18, 1943, the most elite audience in Washington, DC, packed the chamber of the House of Representatives. The charismatic speaker was Song Meiling, Chiang Kai-shek's wife, only the second woman and the first private citizen ever to address a joint session of Congress. She had made the journey to raise China's profile in the US, worried that rumors of corruption and unwillingness to fight might turn American public opinion against financial and military assistance for China. Meiling's appearance created a storm of excitement. Wearing a simple black cheongsam and jade jewelry, she stood next to Vice President Henry Wallace as she charmed, then hectored, the assembled politicians. She told the story of an American pilot who had bailed out over China on his way back from one of the Doolittle Raids and had been greeted by the peasants who saw him "like a long lost brother." She said the pilot later told her that "he thought he had come home when he saw our people; and that was the first time he had ever been to China." Her peroration ended with the demand that "it is necessary for us not only to have ideas and to proclaim that we have them, it is necessary that we act to implement them."[1] It was a clear challenge to her audience: give priority to aid for China, and stop criticizing its policies.

The American policymakers were won over by Madame Chiang, and the fund-raising tour she made saw her mobbed by adoring crowds across the US. But beneath its image as an embattled, embryonic democracy fighting Asian fascism, Free China was more and more strained. Graham Peck, for one, interpreted Song Meiling's seeming triumph as a sign of impending collapse. "I do not think she really began to disintegrate until she went to America," he wrote. "Then, the wild adulation given her seems to have had the same effect that unqualified American support was to have upon the Kuomintang [Nationalists]."[2] Actually, Chiang's view of Meiling's American visit was more sober than Peck realized. "After my wife's visit to the White House," he mused, "I'm certain that it's American policy just to make use of us without any sincerity."[3] The year 1943 would be one of deepening mistrust between the Allies, as China, Britain, and the US circled each other with ever greater wariness. By the end of the year, Chiang would find that the roller coaster of US-China relations would fling him from triumph to disaster, in locations as far apart as the sands of Egypt and the jungles of Burma.

After the Burma debacle in the spring of 1942, relations between the American and Chinese political and military leaders continued to worsen, slowly but perceptibly. However, overall, the global war was turning, just as slowly but also noticeably, in the direction of the Allies. Far from China, the Battle of Stalingrad reached its climax in the first days of February 1943. Zhou Fohai, now playing secretly for both the Nanjing and Chongqing teams, recognized the change in fortunes for the Axis. "The German frontline is in trouble," he observed in late January. "If [the Allies] open a second frontline, Germany will definitely lose." Zhou was prescient: the battle was indeed the turning point, when the Soviet Union began to turn back the Nazi invasion. Yet Zhou still believed that there might be a place for a Japanese-dominated sphere in the postwar world. Rightly suspecting that the Americans and British did not really trust the USSR, he thought they might try and prop up Japanese power to contain the Soviets: "They'll still allow Germany a certain level of power so as to contain the USSR. Otherwise the whole of Europe and Asia will all be controlled by the Soviet Union . . . so the US, Britain, Germany, and Japan will all have to compromise to face the USSR."[4]

Zhou failed to understand the Allies' determination that there would never be a third opportunity for Germany to dominate Europe by military force, and that compromise with Japan had been made immeasurably more difficult by the increasing savagery of the war in the Pacific. But he was prescient in his prediction that containment of the Soviet Union would be a prime concern for the Western powers in a postwar world. In a secret meeting with Liu Baichuan, a representative of Chiang Kai-shek's government in Chongqing, Zhou suggested that if the US and Japan looked likely to reach a compromise agreement, then Chongqing should make the first move toward a peace with Japan, leaping in ahead of the Americans. The idea was clearly in the Wang government's interest in Nanjing, since this would keep it politically relevant in the event that peace broke out in the Pacific. However, Zhou knew the right button to push with Chiang Kai-shek. Chongqing remained paranoid that the US might not insist on unconditional victory against Japan, but arrange a brokered peace.[5] Because the defeat of the Nazis in Europe now seemed a real possibility, the Allies might well decide that the Pacific should be made a secondary priority, and China sidelined even further.

Despite Song Meiling's seeming triumph in Congress, Chiang's attitude toward his allies had become ever more suspicious. "China is the weakest of the four Allies," he wrote. "It's as if a weak person has met a kidnapper, a hooligan, and a bully." No matter whether they claimed to be your friend or your enemy, they might still "regard you as meat on the chopping board."[6]

Criticism was repeatedly heaped on China as a weak and corrupt dictatorship unworthy of alliance with the democracies. Yet the critics included the US, which maintained legal racial segregation across a third of its territory, and Britain, which held colonies across the world; and both countries had of course entered an alliance with the murderous regime of Stalin. The indictments of Nationalist China did of course reflect its often ugly domestic politics, but were also a product of the country's weak geostrategic position. Chiang looked on the United States and its president with a mixture of respect and anger. In February 1943 he fumed that Roosevelt and Stalin had "destroyed our war plan of the last three years" after the two leaders made agreements following the Casablanca Conference of 1943, and drawing on the improvement in the USSR's position at Stalingrad, that tied the Soviets into the defeat of Germany as their top priority. In Chiang's view this commitment reduced the (already very low) possibility that Japan might attack the Soviets, "so the victim is China." The sense that the "Big Three" would continue to treat China as a minor player reinforced Chiang's view that he would have to fight to win his country its rightful prominence. "Previously the US treated China as a decorative object," Chiang brooded, speculating that even financial assistance to China might have been just an indirect way to soften up American public opinion toward increasing Lend-Lease assistance to Britain. Now once again, he declared, "China is clearly being made a sacrificial item." He resented the fact that the United States, intent on controlling the Pacific after the war, did not want China to have an independent air force.[7] Yet Chiang also realized that power in the Pacific was shifting. In one conversation he observed that "we're not afraid that America *will* be the dominant power in East Asia; we're afraid that it *won't* be."[8] If there was to be a hegemonic power, he thought, then better the US than Japan, the USSR, or Britain.

In contrast, if Chiang respected the British, it was mostly for what he saw as their cunning, stubbornness, and arrogance. He believed that their presence in China had little purpose beyond maintaining their own position. Churchill was a particular bugbear. In March 1943 Chiang seethed that Churchill had talked about the "Big Three" countries that would shape the postwar order: "he excludes China completely." A few months later Chiang followed this up with the observation that "all ambassadors are spies by nature, but the British more than most."[9]

Britain's political leadership took an equally dim view of China. "Assistance to China should only be a primary consideration if it is in the interests of strategy," one Foreign Office document declared in July 1943, adding that it was better to let the Chongqing government fall than to disrupt the major effort against Japan. Indeed, Churchill found the idea of China as a great power farcical, and made no secret of the fact that he considered the American aspiration to raise China's global status utterly misconceived. Churchill wrote to Anthony Eden, the foreign secretary, that it was "affectation" on the part of the US "to pretend that China is a power in any way comparable to the other three."[10] Nor did the British trust American intentions: Churchill made it clear that he had no time for Roosevelt's aspiration that Britain might return Hong Kong to China as a goodwill gesture.[11]

From the Opium Wars onward, Britain had been the preeminent Western power in China, and it was Japan, not the US, that seemed to threaten its position in the 1930s. Yet despite Churchill's unwillingness to treat China as a key power in the postwar global order, there was a wider understanding in British circles that China would now have to be treated as an actor in its own right.[12] Britain communicated this with one particularly substantial action. Since 1842, Western imperialism in China had been visible in the most obvious form in the center of China's greatest commercial city, Shanghai. The International Settlement, along with the French Concession, were islands of foreign rule, although the Settlement had fallen to the Japanese as soon as the Pacific War had broken out. Now, the Americans and British offered to end the hated system of extraterritoriality, and to return the International Settlement to Chinese rule. If China won the war, Shanghai would be a city united, for the first time in a century, under Chinese national sovereignty.[13] Under considerable American pressure, the British agreed to new treaties, signed on January 11, 1943, that marked the end of imperialism in China and the replacement of "unequal treaties" with equal ones for the first time. (Not to be outdone, Wang Jingwei had also obtained "sovereignty" over the concessions in a treaty signed two days earlier, on January 9, as part of his price for an official declaration of war by the Nanjing regime against the Allies.[14] But this was a hollow gesture, replacing Western imperialism with a Japanese variant.)

Chiang Kai-shek found much to criticize in his British and American allies, but he reserved his bitterest scorn for his chief of staff. Typical was one diary entry in which Chiang declared "I saw Stilwell today; he disgusts me. I despise him: I've never met anyone like that!"[15] In February 1943 Chiang recorded his version of a conversation between the two of them. Chiang requested 10,000 tons a month of supplies across the Hump, and 500 aircraft; without this, China could not be "responsible" for prosecuting the war further. "Are you saying that if we can't do that," Stilwell replied, "then you can't fight Japan?" Chiang found Stilwell's response "evil and disrespectful." He noted:

> I swallowed it and didn't attack him — but I just replied that China had been fighting for six years; even before the Pacific War had broken out, when the US and Britain were not helping, China had fought alone.[16]

"Vinegar Joe," of course, was equally forthright in his private assessment of Chiang. "We are maneuvered into the position of having to support this rotten regime and glorify its figurehead, the all-wise great patriot and soldier — Peanut. My God."[17]

Chiang's suspicions about Stilwell were nourished when Burma returned to the Allied agenda in spring 1943. At least Stilwell, unlike most of the senior Allied commanders, did believe in the centrality of China as a battleground in Asia, a sentiment shared by his opponents Chennault and Chiang. However, Stilwell was still tied up in his continuing feud with Chennault about the merits of airpower versus land forces in the China Theater. In November 1942 Wendell Willkie, the Republican who ran unsuccessfully against Roosevelt for the presidency in 1940, had been sent to Chongqing on a goodwill mission. (His visit would many years later give rise to a salacious rumor that he had a one-night stand with Song Meiling.) Willkie asked to meet Chennault, who wrote down for the visitor what he claimed to need for victory in China and then the Pacific: 105 fighters and 42 bombers, which would enable him to win the war from the air. The letter was quickly dismissed by Marshall back in

Washington, but he also suggested to Stilwell that he should try and mend his relationship with his American rival.[18]

In May 1943 Chennault and Stilwell were called to Washington to report on what needed to be done in China. Stilwell remained adamant that Chinese troops had to be better trained so that they could launch the assault against the Japanese in north Burma to open up a supply road there. Chennault disagreed. He wrote a memo to Marshall which argued that "the internal situation in China is already critical." He noted increased recruitment to Wang Jingwei's collaborationist armies, and "that progressive inflation, progressive starvation, and increasing disease have at last begun to tell visibly on the Chinese people." He doubted that the time remained to prepare for a land war, and suggested airpower instead. "The risks to be run by launching a China air offensive are relatively slight," he suggested, "compared to the risks that will be run by continued inaction."[19]

Stilwell was acid about his rival's suggestion. "Nobody was interested in the humdrum work of building a ground force but me. Chennault promised to drive the Japs right out of China in six months, so why not give him the stuff to do it? It was the shortcut to victory."[20] The weight of the conference turned against Stilwell's idea of a campaign in north Burma, which they proposed should begin after the monsoon season of autumn 1943. Instead, Chinese forces in Yunnan were to be built up so that they could be used to protect bases for heavy bombers within China. Roosevelt also agreed that there should be a major increase in the tonnage to be flown over the Hump. "Roosevelt wouldn't let me speak my piece," complained Stilwell, who thought the concentration on airpower ill-advised. "I interrupted twice, but Churchill kept pulling away from the subject, and it was impossible."[21]

When it was put to him, Chiang agreed to a Burma campaign, but only if there were to be substantial air, naval, and infantry support from the US.[22] Chiang's wariness about the commitment of the Western Allies to a new venture in Burma was well founded, for the plan did not materialize. By mid-1943 the American and British commanders were concentrating on Operation Overlord, the D-Day landing in Europe that would eventually lead to the defeat of Nazi Germany. China, once again, sat very low on the list of priorities. Then, at the Quadrant Conference held in Quebec in August, a new Southeast Asia Command (SEAC) was established under Lord Louis Mountbatten that separated the region of

Burma from China and India. Some of the pressure came from Churchill, who was concerned that American public opinion might feel that Britain was not playing a sufficiently important role in the war in Asia (leading to the quip in American circles that SEAC stood for "Save England's Asian Colonies").[23] Burma and Thailand were placed under SEAC, separating them from Chiang's sphere of influence, and placing the relief of China even further down the list of important issues. Stilwell was appointed as deputy commander of SEAC under Mountbatten, but retained his command of the China-Burma-India Theater as chief of staff to Chiang Kai-shek, a situation that was complex and not easily workable, not least since "Vinegar Joe" was almost as allergic to the British as he was to Chiang.[24]

During the summer of 1943 Stilwell fantasized about taking command of all Chinese troops, including the Communists, with Chiang and the Nationalist military leadership left as ciphers only. His relationship with Chiang became even more sulphurous. Stilwell gloated that Chiang "had thought that by making me his joint chief of staff I would accept without question any order he chose to give me. He is that dumb."[25] By this stage Stilwell was incapable of taking any of Chiang's suggestions or priorities seriously. He now regarded himself as the only one with any understanding of what the situation demanded, and thought not only Chiang but also the British and most other Americans were misguided.

Stilwell's self-aggrandizement was causing raised eyebrows in Washington. Chiang's brother-in-law T. V. Soong had been appointed foreign minister immediately after Pearl Harbor. In the American capital, Soong used his influence with Harry Hopkins, Roosevelt's close friend and political fixer, to complain about Stilwell and press for the American to be relieved of his command. Hopkins, who regarded Stilwell as a malign influence in China, was sympathetic, and encouraged Soong to propose a change of military leadership. On September 15 Soong suggested to the White House that Mountbatten's appointment as head of SEAC meant that there was no longer any need for Stilwell to remain in China. Instead, a Chinese general should command all troops in China, as well as take over air command of the China-Burma-India Theater.[26] The argument fell on receptive ears in the White House. By mid-September, Roosevelt was ready to call back the troublesome American chief of staff. T. V. Soong returned to Chongqing and on October 15 Chiang made an official request for Stilwell's recall.

Then Chiang hesitated. Although one brother-in-law was agitating for

Stilwell's removal, other family members were equally vociferous in advising that Stilwell should stay. "May" and "Sis" (Song Meiling and Song Ailing, wife of H. H. Kung) unexpectedly took up the chief of staff's cause: Stilwell's assessment was that these "intelligent dames" had worked out "the gravity of the situation," although he wrongly thought they were defending him at T. V. Soong's urging.[27] Chiang's wife and sister-in-law recognized that if Stilwell were removed, it would solve the continuing lack of engagement between him and Chiang, but it would also make public a fundamental divide between the Americans and the Chinese at a time when Japanese forces still threatened to conquer Free China. Song Meiling in particular strongly opposed the recall, and H. H. Kung and Song Ailing may have feared that Stilwell's recall would boost T. V. Soong's power at the expense of his in-laws. Washington regarded H. H. Kung, not without reason, as venal and lacking in vision, unlike the better-liked T. V. Soong, who was perceived as relatively liberal, and potentially a contender for high power in his own right. Chiang did not want to give Soong a political boost over other members of the family. He may also have feared that the loss of Stilwell might make it easier for SEAC (commanded by a Briton, Mountbatten) to pressure China into using troops for British priorities rather than Chinese ones.[28]

On October 16 Mountbatten arrived in Chongqing and met Stilwell, who recorded in gloomy capital letters that "THE G-MO SAYS I MUST BE RELIEVED."[29] But Mountbatten pressed Chiang to retain Stilwell. Pressured on all sides, Chiang met Stilwell on October 17. The two of them talked intensely. "Stilwell came and I advised him on his mistaken views," wrote Chiang. "He admitted it and agreed to obey me from now on."[30] Stilwell did not see it quite this way. He had been called over late at night to see Chiang, who told him that he should "understand the duties of the commander in chief and the chief of staff" and "avoid any superiority complex." Stilwell considered this to be "balderdash," but "listened politely." Overall, he felt "as free as air — no regrets and no self-blame."[31] The two men had postponed confrontation rather than solving the fundamental problem. A few days later Chiang confirmed his change of mind and asked for Stilwell to stay. T. V. Soong was outraged that his efforts in Washington had been overruled, humiliating him in the process, but Chiang was in no mood to listen. He brooded in his diary, going back over past slights: he was sure Soong and Borodin (the Comintern agent who had been sent by the Soviets to train the Nationalists and Communists at the Whampoa Academy) had schemed in the 1920s to bring him down, and Soong had further undermined him by refusing to bankroll him during the Manchurian crisis of 1931. Now Soong was frozen out of power.[32]

During the same week in October 1943, the Chongqing government hedged its bets against its uncertain Allies and kept its line of communication with Wang Jingwei's regime in Nanjing open, sending another representative, Xu Caicheng, to visit their insider, Zhou Fohai. Xu told Zhou that although China had signed the pledge common to all the Allied powers not to make an independent peace with Japan, there might be a get-out clause that enabled them to have such a discussion if it was for the purpose of protecting Chinese territorial sovereignty. Zhou had his doubts. "Thinking on behalf of China is like playing chess," he reflected. "You don't make an irreversible move, but keep some room to maneuver. However, I don't know if Chongqing have thought deeply about this, or whether the Americans and British really have agreed to such a condition."[33] He was right to be doubtful. The Western Allies had no intention of giving China that sort of autonomy to negotiate with Japan.

By November 1943, the Allies and Axis stood at different positions in that chess game. In Europe, the defeat of Hitler's armies at Stalingrad had added to the momentum in the Pacific caused by the victory at Midway in June 1942 and the slow recapture of the Solomon Islands over the following year. In July, Mussolini had been toppled in Italy. The advantage now seemed to be with the Allies, and the Japanese had to demonstrate that Chiang would do better to negotiate with them than to remain tied to the Americans and British. The conference at the Imperial General Headquarters in Tokyo in September 1943 took the view that they could expect no further assistance from Germany. Japan's war economy was under great pressure, with iron ore, steel, coal, and oil all in short supply, and the country had to adjust its strategy to prioritize defense of the home islands and the conquered areas of Southeast Asia rich in oil. Japan would defend Burma and much of its Southeast Asian empire, but would try to make sure that the USSR remained neutral. The conference also stressed the need to avoid escalating the conflict in China.[34]

Now both alliances gathered for summits that would showcase very different visions of Asia after the war. Tokyo declared openly that its aim was the "liberation" of its Asian allies from the Western yoke.[35] As a gesture toward this goal, on November 30, Japan signed a treaty with the

Wang regime that was more equal, at least in phrasing, than the existing humiliating settlement. The next day, Wang Jingwei and Zhou Fohai flew to Tokyo for a conference to celebrate the Greater East Asia Co-Prosperity Sphere, the grandiloquent term that the Japanese used for their empire.

The wartime capital they landed in was an austere place indeed, not yet within range of major American bombing efforts, but slowly becoming hungrier as supplies of rice dwindled. The conference had been called in defiance of the worsening reality to demonstrate the amity between Japan and its allies, and to give some substance to the idea that Japan was launching a new political formation in the region that would supersede the old Western imperialism that had dominated for so long. On November 5, 1943, Premier Tôjô of Japan welcomed a group of leaders to Tokyo who had been gathered from all across Asia. Ba Maw, the Burmese independence leader, was "lively and outgoing, like a student leader," in Zhou Fohai's opinion, whereas José P. Laurel, who led the government of the Philippines now that its American rulers had been drummed out, was "very experienced." But the most charismatic of the delegates was Subhas Chandra Bose, the former Indian Congress president who had defected to Germany in 1941, and subsequently come to Japan as leader of the newly formed Indian National Army, which sought an *Azad Hind* (Free India). "A purposeful revolutionary," noted Zhou enthusiastically, responding to Bose's speech. Bose had praised Japan's role: "This is not the first time that the world has turned to the East for light and guidance . . . in the creation of a new, free and prosperous East, the Government and people of Nippon should play a leading role." Bose also recalled the inspirational example of the 1904–1905 Russo-Japanese War, the first occasion on which an Asian power had defeated a European one. Completing the lineup was Wang Jingwei, there as president of the Reorganized Government of China. Compared to the dynamic Bose and Ba Maw, Wang seemed almost broken. Ba Maw said that he was "strikingly handsome" and "spoke little, but carefully chose his words . . . You soon sensed the Chinese tragedy in his restrained demeanour and trailing words."[36]

Few concrete promises were made at the conference. Yet for the Southeast Asian leaders, and also for Bose, however weak or self-serving the Japanese advocacy of their independence, the conference marked a clear moment when their aspirations to independence were, at last, officially acknowledged, free from British or (in the case of the Philippines) American colonial rule. For Wang, the conference had no such benefit. China's already compromised sovereignty had been weakened, not strengthened, by the outbreak of war, and it was hard to believe that the new alliance with Japan, even if nominally more equal, marked a genuine partnership. Yet however thin a reed the Greater East Asia Co-Prosperity Conference was, it was clearly a challenge to the Allied vision of the postwar era.

Contrary to their name, the Allies were startlingly disunited, and this was a problem for Chiang Kai-shek in particular. The weakness of China's position derived from the peculiar contortions of the partnership itself. Crucially, the USSR remained neutral against Japan. This meant that Stalin could not be seen to appear in public at any conference that included Chiang, since it would imply endorsement of China's war aims against Japan. Yet Stalin clearly had a significant interest in the shaping of a postwar Asia. As a result, almost all the major conferences after 1941 excluded Chiang. This situation was worsened by Churchill's clear contempt for the Chinese in general.

For Chiang, these pressures increased the importance of the Cairo Conference ("Sextant") held between November 22 and 26, 1943, the only major conference of the war that attempted to make a comprehensive settlement of the Sino-Japanese conflict. The meeting in Cairo came at a time of continued tension between the United States and Britain. The two sides had gone back and forth during the winter and spring of 1943 on the question of the best timing for Overlord, the invasion of Western Europe. The Americans insisted on defining strategic priorities, whereas the British wanted to keep their options open. The decision on Overlord would inevitably have a sequential effect on the other theaters of war, including the Mediterranean, the Pacific, and ultimately China. Significant time would also be taken at Cairo to decide on strategy for the Pacific War.[37] Yet the Cairo Conference was hampered by the fact that neither the US nor Britain had a clear idea of exactly how the war in the Pacific would be brought to a conclusion. Even while the role of the Pacific was upgraded by both Washington and London during 1943, the precise significance of China was not defined.[38]

Patrick J. Hurley, who had served as secretary of war under Herbert Hoover, was now a personal international emissary for Roosevelt. On November 12 he spoke to Chiang in Chongqing. In Chiang's eyes, Hurley had come to explain Roosevelt's intentions toward Churchill and Stalin so that there would be no misunderstandings about the upcoming conference. Chiang's interpretation was that the American president was "re-

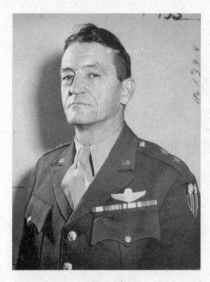

General Claire Lee Chennault.
His "Flying Tigers" were an important
morale-booster for Chinese Nationalist
resistance to Japan.

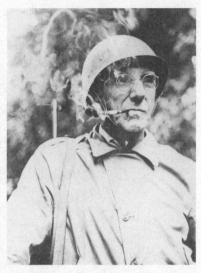

General Joseph W. Stilwell ("Vinegar Joe"),
Chiang's chief of staff. The toxic relationship
between the two would affect US–China
relations for years to come.

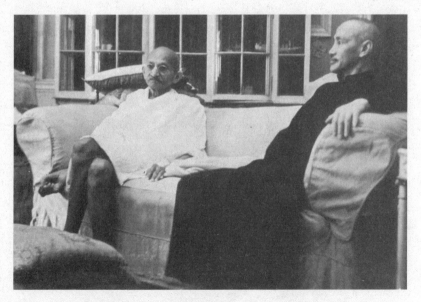

Chiang Kai-shek and Mahatma Gandhi meet near Calcutta, 1942. This was
the first occasion that a non-European national leader had visited a major Indian
anti-imperialist figure.

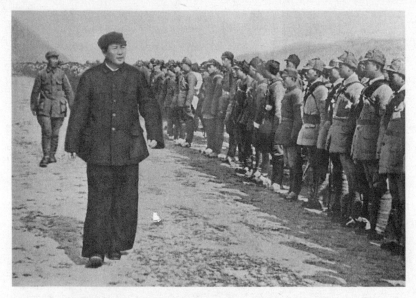

Mao inspects Eighth Route Army troops stationed in Yan'an. Communist troops would carry out important guerrilla attacks throughout the war, though they engaged in few set-piece battles.

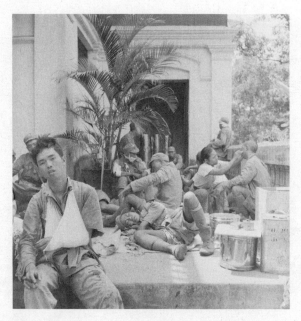

Wounded Chinese troops, Burma, 1942. The retreat from Burma was one of the greatest humiliations for the Allies in the early part of the joint war against Japan.

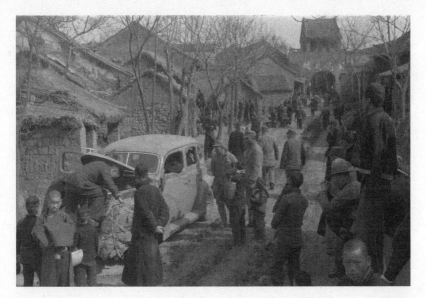

Refugees fleeing famine-stricken Henan province, c. 1943. A combination of natural disaster, incompetence, and factors outside Chinese control led to a devastating famine that eroded Nationalist legitimacy.

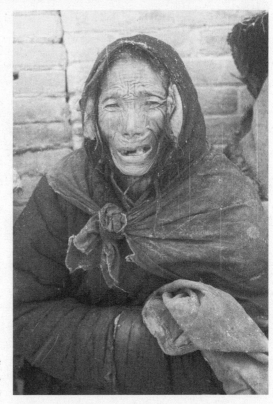

Female famine victim, Henan, c. 1943.

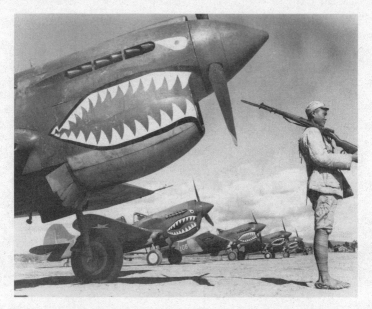

A Chinese soldier guards a squadron of Curtiss P-40 Warhawk fighter planes, 1943.

Colonel David Barrett (*left*) and diplomat John Service outside their Yan'an lodgings. The two were part of the American "Dixie Mission" into Communist territory.

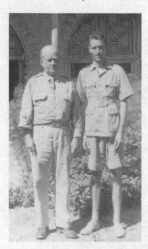

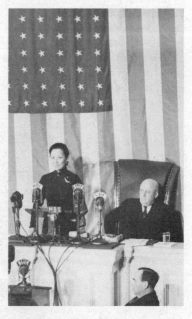

Song Meiling (Madame Chiang) on the rostrum of the US House of Representatives, Washington, January 18, 1943. US aid was critical to China's war effort, but Chiang's reputation faded during the war, despite Song Meiling's attempts to restore it.

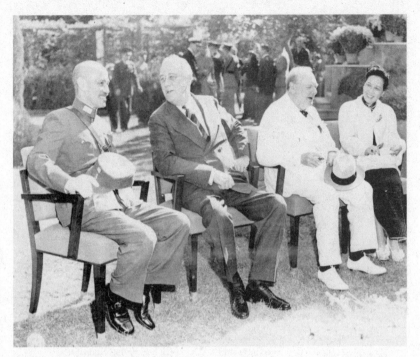

(*left to right*) Chiang Kai-shek, Franklin D. Roosevelt, Winston Churchill, and Song Meiling at the Cairo Conference, 1943. This was the first (and only) conference in which China participated as an equal Allied power.

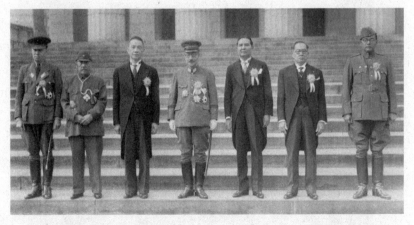

Participants in the Greater East Asia Conference, Tokyo, November 1943 (*left to right*): Ba Maw, Zhang Jinghui, Wang Jingwei, Tôjô Hideki, Wan Waithayakon, José P. Laurel, Subhas Chandra Bose. The conference aimed to project an idea of a Japanese-dominated Asia in contrast to the Allied vision for the region.

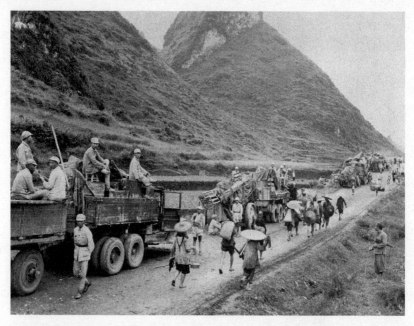

Refugees on foot, November 1944. The Japanese Operation Ichigô tore through central China in 1944 and devastated huge areas that had been held by the Nationalists.

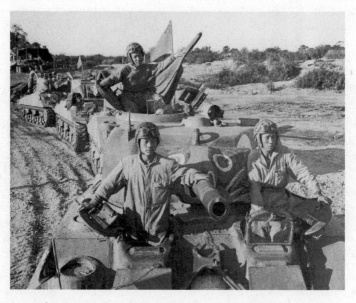

Chinese-manned American tanks enter Burma, January 1945. The Allies had insisted on Chinese participation in the recapture of the country they had lost in 1942.

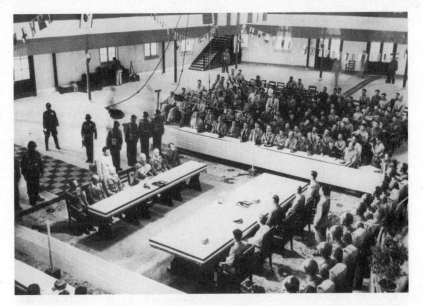

General Okamura Yasuji, head of the Imperial Japanese Army in China, during the surrender ceremony, with the Chinese delegation under General He Yingqin, Nanjing, September 9, 1945.

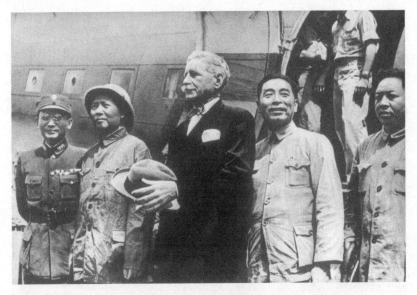

(*left to right*) Zhang Zhizhong, Mao Zedong, Patrick Hurley, Zhou Enlai, and Wang Ruofei, en route to Chongqing for negotiations with Chiang Kai-shek after the Japanese surrender, 1945.

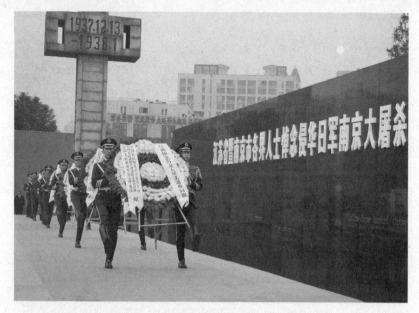

Chinese paramilitary policemen carrying wreaths of flowers march toward the Nanjing Massacre Memorial Hall in Nanjing on December 13, 2012, to mark the seventy-fifth anniversary of the atrocity.

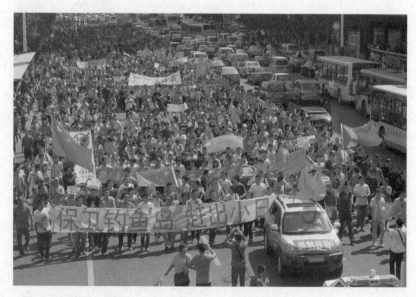

Anti-Japanese demonstration during the Diaoyu islands dispute, Shenzhen, September 16, 2012.

lying on me to dispute with Churchill over East Asian matters," so that Roosevelt could then intervene as mediator. Chiang declared his intention to press home several points at Cairo, including the establishment of a formal United Nations structure to give China equal status in the emergent international order, and the need for naval and air support in any future attempt to recapture Burma.[39] (At this point "United Nations" referred to the Allies; the term was not used in the sense of the United Nations Organization until after 1945.) Chiang also took time to consider the significance of his own role. No non-European leader had ever taken such a personal stake in a major meeting alongside the leaders of the great Western powers. "When I go to the conference," reflected Chiang:

> I want moderation as my only principle. In general, I don't want to bring any great shame upon myself. We should wait for the British and Americans to bring up the treatment of Japan and reparations; we shouldn't do it. This will reassure [them] about us and will make them respect the fact that we don't have any selfish intentions with regard to the global war.[40]

Chiang and Song Meiling landed at Cairo in conditions of strict security, but caused something of a sensation when they appeared in public. General Alan Brooke, chief of the Imperial General Staff, noted that some of the junior officers had given a "suppressed neigh" when they caught sight of Madame Chiang, dressed to kill as usual. Brooke himself thought her "not good looking," noting her "sallow complexion" and her smoking of "continuous cigarettes."[41]

For the first time, Chiang met the figure who had loomed so unpleasantly in his mind for the past three years, Winston Churchill. They talked for around half an hour, with Song Meiling interpreting, and it "went quite smoothly; better than I had expected." The next day they spoke for a full hour, with Meiling and Churchill laughing as the latter declared "You think I'm a terrible old man, don't you?"[42] (The senior British Foreign Office civil servant Alexander Cadogan also noted that "Winston fell for Madame Chiang Kai-shek.")[43] Later that day, Chiang met Roosevelt, who "looked old" (already showing signs of the strain that would kill him). Meiling continued to provide a lively presence, in contrast to the withdrawn Chiang. "During the tea party, my wife worked to entertain everyone," Chiang wrote. "I talked very little and after an hour I withdrew." He was discomforted to note that the British and the Americans appeared already to have set the conference agenda, and that China's proposals and the question of its status had not yet been discussed. "This is very strange," he noted.[44]

There were two major pieces of Asia-related business at Cairo. One was the shape of postwar Asia. The other was the immediate strategy for China and the Southeast Asia Command (SEAC). Chiang recorded his own most important postwar goals for the conference: the return of Manchuria, Taiwan, and the Penghu (Pescadores) islands to China; the establishment of an independent state of Korea; and the handing over of all Japanese factories and shipping in occupied China as part of reparations for China.[45]

But discussions did not go smoothly. The Allies disagreed strongly about the way that the war should be prosecuted in Asia. At Cairo three possibilities were laid out for SEAC: the reoccupation of Burma ("Tarzan"); the invasion of the tip of Sumatra ("Culverin"); and the most ambitious plan, an amphibious operation across the Bay of Bengal to capture the Andaman Islands and threaten Japanese supply lines across Southeast Asia ("Buccaneer").[46] Chiang supported Tarzan, in which Chinese troops were to be deployed alongside British Empire troops under General Slim. But Chiang also wanted a commitment on a push across the Andaman Sea; on arrival at Cairo, he had recorded in his diary that he would advocate joint army and navy moves into Burma, and for making Mandalay the target of the north Burma campaign.[47] Churchill was unwilling to back this idea, but Chiang thought that he sensed that "everyone else gave tacit assent." In fact, the US high command was also unenthusiastic, believing that operations in the Pacific should take priority. Chiang may have had some inkling of this: "I talked to Marshall; his words were long [but vague] . . . I couldn't work out what his main point *was*."[48] Mountbatten also gave an unfavorable verdict on Chiang, declaring that he could not "help wondering how much he knows about soldiering."[49] At the same time Mountbatten clearly gave little thought to the fact that both the US and British sides were being deliberately vague toward Chiang, making it harder for the latter to make serious strategic choices. Then there was a surprising intervention by Roosevelt: he assured Chiang that Buccaneer would indeed be put into action to accompany Tarzan.[50]

Chiang's conversations with Roosevelt gave the Chinese leader reason to believe that his goals for a postwar China with major status in Asia would be fulfilled. In private talks, with Churchill absent, Chiang spoke to the president both about the future of Japan and about the fight against communism and imperialism in the postwar world. "I praised Roosevelt's policy with regard to Soviet communism," he wrote, "but I hope that his policy toward British imperialism can also be successful, to liberate those in the world who are oppressed. Only then can we return the contribution made by the US to this world war."[51] Much of Chiang's concern was about Xinjiang, the northwestern region which the USSR wished to control, and he also repeated his desire for an independent Korea and Vietnam (the latter apparently to be brought about under joint Sino-American tutelage). Chiang's conversation with Roosevelt reinforced his conviction that anti-imperialist nationalism and anticommunism were naturally compatible positions. One intriguing possibility was also discussed, according to Chiang: a suggestion by Roosevelt that the main occupation force in Japan after the war should be made up of Chinese troops. "This was very significant," Chiang observed, "but I didn't say Yes or No clearly."[52] Perhaps this was just as well: Roosevelt's warm but vague passing comment would never have stood up to examination in a conference chamber, and it is doubtful that anyone in the US command would have attributed to the suggestion the significance that Chiang had given it. Chiang was experiencing what dozens of Roosevelt's political friends and foes had observed over decades: the president's ability to utter friendly words that made the person he was talking to believe that the two of them were in perfect agreement, even when Roosevelt had said something almost entirely incompatible to someone else earlier the same day.

Roosevelt was also clearly playing Chiang and Churchill off each other, knowing their mutual distrust. Of Churchill, "I recognize that he's a British-style politician, and a typical example of the Anglo-Saxon race," sniffed Chiang. "But [he] can't be compared with Roosevelt. He can be summed up as narrow-minded, slippery, selfish, and stubborn." Roosevelt fed Chiang's animus at the banquet, claiming (according to Chiang) that "the problem that really makes my head hurt is Mr. Churchill," because Britain still did not want China to be a strong power.[53]

Chiang's concern about the British was shared by many Americans, who were also worried that the US war effort was being used to shore up the British Empire. By the time of the Cairo Conference, it was clear to Churchill that his war aims in Asia were substantially different from Roosevelt's, and that the Americans wanted a great deal more leeway for direct discussions with Stalin about the shape of postwar Europe and Asia. Back in September, Churchill had spoken of the need to maintain "Anglo-Saxon superiority" during a lunch at the White House. There were some in American public life who agreed with this idea, including the former ambassador to China Nelson T. Johnson (although he had always shown a sympathetic attitude to the plight of the Nationalists). But the majority of American opinion, while shaped by its own prejudices, found that the alliance with Britain created an uneasy possibility of alliance with imperialism and the danger of turning the war against Japan into a race war. A. A. (Adolf) Berle, assistant secretary of state and one of Roosevelt's "Brain Trust" of advisers, observed that the two countries were separated in Asia on issues including "the Chinese question, race question, attitude toward Indian aspirations." Beyond Churchill's rhetoric, the reality was that the empire was overstretched and moving into the shadow of its American ally, particularly as Britain's wartime debts continued to mount.[54] The British were also concerned by a real, if not dominant, sentiment in the US that it was the Japanese, rather than the Germans, who were the US's primary enemies: Alan Brooke for one noted in his diary of the American military that "their hearts are really in the Pacific."[55]

Chiang and Song Meiling snatched a quick visit to the pyramids, then departed on November 27. In the aftermath of Cairo, Chiang reflected further on what he had learned. "My first appearance on the diplomatic stage," he observed, also predicting that he would likely be more confident on future outings. If he managed to achieve the territorial gains that he sought, then "it would likely be the greatest foreign policy success in Chinese history."[56] At one level, this was an absurdly grandiose statement, even for his personal diary. It did, however, focus attention on a startling fact: few countries as diplomatically weak as China had ever forced an alliance of much stronger countries to treat it, at least nominally, as an equal. Chiang also reflected, not for the last time, on British influence: "Britain has a power that extends to the furthest part of the world . . . in two continents, Asia and Africa, even the untameable Muslim peoples obey their orders. You can't help admiring their magic powers." Churchill, who spent much of the Cairo Conference fretting that Britain was losing influence with the US, would have been gratified to know of Chiang's appraisal.

Yet Chiang's own story showed how far China had come in its relationship with the Western powers. In less than two decades Chiang himself had risen from provincial military obscurity to become a leader who could sit beside an American president and a British prime minister. Now, Chiang reflected, China must take this opportunity to strengthen itself so that it could serve as an example to other countries seeking independence. In the longer term, the country must improve its quality of education if it truly wished to compete with the US and Britain. But more immediately, he reflected, it was clear that "the British will sacrifice nothing to help others," so it was imperative that Roosevelt guarantee naval support for any land operation in Burma. Chiang's caution turned out to be prophetic.[57]

As his aircraft bore Chiang back to Chongqing, events taking place some 1,800 kilometers from Cairo, in the Persian capital of Teheran, would change the picture significantly. Stalin had refused to join the others at Cairo, but at Teheran, meeting only Roosevelt and Churchill, he made his views clear. Europe must be the absolute priority, he argued, and he promised to strengthen operations on the Eastern Front once Operation Overlord was under way. He did pledge that the USSR would join the fight against Japan, but only after the surrender of Germany. The result was a hasty change in Allied objectives. Operation Buccaneer, which was to have seen a significant amphibious operation across the Bay of Bengal, was canceled on December 5.[58] It would have demanded a huge proportion of all the landing craft that the Royal Navy possessed, and the American command had never been convinced that it was a viable strategy. The abandonment of Buccaneer was yet another indication that promises to China could be made and broken with seemingly little consequence.

Concerned that he would be isolated and left without support, Chiang refused to deploy his Yunnan-based troops (Y Force) into Burma: "You can see that the British don't want to use their strength in the Far East," he complained.[59] Churchill gave Mountbatten permission to use some 20,000 empire troops to support the Chinese forces in a smaller amphibious operation on the Arakan coast, but Chiang rejected the idea. With that decision, Buccaneer was dead. Chiang continued to pledge commitment to Operation Tarzan, the push into Burma, realizing that it was important that China should be seen to make some contribution to Allied campaigns outside its own territory. At the same time he was understandably cautious about the way in which China's interests, and its remaining armed forces, were being used as pawns in a wider geostrategic game.

He continued to blame the British for the change of heart: "Britain is not sincere about advancing into Burma," he wrote, adding that their attitude was "suffocating our economy."[60] Instead of the amphibious attack, Marshall now committed to a north Burma campaign that would lead to the construction of a road across that territory.[61]

The kaleidoscope kept shifting for Chiang. He had been reminded of the precariousness of his command when he stopped over in India on the way back from Cairo, where he spoke to General Zheng Dongguo and inspected the 33,000 men of the Chinese Army in India (X Force), based at Ramgarh in Bihar province. "Stilwell was treating Zheng as a puppet," Chiang lamented, "and would not give him any real command power, or allow him to command the frontline at Ledo. There are many incidents like that—it's truly painful." Yet Chiang was not blind to the problems of developing officers of high quality. "My commanders' spirit, body, and scholarship, to be fair, cannot compete with that of the Americans," he admitted. "How can we nurture such a backward people, feel proud of the country, and seek a true national liberation?"[62]

Meanwhile, doubts were still hardening in some American minds about how far they should support Chiang, and their judgments were becoming harsher. The situation looked very different from Chongqing than it did from Cairo. The American ambassador to China, Clarence Gauss, wrote to Secretary of State Cordell Hull at the end of the Cairo Conference, as the Generalissimo made his way back to Chongqing, expressing concerns about the durability of Chinese resistance. Gauss reported a conversation he had had with Weng Wenhao, the well-respected minister of economic affairs, who had frankly admitted that the gathering of the grain tax in kind had led to deep resentment among the peasantry. "It must be accepted as fact that the Chinese cannot solve their desperate economic problems," Gauss declared. It also had to be accepted that the Chinese government had now become "completely defensive" in its strategy, and "in many respects, passively and complacently so." Gauss argued that the Chinese troops were badly nourished and that the army was riddled with corruption and undertook activities of little military value.[63]

In Chongqing, Gauss was not the only one who perceived the deterioration of Free China. He and Graham Peck were among those who could see that Chiang's regime, propped up with US dollars, was holding on to power with the greatest of difficulty. The many tentacles of Dai Li's MSB arrested numerous dissidents and took them off to torture and execution.

Chiang was still not in the same class of brutality as that other Western ally Stalin, but by the end of 1943 from the American perspective the Nationalist government was nearly impossible to like and almost as difficult to admire. Gauss noted the "fascist-like" actions that would make it an embarrassing ally for a postwar America.

Yet Gauss admitted that although the political situation was dire, "it would be a mistake to assume that the inevitable result will be compromise with Japan." Gauss affirmed that the National Government genuinely believed that the Allies would win the war, and "the necessity of being on the winning side." He also reminded Hull that the Chinese had been fighting for six years and that they were continuing to contain "almost half a million Japanese troops." He also acknowledged that "war weariness" was a powerful deterrent to further Chinese action. (Earlier in the year, of course, Chiang had admitted, "We are exhausted after six years of our war of resistance against Japan.")[64] Many Chinese felt that their country had already played its part in the defense of Asia, and that their government should preserve its strength for the postwar settlement, as well as preventing an occupation of the north by the Communists, assisted by the USSR. Gauss also acknowledged Chiang's great fear that the US might itself make a compromise peace with Japan. There were many reasons to explain the unwillingness of a hollowed-out, battered China to take a more active role in the next stage of the war.

Even with his qualifications, Gauss's criticism was still not fair. Chiang had made it quite clear that he was willing to take part in a joint campaign in the Pacific. But the suggestion that he should do so while the other Allies concentrated their forces in Europe was disingenuous. In the circumstances it was hardly surprising that Chiang had adopted a defensive strategy. Once again the Allies not only told China that it was a secondary, or indeed tertiary priority, which was understandable in terms of their geostrategic goals, but also implied that China should act as if it were a first-rank ally while being treated as a third-rank one. The demand was also hypocritical. The Allied strategy was dependent on there not being further action in China in the period immediately preceding the invasion of Europe.[65] If Chiang had really launched his troops in some sort of solo offensive, they would have been destroyed and the Chongqing regime would have fallen even more swiftly, perhaps allowing the Nanjing regime to gain more of a hold in parts of China, or a faster Communist victory.

In a message to Roosevelt, Chiang was frank about his disappoint-ment that the all-out assault in the Pacific would not now take place, and warned that the Chinese people might not believe that Allied pledges of assistance were sincere, particularly in the face of looming economic col-lapse. Only a loan of a billion gold dollars—along with a doubling of the size of the American air force in China, and an increase in general air transportation to at least 20,000 tons per month—could prevent the imminent implosion of the Chinese economy, and with it, the country's resistance. Otherwise, Chiang feared, Japan would take advantage of the concentration of Allied efforts on the European front to "liquidate" China.[66]

The request was unwise at the very least, and it was taken as a sign that Chiang's greed knew no bounds. But Chiang can be forgiven for perhaps thinking that cash in hand was better than the vague promises of support that seemed to be written in wind and water. After all, his position, which he had thought so strong at Cairo, had been undermined within a matter of days. It was now clear that Europe, and the plans for Overlord, would dominate the global theater of war in 1944.

As the new year dawned, Chiang did not realize that he would soon be fighting for the very survival of his regime. The decision to concentrate troops on the liberation of France and the push toward Berlin would have unexpected, direct, and very dangerous consequences for China within just a few weeks. And Allied, primarily American, decisions forced on Chiang would make matters even worse.

Chapter 17

ONE WAR, TWO FRONTS

H UANG YAOWU'S FIRST AIRPLANE flight took place in a troop convoy to India in June 1944. He knew that the Hump flight was dangerous, but he was young, ready for adventure, and not overly concerned. What bothered him much more was the cold. On the ground, the temperature was high, but in a Douglas C-47 Dakota some 9,000 meters above ground the soldiers were all chilled to the bone, wearing just one layer of clothing. "I was dizzy, my head pounding," Huang recalled. Miserable, he fell asleep, with only the warm air on his body alerting him to their final arrival in India.[1]

Huang's Cantonese parents had immigrated to America but had returned to China after 1911, fired by a desire to help build the new republic. Huang had been born in 1928. His parents died early in the war, and needing to support himself, he signed up for the army, aged only fifteen. He had vivid memories of the early days of his service. His group of recruits sat in front of pictures of Chiang Kai-shek, Mao Zedong, and He Yingqin, placed on the wall as if they were all members of the same party and the bitter conflicts of the 1930s had never happened. Later, he and his friends went out into the mountains and swore blood brotherhood with each other, vowing never to return home until they had killed all the Japanese invaders. Within a few months, Huang would play a crucial role in one of the most heroic and tragic years in China's war against Japan.

China would fight on two fronts. Although on one front it would win a tainted victory, on the other front it would face a disaster that would come close to destroying the Nationalist state. On New Year's Day 1944 Chiang had sent a telegram to Roosevelt, warning that the strategy decided at Teheran, reversing the one proposed at Cairo, would provoke the Japanese to seize their chance in China. "Japan will rightly deduce that practically the entire weight of the UN forces [i.e., the Allies] will be applied to the European Front, thus abandoning the China Theater to the mercy of Japan's mechanised land and air forces," he declared. "Before long Japan will launch an all-out offensive against China."[2] Western intelligence sources disagreed, convinced that the Japanese would take a more defensive position. At the Fourth Nanyue Military Conference in February, Chiang expressed his frustration that his position was not taken more seriously by his allies. "They do not consider the Chinese army to stand equal," he admitted. "This is the most shameful thing . . . The basic reason is that our army is still not strong enough."[3]

By the spring, there were signals that something was brewing in east China. The American ambassador to China, Clarence Gauss, informed Secretary of State Cordell Hull on March 23 that credible intelligence indicated that "Japan is preparing for new drive in Honan."[4] But General Stilwell's attention had turned in a different direction. On February 14 a scorching article had appeared in *Time* magazine, discussing the opening of a supply road from India to Burma:

> For 17 months Lieut. General Joseph W. Stilwell has been under fire in Washington, London and New Delhi. Critics said the new Ledo Road from India to China was not worth the effort . . . In India's capital last week, "Vinegar Joe" Stilwell sat rigidly in his rattan-cane armchair, long fingers playing with his favorite cigaret holder, eyes almost shut. Curtly he replied to his critics: the Ledo Road fulfills two U.S. objectives: 1) to get at least some supplies to blockaded China; 2) to set up a situation in which Japs are killed . . . Admiral the Lord Louis Mountbatten differs with Stilwell . . . The U.S. commander admitted that a southern China port must be opened before the armies of Generalissimo Chiang Kaishek can be rearmed. But "Vinegar Joe," who probably knows China better than any brasshat in New Delhi, stoutly held that the "Hump" air route and the Ledo Road can fill the immediate gap in China's desperate needs, thus fit into the general Asia strategy.[5]

It was an article meant to provoke, and it did just that, infuriating Mountbatten, who tried unsuccessfully to have Stilwell recalled.[6] It also reflected the particular viewpoint of Stilwell and his supporters in the press. Ever since being forced to walk out of the jungle in May 1942, Stilwell had had an obsession with the recovery of Burma. At the Cairo Conference the proposal for Buccaneer had raised his hopes, only for them to be dashed again after its cancellation. All the same, British and Chinese troops had already been moved in preparation for an assault on Burma, and by late December 1943 the Chinese had begun to encounter Japanese outposts in the border areas. But Southeast Asian Command (SEAC), under Mount-batten, vetoed the idea of fighting to reopen the road from Ledo in Assam, in northeast India, through Burma into Yunnan in southwest China. Now a battle between the Allies broke out, as Stilwell insisted on launching an assault as soon as possible on the Ledo Road, whereas Mountbatten and the American Albert Wedemeyer, SEAC's chief of staff, maintained that such a plan was impractical. In the end Stilwell prevailed. He sent representatives to lobby Roosevelt, who did not take a clear stand, but also did not say no to a campaign in north Burma. A major disruption between Stilwell and SEAC would have been highly embarrassing and distracted attention just when the Allied commanders were preoccupied with their top priority: the secret preparations for D-Day just four months away. Stilwell was able to launch his campaign because nobody had the incentive to stop him.

Chiang Kai-shek was still concerned that a major Japanese assault was imminent. But his words did little to convince his Western Allies. On March 27 Chiang suggested that transferring Y Force (some 90,000 men in total) and the American fighter planes to India for the Burma campaign would leave central China vulnerable. Roosevelt replied on April 3 that further aid to China would be "unjustified" unless Chiang agreed to send the troops. Under further pressure from Stilwell (and Marshall), Chiang was forced to acquiesce.[7] Despite his deep misgivings, he sent 40,000 Chinese troops under General Huang Weili to the Burma front. Stilwell sent his troops, Chinese and American, in a bold dash for Myit-kyina in northeast Burma. On May 17 he captured the airfield there, but within a short time history repeated itself. Once again, as in 1942, Stilwell found himself besieged in the city by the Japanese.

This time, however, there was more support coming to Stilwell's rescue. Huang Yaowu was one of the soldiers assigned to the 22nd Division of the New Sixth Army. The troops in India were well drilled and also benefited from information provided by Chinese divisions stationed in India. The intelligence was hardly reassuring. The Japanese were taking advantage of their experience in jungle warfare to place machine-gun nests in trees. On some parts of the road, with dense jungle on one side and, on the other, a sheer cliff, soldiers had to use vines to climb up.[8] The lush, monsoon-nourished jungle of Burma was very different from the plains or forests of China; the territory felt as alien to the Chinese soldiers

318 • THE POISONED ALLIANCE

fighting there as it did to their American and British counterparts. Soon enough, Huang and his comrades were sent into the jungle themselves. They rapidly developed ways to avoid attracting the attention of the Japanese, using a system of "monkey cries" to keep in contact with one another; if Huang gave three cries, and his comrade replied with three, that signaled "all clear."

However, there were advantages to being in Burma. Stilwell's control of Lend-Lease supplies meant that the troops were well resourced. Huang remembered becoming tired of beef and pumpkin at every meal; but this was a diet whose quality would have been the envy of many of the troops who would soon be fighting more than 2,000 kilometers to the east.[9]

Yet the Allies could not know that the Japanese had their own plans: its leaders had made the extraordinary decision to launch a major assault into the Chinese mainland at the same time as a major campaign in Burma. In the autumn of 1943 the Imperial General Headquarters had looked at the increasingly perilous position in Asia. As the Americans advanced in the Pacific, it became clear that the initial Japanese gains of early 1942 were vulnerable. By the spring of 1944 Allied assaults had forced Tokyo to regroup its forces to protect at least some of its empire in the Central Pacific. The loss of the Marshall Islands in February 1944 led General Tôjô to dismiss the head of the Navy and install himself as chief of staff for the Army.[10] Now the Japanese decided, as in 1941, to double their bets and hope that a bold and unexpected move would once again give them the advantage. They resolved to launch one last, massive thrust against the Asian mainland. Operation Ugô was to send 85,000 troops from northern Burma into British India.

Another major campaign was to knock China out of the war for good: Operation Ichigô ["Number One"]. The Imperial General Headquarters in Tokyo approved a military operation that would create a clear corridor of operations in central China. The idea was taken up by Japan's China Expeditionary Command, which had spent much of the last year bogged down trying to keep control over the areas of occupation. On January 4, 1944, the plan was laid out. The key military aims were to destroy the American air bases in central China, and to open up a route between central China and French Indochina using the railway network. Though Prime Minister Tôjô endorsed only the destruction of the air bases, the plan was officially approved and put into action on January 24.[11]

Ichigô was the largest operation ever undertaken by the Japanese Army. Some half a million troops were mobilized across central China to the border with French Indochina. But Ichigô was about much more than named strategic objectives. For both the Japanese and the Nationalists, the campaign was a last-ditch attempt to remain in the war. The attempt to neutralize China completely became an urgent, even desperate priority. If the Japanese could gain the initiative in Asia, they just might be able to negotiate a settlement with the Americans, who were concentrating on Europe.[12]

In mid-April the suspicions of Chiang and Gauss proved devastatingly correct. A mighty assault by the Imperial Japanese Army thrust into Henan. Half a million men and 200 bombers were mobilized, with supplies of fuel for eight months and ammunition for two years.[13] It took a long time for the Nationalist command to understand what the Japanese were doing. Xu Yongchang, minister of military operations, was convinced well into the spring of 1944 that any Japanese assault would come in southern China, and it was not until May that it was clear the attack would be along the Ping–Han (Beiping–Wuhan) railway line in the center of the country.[14] Troops moved to defend central China against the coming storm.

Now the army felt the effects of years of attrition from Japanese assault and governmental corruption and incompetence. Recruitment had been falling since 1941, and press-ganging of new soldiers had become much more common. Conscripts were often marched in gangs tied together with ropes to an area far from home; if they were too close to their own villages, they might simply flee.[15] Inflation had eaten away at military salaries and made service far less attractive. At the same time some of the best Chinese armies that remained, including the Yunnan-based Y Force, were thousands of kilometers away in Burma, by Stilwell's side as he fought to relieve the siege of Myitkyina.

The huge gap between the theoretical strength of the Chinese forces in central China and the ragged reality was exposed in the nightmare days of May 1944. Jiang Dingwen and Tang Enbo were the two generals placed in charge of the First War Zone in northern China, defending the city of Luoyang, on the Yellow River in Henan, the province that had suffered so much from flood and famine. Jiang gave his account of what happened in northern Henan, an area still suffering grievously from the breach of the dike at Huayuankou in 1938. "I'd already thought that there were not enough troops," he wrote, "but when he asked for reinforcements he was not granted them. Other Nationalist troops had been moved away to block off the Communists, he said, and "we faced the enemy on three sides. The area to defend was huge and the troops very few." The Japanese, in contrast, had motorized troops who could operate to full advantage in this flat terrain.

Jiang Dingwen also hinted heavily that the problems lay not with him but his commander in chief. His troops should have attacked on April 23 or 24, early in the campaign, to launch a decisive battle at Luoyang, but he had not received Chiang's permission to attack until May 1. By that time the Japanese had advanced even further, and it was too late. Jiang had to send his army to relieve Tang Enbo, because Tang had set out in another direction to follow Chiang Kai-shek's previous order that they should hold nearby Yu county. These kinds of communications failures were endemic. The 38th and 13th Armies failed to receive the message that they should advance to Luoyang and ended up following the previous order to head to Yu county instead. In the days that followed, the same story came up repeatedly: some of Tang and Jiang's troops made their way to the next crisis area, but too many of the other troops found themselves cut off from communications, and a coordinated strategy became impossible. And, Jiang hinted ("Mr. Chiang, you can still remember this"), Chiang Kai-shek's orders were what had confused the issue.[16]

Yet the most chilling aspect of Jiang's account was his description of the reaction of the local civilian population:

> During this campaign, the unexpected phenomenon was that the people of the mountains in western Henan attacked our troops, taking guns, bullets, and explosives, and even high-powered mortars and radio equipment . . . They surrounded our troops and killed our officers. We heard this pretty often. The heads of the villages and *baojia* (village mutual-responsibility groups) just ran away. At the same time, they took away our stored grain, leaving their houses and fields empty, which meant that our officers and soldiers had no food for many days.[17]

Jiang grudgingly admitted that the army's own behavior may have played a role. "There were certainly a minority of soldiers who did not keep discipline and harassed the villagers," he conceded, "but it was the lack of civilian administration that meant that they could not compete with the military." However, Jiang did see how damaging the breakdown of trust had been. "Actually this is truly painful for me to say: in the end the damages we suffered from the attack by the people were more serious than the losses from battles with the enemy."[18]

Jiang's account was self-serving, placing the blame on Tang, Chiang, and anyone but himself. A document submitted to the government indicting the commanders was unsparing in its accusations. The reason for the failure of the campaign in the First War Zone, they declared, was that "Jiang Dingwen and his deputy Tang Enbo paid no attention to political and military matters," and had instead diverted their time to enriching themselves, thereby encouraging their subordinates to act in the same way. Jiang and Tang's troops had had various advantages, for instance, Czech weapons that might actually have been superior to some of those used by the enemy, yet they were never properly used. They had taken a cut from the ordinary soldiers' salaries, the accusation went, and had padded the official rolls with nonexistent soldiers to claim their salaries, so the divisions were actually undermanned.

While Jiang Dingwen was nominally in command, most observers believed that Tang Enbo was the real authority, and his accusers aimed their fire squarely at him. Heroics at Taierzhuang six years previously now carried no weight. "Tang Enbo had the major responsibility for defeating the enemy in central China," declared his critic, Guo Zhonghuai. "But when the enemy were crossing the Yellow River . . . he didn't himself lead from the front, but retreated . . . relaxing and taking a dip in the hot springs." With the lead officer taking a long soak some 400 *li* away (perhaps 200 kilometers) from the battlefront, the troops scattered and ran: "No wonder they didn't fire even one bullet." Tang's troops, supposedly among the elite of the Nationalist forces, were used alongside civilians to carry the baggage of officials who wanted to escape the combat zone. Tang himself fled, taking with him two telegraphists and about 20–30 personal bodyguards, "running like a rat . . . and completely losing contact with his army." The accusations sharpened: Tang, they said, had faked reports claiming that he had engaged with the enemy, or was going to attack. "But he didn't even know where his armies were," Guo's indictment went on, "so how can he order them to attack? The crime of giving false military information is difficult to forgive."[19]

Tang and Jiang had behaved inexcusably. But in some ways Tang's abandonment of his men had echoes of Stilwell's "walkout" in Burma in 1942. Stilwell was not remotely corrupt, and he could show deep concern for his men. But he was also capricious and capable of driving his men beyond reasonable limits (as he would do soon with the American troops sent to relieve Myitkyina), and letting his personal vendettas overrule his military judgment. Western and Chinese commanders alike in the China-Burma-India Theater were capable of inspired leadership, but also of conduct that demanded a court-martial: Tang and Stilwell were among those clearly capable of both.

The indictment against Tang and Jiang went on. Because the soldiers lacked supplies, they had to "borrow" grain from the farmers, and they were distracted from training by the need to find the grain and mill it. Even when they had done this, the poor quality of the grain meant that they were undernourished, and "their will to fight was exhausted."[20] The relationship between the population and the military was now utterly hollow. When the northern part of Henan fell to the Japanese, the invaders seized much of the grain that had been left in the official government granaries: the million bags of flour captured could have nourished 200,000 soldiers for five months.

Tang's excuse — that the Henan peasants had been deceived by collaborators and were seizing the Nationalist army's weapons — was dismissed by Guo Zhonghuai: "Everyone knows that the Henan people are loyal and brave, and even at a time of drought and famine they offered men and grain." In fact, Tang was right. The locals had simply picked up the weapons that the Nationalist troops had abandoned when they fled, to defend themselves against the Japanese. "Even if there is an Allied victory which changes the war situation, it will still be very difficult to recover the northern provinces and the important area of Henan," Guo admitted.[21]

Jiang Dingwen's account also blamed collaborators with the enemy, who were in the "lower-level administration and police stations," enabling them to harass the army and "mislead" the people. His report shows the breakdown in trust between the state and its population. The locals did not obey the Nationalist army orders to destroy local highways to prevent the Japanese advancing. Sometimes they even went back at night and mended roads which the army had torn up by day.[22]

The Nationalists were reaping the results of the dike-breaking in 1938 and the subsequent famine in Henan in 1942. The famine had not been wholly caused by governmental incompetence (although that was a significant element), and without the Japanese invasion it might not have occurred at all. But this made little difference to the farmers who had endured endless horrors and seen themselves reduced to refugee status or starvation as their crops failed and their grain was seized as tax. Now the Nationalists demanded that they contribute to the defense against the enemy once more. This time the population of Henan declined to do so.

Everett F. Drumright, one of the US embassy staff based in Xi'an (and a future ambassador to Chiang's government on Taiwan), had sent an account of the battle to Gauss, who in turn forwarded it to the State Department. Some 60,000–70,000 Japanese troops had been met with only "token resistance," and the First War Zone was now "shattered," along with the reputations of Jiang Dingwen and Tang Enbo. "Chinese suffered heavy losses in men, material, and crops. Loss of wheat crop, best in years, most serious loss." Shaanxi, the next province to the west, now lay open.[23] Theodore White also observed all the features that had made the defeat in Henan such a rout — commanders absent from the field, officers using military facilities to evacuate their private property, and the seizure of oxen from the peasants — as well as the result: soldiers being disarmed by their fellow Chinese. "Within three weeks the Japanese had seized all their objectives; the railway to the south lay in their hands, and a Chinese army of 300,000 men had ceased to exist."[24]

The fall of Luoyang was rapidly followed by another disaster as the Nationalist military leadership underestimated the strength of the Japanese forces that were ranged against them. At the end of May, General Xue Yue prepared, once again, to defend Changsha, the city that had suffered so grievously after Chiang's retreat from Wuhan in October 1938. Although Xue Yue had previously held the city with great bravery, this time he was hampered by inferior numbers (his 10,000 troops had to match 30,000 Japanese), and the fact that the Japanese were already familiar with his plan to encircle them: he had used it before at Changsha.[25] "His units were three years older," was Theodore White's verdict; "their weapons three years more worn, the soldiers three years hungrier than when they had last won glory."[26] Chiang Kai-shek placed his own judgment in serious question by refusing to send supplies to Xue Yue in Changsha, fearing that Xue was disloyal to him. General Chennault, for one, was outraged at Chiang's behavior.[27] Xue and the general in charge of the defense of the city itself, Zhang Deneng, were unable to hold the line and the city fell to the Japanese, after six years of resistance, in just three weeks, on June 18, 1944. American confidence was now as low as Chinese. It became all the more imperative that the Nationalists should be seen to fight back. On June 15 Gauss wrote of the "general gloom . . . and somewhat defeatist attitude [that] is becoming prevalent at Chungking," adding that the fact that the Henan peasants had turned against their own troops, "due to their own deplorable condition," had particularly harmed official morale. Just a week later, Chiang gave a downbeat speech at the Central Military Training Academy. "Everybody has adopted the mentality that the Japanese are too strong and we are too weak," he declared. "Our current age is an age of science," he continued, "and we must develop a spirit in accordance with it."[28] Yet the reality was a long way from the technological modernity implicit in Chiang's words. In a later address, he too focused on the attack by the people of Henan on their own army, as had happened to the Whites in the Russian Civil War, and admitted that the retreating army had robbed, raped, and murdered. "Of course," he mourned, "this sort of army will lose."[29]

It was fortunate that Chiang, and the Americans, did not see the reaction of their supposed comrade, Mao Zedong. Soviet adviser Peter Vladimirov recorded that "the CCP leadership rejoices at the news of the defeat suffered by Chiang Kai-shek's troops in Honan [Henan] and Hunan . . . His calculations are simple — whenever Chiang Kai-shek suffers a defeat, [Yan'an] benefits from it."[30]

The city of Hengyang was the next probable Japanese target. Eventually, the assault through central China was likely to be accompanied by separate Japanese thrusts north of Guangzhou (Canton) and south of Wuhan, cutting a line right across the country's heartland and leaving Free China even more isolated than before. In addition, the Nationalist war effort was once again under threat because of the toxic relationship between Chiang and Stilwell. Xue Yue now moved to Hengyang, but again Chiang refused to offer him direct assistance because of his suspicions about Xue's loyalties. Chiang did allow a general whom he trusted, Fang Xianjue, to take part in the defense of Hengyang, supported by Chennault's air force, and the Japanese were at first driven back from the city. But soon the Chinese supplies ran out. Chiang did not resupply the defenders, and Chennault went directly to Stilwell, begging him to send a tiny amount of support, some 1,000 tons, to the Chinese front-line troops. Stilwell vetoed the plea with three words: "Let them stew."[31]

Chiang and Stilwell both acted irresponsibly. Their pique and personal prejudices led to decisions that caused the deaths of thousands of the Chinese soldiers both claimed to hold in such high regard. In the end, though, it was Chiang's efforts and not Stilwell's that proved decisive, as Chiang realized how important it was that the Chinese be seen to fight. Rather than flying in new supplies, he sent other armies located nearby to help defend Hengyang. The city was defended heroically but unsuccessfully, and it fell on August 8.[32]

In 1938 a gallant but failed defense had been sufficient to bolster Chiang's case for support. By 1944 it was no longer enough. The Nationalists were drawing strong criticism from one figure whose confidence Chiang needed to maintain: President Roosevelt. Early in the war the Nationalists had been defeated over and over again. Yet their performance in Shanghai and then at Wuhan, even when they were eventually bested, gave the necessary impression that the government was serious about resistance. Now, the sorry defeats at Luoyang and Changsha were causing hostile murmuring in Chongqing and in Washington. General George Marshall told Roosevelt that the time had come to entrust the remaining military resources of China to an "individual capable of directing that effort in a fruitful way against the Japanese." In Marshall's view, only Stilwell fitted the bill. Roosevelt requested that the American be appointed as commander for all forces in China. Chiang had no option but to agree.[33]

Chiang was not oblivious to American attempts to encroach on his command and even his right to rule. He became convinced that Sun Fo (also known as Sun Ke) was being groomed by the Americans as a possible head of the Nationalist Party. As the son of Sun Yat-sen, Sun had an excellent pedigree for this task. His untouchable status also gave him license to advocate liberal policies that had gotten other prominent figures into trouble with Dai Li's secret police. "Sun Ke is flapping around everywhere, using the slogan of 'democracy' to shake up people's hearts," complained Chiang. "Certain Central Government committee members are following along . . . I think a great disaster will happen." In the following months Chiang widened the net of suspicion. "Russia is the master behind the scenes . . . [Sun] is even worse than the traitor Wang!" he wrote, adding a while later, "The US, Britain, and the Soviet Union all use Sun as a puppet . . . and the US is the worst."[34]

But while American confidence in the Nationalists was fast dissipating as the Japanese smashed into central China, it was not Sun Fo to whom most of their eyes turned. (Vice President Henry Wallace, on meeting Sun in China, judged that he "does not impress one as having strength of character needed for leadership.")[35] John S. Service, the second secretary at the US Embassy in Chongqing, attached to Stilwell's staff, reported to Gauss that the consequences of a Nationalist collapse in central China would be severe for the Chinese war effort. The loss of the rice-growing provinces of Jiangxi and Hunan, a new refugee flow, the need to support large armies on ever poorer land in western China, and the influx of Japanese puppet currency would worsen the already soaring inflation in Nationalist China. The collapse of the National Government, he concluded, "might become only a matter of time."[36] This assumption would lead Service to draw daring conclusions about the alternative to the Nationalists as future leaders of China.

In January 1944 John Paton Davies Jr., a US Foreign Service officer, had made the case that the US would be wise to make formal contacts with the Communist headquarters at Yan'an. "Only one official American observer has ever visited the 'Communist' area," he noted. "That was six years ago." Yet even from the secondhand information that the Americans had gleaned since then, Davies argued, certain points about the CCP seemed quite clear. The Communists had a major base near important Japanese military and industrial centers, and they possessed valuable intelligence on Japan. If the USSR were to enter the war, it would have to attack through areas held by the CCP. He declared that they were "the greatest single challenge in China to the Chiang Kai-shek government." More contentiously, he suggested that they ran the "most cohesive, disciplined, and aggressively anti-Japanese regime in China" (with the implication that more active fighting was being done by the CCP than by the Nationalists), and that they might form the "foundation for a *rapprochement* between a new China and the Soviet Union." The Communists had indicated they would be willing to receive American visitors, and the US should seize the opportunity before the Communists changed their minds, as Chiang's blockade of Yan'an made compromise harder. Chiang, of course, would be opposed to any such approach, and "the request should come to him directly from the President, who can overcome any initial refusal by exercise of our ample bargaining power."[37] Gauss, forwarding Davies's message to Washington, observed that Chiang's position was under threat from several directions. For instance, there had recently been an attempted coup by young officers who wanted to revitalize the Nationalist regime. An effort to crush the CCP might provoke a civil war, particularly as some Nationalist generals, such as Hu Zongnan, stationed in the northwest, were reported to have cooperative agreements with the Communists.[38]

Stilwell was also convinced that the Communists must be brought more fully into the conflict and that they had an understanding of Chinese society that the Nationalists lacked. Although a Republican at home, Stilwell's disgust at Chiang's regime led him away from his usual political tendencies. "He can't see that the mass of Chinese people welcome the Reds," Stilwell wrote, "as being the only visible hope of relief from crushing taxation, the abuses of the Army, and Tai Li [Dai Li]'s Gestapo."[39]

At first, Chiang fiercely resisted any suggestion that there should be formal contact between the US and the CCP. "It's only reasonable that I should strongly refuse," he wrote.[40] However, the visit of US vice president Henry Wallace in June 1944 helped to sway him. Wallace sent a deeply gloomy report to Roosevelt about the state of Chinese resistance, condemning Chiang as surrounded by "reactionary" figures, and judging that he "showed himself so prejudiced against the Communists that there seemed little prospect of satisfactory or enduring settlement as a result of the negotiations now under way."[41] Chiang had to give way to American pressure to make contact with the CCP.

The events of the long summer of 1944 began to induce paranoia in Chiang. "For twenty years, the Communist bandits and the Russians have been plotting against me," he wrote. "But now the British and Americans are plotting with the Communists — this is like world imperialism ambushing me!"[42] Stilwell might regard Chiang as "the Peanut," a buffoon who was unwilling to fight. But from Chiang's point of view, his fear of his own allies was perfectly rational. He was seeking to resist a major Japanese incursion with reduced troops at the same time that he had been pressured to support a campaign in Burma of which he did not approve. Simultaneously, his rule was also being undermined by American attempts to find other bases of power.

Yet Chiang's great opponent was nervous too. Peter Vladimirov, Soviet adviser to the CCP in Yan'an, saw Mao on July 15. "He looked tired," the

Russian noted, observing Mao dropping cigarette ash everywhere while pacing up and down during a long nighttime conversation. "America's position is of tremendous importance to our future," Mao told him. Vladimirov felt that Mao was willing to try and make some sort of accommodation with the US and Britain to lessen his dependence on the Soviet Union.[43]

On July 22, 1944, a Douglas DC-3 aircraft came in to land on the yellow loess soil of Yan'an, bearing the United States Army Observation Group. Mao and Zhu De had come to the airfield to meet them, wearing new matching uniforms for the occasion. There was martial music, a parade of soldiers, and Vladimirov himself (in his role as correspondent for the official Soviet news agency, TASS) waiting to record the historic moment with his Leica camera. History threatened to turn into farce or even tragedy as the Douglas veered off the runway in a cloud of dust and made an abrupt stop as the propeller fell off noisily. Fortunately, there were no injuries and the party emerged unscathed.[44]

The visiting American party would become known as the "Dixie Mission," a joking reference to Union missions behind Confederate lines during the American Civil War. The group of nine, supplemented a month later by another ten, was led by John Service, who undertook political analysis, and Colonel David Barrett, in charge of military information-gathering. Service made a particular impression on Vladimirov: "young, full of bounce, and has a good retentive memory." Service made good use of those qualities as he traveled throughout the area, asking endless questions.[45] Service's reports were sent back to Chongqing, where Gauss passed them on to Washington. It was all new, for little was known about the reality of Yan'an. From the discomfort of the caves to the terror of Rectification, the politics of the Communist base lay behind a veil of secrecy, in sharp contrast to the fierce light that shone on the decay in Chongqing. Service observed that he was at pains not to be taken in by the "spell of the Chinese Communists." Nonetheless, the first impressions of the Observation Group were immensely positive, with a universal sense that they had "come into a different country and are meeting a different people." The differences between Yan'an and the Nationalist areas were obvious at every level. "Bodyguards, gendarmes and the clap-trap of Chungking officialdom are . . . completely lacking," Service wrote. "Mao and the other leaders are universally spoken of with respect . . . but these men are approachable and subservience toward them is completely lacking." Also impressive were the simplicity of life and clothing, and the lack of beggars and desperate poverty. Service also noticed the similarity in clothes and manners, at least ostensibly, between men and women. He even remarked on the absence of the "spooning couples seen in parks or quiet streets in Chungking," echoing the activist who had commented that "Yan'an was really not a sexy town."[46]

Service also noticed many of the other social changes the Communists had fostered: the stress on peasant art forms such as folk dancing, for example, a product of Mao's demand in 1942 for art and culture to find more points of connection with the culture of the peasantry.[47] Service also reported a lack of censorship, and a sense of freedom. "Morale is very high," he wrote. "The war seems close and real. There is no defeatism, but rather confidence."[48] "To the casual eye there are no police in Yenan," he observed. Over the months, Service attempted to get some measure of the Communist leaders and their system. He described them as having a "lack of striking individuality" but giving an overall impression of youth and vigor, as well as pragmatism. "The test of everything," he suggested, "was whether it works — in China." He did observe that there was a certain "uniformity" in their way of thought.[49] But in general, the assessments of Service praised Mao's achievements and contrasted them unfavorably with Chiang's. The views of Service differed strongly from Vladimirov's, who wrote that anti-Nationalist propaganda and the Rectification movements had led to an "oppressive, suffocating atmosphere in the party": people "abandoned any initiative" in their haste to "redeem themselves from their nonexistent sins."[50]

On July 26, Service was seated next to Mao at a banquet given in honor of the American visitors. The Communist leader asked Service whether there was any prospect of an American consulate being set up at Yan'an. Service spoke diplomatically of the obstacles to such a plan, but Mao stressed that if the Americans left immediately on cessation of the war with Japan, then it would be at "just the time of greatest danger of a Kuomintang attack and civil war."[51]

In the Cold War years, Service, Barrett, and the other Americans involved with the Dixie Mission would find themselves in deep trouble as political warmth between the US and China turned to icy enmity, poisoned by the politically barbed and misleading question of "Who lost

China?" Their defenders argued that there had been a realistic hope of cooperation between the United States and Mao's party. Those who attacked them argued that they had become dupes of a Communist campaign of deception.

Neither interpretation seems convincing. Service and his colleagues were right to argue that the Communist areas had better-disciplined troops and that their policies were more economically just than those in the Nationalist zone, because this was demonstrably true. In particular, the successful implementation of tax reform marked a real socioeconomic change that the Nationalists had never managed, and was to the Communists' credit. But despite their close observation, Service's group were not comparing like with like: their long years and inside knowledge of the Nationalist areas were being contrasted with a short and selective visit to Yan'an. After years of close-up experience of Chongqing, with its "reek of corruption," and knowledge of horrors such as the famine in Henan, it was not surprising that they found the Communist areas much more impressive.[52] Their view of the Communist presence was overly rosy, but the brutality of the Rectification movements does not in itself invalidate their views: it is possible for a regime to be repressive and genuinely popular among its own people at the same time. Yet Service's group also underestimated the advantage that Mao gained by avoiding the massive air raids and refugee flight that had hampered the Chongqing regime from the start of the war. Furthermore, they were not privy to intraparty discussions that made it clear Mao would never genuinely entertain an alliance with Washington.[53] His ideological alignments were toward Stalin and toward a radical, violent, indigenous revolution.

Nor did Service's group acknowledge the extent to which Western and particularly American action and inaction were responsible for the decayed and flawed state of Chiang's regime. The years of isolation, and the acceptance of an alliance that placed China far down the list of Allied priorities, put Chiang in an impossible position. Just at the time that Service and Barrett were visiting Yan'an, Nationalist armies were attempting to hold the line at Hengyang, at the same time that some of their best troops were following Stilwell on his quixotic journey into Burma. Gauss, who was much less starry-eyed about the CCP than Stilwell and Service were, passed on Service's enthusiastic accounts faithfully to Washington, but added a rider in which he cautioned against taking the CCP's assessment of its own contributions too literally. "Recent Chinese Communist claims of military achievements against Japan seem to have been exaggerated," Gauss cautioned. He acknowledged that the Communists had "unquestionably" set up valuable sites of resistance in north China, and also contained "some" Japanese troops in north and central China:

> They appear to have avoided meeting the Japanese in frontal clashes, confining themselves in the main to occasional attacks against small elements of the enemy. In reviewing the battles of the past seven years in China, it would seem safe to say that Communist participation has been on a relatively minor scale. The Communist[s] have fought no battles comparable in scope and intensity to those of the Shanghai, Hsuchow [Xuzhou], Hankow [Wuhan], and Changsha campaigns; and their claims to the contrary notwithstanding, they appear to have contained but a minor proportion of the Japanese military forces operating in China.[54]

A minor proportion, that is, in comparison to the Nationalists. Gauss was no admirer of Chiang, but he could see that the CCP was not the magic key that could transform the worsening war situation in China. In Yan'an, Vladimirov, who could see the CCP close up, agreed. "The Eighth Route Army and New Fourth Army have actually folded up military operations since 1941," he stated flatly in his report to Moscow.[55]

While central China continued to collapse, the campaign in Burma ground on. Huang Yaowu had no doubt that death could come to him and his friends at any moment. One of Huang's comrades suffered from night blindness; he disappeared at night in the forest and was never seen again. Huang's commander, knowing that his men were in unfamiliar territory, gave orders on setting up camp: first array machine guns, then set up defense works, and only then set up shelter. The bedding was often elementary, as soldiers simply threw down sheets and blankets between trees. The enemy threat was present and real. One night skirmish saw 100 Japanese dead, but 30 Allied troops were also killed. One of the dead was an American liaison officer. He had used his parachute as a makeshift tent, but in doing so had made himself a particularly visible target.[56]

The siege of Myitkyina in northeast Burma showed no signs of ending. Stilwell might have used British troops to relieve the siege, but his mind was still on public relations and he insisted that American troops must retake the city. Stilwell's troops included the crack unit known as Merrill's Marauders, which had been supplemented with Chinese and native Burmese troops, but they had already been seriously reduced in number as they fought their way across the mountains. By the time they reached Myitkyina, many of them were extremely ill, and the siege cut them off from supplies. Mountbatten was outraged at Stilwell's willingness to sacrifice his men and once again tried to have him recalled.[57] Stilwell's diaries show concern at the pounding his men were taking, and he had generous words for the Chinese soldiers (the "pings" as he called them, using the normal — and perfectly respectful — Chinese word for "soldier") who had tracked down and liquidated Japanese soldiers attempting to enter the town. But he also found time to complain about an edition of the *Saturday Evening Post* that had been flown in. "The one man of genius in Asia is Chennault," he fumed ironically, referring to the paper's judgment on his great rival; Stilwell was "just a dumb bastard" (Stilwell's words, not those of the *Post*). Even in the midst of a hellish siege, Stilwell was concerned about his press.[58] He also found time to vent his scorn at Mountbatten, writing that "he had the nerve to make a speech at our headquarters but he don't fool our GIs much. They are getting a look at the British Empah with its pants down and the aspect is not so pretty."[59]

Yet in that same week it was the British troops so despised by Stilwell who turned the tide in Burma with a hard-won victory at Imphal on June 22. Lieutenant General Slim's armies were known for their pitiless treatment of any Japanese they might find in their advance: the enemy was to be killed, not captured. Some 80,000 Japanese died during the recapture of Burma.[60] Stilwell's troops, American, Chinese, and Kachin, advanced from the north, inflicting further destruction on the Japanese. By August 3 they knew that they were beaten. The monsoon was coming, and they retreated, leaving Myitkyina to Stilwell's men. Of those troops who had started out with Stilwell, during the three months of the siege, four out of every five had been wounded or died.[61]

The tide had turned in Burma, though far less of the credit was due to Stilwell than the American press made out. Gauss was scathing about Nationalist failings, but also made another sharp point. Informed critics, he observed, were arguing that "we have not supplied the Chinese armies with arms; that the excursion into northern Burma was a mistake;

and that the forces on the Salween which we did equip should have been assigned to the eastern front."[62] He did not need to point out that these decisions had not been Chiang's, but Stilwell's, backed by the SEAC commanders. The eventual victory had come at the same time that the Nationalists were paying a terrible price in east China. On August 8, just five days after the siege in Myitkyina was lifted, the siege of Hengyang ended with the fall of the city. The poor performance of troops in the Henan offensive showed that more troops might not have reversed the Japanese onslaught. But the Ichigô offensive — which Chiang had warned about, only to be discounted by Allied intelligence — was surely even more brutal because of the lack of the higher-quality Chinese troops that the Japanese faced in Burma. Stilwell had gotten his road and his revenge. Yet it would be December before the legacy of his obsessive project finally came to fruition. The Ledo Road from Assam had been connected to the Burma Road at Lashio, allowing supplies to move overland again from India to China. In the month of July 1945 some 5,900 tons of supplies were moved along the road. But by this stage the amounts of freight carried on the Hump flights dwarfed what the road could carry.[63] Had the war lasted longer, of course, the road might have played a more significant role. The Ledo Road was renamed the Stilwell Road by Chiang Kai-shek, ostensibly as a tribute to the American's determination in having it built, but perhaps with the implication that such a folly should bear the name of its author. By the time the road was any use, Stilwell himself had met a fate that he could not foresee as he fought in the jungles of Burma in the sweltering summer of 1944.

The road is known as Stilwell's to this day. Huang Yaowu, just sixteen years old, gave a thought to those whose names would never be remembered. "I was very upset about my comrades who had sacrificed themselves. They had all come from Guangdong, and now they were no more." He continued: "War is like this. Victory is hard to achieve, and once they are sacrificed, they are not even buried, because the advancing troops have no time to do it. Their bodies will be eaten by insects in half a day, and their families will never be notified or compensated."

Huang's blood brothers, with whom he swore that oath in the mountains, and whose bones still lie in the forests of north Burma, might at least have hoped that their deaths would be remembered by a grateful country. But fate had dealt them one more cruel blow. They had fought with the

Nationalist Sixth Army, not the Communist Eighth Route or New Fourth Army, and within a few years they would be written out of the record in Mao's China. "Really, later history has forgotten them," Huang admitted many years later. "In my heart, they are martyrs who died for the motherland. They died for a good cause. But who remembers them now?"[64]

Chapter 18

SHOWDOWN WITH STILWELL

O N SEPTEMBER 19, 1944, a car drew up at Huangshan, the mountain retreat of Chiang Kai-shek and Song Meiling near Chongqing. Out of the vehicle stepped General Joseph Stilwell, in a state of high excitement, with a message from President Roosevelt in his hand.

Stilwell knew that the note was explosive. "Mark this day in red on the calendar of life," he gloated in his diary. "At last, at long last, F.D.R. has finally spoken plain words, and plenty of them, with a firecracker in every sentence."[1] At Huangshan a meeting was in progress between Chiang, Roosevelt's personal emissary to Chongqing, Patrick J. Hurley, and senior officials including T. V. Soong, now back in favor, and the minister of war, He Yingqin. Stilwell called Hurley out of the meeting and showed him the message, saying that he had been ordered to deliver it to Chiang in person.

Hurley urged caution. The very same meeting from which he had been called was working out the new parameters of Stilwell's responsibilities, as laid out in Roosevelt's message. Reinforcements were going to be sent to Burma and Stilwell was to be made commander in chief. "Joe, you have won this ball game," pleaded Hurley. If Stilwell delivered the message directly, he risked permanently damaging Chinese-American relations, potentially for generations to come.[2]

That moment in September came after one of the worst years in the already wrenching Chinese war experience. That autumn, Japan's Ichigô campaign was still driving a deadly path through central China, yet many of Chiang's best troops remained in Burma. After the fall of Hengyang in August 1944, Chiang was in the depths of despair. The current disastrous situation, he wrote, was caused "not by [Japan] but by our Allies." By now, he was convinced that "Roosevelt has already determined that he *has* to overthrow me." Assailed by Sun Fo and the CCP, Chiang wallowed in self-pity. "The evil forces of the whole world are uniting to oppress and insult me," he spat. "It's like hell has opened up to swallow me."[3]

In private, Chiang contemplated taking a very bold step. "If it's necessary at last," he wrote, "I should prepare to resign my military and political positions." To do so would force the Americans' hand. "Roosevelt thinks I can't and don't want to resign, so he oppresses me without any concern . . . He wants to use Chinese troops to make war, otherwise he'd have to send over a million American troops to East Asia to sacrifice themselves." Chiang mulled over the possible responses to the pressure that he felt Roosevelt was placing on him. At this point some 27,739 US troops were stationed in China, of whom 17,723 were Army Air Force troops.[4] Roosevelt might take the opportunity to brush Chiang aside. On the other hand, it was possible that his "resignation might be a disadvantage to the US war effort against Japan, so they would have to change their attitude toward me," and cease to insult Chiang and China. Or the US might sit by while a "puppet" such as Sun Fo was placed in office. Then, as the military and political situation worsened, the Americans would call on Chiang again, as "they would have no choice but me," and would deal with him with a new sincerity.[5] Two days later, Chiang decided that resignation was not an option: "it's too dangerous for the country." He reflected on the many problems that might flow from his departure, from Sun Fo's supposed closeness to the USSR to the threat of provincial militarists uniting with the CCP and the Japanese against the National Government, and the CCP contaminating the nation's youth and education system with their thinking.[6]

This appeared a self-serving (if private) decision, but Chiang's threat was not an idle one. He had resigned before, most notably at the height of the Manchurian crisis in winter 1931. On that occasion, Sun Fo had indeed taken over as premier, only to find that none of the Nationalist factions, whether their power lay with the military or finance, would accept his rule. Chiang was back in power by the start of 1932, and Chinese politics had learned that Chiang was the indispensable man who could hold the country together. If Roosevelt was now flirting with Sun Fo, then perhaps he needed to be taught the same lesson.

But in 1944 the situation was very different from 1932. Sun Fo was still not a credible alternative, nor were the Americans as close to him as Chiang imagined, but the same was not true of the CCP. On August 31, the same day that Chiang decided against resignation, the American ambassador, Clarence Gauss, met him to discuss the need for compromise between the Nationalists and the Communists. Chiang "did not seem to realize that time is on the side of the Chinese Communists," Gauss wrote later, nor that the "Government's influence and control in Free China is deteriorating if not yet disintegrating." Gauss suggested that the solution might be some kind of cross-party war council, but Chiang had given the idea no more than polite acknowledgment.[7]

Actually, Chiang understood the agenda very well. All of this drove him into an even greater rage:

> Pressure has become greater every day, both internally and from abroad. The psychological pressure from the Americans is especially great. They're hoping to force me to cooperate unconditionally with the Communists, hoping I'll accept Stilwell . . . This is imperialism fully-exposed.[8]

Stilwell was unquestionably winning the war for Washington's ear. He made it clear that he regarded the critical situation in Burma as having been caused by Chiang's unwillingness to offer him further support. On September 7 Hurley had arrived at Chongqing to firm up details of the new structure under which Stilwell would be given operational command of all Chinese troops, including (supposedly) the Communists. Just over a week later, Chiang and Stilwell confronted each other once again at a meeting called by the former. Stilwell had returned from Guilin, a city on the edge of collapse in the face of Japanese invasion, and in his diary he made no secret of the fact that he considered Chiang responsible: "Disaster approaching at Kweilin [Guilin] . . . what they ought to do is shoot the G-mo and Ho [Minister of War He Yingqin] and the rest of the gang."[9] Now Chiang asked for the X Force in northeast Burma at Myitkyina to move further east and relieve the village of Longling. Stilwell refused, insisting that the troops needed to rest, but Chiang declared that unless the troops moved within a week he would have to withdraw the Y Force from Burma and use it to defend Kunming, the capital of Yunnan. "Crap and nonsense" was Stilwell's verdict.[10] Following this confrontation, on September 15, Gauss came to see Chiang to press again for a broadening of the leadership to include members of the other parties. Chiang was angered at the request.[11] However, the pressure was about to mount yet further.

On September 16 Roosevelt and Churchill were at the second Quebec Conference ("Octagon") discussing major decisions about the European front, including the establishment of occupation zones in Germany after the defeat of Hitler's regime. The president's mind was on other matters when he received Stilwell's complaint, passed on by George Marshall, that Chiang was refusing to provide relief for the troops in Burma. (The fact that Chiang had sent the 200th Division and 10,000 fresh troops was not mentioned.)[12] Roosevelt's reaction, understandably, was fear that a disaster might be about to happen in Burma, a particularly unattractive prospect just a few weeks before the presidential election. Marshall's staff now drafted a note, to be signed off by the president, to express his deep concern at the turn of events in Burma (at least as they had been reported). This note demanded that not only should Chiang not withdraw his troops from north Burma, but that he should send yet more reinforcements to back them up. Roosevelt declared that if Chiang cooperated with Stilwell and Mountbatten, then "the land line to China will be opened in early 1945 and the continued resistance of China and maintenance of your control will be assured." But if Chiang did not provide ground support for the Burma offensive, then land communications with Free China would be cut off. The warning became starker: "For this you must yourself be prepared to accept the consequences and assume the personal responsibility." Roosevelt's tone was firm: "I have urged time and time again in recent months that you take drastic action to resist the disaster which had been moving closer to China and to you." One demand, above all, was made clear: to place "General Stilwell in unrestricted command of all your forces."[13] The note was perhaps the most uncompromising that had even been written to Chiang.

This was the message that Stilwell insisted on delivering in person that September day in 1944. The irony was that Chiang was about to concede all of Stilwell's key demands: the command of the Chinese armies was to be handed over to a foreigner. There was therefore no need for the note —written in such hard, indeed offensive, terms toward a fellow head of state—to be delivered verbatim. Yet Stilwell insisted. Hurley attempted to soften the blow by asking that Chiang read the Chinese translation, which later turned out to have been even more blunt than the original. Chiang read the note and said simply "I understand," while appearing nervous. Then he turned his teacup upside down. The gesture indicated that the meeting was over, and with it, any chance whatsoever of continued cooperation with Stilwell, or of the American being placed in command of the millions of men who made up the armed forces of the Republic of China.[14]

The delivery of Roosevelt's note was a watershed. For this short moment of satisfaction, Stilwell would pay a very heavy price. US-China relations for the next quarter century would pay an even heavier one. Arguably they are still paying some of that price today.

Chiang showed no emotion when Stilwell presented him with the letter, but once he was alone with his brother-in-law T. V. Soong, he burst into tears, and raged that the letter was the product of Stilwell's actions. It was a fair accusation, since Roosevelt and Marshall had believed Stilwell's implication that it had been Chiang's refusal of support that had worsened the Burma situation. Soong called up Joseph Alsop, the American journalist who was close to both Soong and Chennault, and asked him for help in drafting a response. The letter to Roosevelt made it clear that Stilwell was no longer welcome in China. Yet Chiang delayed sending it, and meanwhile took pains to strengthen the southwestern front in Guangxi, persuading General Bai Chongxi to accept command in the Fourth and Ninth War Zones.[15] Meanwhile Stilwell gloated, sending his wife a letter containing a five-verse piece of doggerel. The first stanza gives the flavor of the acid whole:

> I have waited long for vengeance —
> At last I've had my chance
> I've looked the Peanut in the eye
> And kicked him in the pants.[16]

The relationship between America and China had now become poisoned almost beyond recognition. In the eyes of many Americans, Chiang's government was an ungrateful, corrupt state of secondary importance, a distraction at a time when the most important campaign of the Western European Theater — Overlord — had started. A diplomat at the US Embassy sent a dispirited assessment from Xi'an in October 1944: of the many American servicemen to whom he had spoken, "almost all [were] adversely and often bitterly critical of China and the Chinese." Among the sights that had shocked them were corruption (including wives of high officials buying gasoline originally supplied under Lend-Lease agreements) and collaboration (as suspected spies for the Japanese were released without being properly questioned). The diplomat did admit that these views were combined with a more general dislike of the "dirt, disease, and squalor" of Chinese towns, and habits such as spitting in the street. He observed that many of the servicemen also admitted they had lost their sympathy for the Indian cause, having served in India itself and seen its realities close up.[17] Rice reflected with some prescience that, just as Americans who had occupied Germany after the Great War were sometimes more sympathetic to the Germans than to their own allies, the French, so Americans garrisoning a postwar Japan might find themselves comparing it favorably to China. "Certainly," he wrote, "it will influence American public opinion in the postwar period."[18]

Yet at the same time the Chinese leadership had begun to regard the Americans as a burdensome presence, an ever-increasing number of troops who were not fighting within China, but who also refused to adapt to the reality that China was a state under siege. The US had begun to build up its military presence within China, as it was anticipated that at some stage, when the Nazis had been defeated, American ground troops would be needed there. Some 10,600 US soldiers were now based in Kunming, the capital of Yunnan province. In early 1944 War Minister He Yingqin cabled Yunnan governor Long Yun to ask him to increase the supply of beef for the American troops both in his own province and in India. Long Yun replied that "the American army in Kunming have been here over a year, and consume huge amounts." He went on:

> Since spring 1943, every single day the Americans have needed nearly thirty oxen every day, over 1,000 chickens, and several thousand eggs, not even counting pigs and sheep. The oxen that plough the fields have all been bought up. It's been a huge and surprising expense . . . not only can we not supply India, but even supplying Yunnan will be a real problem.[19]

Chiang himself intervened on the question later in the year, stressing that the Americans needed a much more meat-based diet than the Chinese to maintain their fighting capacity. Long Yun continued to point out that by requisitioning so many oxen for beef, there would be fewer left to till the land, which was essential if grain supplies were to be maintained. Nor could the supply of meat be supplemented with pigs and chickens; these animals were only raised in individual households, not on an industrial scale, and it would be very difficult to buy more of them.[20] It was not un-reasonable that the Americans wanted to give their troops a familiar diet that would keep morale high; but the cost to China was rarely acknowledged. In January 1945 there were 32,956 US soldiers in China, a number that had risen to 60,369 by August; over the period from November 1944 to May 1945 the cost of the (as yet noncombatant) American presence soared from 1 billion to 20 billion yuan per month.[21]

Chiang may have been particularly irked to have to send messages about beef supplies for the Americans at a moment when he and his state were fighting for survival in the face of a Japanese onslaught. He believed that the Western Allies were once again dismissing his priorities, and those of China, to preserve their own interests. By forcing Chinese troops to participate in the Ledo Road campaign, the Allies had distracted attention from the real threat: the massive incursions into central China that came with Ichigô. Chiang was not overconfident that Stilwell's recall would shore up his position: "Even if [the US] gives way now on the recall of Stilwell, they will still . . . hope to overthrow me."[22] The American general seemed oblivious to the damage that he had caused. He set to work on a plan for Communist troops to be brought into an overall national command structure in which they would report to Chiang through him. In return the CCP would receive five divisions' worth of equipment and supplies, and the right to deploy troops north of the Yellow River.[23]

But Chiang insisted that Stilwell must go. On September 25 his official request for the general's recall was transmitted to Washington.[24] On October 5 Roosevelt and Chiang had one of the frankest exchanges in their relationship, unusual for these two politicians who specialized in trying to avoid verbal confrontation rather than invite it. (Roosevelt's words were in fact written for him by Marshall.) "I must state my surprise and regret at the reversal of your agreement of August 12th to accept Stilwell for the command of all forces in China," wrote Roosevelt. The president warned that he felt the situation in China, post-Ichigô, had become so dangerous that he would rather keep the United States out of any command structure on the ground at all. But because the maintenance of Hump tonnage was so important, the situation demanded that "Stilwell be placed in direct command under you of the Chinese forces in Burma and of all Chinese ground forces in Yunnan Province." Roosevelt did concede that Stilwell should not remain Chiang's chief of staff or have direct authority over Lend-Lease. (Chiang was well aware that Stilwell's control of Lend-Lease explained why so little of it was available to the Chinese during Ichigô.) But Roosevelt ended on a note of warning: "I feel that should we remove Stilwell from the Burma campaign the results would be far more serious than you apparently realize."[25]

Stilwell himself knew that his recall was in the air. By now his comments on Chiang Kai-shek seemed to imply that there was almost no chance of the two of them cooperating: Chiang, in Stilwell's view, was "responsible for the major disasters of the war," had "spoken contemptuously of American efforts," and "will not make an effort to fight seriously." Stilwell was also disgusted by Roosevelt, who he felt had not backed him up: "F.D.R. proceeds to cut my throat and throw me out . . . They just can't hurt me. To hell with them."[26] Then on October 7 Stilwell had sight of Roosevelt's message to Chiang, which he thought "rather encouraging." He was particularly pleased about the comment recommending against removing him from Burma ("a stiff one on the end," as he described this parting shot).[27]

Chiang did not share Stilwell's assessment of the message from the American president. He sent back his reply through Hurley. Chiang was still willing to give command to an American officer, but it had to be "one in whom I can repose confidence, and must be capable of frank and sincere cooperation." Chiang was unequivocal: "General Stilwell has shown himself conspicuously lacking in those all-important qualifications." He concluded by making his request crystal clear: Chiang wanted Stilwell recalled, immediately.

There was a sting in the tail. Chiang had given Hurley a more informal note which was supposed to make his justifications—in particular, Chiang's lack of trust in Stilwell's military judgment—clearer to Roosevelt. "General Stilwell and I have never agreed about the Burma campaign," Chiang declared. He understood the importance of reopening land communication across Burma. But he was adamant that it could only be achieved with amphibious support in the south of Burma, as had been proposed at Cairo, and then reversed after Teheran. "A limited offensive in north Burma" alone would be "more costly than could be justified by the results and might even be exceedingly dangerous." When Stilwell had proposed just such an offensive in the summer of 1944, and Chiang had demurred, Stilwell had suggested that "China would be suspected of wishing to withhold any real contribution to the Allied cause." So Chiang had in the end consented, letting troops trained at Ramgarh in Bihar province, eastern Burma, be used in the campaign for the Ledo Road. Stilwell had then demanded that more Chinese reserves be sent into Burma, and had commandeered Hump tonnage to use there.

In Chiang's view, these actions had a direct consequence: "the Japanese took advantage of the opportunity thus offered to launch an offensive within China attacking first in Honan [i.e., Henan] and then in Hunan." The Burma campaign had sucked away both men and supplies. Stilwell had displayed "complete indifference," despite the fact that the National-ist armies in east China faced six times the number of forces that Stil-well had to cope with in Burma. Chiang's most pointed accusation was that Stilwell had refused to release Lend-Lease supplies even when they were readily available in Yunnan. Chiang argued that only a minuscule number of arms had been released for China's use: "60 mountain guns, 320 antitank rifles, and 506 bazookas." As a result, he declared, "we have taken Myitkyina, but we have lost almost all of east China, and in this, General Stilwell cannot be absolved of grave responsibility." Chiang went on to express dismay at the implications of the message from Roosevelt that Stilwell had rudely delivered. He rejected the idea that China was in danger of fundamental collapse, and found it objectionable that Roo-sevelt should suggest withdrawal of aid from China precisely *because* it was in trouble. Hurley forwarded the note with his own, blunt comment: "Chiang Kai-shek and Stilwell are fundamentally incompatible. Today you are confronted with a choice between Chiang Kai-shek and Stilwell." Adding that there was no other Chinese leader who could offer what Chiang could, it was clear what choice he thought Roosevelt should make.[28]

"THE AX FALLS," Stilwell wrote on October 19. "I am 'recalled.'" The next day, at 5:00 p.m., Stilwell had one final meeting with the "Peanut." Both sides mouthed the necessary hypocrisies: Chiang claimed that he regretted everything that had happened, and Stilwell asked him to re-member that he had only ever acted for "China's good." Chiang offered Stilwell the Grand Cordon of the Blue Sky and White Sun, the highest honor that China could offer a foreigner: Stilwell declined it ("Told him to stick it up his ___!").[29] Four days later, on October 24, Stilwell took off for Delhi. He would never again set foot in China.[30]

The bad blood between Chiang Kai-shek and Joseph Stilwell was the most colorful and ultimately the most public face of Sino-American dis-cord during the wartime alliance. But it was only part of a series of mis-understandings that dogged the war in China, from turf wars over intel-ligence to arguments over financial assistance and troop commitments. The personal clash between Stilwell and Chiang was important, but it should not distract attention from the wider strategic decision that Marshall and the other Allied leaders had made at the start of the war: China was not going to be a major theater of war in the Allied effort.[31] This was perfectly understandable, but it could hardly be expected that the Chinese should consider themselves expendable. By creating a fiction that Chiang had to fight to show his value to the alliance, the Allies allowed the relationship between the US and China to erode. Rather than trying repeatedly to take Burma, a target of dubious value, it would have been perfectly reasonable to let Chiang use his limited resources to defend China, even if, in publicity terms, it appeared that China was not playing an active role in the wider war effort. It would also have been better, had Winston Churchill been willing, to use Chiang more as a credible envoy to other non-European peoples, a genuine symbol of nationalist nonwhite resistance who could have challenged Japanese pan-Asianism and communism alike. Instead, Chiang's regime was made complicit in thankless and overly ambitious goals, giving the impression that China's own aims and priorities always had to give way to those of the Western Allies and the USSR. The seeds were sown for mistrust between the US and China that would continue after the eventual Communist victory in 1949. Even today, the state of US-China relations shows that those wounds are a long way from being healed.

Meanwhile, the Japanese Ichigô advance continued to drive onward through south-central China. The atmosphere in the Nationalist zone became feverish as the prospect of a Japanese victory seemed suddenly more likely. In Guilin in November 1944 Graham Peck sensed a shrill hysteria. The city was like "a floating amusement park, adrift in a stormy sea," populated by swarms of refugees. The railway station was full to bursting with people fleeing the city, running from the oncoming Japanese assault as fast they could be transported further west.[32] The city fell on November 24, and the Japanese onslaught moved yet another step closer to Chongqing. The war that had turned into stalemate might suddenly be resolved with violent swiftness.

Chapter 19

UNEXPECTED VICTORY

U NLIKE F.D.R.'S PREVIOUS THREE campaigns, the result of the 1944 presidential election was hard to predict. A dynamic reforming Republican governor, Thomas E. Dewey of New York, seemed to have a plausible chance of deposing the aging and ailing president. Now the Stilwell crisis had contributed to the already feverish atmosphere around the election. By having to recall Stilwell, American policymakers in China seemed to be at the beck and call of an ally who —thanks in part to "Vinegar Joe's" supporters in the press—was now considered an unworthy partner for the United States. Brooks Atkinson of the *New York Times* returned from China ready to report the story. He had already composed his text by the time he evaded military censorship on a stopover at Cairo, keeping his draft in his jacket pocket while his bags were searched. Even back home in the US his story was stopped by censors once again, until on October 31 Roosevelt personally approved the lifting of the ban on the story. Atkinson's article was devastating. It suggested that Stilwell's recall was "the political triumph of a moribund anti-democratic regime," and described Chiang Kai-shek as running a government that was "unenlightened, cold-hearted," and "autocratic." Above all, the article accused Chiang of a "basic unwillingness" to fight the Japanese.[1]

Roosevelt had calculated correctly that the story would reflect badly on Chiang, rather than on the president's American advisers. On November 7 the president was reelected by 432 electoral college votes to Dewey's 99. Although Roosevelt won the popular vote by only 2 million votes, it was still a comfortable mandate, and he had a new vice president, Harry S. Truman, at his side. (Henry Wallace had been dumped after Democratic Party power brokers made it clear that they regarded him as a leftist eccentric who was unfit for the presidency.) China was clearly not the decisive issue; the world war in Europe and the Pacific was occupying the minds of the public much more. The Stilwell crisis had not turned the tide further against Roosevelt. Nonetheless, the relationship of the United States with Chiang Kai-shek's government had now reached a new low.

Then, unexpectedly, relations between Chongqing and Washington got a boost. As it turned out, the new warmth would have its own dangers. But for a short period, it looked as if the recall of Stilwell and the reelection of Roosevelt might just have lanced the boil that had aggravated the US-China partnership.

Most important of all in changing the temperature was the sudden halt in December of the Ichigô advance (although it did not end formally until February 1945). Ichigô marked the furthest penetration of Japanese troops into Chinese territory during the entire war, putting the enemy in control of even more territory than they had held in summer 1938, when Japan had thrust so deep into central China. Nonetheless, the campaign failed to achieve most of its long-term aims. Although it did place the US air bases near Guilin out of use, these were simply relocated further inland. More importantly, the American capture of Saipan in the Pacific meant that there was another site outside China from which the US could bomb the Japanese home islands, a campaign which included the fierce firebombing of Tokyo in 1944–1945. And while Ichigô did open up the link between French Indochina (under Vichy control) and central and north China, the ragged state of the Japanese army on the Chinese mainland by early 1945 made the connection of little use.[2] Some 23,000 Japanese troops were lost during the campaign.[3] Yet while Ichigô failed to help the Japanese gain outright victory, it also crippled the Nationalists. The great breadbasket and recruitment provinces of Henan and Hunan were lost, and the campaign cost the Nationalists a further 750,000 casualties.[4]

The halting of Japanese forces was something Chiang Kai-shek could cling to at the start of 1945, and he also found other grounds for cautious optimism. Chiang took Stilwell's recall as a sign that America was "sincere" about helping China: "This is the greatest comfort for me in the new year." He was still concerned about American attempts to arm militarist rivals such as Xue Yue and Long Yun, but told himself that the American attitude was "completely different" from the type of imperialism advocated by the British.[5] Chiang was still persuaded that the US wanted to raise China's status in the world, whereas the British had no intention of taking the country seriously in any postwar settlement.

Stilwell had left without waiting to brief his successor, General Albert Wedemeyer, nor had he left behind much in the way of paperwork ("Stilwell kept it all in his hip pocket," observed one cynical veteran.)[6] Wedemeyer was impressed by Chiang Kai-shek, but shocked by the state of the overall military command in China. Chiang also balked at the discovery that Wedemeyer intended to continue Stilwell's policy of controlling Lend-Lease supplies. "It's clear US policy hasn't changed at all," he wrote. "This makes my heart bitter."[7] Chiang remained convinced that the US was attempting to arm rival militarists, "distributing weapons as a bait, so the military will worship foreigners and disobey orders."[8] After his humiliation at Stilwell's hands, Chiang was now ready to be suspicious at the slightest sign of disrespect from his allies.

Chiang's rivals might have been surprised to know of his anger at the United States. Ambassador Clarence Gauss, whose increasingly despairing messages back to Washington showed his lack of confidence about the situation in China, resigned shortly after Stilwell's recall, and Patrick Hurley was promoted from presidential envoy to full ambassador. Hurley's arrival in post ended the policy of warmth toward the Communists advocated by John Service and supported at least tacitly by Gauss, and strengthened Chiang's hand. Chiang had never had a clear understanding of the way that public opinion worked in a democracy. (That was his wife Song Meiling's specialty, hence her assiduous courting of the American press and public.) Chiang also failed to understand how damaging the recall of Stilwell had been for his cause in the United States. Unfortunately, Hurley lacked the analytical abilities of his predecessors, and their experience of China. Whereas Gauss tended to think the worst of Chiang, Hurley thought the best, and not always to Chiang's benefit. An Oklahoma oilman with a rambunctious manner, Hurley was known for his careless mangling of Chinese names, at first referring to the generalissimo as "Mr. Shek" and the Communist leader as "Moose Dung." Hurley had excessive confidence in Chiang's ability to unite China, and did not understand that the Communists were serious contenders for power. And understanding this immensely complex and delicate political situation was now critical to avoiding a civil war between the Nationalists and Communists.

Chiang was worried about the intentions of the CCP, and with good reason. The waning of his power had been matched by a steady growth in Mao's. With party membership of over a million people, and some 900,000 regular troops supplemented by a similar number of militia troops, the Communists would clearly be a major force in the postwar order. Yet at this point, all Chinese parties assumed that the war against

Japan would continue for at least one or two more years. This created a dilemma for Mao as to how best to orient his party toward the new world. The Communists had to be seen to support the war effort against Japan. To move openly against Chiang would rob them of the moral high ground from which they could accuse him of emphasizing the fight against the Communists over the war against Japan. (This accusation remained powerful even though Nationalist troops were fighting the Japanese in both the Ichigô assault and in Burma, and the CCP had contributed to neither of these campaigns.) On the other hand, Mao was determined that "this time, we must take over China."[9] The party debated how far it could exploit the opportunities afforded by Ichigô. With the Nationalists on the back foot, and the Japanese close to exhaustion, might there be an opportunity for the Communists to place themselves in a better position for the postwar conflict, now surely just a year or so away? Mao advocated caution, noting that "our party is not yet sufficiently strong, not yet sufficiently united or consolidated," a warning that the party should not try to occupy areas where its power was not completely assured. It still expanded cautiously into areas where the Nationalists had retreated, although implementation of its social policies was patchy.[10]

The Dixie Mission had been one crucial part of the strategy, an attempt to create a new warmth with the US, and to persuade its American contacts that the CCP could provide behind-the-lines assistance for an American invasion of the Chinese coast. But the fallout from Stilwell's recall in October 1944 now changed the relationship between Chiang and the Americans. Until autumn 1944 both the then American chief of staff (Stilwell) and the US ambassador (Gauss) had been hostile to Chiang, and although they did not sympathize with the aims of the Communists, they had admired aspects of what they knew about the party. But Stilwell's replacement, Wedemeyer, was much less abrasive in his dealings with Chiang, and Hurley, who took over from Gauss, strongly favored him, putting him in the position both of holding the ring between the parties as well as advocating Chiang's viewpoint.

Hurley did start well. On November 7, 1944, against Chiang's wishes, the new ambassador made his own journey to Dixie. When his flight touched down at Yan'an, he emerged at the top of the aircraft steps and disconcerted the waiting welcome party, including Mao Zedong, by giving a Choctaw war cry (a nod to his Oklahoma heritage). Peter Vladimirov, the Soviet agent sent to Mao's base area at Yan'an, was impressed by the way that Hurley handled himself in discussions with the CCP's top leaders: "Well groomed and self confident," he allowed, although adding (perhaps thinking of the war cry) "slightly eccentric manners."[11] The negotiations were lively and the two sides came up with a five-point plan that would allow the Communists to enter a coalition government under Chiang Kai-shek's leadership, while retaining their own armed forces. However, when Hurley returned to Chongqing, Chiang turned the proposal down flat. Unless the CCP placed its troops directly under Nationalist command, there would be no place for it in a new government.

Hurley reversed course and insisted on the generalissimo's preferred option: the CCP must merge its forces with the Nationalist military before entering a coalition.[12] Accusations flew back and forth. Chiang "had the audacity to say that the Chinese Communist Party must hand over its troops before he would bestow 'legal status' upon it," Mao scoffed.[13] Hurley, for his part, made his view clear in a telegram to acting secretary of state Edward Stettinius (who had taken over from a weary Cordell Hull in December 1944): "In all my negotiations with the Communists, I have insisted that the United States will not supply or otherwise aid the Chinese Communists as a political party or as an insurrection against the National Government." Other officers disagreed strongly: Service argued that "as we did in the case of Yugoslavia," the Americans should simply tell Chiang that they would arm any forces that were anti-Japanese.[14] Late in the previous year, Service had sent a telegram to Stilwell declaring "The Kuomintang [Nationalist Party] is dependent on American support for survival. But we are in no way dependent on the Kuomintang," adding that "we need feel no ties of gratitude to Chiang."[15] Even in a private telegram, this was an astounding thing to say of a regime that had been resisting Japan for over seven years. At least one group within the US wartime intelligence agency, the Office of Strategic Services (OSS), also advocated the establishment of "a major intelligence organization in North China based at . . . Yenan, and operating through four main forward bases in 8th Route Army or guerrilla areas in Shansi, Hopei, Shantung, and Jehol, with seventeen advanced teams, and a large number of native agents."[16] This level of recognition from the Americans would have raised the status of the Communists to an even higher level.

In March 1945 Service reported on a conversation with Mao in which the Communist leader made it clear that he thought that America was making a foolish move by backing Chiang. The CCP, Mao claimed, was the only party that truly represented the interests of the peasantry, the largest section of the country's population. Stressing again the goodwill that Hurley had earned with his "five points," Mao complained, "We don't understand why America's policy seemed to waver after a good start."[17]

Neither Hurley's nor Service's analysis was wholly wrong. It was true, as Hurley had it, that if the CCP did not merge its forces with the Nationalists, then it would use those forces to launch an attack on them. It was also true, as Service had it, that Chiang was desperate for the Communists not to be seen as an independent power base, even if it would aid the anti-Japanese cause. But both American viewpoints, widely differing though they were, understandably assumed that the best policy was the one that helped defeat Japan as fast as possible. This was, of course, by far the best outcome for the war-weary Allies as a whole. The price for China, however, might well be the swift outbreak of civil war. At the heart of the problem was a stubborn fact that the Americans could not or would not see. Neither Chinese side was sincere about a coalition government for its own sake. Both Chiang and Mao saw it as a temporary arrangement while their parties prepared to vie for absolute power.

But Chiang and Mao were not the only ones weighing up the new realities of power in China. In Nanjing, Zhou Fohai was also trying to protect himself. Throughout 1944 Wang Jingwei's health had been failing. From the very start of the Nanjing government's life, Wang had been a forlorn and faded figure, with Zhou, Chen Gongbo, and others bearing most of the burden. On realizing how hollow Japan's promises of autonomy for the regime had been, Wang seems simply to have lost heart, and by the end of his time in office he was little more than a figurehead. Along with psychological despondency, Wang's physical ailments also came back to haunt him. He had never really recovered from the assassination attempt in 1935, and in March of 1944 he was flown to Japan and was confined in the Imperial University hospital at Nagoya, where he became almost entirely bedridden. Zhou flew to Japan to see him in August. Wang was shockingly gaunt, but able to express his wish that Zhou and Chen Gongbo should take over the government in Nanjing. Chen Bijun, Wang's loyal wife, made clear her fury at the thought of her rivals achieving ascendancy.[18]

On November 10 Wang died of complications from pneumonia. Zhou Fohai was told the news the next day through the Japanese Embassy in

Nanjing. "When I think about our journey together from Kunming to Hanoi, I can't help but be sad," he wrote. "Human affairs are not consistent."[19] Wang's remains were flown back to Nanjing. In death he finally achieved what he had tried to do in life: he was reunited with Sun Yat-sen. A huge new mausoleum was built on top of the Purple and Gold Mountain just outside Nanjing, and Wang's body was laid to rest just a short distance away from the last resting place of his old political master. Wang's political journey had seen him move huge distances both politically—from radical revolutionary to collaborator with the Japanese—and geographically—from Nanjing to Europe, Chongqing to Hanoi to Nanjing again, and then Japan before coming to rest once more in Nanjing. Fourteen months later, he would be subjected to one final journey.

Chen Gongbo had taken over as acting head of the Reorganized Government. Zhou Fohai, meanwhile, remained fully engaged in his double game. While second-in-command to Chen Gongbo, he was also in constant communication with Dai Li, as they planned for the occupation of eastern China by Allied (US) forces. (By the summer of 1945, over 60,000 US military personnel, including 34,726 air troops and 22,151 ground troops, were present in the China Theater.)[20] Zhou guaranteed that the soldiers of the Reorganized Government would join in alongside the regular American troops, and also that they would reject any alliance with the CCP. Zhou and Gu Zhutong, commander of the Nationalist Third War Zone (in eastern China), engaged in lengthy discussion about securing the coastline from Shanghai to Zhejiang in advance of an Allied invasion.[21] The fraternization between the Nationalists and the Wang regime disconcerted many outside observers. John Paton Davies, for one, wrote of Gu Zhutong in a slightly bewildered fashion: "He is not particularly disloyal—or loyal—he is too busy trading with the Japanese."[22] But Zhou Fohai found a comparison that seemed to make sense to him. On August 21 Zhou observed that the Vichy government had had to relocate in the face of Operation Overlord. "Their situation is similar to ours," he noted, adding "they don't have time to mourn themselves, so we will mourn them." In the last days of the war in Europe, the French collaborationist government would argue that its cooperation with Germany had been a means of protecting France when no outside help was forthcoming: Marshal Pétain would famously claim that when General de Gaulle had been France's "sword," he himself, as the head of the Vichy government, had been France's "shield."[23] Wang's regime had of course used the same argument two years before the Vichy government had even been formed, seeing itself as engaged in the same task as Chongqing but through different means. Zhou saw other worrying parallels with the French situation. The Americans were still stuck in the French countryside outside Paris, and the streets of the capital were filled with Resistance fighters attacking the Germans. "This could happen in Nanjing and Shanghai," Zhou wrote. "We can't imagine how chaotic that would be."[24]

Davies expressed dismay that Chiang's regime was talking to the collaborators. He would have been even more aghast if he had known of another set of even more confidential meetings in the spring of 1945. There is intriguing though still incomplete evidence that the Communists were engaged in talks with the Japanese at a small village in Jiangsu province, in anticipation of a land campaign in eastern China in the coming year. The Japanese proposed that they would not stand in the way of the Communist New Fourth Army or the 700,000-odd troops still under the control of the Nanjing regime, instead concentrating their fire on the Nationalists. It is hard to know how far these talks would have gone. As with Chiang, talking to the Japanese did not equate to surrendering to them, and the CCP should be given the benefit of the doubt as genuine anti-imperialists. Yet the Communists were, like the Nationalists and Wang's regime, keen to make the most of a changing and unpredictable situation.[25]

By the start of 1945 it seemed clear that the Nazi grip on Europe would end within months. Roosevelt, Stalin, and Churchill turned their attention to concluding the war in Asia as swiftly as possible. At Teheran, in November 1943, Stalin had pledged an eventual Soviet entry into the Pacific War when the European tide had turned, and now Roosevelt wanted to make sure that commitment was acted on. Far off in the New Mexico desert, an extraordinary experiment was taking place to develop an atomic bomb. But in early 1945 it was still unclear whether it would work, and the Allies had to make plans for a campaign to conquer Japan that might involve a long and extremely bloody campaign. The fate of much of Europe and Asia was to be decided at a conference that began on February 4, 1945, at Yalta, on the Black Sea, in the Crimea region of the USSR.

Much of the conversation at Yalta was about the fate of postwar Europe, with the division of the Continent into zones under Western and

Soviet influence. But Asia was also a major topic of discussion. The Combined Chiefs of Staff were convinced that victory would not come until mid-1947, and told Roosevelt and Churchill so, increasing the pressure on them to make sure that Stalin would participate in the war in Asia.

However, Stalin's participation came with conditions. He demanded control of the Kurile Islands, an archipelago stretching from the north coast of Japan to Russia's Kamchatka Peninsula, and the southern part of Sakhalin Island, just off Russia's coast. He also asked for a variety of military and transport concessions in Manchuria, as well as the maintenance of Outer Mongolia under de facto Soviet control. (The Nationalists still laid claim to all of Mongolia.) While Chinese sovereignty in Manchuria would be fully acknowledged, Soviet influence in the region would also be confirmed. Stalin wanted the other leaders to agree to these demands without any prior consultation with China. In return, Stalin would pledge to enter the war against Japan no more than ninety days after the end of the war in Europe. The deal was made in a series of secret agreements that supplemented the official record of the conference.[26]

Chiang Kai-shek was not privy to any of the Yalta discussions about China's future, but he had his suspicions. "The influence of this conference on China will be great," he acknowledged. "I hope Roosevelt isn't plotting with Churchill and Stalin against me." When he heard even the public terms of the agreement, Chiang was plunged into gloom, thinking that the world would be thrown back into the same race for dominance that had marked the aftermath of the Great War. "This meeting of the three leaders has already carved the seeds of the Third World War," he wrote. "Roosevelt is still calling this a diplomatic victory — this is really laughable."[27]

Chiang's suspicions were fueled by rumors that there were secret clauses attached to the Yalta agreement. Finally, Roosevelt met the Chinese ambassador to the US, Wei Daoming, and admitted that there were indeed hidden agreements relating to Manchuria; on learning this, Chiang was furious. Meanwhile, Hurley had returned to Washington. He too was concerned at rumors of concessions to the Soviets, and after some delay Roosevelt allowed him to see the details of the Yalta agreements. Hurley was shocked by what he read, as he was by a State Department paper that suggested the Americans might arm the Communists if the former landed on the Chinese coast. Roosevelt supported Hurley's views

on Chiang, although he cautioned him not to say anything in public that
might make the job of reconciliation between the Nationalists and the
Communists harder. But on April 2 Hurley held a press conference in
Washington at which he declared that the United States would recognize
only the National Government and have no further dealings with the
Communists.[28]

Even if Roosevelt had wished to soften the stark position that Hurley
had outlined, he had little chance to do so. The ailing president had used
the last reserves of his energy in fighting the global war, and on April 12,
1945, just ten days after Hurley's announcement, Roosevelt died of a ce-
rebral hemorrhage at his home in Warm Springs, Georgia. As the nation
mourned, Harry S. Truman was sworn in as president. Among the problems the shrewd but underbriefed new commander in chief had to deal
with was the growing crisis in China. For just as American intelligence in
China had been weakened by the turf war between the OSS and Milton
Miles's SACO (Sino-American Cooperative Organization), so differing
voices continued to emerge from the State Department. Hurley clung to
a position of absolute support for Chiang. Service and Davies continued
to speak out in favor of alternatives in case Chiang proved recalcitrant or
just collapsed. In turn, Hurley became more convinced that opposition to
him was personal.[29] These character-driven squabbles would lead to one
of the postwar tragedies in American politics: the sterile debate on "Who
Lost China?"

Although Hurley's declaration of faith in the Nationalists had been
made in public, he still failed to understand that power had shifted within
China and that he might have done better to advise Chiang to form a
coalition government that would allow him room to regroup. Mao denounced the American's move angrily. "For all its high-sounding language," he fumed, "the Hurley-Chiang racket is designed to sacrifice the
interests of the Chinese people, further wreck their unity, and . . . lay a
mine to set off large-scale civil war in China."[30] Throughout the speech
Mao denounced Chiang as "His Majesty," and poured scorn on his ideas
for constitutional renewal through a National Assembly as no better than
the paper-thin parliaments that had been convened during the warlord
era of the 1920s. He added, a couple of days later, that "the policy of the
United States toward China as represented by its ambassador Patrick J.
Hurley is creating a civil war crisis in China."[31]

Mao's confidence was fueled, in part, by a conviction that the entry of the Soviet Union into the war would tilt the balance of power toward the CCP. But the Communist leader underestimated the protean pragmatism of Joseph Stalin. During the Yalta discussions, Roosevelt had ceded to Stalin a restoration of the rights in East Asia that Russia had lost after the 1904–1905 Russo-Japanese War. But Roosevelt secured an assurance that the USSR would not actively support the Communists against the Nationalists. Roosevelt told Chiang about this condition, but Stalin did not tell Mao.[32] The Communist leader was unaware of Stalin's betrayal.

Not that Chiang was happy to trust Stalin's good faith, and as it turned out, with good reason. On April 30 Adolf Hitler killed himself in his bunker under the ruins of Berlin. On May 8, 1945, the war in Europe ended. Now, at last, Asia would be at the center of the conflict, and the USSR would be part of that effort. In early July Chiang sent T. V. Soong, along with his Russian-speaking son Ching-kuo, to Moscow to negotiate terms with Stalin. Stalin agreed to recognize only Chiang as the ruler of China, but made extensive demands in return, including China's recognition of Outer Mongolia's independence and the granting of a privileged status for the USSR in Manchuria. The question of what China would cede to the Soviets was still unresolved when Stalin left for the Allied conference at Potsdam in the middle of the month.

Chiang was angered at Truman's refusal to intervene in the Sino-Soviet negotiations. "This is an insult," he fumed. "I didn't acknowledge Yalta. I didn't take part, I don't have responsibility for it, so why should I carry it out? They really do think that China is their vassal." Echoing his thoughts at the deepest moment of the Stilwell crisis, Chiang brooded: "American diplomacy really has no center, no policy, no morals."[33]

The Ichigô campaign had been just as destructive to Chinese society as it had to its military, creating yet more deprivation and destruction in China's most fertile areas. The efforts in the early war years to create a more integrated system of welfare provision had always become weaker the further one traveled from Chongqing, but by the last year of the war, they seemed a hollow mockery in the face of massive need. To tackle the problem, China engaged with a remarkable new organization: the United Nations Relief and Rehabilitation Agency (UNRRA). Roosevelt had realized that in the areas liberated from the Axis powers, there would be immense misery, and a formally coordinated effort was needed to make provision to feed starving people and enable countries to rebuild their societies. Although some forty-four countries signed UNRRA's founding document at the White House on November 9, 1943, it was always heavily bankrolled by the US and run primarily by American administrators.

The China office was headed by the American Benjamin H. Kizer, who arrived in Chongqing in December 1944. Kizer had been warned repeatedly that it was one of the worst postings possible: hot, hilly, and lacking in any workable transport network. The buildings he was assigned were better than many, however. "On clear days, which are rare at this season," he noted, "they command a fine view of the river and the hills beyond."[34] His personal comfort, however, was of trivial importance in comparison to the task he had been set. And the task was made more difficult from the beginning because the American and Chinese sides had such widely differing interpretations of UNRRA's role.

The crossed wires between the Chinese government and UNRRA were evident in declarations made just a few months after the two sides had begun working with each other. Jiang Tingfu was a distinguished Nationalist figure who had been made head of CNRRA (Chinese National Relief and Rehabilitation Agency), the partner organization that was supposed to coordinate with UNRRA within China's territory. Jiang declared on July 3, 1945, that the success of relief and rehabilitation efforts in Guizhou and Guangxi provinces showed that "China is demonstrating a determination to help herself before aid can reach her from outside." Jiang detailed the way in which the Chinese government agencies were working alongside major NGOs such as the American Red Cross, the Chinese Red Cross, and the Associated Christian Colleges. Overall, Jiang declared, the joint effort was paying "enormous dividends" in "experience and 'know-how' gained."[35] Yet despite the geniality of tone, Jiang was signaling an expectation of much greater provision by UNRRA. He expressed a widely held belief in official Chinese circles that if the US wanted a progressive government to emerge, they should also help pay the price. It was not the fault of the Chinese that their country had been battered into submission in the first place. Kizer, on the other hand, had reason to assume that UNRRA material would feed the maw of a ravenous and corrupt state, and his letters suggest that he was unable to take the Nationalist government entirely seriously. In May 1945, six months after the establishment of the UNRRA China offices, Kizer characterized Jiang as "dragging his feet," an example of how the Chinese side wanted to "do nothing."[36]

However, the Nationalists had good reason to fear that the relief effort might be seen purely as largesse from the US. The blame for the failures of Nationalist provision (most notably the Henan famine) had fallen almost exclusively on the shoulders of Chiang Kai-shek's regime, and corruption and incompetence had played a serious part in causing the disaster. Yet this explanation did not acknowledge that the wider constraints of the war had forced the government to make a series of deeply unappetizing choices. If food relief was now portrayed purely as a piece of American generosity that had no connection with sacrifices made by the ruling party, then Chiang's government might well lose all of its legitimacy, be blamed for what went wrong, and be given no credit for any successes.

The Nationalists did not see themselves as a bankrupt and hollow regime. Chiang's government was still determined to rule over a postwar China very different from the one that had gone to war with Japan in 1937. Many of the party's planners saw the need to create a state where the obligations that government and the people had to one another were greater and more clearly defined. In this they were not alone. Roosevelt's administration passed the G. I. Bill in 1944, providing training and education for returning veterans. In July 1945 the British people voted out the deeply admired wartime leader, Churchill, in favor of a Labour Party government under Clement Attlee with a program of extensive social welfare. One British example was particularly intriguing to some Nationalist planners. The Beveridge Plan, authored by a distinguished Liberal Party politician, had created huge enthusiasm on its publication in 1942, with its advocacy of a welfare state providing full unemployment and health benefits. It was adopted by all the main political parties and heavily influenced Labour's winning election manifesto. Back in Chongqing, bureaucrats thinking about the shape of a postwar China noted with approval the "world-famous Beveridge Report."[37]

Despite Western imputation that the Nationalists were capable of little but corruption and chaos, these proposals were not out of character. From the start of the war, Chiang's technocrats had linked the provision of welfare and refugee relief with the creation of a stronger, more united national body.[38] Health care was part of the agenda of "hygienic modernity" which underpinned the Chinese sense of national identity, stimulated by global initiatives such as the Health Organization of the League of Nations (predecessor of the World Health Organization).[39] The Executive Yuan (the Cabinet-level body) of the government even argued that in time it would seek to provide greater health-care provision for the population, "in which the private and voluntary agencies will be encouraged to play their part."[40] This was clearly something rather less all-encompassing than a postwar European-style socialized health system, although the plans did include ideas such as the provision of health care "free of charge" to those who could not pay.[41] Concerns over health care were linked to a concern to create a modern, rational state in Nationalist China, even in the last desperate year of the war against Japan. Visible, if patchy, programs of vaccination and education for rural women on health-care issues continued all the way up to 1945, along with a seemingly more quixotic-seeming campaign to replace public lavatories in various Sichuan counties.[42] In fact, these were among the more logical campaigns at a time of great financial and political pressure: they were low-cost, dealt with real problems of hygiene (dirty lavatories in the 40-degree Celsius heat of rural Sichuan were a sure recipe for an epidemic), and demonstrated a continued commitment, however flawed, to renewal at the grassroots level.[43]

The Nationalists had always had an interest in projecting the image of a modernizing, active state. However, the issue of social welfare had a particular resonance because it was a response to the Communist challenge. Not only to John Service and Colonel David D. Barrett, commander of the US Army Observation Group that was sent to Yan'an (the "Dixie Mission") but also to millions of Chinese, the Communist system appeared to offer an egalitarian vision in which provision would be made for all. The Nationalists had to make at least some effort to compete. Yet stark reality blocked these good intentions. The basic reason for lack of progress was simple: there was no money. By 1945 the Nationalist government was undeniably riddled with corruption. But the total financial commitment of the Allies to the reconstruction of China was tiny, compared to the actual costs involved.[44] Even if Chiang deserved his nickname of "Cash My Check," others, notably the British Empire and Stalin's Soviet Union, were making much heavier calls on the American bank account. In a private letter James Johnson, American legal counsel to UNRRA, acknowledged the roadblocks standing in the way of the Allies' vision for postwar China:

There is . . . the fundamental problem of China's difficult financial circumstances, which has all the government bureaus operating far below their potential efficiency. The picture of a fully equipped, fully staffed public hospital with virtually no patients is not uncommon, the reason being that there isn't enough money available for the hospital to feed its patients after paying its staff even on a thoroughly inadequate basis. This difficulty has come up over and over again in connection with every conceivable aspect of CNRRA operations and preparatory work.[45]

The investigations of UNRRA also found the war-torn zones of China blighted by famine. In Henan UNRRA detailed cases of starvation that had been made worse by the massive destruction caused by the Ichigô campaign. UNRRA figures suggested that some 70 percent of the population in the province were in dire need in 1945; cases of malaria were reckoned at 130,000, and the number of people starving at over 2 million.[46] The Nationalist aspirations toward social reform — though hampered by financial realities, political disintegration, and corruption — were matched by gestures that seemed to indicate political reform. In April 1945 Chiang called the Sixth Party Congress (May 5–21), the first since 1938. The proposed reforms had a liberal gloss, including a move toward the formalizing of multiple parties in the National Assembly, and for multiparty elections (though at the regional and local rather than national level). The Congress also declared its intention to reduce rents and reform land taxes. There were loud public attacks on the corruption that blighted public life.[47] Clearly the Communist challenge had influenced the Nationalist program. Yet there were signs of something darker in the declaration, too — notably, Chiang's intention to set up committees to oversee (and limit) the democratization process.

The CCP responded in kind with its Seventh Congress, timed to overlap with the Nationalist Sixth Party Congress, from April 23 to June 11, 1945. It had been even longer since the Communists had held their most recent Congress (in Moscow in 1928, in exile from the Nationalist purge), and even the last Plenum had been in 1938. The tone was confident, even aggressive. "Our Communist Party has never been so powerful, the revolutionary base areas have never had so large a population and so large an army," Mao announced on the opening day. And Mao himself was central to the proceedings, officially acknowledged as the paramount party leader. The process that had begun with the Rectification movements now came to its climax. The Congress ended with one of the whimsical tales that Mao liked to tell to leaven his theory-laden language. A foolish old man of ancient legend, Mao began, found that his way forward was blocked by two mountains. So he began to dig away at them. His neighbors mocked him for engaging in such an endless task, but the foolish old man replied that even if he died before completing his task, then his sons and grandsons would carry on. "God was moved by this," said Mao, "and he sent down two angels, who carried away the mountains on their backs." In Mao's atheistic interpretation of the fable, God was none other than "the masses of the Chinese people," who would remove the twin mountains of imperialism and feudalism. With the masses behind them, "why can't these two mountains be cleared away?"[48]

The relationship between the CCP and the Americans had now become more strained. In July, Wedemeyer wrote to Mao to inquire about the fate of four American soldiers and their Chinese interpreters who had accidentally parachuted into Communist territory in May and been placed in "protective custody." The American went on, "In view of our common desire to defeat the Japanese, it is my hope that incidents of this kind will not arise in future," but it was clear that the warmth which had been developing between the two sides had decidedly cooled.[49]

Meanwhile, Allied plans developed for the push against the Japanese. In Potsdam, the leaders concentrated on the settlement for peace in Europe. But the US, Britain, and China also issued a declaration that called for "the unconditional surrender of all Japanese armed forces," warning that "the alternative for Japan is prompt and utter destruction."[50] In China itself, Wedemeyer was drawing on Stilwell's plans to train thirty-nine new divisions of Chinese troops for the recapture of eastern China, although Chiang Kai-shek rejected any suggestion that Stilwell himself might return to China for a land invasion in 1946. In turn, at Marshall's suggestion (prompted by Stilwell in a final act of revenge), General Claire Chennault was also recalled to the US at the end of July.[51] There was anticipation in the air but also a sense of weariness. With peace now settled in Europe, the prospect of a war in Asia that might stretch into 1946 or 1947 was deeply depressing.

For both the Chinese and the Japanese armies were exhausted beyond measure. By the middle of 1945, the Japanese had been driven back from their most important Pacific conquests. From November 1944, American bombers used the recaptured island of Saipan as their base for increasingly ferocious attacks on the Japanese home islands. From spring 1945, their payload included incendiary bombs that unleashed devastation on major cities including Tokyo, Nagoya, and Osaka. Between April and June, the Americans captured Okinawa in fighting of immense savagery, which ended with the suicide of the Japanese commander, General Ushijima Mitsuru. Japan's war economy stood close to collapse. Its shipping was decimated, meaning that the precious supplies that kept its war economy going became ever scarcer. But on the Chinese side, the Nationalist armies were also in a state of near collapse after Ichigô. The state for which they fought was riddled with corruption, inflation, and sheer battle-weariness. Yet somehow both sides insisted, at least outwardly, that they would continue to fight on the Chinese mainland.

Then, on August 6, 1945, a US Air Force aircraft named *Enola Gay* flew over the Japanese city of Hiroshima and released a 4,400-kilogram bomb nicknamed "Little Boy." The first atomic bomb to be used against a human population instantly burned some 66,000 people to death. Truman promised a "rain of ruin from the air, the like of which has never been seen on this earth," if Japan did not surrender unconditionally.[52] While Japan started to come to terms with the destruction of a city by a force greater than any that science had previously created, events were also moving fast in Moscow. The Japanese ambassador, Satô Naotake, had been trying to discuss a negotiated agreement with the US using Soviet good offices. But at 5:00 p.m. on August 8 Foreign Minister Vyacheslav Molotov called Satô in and asked him to have a seat. Molotov then delivered an uncompromising message. "Taking into account the refusal of Japan to capitulate, the Allies approached the Soviet government with a proposal to join the war against Japanese aggression," he read. "The Soviet Government has accepted the proposal of the Allies . . . from August 9, the Soviet Union will consider herself in a state of war against Japan."[53] At 1:00 a.m. on that day the Soviet Union launched its troops into Manchuria. On the same day a second atomic bomb, "Fat Man," was dropped on Nagasaki, killing a further 40,000 people or more. The Japanese government was now in a state of utter panic. A few diehards tried to make the case for fighting on, issuing a chilling statement in the name of the minister of war, General Anami (who turned out not fully to have known what was being done in his name), that "even though we may have to eat grass, swallow dirt, and lie in the fields, we shall fight on to the bitter

362 • THE POISONED ALLIANCE

end."[54] But the conclusion was inevitable. On August 14, at 10:50 a.m., the emperor declared, in a prerecorded statement, that it was time to "endure the unendurable and suffer the insufferable." Few Japanese understood the full import of the broadcast at the time; the emperor spoke in a form of courtly classical Japanese, and the sound quality of the recording was poor. But the meaning was unequivocal. Japan would accept the terms of the Potsdam Declaration and surrender without conditions.

The next morning Chiang Kai-shek rose at his usual early hour. "I thanked God that the mercy he gave me was so great," he wrote. "Every word in Psalm 9 is true, in my experience."[55] Psalm 9 contains the lines "Thou has destroyed the wicked, thou hast put out their name for ever and ever." Chiang continued with his prayer and, while meditating, heard the recording of the Japanese surrender broadcast. Chiang headed to the radio studios to make his own victory broadcast at 10:00 a.m. "Our faith in justice through black and hopeless days and eight long years of struggle has today been rewarded," he declared. In the course of the speech Chiang gave special mention to two people: Jesus Christ and Sun Yat-sen. Solemnly he declared, "the historical mission of our National Revolution has at last been fulfilled."[56]

The end had come, suddenly and unexpectedly. The war had broken out almost by accident in July 1937, escalating within weeks from a skirmish near Beiping to an exile from eastern China that would last eight years. China had changed immensely. In August 1945 China was simultaneously in the strongest global position it had ever occupied and weaker than it had been for nearly a century. When the war began, it had still been subject to extraterritoriality and imperialism. Now, not only had the much-hated system of legal immunity for foreigners ended, but China was about to make its mark on the postwar world. For the first time since 1842, when the Qing empire had signed the Treaty of Nanjing, the country was fully sovereign once again. Furthermore, China was now one of the "Big Four," one of the powers that would play a permanent and central role in the formation of the new United Nations Organization, and the only non-European one. In Asia the decades of power enjoyed by Britain and by Japan were at an end. While the US and USSR would take their place at the center of the new international order, China would now have an autonomous role that had eluded it throughout the republican era. The war with Japan was fought for Chinese nationhood and sovereignty, the inheritance of the 1911 revolution, and China had achieved that goal.

Yet China had also paid a terrible price. The war with Japan had hollowed China out. Not since the Taiping War of the 1860s had China come so close to disintegration; then, only the decision of the Qing dynasty to devolve the power of warfare to new provincial armies had prevented collapse. The war with Japan had brought China very close to the same abyss. Even now, at the moment of victory, the country was split. It was divided between parties, Nationalist and Communist, who talked about compromise but seemed set for civil war. And it was distorted by an utterly changed geography. For centuries China had been controlled from the north and the east. The war had forced the Nationalists to redefine their mission in the unfamiliar territory of the far southwest. And as he tasted the moment of victory, Chiang Kai-shek looked out over ruin both foreign and domestic. So many people had died: bombed, slaughtered in Japanese war crimes, drowned, starved, or killed in combat. Even now, the numbers are not clear, but some 14 million to 20 million Chinese seem to have perished during the eight years of conflict. The relationship with the US had become bitter, poisoned by the Stilwell fiasco. American disillusionment with the Chongqing government was fueled by the wreck of the regime that ruled China. The nation had grand visions, but the reality was mass hunger, official corruption, and a brutal security state that tried in vain to suppress the aspirations of a people who had been exhorted to develop a sense of national identity and now demanded a state that matched their new sense of themselves. There was a widespread feeling within the country of change abroad. China could not avoid it. And what seemed deeply ironic was that a triumphant Mao Zedong might now reap the fruits of Chiang Kai-shek's victory.

And what of those who had taken the wrong turn in 1938? Zhou Fohai had realized long ago that his allegiance to Wang Jingwei and the Japanese-sponsored regime in Nanjing was a historical dead end. Zhou's diary ends in June 1945 and we do not have a direct record of his sentiments about the end of the war. Yet he must have reflected on the changes in the world since his flight from Chongqing in 1938. Perhaps he would have been pleased to see that Chiang, who was after all his old friend, had achieved nationhood. Perhaps he would have been disconcerted to think about how far the Communists had advanced.

Chiang had plenty of tasks to attend to on the first day of peace. At noon he drafted a version of the surrender document that would go to General Okamura Yasuji, commander in chief of Japan's China Expeditionary Command. He also started to put together a list of the officials who would receive the Japanese surrender in each province.[57] By early the next morning he had also signed off on the Chinese-Soviet mutual assistance agreement, although it still left the exact nature of Soviet support for Chiang's government ominously murky.[58]

But there was one piece of Sun Yat-sen's unfinished business that Chiang turned to without any further delay: reunification. After finishing his radio broadcast, he cabled Mao, inviting him to come to Chongqing "to talk about his big plans." Mao replied that he would have Zhou Enlai represent him in the talks, but Chiang cabled back that Mao himself should make the journey to the meetings that would decide the shape of China's postwar government.[59]

China's long, eight-year war with Japan was over. The Chinese themselves at last had the power to write the next chapter of their story.

EPILOGUE: THE ENDURING WAR

T HE FIGHTING HAD ENDED so suddenly. Even in early August 1945, Mao Zedong perhaps even hoped that the war against Japan would go on late into 1946, and that this would give the CCP time to consolidate its position.[1] Meanwhile, Chiang Kai-shek moved fast to try and prevent encroachments on his territory. His first target was the British. Chiang hoped to occupy Hong Kong, returning it to de facto Chinese sovereignty. Had the British known (they suspected, certainly), the first serious confrontation of the postwar era might have emerged. In fact, the suspicion alone was enough to compel the British to rush to reoccupy Hong Kong.[2] But most of Chiang's attention was on the Communists. On August 12 he told Communist troops that they were not authorized to accept any surrender from the Japanese or collaborationist troops. On August 14 he made an even more significant move, signing a Sino-Soviet Treaty of Friendship, which gave various privileges to the Soviets in northeast China, as well as renouncing any claim to Outer Mongolia. The very next day he invited Mao to come to Chongqing to negotiate a postwar settlement. Mao was reluctant until the US ambassador, Patrick Hurley, himself agreed to accompany him.[3]

Mao was shell-shocked. He had never imagined that Stalin would betray him by signing a separate agreement with Chiang. However, Stalin did not have faith that the CCP really could defeat the Nationalist armies. Focusing on building his new empire in Europe, he did not want to waste time and energy supporting allies who would be pitting themselves against the might of the US, and Mao was left in a weak position. Still, the encounter between Mao and Chiang was historic. It was nearly two decades since they had met.

Mao stayed for six weeks in Chongqing, and in their discussions both sides made some show of compromise. Mao did not insist on a full coalition government, and Chiang conceded that the CCP could maintain twelve divisions of its own. Both Chiang and Mao knew it was vital that they should be seen to attempt to negotiate a solution, but they were also convinced that a civil war was inevitable. Overall, the meetings did not produce a firm agreement that would have maintained stability.

The resulting stalemate was fragile indeed. The CCP began to consolidate its position in the northeast of China, at first attempting to secure the whole region. But the Communists clashed with some of the Nationalist troops being flown back into the region with American help. As it became clear that this might spark a civil war almost at once, the CCP scaled back its ambitions — at least for the moment. Meanwhile the Soviets, now aware that the Americans had no intention of allowing a joint Allied command structure in Japan, were less inclined to follow the Sino-Soviet agreement with the Nationalists to the letter. At the same time, they were at pains not to force a showdown with the Americans.[4]

As 1945 turned into 1946, President Truman made it clear that he would not allow American military forces to fight for the Nationalist government. He was taken aback by the sudden resignation of Patrick Hurley, who accused left-leaning colleagues in the State Department of undermining his position from within.[5] Truman therefore decided to send to China the most prestigious envoy possible: General George C. Marshall, who had just left his post as the chief of staff of the US Army, would try to negotiate an agreement between the two sides.

Over the next few months, Marshall's mission became an exercise in frustration. Neither side was genuinely willing to compromise. The Nationalists refused to allow the Communists to run a parallel military and political organization within their territory. The Communists baulked at the idea of handing over their autonomous military power to an ill-defined Nationalist structure. Both sides agreed to an armistice on January 10, 1946, yet Marshall found it impossible to get them to settle on the next steps.[6] During the first six months of 1946, Marshall's attempts to achieve a real breakthrough were undermined by the escalation of fighting both by the Nationalists and Communists. By the summer of 1946 the Communists were firmly entrenched in the northeast (Manchuria). Chiang continued to demand that the Communists give up their arms (believing that they were weak and would be unable to sustain themselves), while the Communists insisted that the Nationalists must give up the advances that they had made during the course of 1946.[7] On January 7, 1947, Marshall announced that he was ending his attempts to mediate between the two parties.

The behavior of the Nationalists hardly reassured the Chinese people that their fate was in safe hands. The economy was in a parlous situation at the end of the war against Japan, but not irrecoverable. But Chiang refused to reduce military spending, sure that an armed victory over the CCP was the only way that he could stamp his control over the country.

Chiang attempted to impose government price controls, with little effect, and issued new bonds which found few takers among the wealthy, who saw that the bonds issued during the War of Resistance had not been honored by the government.[8] From 1947 inflation, which had been bad during the last years of the war, ran fatally out of control. The returning government also lost much of the goodwill of victory by its arbitrary and corrupt actions, regularly expropriating property and acting with arrogance in the territories it had reconquered.

The treatment of collaborators was a particularly painful question. When Wang Jingwei had died in Nagoya in November 1944, his body had been shipped back to China and interred beside that of his revolutionary comrade Sun Yat-sen. On his return to Nanjing, Chiang made it a first item of business to destroy this symbol in the most final form possible: he gave orders to use high explosives to blow up Wang Jingwei's tomb. Chen Gongbo, who had become the head of the Reorganized Nationalist government after Wang's death, was tried and executed in the spring of 1946.

There was more ambiguity in the way that some collaborators were dealt with. Chen Bijun, Wang Jingwei's widow, was tried (like Chen Gongbo) in the spring of 1946, and she defended herself strongly, arguing that her husband had taken back sovereignty over territories already abandoned by Chiang's government. Spectators at the trial applauded her and asked for her autograph. She was sentenced to prison, but not executed, and died in a Shanghai jail under Communist rule in 1959.[9] And Zhou Fohai, who had been playing a double game for most of the last part of the war, was also spared execution. He might have expected even more lenient treatment, but his ambivalent protector, Dai Li, died in an air crash in 1946, and there were no other powerful figures in the regime who wished to use their political capital on behalf of Zhou. He died of a heart attack in prison in 1948. Overall, the collaborators became hidden and marginal figures as China was engulfed in the new crisis of civil war.

The Japanese were also condemned for their invasion of China. At the International Military Tribunal for the Far East (the "Tokyo Trial") in 1948, the Nanjing Massacre was just one of the events of the China War used to indict the defendants. Seven defendants were sentenced to death, including General Matsui Iwane and former foreign minister Hirota Kôki, both closely associated with the escalation of the war with China.[10]

The social critic Xu Wancheng had made his name in the pre-war period with his investigations of change within Chinese society. Now, in the aftermath of the war, he gave a gloomy assessment of the various political actors and their promises for China. He mourned the "furnace of parties" that had emerged from the war. "Today's Nationalist party authority as compared to Sun's National Revolutionary goals have become . . . ," he wrote, deliberately letting the sentence fade into nothing. As an example, he cited the way the Nationalists had ruined the value of the meager savings of those who had been left behind in the occupied areas by giving a miserly exchange rate for their banknotes. "Heaven and earth are confused," Xu chided, "as if they are saying: 'This victory of China's, is it solely the contribution of the "resistance and construction officials" who escaped to the interior?'" The returning Nationalist officials were treating their compatriots who had been left behind as if they were traitors or conquered peoples, and this was hardly conducive to the weaving of national unity. As Xu pointed out, "among the 'collaborator leaders,' weren't a good number of them Guomindang officials?" He concluded: "In the Nationalist dictatorship, corruption is huge, and they have forgotten the goals of the National Revolution. They only plan for their own big bellies, and their own households' wealth."

Yet Xu felt no greater faith in the Nationalists' great rivals. "The Chinese, talking about communism, are talking about a tiger's face and skin! Why? Because the CCP sets fires and kills people, and in everything its talents are for destruction:"

> Whoever in a place has money or power, they class them as gentry who are all vile and they kill them all, not asking the right or wrongs of it. They will kill the landlords, kill the rich old men, and burn all the big houses . . . This sort of behavior is worse than [the first emperor] Qin Shihuang burning the books and walling up the scholars. By carrying out this policy . . . do they want to rule the empire? Is this really right?[11]

Xu noted the cynical element in the CCP's strategy (as had Peter Vladimirov before him):

> The CCP is happy at disasters and delighted at calamities. Their only fear is that the empire is *not* in chaos. When Dushan was lost, the *Xinhua ribao* put this in big-character headlines, that Dushan had been overcome, and then was silent and said nothing more. The previous year, in this same newspaper, the CCP had said: "We are making efforts for the war of resistance." How much effort *were* they making?[12]

Xu was equally dismissive of the smaller parties such as the China Youth Party. "They have many theories, but have no military authority, and thus no political authority." He summarized, despairingly: "The first to suffer are the good ordinary people! As the blood flows between Nationalists and CCP, the ordinary people are suffering!"[13]

To be fair, there were real achievements made under the Nationalists in the immediate postwar period, but more in the international arena than the domestic. China's wartime contribution meant that it was defined as one of the five permanent powers on the Security Council of the new United Nations, each of which had the right to veto resolutions put before the council. China also had a place within a whole range of other new international organizations. Even in 1945 there were still very few non-Western nations that had full and equal sovereignty in world affairs (and Britain and France continued to maintain large parts of their empire, even if India would be given independence shortly). China's status was significant well beyond the country itself, and formed a startling contrast to the semicolonized and prostrate state that had gone to war in 1937.

Yet the Civil War, once started, went badly for the Nationalists, in large part because of Chiang Kai-shek's judgments. During the war against Japan, Chiang had played an appallingly bad hand much better than might have been expected. During the Civil War, his judgment appears to have deserted him. In particular, his decision to extend his lines to try and recapture the northeast — the region which was the Communist heartland where Mao was underpinned by strong support from the neighboring USSR — was spectacularly ill-judged. In 1945–1946 George Marshall had encouraged Chiang to try and recapture the region, but had become much more pessimistic about the possibility by the spring of 1946.[14]

As 1947 ground on, the Communist general Lin Biao's brilliant campaigning in north China drove the Nationalists further and further back. While major cities were still under Nationalist control, along with the rail lines, the territory was now Communist — an echo of the situation under the Japanese just a few years earlier. In the autumn of 1948 General Wei Lihuang found himself with some 300,000 Nationalist troops facing some 700,000 under Lin Biao.[15] By November the region's major city of Shenyang (Mukden) had been lost, and the northeast with it. Lin's troops of the People's Liberation Army (PLA) drove on further, taking north China, and were poised for the conquest of central China too. During the first half of 1949 Chiang transferred his naval and air force headquarters to the island of Taiwan; many civilians followed suit. In May Chiang set sail for Taiwan. He would never return to the mainland.

The war continued through the summer, but Chiang knew that the game was up and all sides expected a Communist victory, as cities fell one by one — Nanjing, Shanghai, and Chongqing. On October 1, 1949, the People's Republic of China was declared, its capital once more in Beijing.

The Communist victory on the Chinese mainland shaped the politics of East Asia, and of US-China relations, for decades. In the US the "loss" of China (although it was a country that had never really been the Americans' to lose in the first place) began to poison the political atmosphere of the early Cold War.

Chiang Kai-shek's critics made their voices heard. Tired of being forced to restrain his indictments of Chiang, Theodore White had left *Time* magazine and used his new freedom to publish a devastating indictment of Chiang in book form (coauthored with Annalee Jacoby), *Thunder out of China* (1946). "The greatest danger to China," he wrote, "is the right wing of the Kuomintang [Nationalists]."[16] The book was a best seller. There were other critical accounts. Graham Peck, who had spent much of the war working for the Office of War Information (OWI) in Chongqing, wrote a brilliant memoir entitled *Two Kinds of Time.* It was equally unsparing of Chiang, judging that by the time he fled the mainland in 1949 "the Generalissimo was virtually the only man who got satisfaction from his own regime."[17]

The right wing was able to use the issue to accuse American liberals of being soft on communism. The "red scare" tactics of Senator Joseph McCarthy, who claimed to have lists of Communists supposedly hidden in US government institutions, brought a chill to American public life. There was a strong suspicion that key advisers to Roosevelt on China, including Harry Dexter White and Laughlin Currie, had been actively part of a network of Soviet agents. (However, it is worth remembering that the USSR had no immediate wartime interest in the weakening of the Nationalist war effort, and both White and Currie were actively involved in providing material assistance to the National Government.)[18] But those who were guilty of little more than naîveté about the CCP and its intentions, including John Service, were persecuted and accused of betraying their country's interests by undermining the Nationalists. The Nationalists themselves had established a coterie of figures known as the

"China Lobby," who had influence largely with Republican politicians, including Anna Chennault (widow of General Claire Chennault), T. V. Soong, and, of course Henry Luce. The US also encountered one of the most immediate effects of Chiang's failure just months after Mao's victory on the mainland, when the Korean War broke out in 1950. The experience of war on the Korean Peninsula was instrumental in hardening American attitudes toward the new Chinese Communist state.

The grip of McCarthyism had begun to fade by the early 1960s, and it became clear that the Communist regime on the mainland was there to stay. This development had a strong effect on academic analysis of the war against Japan in the West, and in the United States in particular. Since Mao's regime had clearly won, the important question was why he had succeeded. Chalmers Johnson wrote a groundbreaking and courageous book which argued that the origins of Mao's victory in 1949 lay in the ability of his wartime regime in Yan'an to mobilize peasants through nationalism, which further inspired them to embrace the social revolution of communism.[19] The book created a storm of debate, and one of the most important responses, a decade later, came from the historian Mark Selden, whose book *The Yenan Way* argued that the wartime social revolution itself, rather than peasant nationalism, was at the heart of Mao's victory. By that stage, American life had been convulsed by the Vietnam War. For many, the experience of China's Communists in the 1940s was an account that could help to deepen their understandings of the Indochinese Communists some thirty years later. For those who saw Vietnam as an unjust war, Mao's social experiment during the war against Japan helped to burnish the idea that indigenous social revolution should be understood rather than opposed. However, with this "Yan'an-centered" history of the wartime period, the record of the Nationalists was mostly dismissed.

Other progressive critics attacked the right-wing version of history presented by the China Lobby, which held that Chiang had merely been a victim of Communist duplicity. The renowned historian Barbara Tuchman wrote a classic book that used Stilwell's papers to make a devastating case against Chiang's regime. Published just as Nixon began his opening to China, it further demolished Chiang's reputation.[20]

In China itself discussion of the history of the wartime years was even more restricted. Mao's China had no place for any description of the Nationalists except as enemies who did little to defend China against Japan and had rightly been routed in 1949. All credit for leading the Chinese people in the "war of resistance against Japan" went to the CCP alone, and more specifically to Mao himself.

The myths surrounding Mao's revolution in Yan'an became central to the country's identity. But huge swathes of people were excluded from the narrative. At a time when Britain, the US, Germany, France, and Japan came to terms, joyously or painfully, with the titanic changes that the war had wrought on their societies, the experience of eight years of resistance was almost entirely removed from the public sphere in China. The Nanjing Massacre, the bombing of Chongqing, the collaboration of Wang Jingwei, the Communist areas that had not been under Mao's control: all were sidelined or not even mentioned. The Japanese did turn up, often in somewhat stylized form, as the enemy (as in the Chinese opera *The Legend of the Red Lantern,* designated one of the "eight model operas" during the Cultural Revolution), but during most of the 1950s to the 1970s Mao's government was trying to detach Tokyo from the Cold War embrace of the US, and there was no sustained effort to whip up genuine hatred of the defeated enemy. Much of the discussion about the Japanese circled around the need to establish "reconciliation" with those who had genuinely repented. The real venom was reserved for the Nationalists across the water in Taiwan, where they remained protected by the US Navy.

Many aspects of Chinese society and culture seemed to reflect changes that had happened during the war. Military service had habituated the Chinese to more collective ways of living, as had the trend toward living and working in the same place to avoid being caught traveling during bombings. More than that, the atmosphere of political mobilization that the war had brought about remained a constant in Chinese life. From the Aid Korea Resist America Campaign during the Korean War (1950–1953) to the Great Leap Forward (1958–1961), Chinese life was characterized by constant campaigns. In the latter case, the drive to increase economic growth gave rise to a horrific famine that killed some 20 million people or more. Yet of all Maoist China's campaigns, the most intense was the Cultural Revolution of the 1960s.

Ostensibly, the great upheaval of the Cultural Revolution, when Mao declared war on his own party, had little to do with the legacy of the Sino-Japanese War. But two of the cities where the fighting would be fiercest —with tanks in the streets— were Chongqing and Chengdu.[21] During the Cultural Revolution younger Communist cadres from ideologically "bad" families took the opportunity to seek revenge against cadres from "good" families who had been privileged since the Communist revolution in 1949. By 1966, when the Cultural Revolution was launched, the "bad" cadres came from families who had had bourgeois connections before 1949, and in many cases these would have been people associated with the Nationalist Party in particular. After 1949 the Nationalist record in Sichuan was associated with nothing except corruption and a supposed refusal to fight: the sacrifices the province and its people had made during the war years had little connection with the CCP, so they were written out of the narrative. While many factors shaped the savagery of the Cultural Revolution in Sichuan's cities, it is not implausible to see at least the ghosts of the wartime trauma writing part of the story for the generation that was born after the war itself had ended.

Then the Cold War unfroze. President Richard Nixon visited Beijing in 1972 and the contours of global conflict started to shift. Chiang Kai-shek died in 1975, Mao in 1976. The duel across the Straits had lost its fire. By the early 1980s the historical narrative of the war had begun to shift significantly.

Among the most important signs of the new policy were the establishment of new museums commemorating different aspects of the war. At Wanping, where the fighting had broken out in July 1937, a major museum opened in 1987 covering the events of the whole war, dated from the invasion of Manchuria in 1931 to victory over Japan in 1945. Although the CCP was still given the credit for leading the victory against Japan, the Beijing museum stressed the contribution of Nationalist generals and the importance of victories such as Taierzhuang. In the suburbs of Shenyang, a museum commemorated the explosion on the railway track that launched the Manchurian crisis of 1931. (The facade of the museum is designed to resemble a desk calendar opened at September 18, 1931, the date of the attack.) And perhaps most resonant of all, in 1985, there opened a memorial museum to the Nanjing Massacre, on the site of one of the particularly horrific killings. It was remarkable that it took some four decades to pass after the war had ended for such a site to be created.[22]

As the 1990s drew on, various parts of China took advantage of the new historical openness to discuss previously taboo topics. Chongqing, in particular, took full advantage of the new possibilities. Of all the Allied wartime capitals, it was the only one that had been given no chance to celebrate its resistance or to mourn its losses. Even the Monument to Victory in the Anti-Japanese War set up in the city center was renamed the Liberation Monument (as in liberation by the CCP from the Nationalists) after 1949. In the early twenty-first century Chongqing made up for lost time. The city burnished its reputation as the last redoubt of resistance. Chiang Kai-shek's old mansion at Huangshan, from where he had seen the city on fire during the war, is now handsomely restored. The historical narratives inside portray him as China's national leader of resistance; his political and military shortcomings play little part in the description. The city's Three Gorges Museum has featured displays including dioramas of the bombing of Chongqing and a reconstruction of the great tunnel suffocation disaster of 1941.

Mass media have also been used to send out messages about the new interpretation of history. A series entitled "Temporary Wartime Capital" was made by the local television station in 2005, to mark the sixtieth anniversary of the end of the war and celebrate Chongqing's role. The marketing of the DVD was revealing. The cover showed images, familiar in the West, of three great wartime capitals — London's Houses of Parliament, the US Capitol in Washington, DC, and the clock tower in Red Square in Moscow. But it also showed, portrayed twice as high as the other structures, the Anti-Japanese Victory Monument in the center of Chongqing. The international message was clear: the Second World War had been won by four, not three great Allies. And the domestic message was also pointed: Chongqing had had a role of global significance in the recent past, and this should be acknowledged by all Chinese.

Yet convergence still seems far off when it comes to the most contentious areas of wartime history. A joint committee of top Japanese and Chinese scholars was established in 2006 to provide an agreed version of a variety of questions in the history of the two countries. Despite efforts to reconcile views, disagreements over the way that the war was interpreted (particularly the issue of whether Japanese aggression was preplanned or not) meant that the report was never officially adopted by the Chinese government after it was presented in 2009.[23]

As in China, historical memory of the war in Japan itself has been complicated. One version of events, often heard in China and sometimes in the West, is that Japan has simply refused to acknowledge its own war crimes. This view is too simple. It is true that there was and is a vocal right wing in Japan that downplays or denies wartime atrocities. The Japanese conservative mainstream is also often too quick to dismiss the enormity of Japanese crimes. Japan has also pointed to its sad distinction as the only country ever to have been attacked with atomic weapons to make a case for itself as a "peace nation" — but often with little context or explanation given for the events that led to the dropping of two atomic bombs.[24] However, it is also true that there is a wide and lively public sphere in Japan which examines and in no way excuses the Japanese war record in China and elsewhere. The Japanese left, notably the journalist Honda Katsuichi, was instrumental in forcing their own country to re-examine the Nanjing Massacre in the 1970s, long before the issue was brought back to the public gaze in the West or China. Although there have been attempts in Japanese schools to introduce "revisionist" textbooks that minimize Japanese atrocities in China, they have not been widely adopted within the school system.

The first decade of the twenty-first century has seen China's inexorable rise to greater global influence, and part of that rise has been a new assertiveness about foreign relations, and relations with Japan in particular. Repeated events showed that memories of the war remain a flash point. Around the time of the handover of power from Hu Jintao to Xi Jinping in late 2012, tensions over the sovereignty of the Diaoyutai Senkaku Islands in the East China Sea spilled over into Chinese streets. The islands are part of the unfinished business in the Asia Pacific region, claimed by Japan, China, and Taiwan. Informed by popular memories of Japan's wartime record in China, protesters railed against Japan's claims to the islands in massive demonstrations across Chinese cities. Young people with no possible personal memory of the war were using its legacy to make a statement about contemporary East Asian international relations.

But rather more noticeable within China, and more significant in the longer term, is the use of the war to unite people within China and to position the country as a cooperative rather than confrontational actor in world politics. The term "war of resistance against Japan" (*KangRi zhanzheng* or just *Kangzhan*) remains the commonest term to describe the war in China. However, the term "antifascist war" has also become more commonplace, particularly as writers seek to portray Chinese resistance not simply as a solo act of opposition to Japan, but rather as part of an act of collective resistance to the Axis powers. The implication is clear: at an earlier time when its contribution was needed, China delivered, and it should now be trusted as it seeks, once again, to enter international society playing a wider role. The new interpretations of history acknowledge the role of the United States in China during the war, but not always to the advantage of the US. One Chinese historian concluded that the aim of the United States in making China one of the major world powers was to create a "vassal" for the US in the postwar world (an echo of Churchill's anxieties on the same question). Another agreed, declaring that America had defined its foreign policy simply "to maintain its own national interests."[25]

The war has also become a fixture in popular culture. In 1986 one of the first revisionist films about the war was entitled *The Great Battle of Taierzhuang,* celebrating the major Nationalist victory in April 1938. The Nanjing Massacre has been re-created on film several times, including Lu Chang's *City of Life and Death* (2009) and Zhang Yimou's *Flowers of War* (2012). Even video games have taken the war on board; multiplayer games allow enthusiasts to fight the Japanese Imperial Army.[26]

Given the tacit permission to rehabilitate the record of the Nationalists, however, not all new interpretations of the war have made entirely comfortable reading for the Chinese Communist Party. Fan Jianchuan, a former soldier turned wealthy businessman in Chengdu, used his fortune to set up a series of private museums outside the city. One of these commemorated Sichuan's contribution during the wartime period, showcasing identity documents and uniforms from the Nationalist areas. Fan published a book entitled *One Person's War of Resistance* in which he showed off some of his artifacts. In his reflections he talked about a cup he had found which dated from the Cultural Revolution era. It was inscribed with a heartfelt, semiliterate message from a victim of persecution: "I fought the Japanese, and I took a bullet in my leg." Yet in 1966 the old soldier was being attacked because he had fought for the Nationalists, not the Communists. "For the eight years of the War of Resistance," reflected Fan Jianchuan, "he had dodged death . . . and suddenly, overnight, [his war record] was considered shameful?"[27]

In more recent years Nationalist soldiers may not have been persecuted, but instead they were being ignored as they died off. In 2010 Cui Yongyuan, one of China's best-known television hosts, gave an interview in which he talked at length about his rediscovery of the Nationalist role in the war. As a child he had seen films that implied that the Nationalists had collaborated with the Japanese, and it was only as an adult that he gained a greater understanding of their role when he toured a battlefield with a Nationalist veteran who showed Cui where his comrades had fallen.

"This was perhaps the first time that I had met a Nationalist soldier," Cui recalled. "I really began to feel respect for them." Cui interviewed over a hundred Nationalist veterans in Yunnan province. He suggested that individual stories were the best way to explain the complexities of the war, whether it was occasions when the locals had pointed out members of the Eighth Route Army to the Japanese rather than hiding them, or occasions when even collaborators might have shown some conscience. "Memoirs from collaborators give a variety of self-justifications," he observed, "but it's not always as simple as betraying your country. There were even some collaborators who did what they did as a version of the war of resistance, trading space for time."[28]

The unquiet spirits of the war against Japan were beginning to rise, some seventy years after laying down their swords — or their lives.

Modern China has been marked by massive upheavals and destruction that are just starting to be discussed openly. The devastating famine of the Great Leap Forward and the destruction caused by the Cultural Revolution have only been partially acknowledged in China. Likewise, the war against Japan, until recently, was only discussed in very limited terms. The opening up of dialogue on the war, and in particular the role of the Nationalists and of China as an international actor at that time, indicates significant change in the way that China conducts its contemporary politics, both domestic and international.

Yet one of the most important conclusions we can draw from China's wartime history may still be unwelcome in China. And that is the contingent nature of China's path to modernity. The three men who sought to rule China during the war — Chiang Kai-shek, Mao Zedong, and Wang Jingwei — each embodied a different path to the same goal: a modern, nationalist Chinese state. There was nothing inevitable about the Chinese Communist Party's coming to power in 1949. Without the war with Japan, there would have been a greater possibility of an anti-imperialist, anti-Communist Nationalist government consolidating power. It would have still been an immensely hard task, not least because of the Nationalists' own huge flaws, but the war made it nearly impossible. Of course, in an Asia ruled by Japan, China would have remained colonized for decades or more. The political conditions of China today are not the only possible ones that history could have produced. One of the great lost opportunities of the war was the tentative move toward pluralism both by the Nationalists and the Communists. The increasing harshness of the war, along with a reluctance by either party to surrender ultimate power, made this a green shoot that withered quickly. But it was there, and deserves to be remembered, and considered afresh.

Another topic that is more widely discussed in China today is the danger of an economic crisis leading to social unrest. Large parts of the old "iron rice bowl" of guaranteed employment, healthcare, and pensions, which were instituted during Mao's years of rule, were abolished as part of the price of economic reform in the 1990s. From the mid-2000s, the government of Hu Jintao made moves to mend some of the holes in China's social-welfare safety net, with new plans to subsidize support for the elderly and the ill. Yet the debates of the early twenty-first century on this issue are not new. The war with Japan pressured both the Nationalists and the Communists to create a new social contract based on greater obligations between the state and the citizen. Today's debates are in part a legacy of that eight-year period of war when the state became more demanding of its people, but was also obliged to shoulder greater responsibilities toward them.

As the war comes to matter to China again, it will affect Western perceptions of China too. The immediate need to understand the continuing flare-ups in Chinese-Japanese relations provides a pressing reason to reevaluate the war. But there is also a more profound reason, one that has to do with historical completeness, even justice. Our collective history of the Allied contribution to the Second World War has moved a tremendous distance in the past few decades. The American role is now seen as part of a global war effort. The British have come to acknowledge the massive contribution of the empire and commonwealth in underpinning their decision to continue fighting. The Soviet Union's great resistance, costing some 20 million lives, now stands central to the understanding of the Allied war effort.

China remains the forgotten ally, its contribution only slowly being remembered as its experience fades out of living memory. Its involvement in the war was not as harrowing as that of the Soviet Union, which was engaged in a struggle to the death, a fight about race and power. But the suffering endured by China was still unimaginably great: the war against Japan left 15 million to 20 million dead, and 80 million to 100 million refugees. The flawed but real economic development that the Nationalists had begun in 1928 was destroyed. For eight years brutal death was an everyday possibility for ordinary Chinese, whether from the swords in Nanjing or the bombs dropping on Chongqing, or even the dams, destroyed in desperation by their own government.

Yet this weakened and crippled state, whose centers of gravity moved at huge speed from Nanjing and Shanghai to Chongqing and Yan'an, still fought for eight years when it could have surrendered to the enemy. The Chinese Nationalists and Communists were the only two major political groupings in East Asia to maintain a consistent opposition to the Japanese Empire through the whole period from 1937 to 1945. The Nationalists maintained some 4 million troops in China through the war, helping to tie down some half a million or more Japanese soldiers who could otherwise have been transferred elsewhere. The Communists maintained a guerrilla campaign that prevented the Japanese from gaining control of large parts of northern China, tying down troops and resources.

Without Chinese resistance, China would have become a Japanese colony as early as 1938. This would have allowed Japan dominance over the mainland, and would have allowed Tokyo to turn its attention to expansion in Southeast Asia even more swiftly, and with less distraction. A pacified China would also have made the invasion of British India much more plausible. Without the "China Quagmire" — a quagmire caused by the refusal of the Chinese to stop fighting — Japan's imperial ambitions would have been much easier to fulfill.

Throughout the war, Chiang Kai-shek's master of propaganda, Hollington Tong, created a variety of characters who were meant to represent China's continuing struggle to the outside world. The name he gave to one such character was highly symbolic: Yu Kangming, a name meaning "I fight fate."[29]

Both the Nationalists and the Communists did fight a fate that they had never sought. And in acknowledging their suffering, their resistance, and the terrible choices they were forced to make, we in the West also do greater honor to our own collective memories and understandings of the Second World War.

NOTES

Abbreviations are given below for source references found in more than one chapter.

CKSD: Chiang Kai-shek diary

CQA: Chongqing Municipal Archive

CQDH: Southwestern Normal University Chongqing Bombing Research Center et al., ed., *Chongqing da hongzha* [*The Great Chongqing Bombings*] (Chongqing, 2002)

CQHX: Xu Wancheng, *Chongqing Huaxu* [*Chongqing Gossip*] (Shanghai, 1946)

DBPO: *Documents on British Policy Overseas*

DZY: Du Yi and Du Ying, eds., *Huan wo heshan: Du Zhongyuan wenji* [*Return our Rivers and Mountains: The Collected Essays of Du Zhongyuan*] (Shanghai, 1998)

FRUS: *Foreign Relations of the United States*

GZW: Gao Zongwu, *Gao Zongwu huiyilu* [*The Memoirs of Gao Zongwu*] (Beijing, 2009)

MSW: Mao Zedong, *Selected Works,* vol. III (Beijing, 1967)

MZD: Stuart R. Schram, ed., *Mao's Road to Power: Revolutionary Writings, 1912–1949,* 7 vols. (Armonk, NY, 1992–)

NARA: National Archives and Records Administration, Washington, DC

NCH: *North-China Herald*

PVD: Peter Vladimirov, *The Vladimirov Diaries: Yenan, 1942–1945* (New York, 1975)

QDHF: Yang Lin et al., *Qu da houfang: Zhongguo kangzhan neiqian shilu* [*Going to the Interior: True Stories of the Journey Inland during the War of Resistance*] (Shanghai, 2005)

SMA: Shanghai Municipal Archive

SP: Joseph W. Stilwell, ed. Theodore H. White, *The Stilwell Papers* (Beijing, 2003) [originally New York, 1948]

UNA: United Nations Archives, New York

ZFHR: Cai Dejin, ed., *Zhou Fohai riji* [*Zhou Fohai's Diary*], 2 vols. (Beijing, 1986)

ZHRB: *Zhonghua ribao* (newspaper)

ZT: Qin Shaoyi, ed., *Xian zongtong Jianggong sixiang lun zongji* [*The Thought and Speeches of President Chiang Kai-shek*] (Taipei, 1984)

PROLOGUE: CITY ON FIRE

1. Southwestern Normal University Chongqing Bombing Research Center et al., ed., *Chongqing da hongzha* [*The Great Chongqing Bombings*] (Chongqing, 2002) [hereafter CQDH], 106, 101–102, 111.
2. Ibid., 106–107.
3. Ibid., 111, 103.
4. Tetsuo Maeda, "Strategic Bombing of Chongqing by Imperial Japanese Army and Naval Forces," in Yuki Tanaka and Marilyn B. Young, eds., *Bombing Civilians: A Twentieth-Century History* (New York, 2009), 141.
5. CQDH, 109.
6. Chiang Kai-shek diary [hereafter CKSD] (Hoover Institution Archives) [Box 40, folder 8], May 3 and 4, 1939.
7. CQDH, 85.
8. The number of Chinese deaths in war between 1937 and 1945 continues to be unclear, although the figures are very large. Odd Arne Westad, *Restless Empire: China and the World since 1750* (London, 2012), 249, draws on careful scholarship to posit some 2 million Chinese combat deaths and 12 million civilian deaths caused directly by warfare, citing Rudolph J. Rummel, *China's Bloody Century: Genocide and Mass Murder Since 1900* (New York, 1991), and Guo Rugui, *Zhongguo kangRi zhanzheng zhengmian zhancheng zuozhan ji* (Nanjing, 2006). Meng Guoxiang's extremely useful review article gives a variety of statistical bases for counting deaths and injuries, with figures ranging from some 8 million to 10 million deaths (Meng Guoxiang, "Zhongguo kangRi sunshi yanjiu de huigu yu sikao" ["Reviewing Research on Losses during China's War of Resistance"], *KangRi zhanzheng yanjiu* 2006:4). Diana Lary, *The Chinese People at War: Human Suffering and Social Transformation, 1937–1945* (Cambridge, 2010), 173, acknowledges the immense difficulty of compiling accurate statistics, but notes that the official postwar figures for the total population of China show a drop of some 18 million people since 1937.
9. Huang Meizhen, *Ri-wei dui Huazhong lunxianqu jingji de lueduo yu tongzhi* [*The Japanese and Puppet Plunder and Control of the Occupied Areas of Central China*] (Beijing, 2004), 36.
10. This number refers to the total of Japanese troops at their height. Edward J. Drea and Hans van de Ven, "Overview of Major Military Campaigns," in Mark Peattie, Edward Drea, and Hans van de Ven, *The Battle for China: Essays on the Military History of the Sino-Japanese War* (Stanford, CA, 2011), 39.
11. Lyman P. Van Slyke, "The Chinese Communist Movement during the Sino-Japanese War, 1937–1945," in Lloyd E. Eastman et al., *The Nationalist Era in China, 1927–1949* (Cambridge, 1991), 277.
12. Rana Mitter, "China's 'Good War': Voices, Locations, and Generations in the Interpretation of the War of Resistance to Japan," in Sheila Jager and Rana Mitter,

382 • Notes

Ruptured Histories: War, Memory and the Post–Cold War in Asia (Cambridge, MA, 2009), 179.

13. Recent histories of the global war have begun to incorporate the China theater more fully into their analyses, for example Niall Ferguson, *The War of the World: History's Age of Hatred* (London, 2006), Evan Mawdsley, *World War II: A New History* (Cambridge, 2009), and Antony Beevor, *The Second World War* (London, 2012).

14. Theodore White and Annalee Jacoby, *Thunder out of China* (New York, 1946), 3.

15. For an analysis of the effect of the China wars on British public opinion, see Tom Buchanan, *East Wind: China and the British Left* (Oxford, 2012), especially chapter 2.

16. Important work suggesting that the origins of Communist social structures lie in the wartime Nationalist period include Mark W. Frazier, *The Making of the Chinese Industrial Workplace: State, Revolution, and Labor Management* (Cambridge, 2002), and Morris Bian, *The Making of the State Enterprise System in Modern China: The Dynamics of Institutional Change* (Cambridge, MA, 2005).

1. AS CLOSE AS LIPS AND TEETH: CHINA'S FALL, JAPAN'S RISE

1. One analysis that emphasizes the closeness of the relationship between the two countries is Joshua Fogel, *Articulating the Sinosphere: Sino-Japanese Relations in Space and Time* (Cambridge, MA, 2009).

2. Ronald P. Toby, *State and Diplomacy in Early Modern Japan* (Princeton, NJ, 1984), is the classic work that complicates the idea that Japan was truly "isolated" during this period.

3. Jonathan D. Spence, *The Search for Modern China* (New York, 1990), 122.

4. Susan Naquin and Evelyn Rawski, *Chinese Society in the Eighteenth Century* (New Haven, CT, 1989).

5. The most thoughtful recent reassessment of China's changing foreign relations over the longer term is Odd Arne Westad, *Restless Empire: China and the World since 1750* (London, 2012).

6. For the effects of imperialism on the Qing polity, see Robert Bickers, *The Scramble for China: Foreign Devils in the Qing Empire, 1832–1914* (London, 2011).

7. Ssu-yu Teng and John King Fairbank, *China's Response to the West: A Documentary Survey* (Cambridge, MA, 1954), 39–40.

8. Spence, *Search for Modern China*, 175. On the Taiping, see also Spence's *God's Chinese Son: The Heavenly Kingdom of Hong Xiuquan* (New York, 1996) and Stephen R. Platt, *Autumn in the Heavenly Kingdom: China, the West and the Epic Story of the Taiping Civil War* (New York, 2012).

9. Philip A. Kuhn, *Rebellion and its Enemies in Late Imperial China: Militarization and Social Structure, 1796–1864* (Cambridge, MA, 1970).

10. Paul Cohen, *History in Three Keys: The Boxers as Experience, Memory, and Myth* (New York, 1997), 85.

11. J. M. D. Pringle, *China Struggles for Unity* (London, 1939), 71.

12. Jay Taylor, *The Generalissimo: Chiang Kai-shek and the Making of Modern China* (Cambridge, MA, 2009), 52.

13. Mikiso Hane, *Modern Japan: A Historical Survey* (Boulder, CO, 1992), 68.

14. Hane, *Modern Japan*, 86.

15. Ibid., 141–142.

16. Spence, *Search for Modern China*, 223.

17. Naoko Shimazu, *Japanese Society at War: Death, Memory and the Russo-Japanese War* (Cambridge, 2009).

18. Louise Young, *Japan's Total Empire: Manchuria and the Culture of Wartime Imperialism* (Berkeley, CA, 1998), 91.

19. Rana Mitter, *The Manchurian Myth: Nationalism, Resistance, and Collaboration in Modern China* (Berkeley, CA, 2000).

20. Teng and Fairbank, *China's Response*, 180.

21. Rana Mitter, *A Bitter Revolution: China's Struggle with the Modern World* (Oxford, 2004), 109.

22. On Chiang's early life, see Taylor, *Generalissimo*, chapter 1.

23. On Sun, see Marie-Claire Bergère, *Sun Yat-sen* (Stanford, CA, 2000).

24. John Hunter Boyle, *China and Japan at War, 1937–1945: The Politics of Collaboration* (Stanford, CA, 1972), 16.

25. Ibid., 20.

26. Ibid., 16–18.

27. Ibid., 19.

28. On the May Fourth Movement, see Mitter, *Bitter Revolution*.

29. Li Dazhao, "The Victory of Bolshevism" (November 15, 1918), Teng and Fairbank, *China's Response*, 249.

2. A NEW REVOLUTION

1. Sidney H. Chang and Leonard H. G. Gordon, *All Under Heaven . . . : Sun Yat-sen and his Revolutionary Thought* (Hoover Institution, Stanford, CA, 1991), 86.

2. Ibid., 87.

3. Jay Taylor, *The Generalissimo: Chiang Kai-shek and the Making of Modern China* (Cambridge, MA, 2009), 44.

4. John Fitzgerald, *Awakening China: Politics, Culture, and Class in the Nationalist Revolution* (Stanford, CA, 1998).

5. Ibid., 237.

6. Stuart R. Schram, ed., *Mao's Road to Power: Revolutionary Writings, 1912–1949*, 7 vols. (Armonk, NY, 1992–) [hereafter MZD], "The Question of Miss Zhao's Personality" (18 November 1919), vol. 1, 423.

7. "A Study of Physical Education" (1 April 1917), MZD, vol. 1, 126.

8. Edgar Snow, *Red Star over China* (London, 1973), 92, 94.

9. "Peking Professors on the Shameen Massacre," in Pei-kai Cheng and Michael Lestz

with Jonathan D. Spence, *The Search for Modern China: A Documentary Collection* (New York, 1999), 258.

10. Taylor, *Generalissimo,* 50.

11. Ibid., 54.

12. "Analysis of all the Classes in Chinese Society" (1 December 1925), MZD, vol. 2, 261.

13. Hans J. van de Ven, *War and Nationalism in China, 1925–45* (London, 2003), chapter 3.

14. Taylor, *Generalissimo,* 68.

15. On militarism in the Republican era, see Edward McCord, *The Power of the Gun: The Emergence of Modern Chinese Warlordism* (Berkeley, CA, 1993).

16. On the British role in China, see Robert Bickers, *Britain in China: Community, Culture, and Colonialism, 1900–49* (Manchester, 1999).

17. C. Martin Wilbur, *The Nationalist Revolution in China, 1923–1928* (Cambridge, 1984), 72.

18. Richard Madsen, *China and the American Dream: A Moral Inquiry* (Berkeley, CA, 1995), 30.

19. On Wilsonian thought in the colonial world, see Erez Manela, *The Wilsonian Moment: Self-Determination and the International Origins of Anticolonial Nationalism* (Oxford, 2007); on the racial-equality clause, Naoko Shimazu, *Japan, Race, and Equality: The Racial Equality Proposal of 1919* (London, 1998).

20. Eri Hotta, *Pan-Asianism and Japan's War, 1931–1945* (Basingstoke, 2007), 71.

21. Louise Young, *Japan's Total Empire: Manchuria and the Culture of Wartime Imperialism* (Berkeley, CA, 1998), 89.

3. THE PATH TO CONFRONTATION

1. Academia Historica archives, Taipei: T-172–1: 1068 (Lewis report to Nanjing).

2. The classic scholarly indictment of the Nationalists' record before 1937 is Lloyd C. Eastman, *The Abortive Revolution: China under Nationalist Rule, 1927–1937* (Cambridge, MA, 1974). For a more positive and revisionist interpretation, see Frederic Wakeman, Jr. and Richard Louis Edmonds, eds., *Reappraising Republican China* (Cambridge, 2000).

3. Special Collections, Yale Divinity School Library (RG08, Box 91, folder 21): Katharine W. Hand [KH]: letter of September 14, 1935.

4. On the Chinese Maritime Customs, see the special edition of *Modern Asian Studies,* 40:3 (July 2006).

5. David A. Titus, "Introduction," in James W. Morley, ed., *The Final Confrontation: Japan's Negotiations with the United States, 1941* (New York, 1994), xxii.

6. Two biographies have examined the life of Song Meiling in depth: Hannah Pakula, *The Last Empress: Madame Chiang Kai-shek and the Birth of Modern China* (New York, 2009), and Laura Tyson Li, *Madame Chiang Kai-shek: China's Eternal First Lady* (New York, 2006).

7. *Documents on British Policy Overseas* (DBPO), series 2, vol. 21 (Far Eastern Affairs, 1936–1938), (October 5, 1937), 368–369.

8. On Dai, see Frederic Wakeman Jr., *Spymaster: Dai Li and the Chinese Secret Service* (Berkeley, CA, 2003).

9. Parks M. Coble, *Facing Japan: Chinese Politics and Japanese Imperialism, 1931–1937* (Cambridge, MA, 1991), 33–34.

10. Rana Mitter, *The Manchurian Myth: Nationalism, Resistance, and Collaboration in Modern China* (Berkeley, CA, 2000), 171.

11. Ibid., 112.

12. Coble, *Facing Japan,* 25.

13. Donald Jordan, *China's Trial by Fire: The Shanghai War of 1932* (Ann Arbor, MI, 2001); Coble, *Facing Japan,* 39–50.

14. Mao Tse-tung (Mao Zedong), "Analysis of the Classes in Chinese Society" (March 1926), *Selected Writings* (Calcutta, 1967).

15. William C. Kirby, "The Chinese War Economy," in James C. Hsiung and Steven I. Levine, eds., *China's Bitter Victory: The War with Japan, 1937–1945* (Armonk, NY, 1992), 187–189; Hans J. van de Ven, *War and Nationalism in China, 1925–45* (London, 2003), 151, 132, 156–157, 136, 143.

16. John Garver, "China's Wartime Diplomacy," in Hsiung and Levine, eds., *China's Bitter Victory,* 6.

17. Coble, *Facing Japan,* 113.

18. Ibid., 217. On Du Zhongyuan, see Rana Mitter, "Manchuria in Mind: Press, Propaganda, and Northeast China in the Age of Empire, 1930–1937," in Mariko Asano Tamanoi, ed., *Crossed Histories: Manchuria in the Age of Empire* (Honolulu, 2005).

19. Wang Ching-wei [Wang Jingwei], *China's Problems and Their Solutions* (Shanghai, 1934), 104, 113, 117.

20. "How to Analyze Classes" (October 1933), MZD, vol. 4, 546.

21. On this period, see Stephen C. Averill, *Revolution in the Highlands: China's Jinggangshan Base Area* (Lanham, MD, 2005).

22. Sun Shuyun, *The Long March: The True History of Communist China's Founding Myth* (London, 2007), 169.

23. Van de Ven, *War and Nationalism,* 183–188. Jay Taylor, *The Generalissimo: Chiang Kai-shek and the Making of Modern China* (Cambridge, MA, 2009), 125–137.

24. On the Xi'an Incident, see Taylor, *Generalissimo,* 117–137.

25. James M. Bertram, *First Act in China: The Story of the Sian Mutiny* (New York, 1938), 118.

26. Bertram, *First Act,* 122.

27. Michael Sheng, *Battling Western Imperialism: Mao, Stalin, and the United States* (Princeton, NJ, 1997), 35–39; Van de Ven, *War and Nationalism,* 171.

28. *Foreign Relations of the United States* [hereafter FRUS], 1936, vol. IV (January 12, 1937), 453.

29. James B. Crowley, *Japan's Quest for Autonomy: National Security and Foreign Policy* (Princeton, NJ, 1966).
30. Shimada Toshihiko, "Designs on North China, 1933–1937," in James W. Morley, ed., *The China Quagmire: Japan's Expansion on the Asian Continent, 1933–1941* (New York, 1983), 196.
31. Shimada, "Designs," 174–176.
32. Ibid., 199–201.
33. Coble, *Facing Japan,* 366–368.

4. THIRTY-SEVEN DAYS IN SUMMER: THE OUTBREAK OF WAR

1. Parks M. Coble, *Facing Japan: Chinese Politics and Japanese Imperialism, 1931–1937* (Cambridge, MA, 1991), 368. Marjorie Dryburgh, *North China and Japanese Expansion 1933–1937: Regional Power and the National Interest* (Richmond, UK, 2000), 142–151.
2. FRUS, 1937, vol. III (July 2, 1937), 128.
3. Zhou Tiandu, "Cong 7.7 shibian qianhou Jiang Jieshi riji kan ta de KangRi zhuzhang" ["Chiang Kai-shek's Advocacy of Resistance to Japan as Seen from His Diary around July 7, 1937"], *KangRi zhanzheng yanjiu* 2 (2008), 137.
4. Zhou, "Cong 7.7 shibian," 138.
5. Yang Tianshi, *Zhaoxun zhenshi de Jiang Jieshi* [*Searching for the Real Chiang Kai-shek*] (Taiyuan, 2008), 219.
6. Hans J. van de Ven, *War and Nationalism in China, 1925–1945* (London, 2003), 188.
7. Ibid., 190.
8. Yang, *Zhaoxun,* 221. Zhou, "Cong 7.7 shibian," 138.
9. *Shenbao,* July 9, 1937.
10. Jay Taylor, *The Generalissimo: Chiang Kai-shek and the Making of Modern China* (Cambridge, MA, 2009), 146.
11. On German influence in the army, see Chang Jui-te, "The Nationalist Army on the Eve of the War," in Mark Peattie, Edward Drea and Hans van de Ven, *The Battle for China: Essays on the Military History of the Sino-Japanese War of 1937–1945* (Stanford, CA, 2011).
12. Dryburgh, *North China,* chapter 3.
13. Van de Ven, *War and Nationalism,* 193.
14. In the year leading up to Pearl Harbor, some 70 percent of Japan's government spending would be on the military. Christopher Bayly and Tim Harper, *Forgotten Armies: Britain's Asian Empire and the War with Japan* (London, 2004), 3.
15. John Hunter Boyle, *China and Japan at War, 1937–1945: The Politics of Collaboration* (Stanford, CA, 1972), 144.
16. Boyle, *China and Japan at War,* 51–52.
17. *North-China Herald* [hereafter NCH], July 14, 1937 (original report in *North-China Daily News,* July 10, 1937).
18. Zhou, "Cong 7.7 shibian," 138.

19. FRUS, 1937, vol. III (July 12, 1937), 138.

20. Cai Dejin, ed., *Zhou Fohai riji [Zhou Fohai's Diary]*, 2 vols. (Beijing, 1986) [hereafter ZFHR], July 14, 1937.

21. ZFHR, July 16, 17, and 18, 1937.

22. Zhou, "Cong 7.7 shibian," 141.

23. NCH, July 14, 1937 (original report from July 6, 1937), 46.

24. FRUS, 1937, vol. III (July 10, 1937), 134.

25. NCH, July 21, 1937 (report from July 15, 1937), 103.

26. Ibid. (report from July 13, 1937), 103.

27. Ibid. (reports from July 13 and 18, 1937), 104.

28. Ibid. (report from July 13, 1937), 103.

29. Ibid. (original report from July 14, 1937), 104.

30. Ibid., 86.

31. Van de Ven, *War and Nationalism,* 188–189, 194.

32. Ibid., 194.

33. NCH, August 4, 1937 (original report from July 29, 1937), 177.

34. Zhou, "Cong 7.7 shibian," 144.

35. "Telegram of July 8 to Chairman Chiang . . ." (July 8, 1937), MZD, vol. V, 695.

36. Zhou, "Cong 7.7 shibian," 146.

37. "No more negotiations if Chiang Kai-shek refuses to compromise" (July 20, 1937), MZD, vol. V, 701.

38. "Convey to Chiang Kai-shek the plan to reorganize the Red Army" (July 28, 1937), MZD, vol. V, 711.

39. Lyman P. Van Slyke, "The Chinese Communist Movement during the Sino-Japanese War, 1937–1945," in Lloyd E. Eastman et al., *The Nationalist Era in China, 1927–1949* (Cambridge, 1991), 181. Stephen Mackinnon, "The Defense of the Central Yangtze," in Peattie, Drea, and Van de Ven, *Battle for China,* 205.

40. Van de Ven, *War and Nationalism,* 200.

41. "Our Views Regarding the Problem of National Defense" (August 4, 1937), MZD, vol. VI, 10–11.

42. Zhou, "Cong 7.7 shibian," 148.

43. "The Red Army's Operational Tasks, and Principles Relating to the Use of Our Troops" (August 1, 1937), MZD, vol. VI, 5.

44. NCH, July 28, 1937 (original report from July 21, 1937), 133.

45. Ibid., August 4, 1937 (original report from July 29, 1937), 173.

46. No. 2 National Archives of China, "Kangzhan baofa hou Nanjing guomin zhengfu guofang lianxi huiyi jilu" ["Records of the National Government's National Defense Liaison Committee before the Outbreak of the War of Resistance"], *Minguo dang'an* 1:43 (1996), 31.

47. Yang, *Zhaoxun,* 220.

48. "Kangzhan baofa," 31.

49. Ibid., 33.

50. Van de Ven, *War and Nationalism,* 197.

5. THE BATTLE FOR SHANGHAI

1. NCH, November 3, 1937 (original report from 28 October 1937).

2. Hans J. van de Ven, *War and Nationalism in China, 1925–1945* (London, 2003), 197.

3. Ibid.

4. NCH, August 11, 1937, 217.

5. Ibid., 231.

6. Ibid., August 18, 1937, 267 (original report from August 12, 1937).

7. Ibid., 259.

8. SMA (Shanghai Municipal Archive), U1–16–217, p. 23.

9. NCH, August 18, 1937.

10. SMA U1–16–217, p. 29.

11. NCH, August 18, 1937 (original report from August 15, 1937).

12. Ibid., September 29, 1937.

13. Ibid., October 20, 1937, 93.

14. Yang Tianshi, *Zhaoxun zhenshi de Jiang Jieshi* [*Searching for the Real Chiang Kai-shek*] (Taiyuan, 2008), 229.

15. Van de Ven, *War and Nationalism,* 154–155.

16. Rana Mitter, *The Manchurian Myth: Nationalism, Resistance, and Collaboration in Modern China* (Berkeley, CA, 2000), chapter 5.

17. Yang, *Zhaoxun,* 231.

18. NCH, September 15, 1937 (report from September 12, 1937), 394.

19. Ibid., September 28, 1937, 2.

20. *Documents on British Policy Overseas* (DBPO), series 2, vol. 21 (Far Eastern Affairs, 1936–1938) (November 11, 1937), 470–471.

21. DBPO, series 2, vol. 21 (November 11, 1937), 470–471.

22. Van de Ven, *War and Nationalism,* 215–216.

23. Jay Taylor, *The Generalissimo: Chiang Kai-shek and the Making of Modern China* (Cambridge, MA, 2009), 149.

24. ZFHR, September 27, 1937, October 3, 1937, and October 23, 1937.

25. NCH, October 2, 1937, 17–18.

26. Ibid., October 13, 1937 (report from October 6, 1937).

27. Van de Ven, *War and Nationalism,* 216.

28. Ibid., 213.

29. *Zhongyang ribao,* November 9, 1937.

30. NCH, November 15, 1937, 255.

31. *Zhonghua ribao,* November 21, 1937.

32. ZFHR, November 16, 1937.

33. *Zhonghua ribao,* November 28, 1937.

34. Taylor, *Generalissimo,* 150.

35. DBPO, series 2, vol. 21 (December 17, 1937), 593–594.

36. Ibid. (December 18, 1937), 598–603.

37. W. H. Auden and Christopher Isherwood, *Journey to a War* (London, 1938), 240.

38. ZFHR, December 11, 1937. For a rich account of the fall of Shanghai and life in the period after occupation, see Christian Henriot and Wen-hsin Yeh, eds., *In the Shadow of the Rising Sun: Shanghai under Japanese Occupation* (Cambridge, 2004).

6. REFUGEES AND RESISTANCE

1. Special Collections, Yale Divinity School Library (RG08, Box 173, folder 7), M. M. Rue papers, "Flight" (account of Mrs. Yang), 2–3.

2. Ibid., 4.

3. Stephen R. Mackinnon, *Wuhan 1938: War, Refugees, and the Making of Modern China* (Berkeley, CA, 2008), 45–54.

4. "Flight" (account of Mrs. Yang), 5.

5. Ibid. On the refugee crisis, see also MacKinnon, *Wuhan 1938*; R. Keith Schoppa, *In a Sea of Bitterness: Refugees during the Sino-Japanese War* (Cambridge, MA, 2011); Diana Lary, *The Chinese People at War: Human Suffering and Social Transformation, 1937–1945* (Cambridge, 2010).

6. Marvin Williamsen, "The Military Dimension, 1937–1941," in James C. Hsiung and Steven I. Levine, eds., *China's Bitter Victory: The War with Japan, 1937–1945* (Armonk, NY, 1992), 137.

7. Du Zhongyuan, "Dao Datong qu" ["Going to Datong"] (September 23, 1937), in Du Yi and Du Ying, eds., *Huan wo heshan: Du Zhongyuan wenji [Return our Rivers and Mountains: The Collected Essays of Du Zhongyuan]* [hereafter DZY] (Shanghai, 1998), 257.

8. Du Zhongyuan, "Dao Datong qu," 257–258.

9. Du Zhongyuan, "You Taiyuan dao Fengzhen" ["From Taiyuan to Fengzhen"] (September 26, 1937), DZY, 260.

10. DBPO, series 2, vol. 21 (January 31, 1938), 676–677.

11. Ibid. (February 2, 1938), 679–680.

12. Ibid. (February 3, 1938), 682–684.

13. Du Zhongyuan, "You Taiyuan dao Fengzhen," 264.

14. "Opinions Regarding Strategic Deployment in North China after the Fall of Taiyuan" (October 13, 1937), MZD, vol. VI, 93.

15. "Urgent Tasks of the Chinese Revolution Following the Establishment of Guomindang-Communist Cooperation" (September 29, 1937), MZD, vol. VI, 71.

16. "Guerrilla warfare should be carried out mainly on the flanks in the rear of the enemy" (October 23, 1937), MZD, vol. VI, 107.

17. MacKinnon, *Wuhan*, 18.

18. Katharine Hand, "Extracts from a Diary" (December 25, 1937).

19. Du Zhongyuan, "Jing Taiyuan" ["Going through Taiyuan"], DZY, 262.

20. Joshua H. Howard, *Workers at War: Labor in China's Arsenals, 1937–1953* (Stanford, CA, 2004).

21. Yang Lin et al., *Qu da houfang: Zhongguo kangzhan neiqian shilu* [*Going to the Interior: True Stories of the Journey Inland during the War of Resistance*] (Shanghai, 2005) [hereafter QDHF], 56.

22. Ibid., 68.

23. Ibid., 153–154.

24. Lu Liu, "A Whole Nation Walking: The 'Great Retreat' in the War of Resistance, 1937–1945," PhD diss., University of California, San Diego, 202–203, 210, 250, 287.

25. "Flight" (account of Mrs. Yang), 5–6.

26. Du Zhongyuan, "Jing Taiyuan," 261.

27. Du Zhongyuan, "You Taiyuan dao Fengzhen," 265.

28. Hsi-sheng Ch'i, "The Military Dimension, 1942–1945," in Hsiung and Levine, *China's Bitter Victory*, 180, cites an archival document suggesting some 95.45 million refugees over the 1937–1945 period.

7. MASSACRE AT NANJING

1. Iechika Ryôko (tr. Wang Xueping), "Cong 'Jiang Jieshi riji' jiedu 1937 nian 12 yue de Nanjing xingshi" ["The Situation in Nanjing in December 1937 from a Reading of Chiang Kai-shek's Diary"], *Minguo dang'an* 2 (2009), 111.

2. NCH, August 15, 1937, 262.

3. Du Zhongyuan, "Dao Datong qu" ["Going to Datong"] (September 23, 1937), in Du Yi and Du Ying, eds., *Huan wo heshan: Du Zhongyuan wenji* [*Return our Rivers and Mountains: The Collected Essays of Du Zhongyuan*] [hereafter DZY] (Shanghai, 1998), 258–259.

4. ZFHR, August 15, 1937.

5. NCH, November 20, 1937.

6. Ibid., December 1, 1937 (original report from November 25, 1937), 322.

7. William C. Kirby, "Engineering China: Birth of the Developmental State, 1928–1937," in Wen-hsin Yeh, ed., *Becoming Chinese: Passages to Modernity and Beyond* (Berkeley, CA, 2000), 140.

8. Fujiwara Akira, "The Nanking Atrocity: An Interpretative Overview," in Bob Tadashi Wakabayashi, ed., *The Nanking Atrocity 1937–38: Complicating the Picture* (New York, 2007), 35–36, 30. Hattori Satoshi with Edward J. Drea, "Japanese Operations from July to December 1937," in Mark Peattie, Edward Drea, and Hans van de Ven, eds., *The Battle for China: Essays on the Military History of the Sino-Japanese War of 1937–1945* (Stanford, CA, 2011), 175.

9. NCH, December 1, 1937 (original report from November 25, 1937), 333.

10. Margherita Zanasi, "Exporting Development: The League of Nations and Republican China," *Comparative Studies in Society and History* 49:1 (January 2007).

11. John Rabe, *The Good Man of Nanking: The Diaries of John Rabe*, ed. Edwin Wickert, trans. John E. Woods (New York, 2000).

12. Ibid., 11.
13. The idea was based on a similar zone that had been established earlier in Shanghai by a French Jesuit priest, Robert Jacquinot. Marcia R. Ristaino, *The Jacquinot Safety Zone: Wartime Refugees in Shanghai* (Stanford, CA, 2008), chapters 4 and 5.
14. Rabe, *Good Man*, 53.
15. Ibid., 46–48.
16. Iechika, "Nanjing xingshi," 111.
17. Ibid.
18. Tom Buchanan, *East Wind: China and the British Left* (Oxford, 2012), 62–63.
19. Iechika, "Nanjing xingshi."
20. F. Tillman Durdin, "All Captives Slain," *New York Times* (December 18, 1937).
21. No. 2 National Archives of China, ed., "Cheng Ruifang riji" ["The Diary of Cheng Ruifang"], *Minguo dang'an* 4 (2004) [hereafter CRF], (December 10, 1937), 26.
22. Minnie Vautrin diary in Zhang Kaiyuan, ed., *Eyewitnesses to Massacre: American Missionaries Bear Witness to Japanese Atrocities in Nanjing* (Armonk, NY, 2001) [hereafter MV], 340.
23. On premodern modes of philanthropy in China, see Joanna Handlin Smith, *The Art of Doing Good: Charity in Late Ming China* (Berkeley, CA, 2009); Kathryn Edgerton-Tarpley, *Tears from Iron: Cultural Responses to Famine in Nineteenth-Century China* (Berkeley, CA, 2009).
24. CRF (December 10, 1937), 27.
25. See Ruth Rogaski, *Hygienic Modernity: Meanings of Health and Disease in Treaty-Port China* (Berkeley, CA, 2004).
26. Akira Iriye, "The Role of the United States Embassy in Tokyo," in Dorothy Borg and Shumpei Okamoto, eds., *Pearl Harbor as History: Japanese-American Relations, 1931–1941* (New York, 1973), 119–120.
27. CRF (December 12, 1937), 27.
28. Jay Taylor, *The Generalissimo: Chiang Kai-shek and the Making of Modern China* (Cambridge, MA, 2009), 151–152.
29. Durdin, "All Captives Slain" (December 18, 1937).
30. CRF (December 14, 1937), 28.
31. Ibid. (December 18, 1937), 30.
32. MV, 362.
33. Rabe, *Good Man*, 81.
34. George Fitch diary in Zhang Kaiyuan, *Eyewitnesses* [hereafter GF] (December 18, 1937), 92.
35. Ibid. (December 22, 1937), 93.
36. Ibid. (December 23, 1937), 94.
37. Rabe, *Good Man*, 77.
38. GF (December 19, 1937), 92.
39. MV (December 17, 1937), 358.
40. Ibid. (December 19, 1937), 361.

41. Ibid. (December 17, 1937), 359, CRF (December 17, 1937), 29.

42. MV (December 27, 1937), 366.

43. CRF (December 19, 21, and 22, 1937), 30–32.

44. Ibid. (December 20, 1937), 31.

45. Ibid. (January 1, 1938), 10.

46. Rabe, *Good Man*, 92.

47. CRF (December 15, 1937), 28.

48. Ibid. (December 26 and 29, 1937), 33–34.

49. Ibid. (January 3, 1938), 11.

50. Neil Boister and Robert Cryer, eds., *The Tokyo International Military Tribunal: A Reappraisal* (Oxford, 2008), 191.

51. A variety of rigorous studies have emerged in recent years that give a clear account of what the historically valid parameters of debate on these and related questions are. Among them are Wakabayashi, *The Nanking Atrocity*; Joshua Fogel, ed., *The Nanjing Massacre in History and Historiography* (Berkeley, CA, 2000); Takashi Yoshida, *The Making of the "Rape of Nanking": History and Memory in Japan, China, and the United States* (New York, 2006); and Daqing Yang, "Convergence or Divergence? Recent Historical Writings on the Rape of Nanjing," *American Historical Review* 104:3, 1,999.

52. GF, n.d., 84.

53. Ibid., December 19, 1937, 92.

54. Ibid., December 22, 1937, 94.

55. CRF (December 29, 1937), 34.

56. For the initial phase of life after the occupation of Nanjing, see Timothy Brook, *Collaboration: Japanese Agents and Local Elites in Wartime China* (Cambridge, MA, 2005), chapter 5.

57. CRF (January 2, 1938), 11.

58. Durdin, "All Captives Slain" (December 18, 1937).

59. Ibid.

60. FRUS, 1937, vol. III (December 14, 1937), 806.

61. Ibid., 1938, vol. III (January 11, 1938), 13.

62. NCH, December 29, 1937 (original report from December 25, 1937), 477, 484.

63. On Pan-Asianism, see Eri Hotta, *Pan-Asianism and Japan's War, 1931–1945* (Basingstoke, 2007).

64. Iechika, "Nanjing xingshi," 113.

65. Ibid., 114.

66. Ibid.

8. THE BATTLE OF TAIERZHUANG

1. W. H. Auden and Christopher Isherwood, *Journey to a War* (London, 1938), 39.

2. See Stephen R. MacKinnon, *Wuhan 1938: War, Refugees, and the Making of Modern China* (Berkeley, CA, 2008), chapter 1.

3. Ibid., 11–13.
4. John Hunter Boyle, *China and Japan at War, 1937–1945: The Politics of Collaboration* (Stanford, CA, 1972), 78–81.
5. MacKinnon, *Wuhan 1938,* 20–28.
6. Ibid., 74–75.
7. Ibid., 68–69.
8. Marvin Williamsen, "The Military Dimension, 1937–1941," in James C. Hsiung and Steven I. Levine, eds., *China's Bitter Victory: The War with Japan, 1937–1945* (Armonk, NY, 1992), 139; MacKinnon, *Wuhan 1938,* 34.
9. Stephen Mackinnon, "The Defense of the Central Yangtze," in Mark Peattie, Edward Drea, and Hans van de Ven, *The Battle for China: Essays on the Military History of the Sino-Japanese War* (Stanford, CA, 2011), 194.
10. "Duiri kangzhan yu bendang qiantu" ("On the War of Resistance against Japan and the Future of this Party"), ZT (April 1, 1938), vol. 15, 197.
11. On Li Zongren and the role of Guangxi, see Graham Hutchings, "A Province at War: Guangxi During the Sino-Japanese Conflict, 1937–1945," *China Quarterly* 108 (December 1986).
12. Chang Jui-te, "Chiang Kai-shek's Coordination by Personal Directives," in Stephen R. MacKinnon, Diana Lary, and Ezra Vogel, eds., *China at War: Regions of China, 1937–1945* (Stanford, CA, 2007), 78–79.
13. Du Yi and Du Ying, eds., *Huan wo heshan: Du Zhongyuan wenji* [*Return Our Rivers and Mountains: The Collected Essays of Du Zhongyuan*] [hereafter DZY] (Shanghai, 1998), "Jiang taigong," 273.
14. Ibid., 274.
15. Stephen Mackinnon, "Defense of the Central Yangtze," 1919.
16. Hans J. van de Ven, *War and Nationalism in China, 1925–1945* (London, 2003), 224.
17. Sheng Cheng, *Taierzhuang jishi* [*Taierzhuang Memoir*] (Beijing, 2007), 36.
18. Katharine W. Hand, "Diary," April 8, 1938. DZY, "Jiang taigong," 273.
19. Sheng Cheng, *Taierzhuang jishi,* 48–49, 236.
20. FRUS, 1938, vol. III (April 19, 1938), 154.
21. DBPO, series 2, vol. 21 (April 29, 1938), 744–746.
22. Van de Ven, *War and Nationalism,* 225; Williamsen, "The Military Dimension," 140; MacKinnon, *Wuhan 1938,* 35.
23. DZY, "'Jang taigong' wei jianji" ["Meeting 'Duke Jiang'"] (April 6, 1938), 274.
24. Diana Lary, "A Ravaged Place: The Devastation of the Xuzhou Region, 1938," in Diana Lary and Stephen MacKinnon, eds., *Scars of War: The Impact of Warfare on Modern China* (Vancouver, 2001), 102.
25. Ibid., 113–114.
26. "On Protracted War" (May 26 to June 3, 1938), MZD, vol. VI, 322.

9. THE DEADLY RIVER

1. FRUS, 1938, vol. III (7 June 1938), 194.

2. Ibid. (July 19, 1938), 232–233, 236.

3. Ibid. (July 23, 1938), 234–235.

4. Stephen R. Mackinnon, *Wuhan 1938: War, Refugees, and the Making of Modern China* (Berkeley, CA, 2008), 57.

5. No. 2 Historical Archives of China, ed., "Deguo zongguwen Fakenhaosen guanyu Zhongguo kangRi zhanlue zhi liang fen jianyishu" ["Two Documents with Suggestions on Policy for China's War of Resistance from German General Adviser Falkenhausen"] (August 20, 1935), *Minguo dang'an* 2 (1991), 26.

6. Yet recent work has suggested that the French Army might have had a better chance of defeating the Germans in 1940 than was realized or admitted at the time. See Ernest R. May, *Strange Victory: Hitler's Conquest of France* (New York, 2001).

7. Liang Changgen also argues that the blasting of the dikes was a turning point in terms of the Nationalist government's attitude toward refugees and the need for the government to provide welfare provision for them. Liang Changgen, "Kangzhan qijian guomin zhengfu zai Huangfanqu de ziyuan zhenghe yu guojia diaodu" ["Resource Allocation and State Control of Yellow River Flood Zones by the National Government during the War of Resistance"], *Junshi lishi yanjiu* 1 (2007), 57.

8. No. 2 Historical Archives of China, ed., "1938 nian Huanghe jueti shiliao yi zu" ["Material on the Breaching of the Yellow River Dikes, 1938: 1, Selections from Xiong Xianyi's Diary, June 1938"], *Minguo dang'an* 3 (1997), 9.

9. Xiong diary (June 9, 1938), 10; Diana Lary, "Drowned Earth: The Strategic Breaching of the Yellow River Dyke, 1938," *War in History* 8 (2001), 198–199.

10. "Japan's Sorrow," *Time*, June 27, 1938.

11. Ibid.

12. FRUS, 1938, vol. III (July 19, 1938), 230.

13. Lary, "Drowned Earth," 205–206.

14. FRUS, 1938, vol. III (June 15, 1938), 197.

15. Diana Lary argues that the Japanese were not defeated in any of their overall objectives ("Drowned Earth," 201). Ma Zhonglian suggests that the Japanese had decided to change their path toward Wuhan before the flood, and that there was little strategic value to the flooding ("Huayuankou jueti de junshi yiyi" ["The Military Significance of the Breach of the Dikes at Huayuankou"], *KangRi zhanzheng yanjiu* 4 (1999). Hans van de Ven gives more credit to the decision in military terms, in *War and Nationalism in China, 1925–1945* (London, 2003), 226.

16. "Yanbie deji guwen zhici" ["Speech of Farewell to the German Adviser"], *ZT* (July 2, 1938), 330.

17. FRUS, 1938, vol. III (June 22, 1938), 202.

18. Edna Tow, "The Great Bombing of Chongqing and the Anti-Japanese War, 1937–1945," in Mark Peattie, Edward Drea and Hans van de Ven, *The Battle for China: Essays on the Military History of the Sino-Japanese War* (Stanford, CA, 2011), 265.

19. Qin Shaoyi, ed., *Xian zongtong Jianggong sixiang lun zongji* [*The Thought and*

Speeches of President Chiang Kai-shek] (Taipei, 1984) [hereafter ZT]. "Fayang geming lishi de guangrong baowei geming genjudi de Wuhan" ["Wuhan, Developing Revolutionary History, Gloriously Defending the Revolutionary Base"], (July 31, 1938), 410–421.

20. MacKinnon, *Wuhan 1938*, 96.

21. "Renqing muqian kangzhan xingshi he suo fuze ren nuli zhunbei baowei Wuhan" ["Clearly Recognizing the Current Situation of the War of Resistance and Those Taking the Responsibility to Work Hard to Prepare to Defend Wuhan"], ZT (August 28, 1938), 461–466.

22. "On the New Stage" (October 12–14, 1938), MZD, vol. VI, 478–479.

23. Jay Taylor, *The Generalissimo: Chiang Kai-shek and the Making of Modern China* (Cambridge, MA, 2009), 158

24. Taylor, *Generalissimo*, 159–160.

10. "A SORT OF WARTIME NORMAL"

1. See Lee McIsaac, "The City as Nation: Creating a Wartime Capital in Chongqing," in Joseph W. Esherick, ed., *Remaking the Chinese City: Modernity and National Identity, 1900–1950* (Honolulu: University of Hawai'i Press, 2000).

2. Du Zhongyuan, "Diren neibu yanzhong zhuangkuang de xin baogao" ["A New Report on the Serious Situation of the Enemy in the Interior"] (24 April 1938), DZY, 276.

3. On Xinjiang, see James Millward, *Eurasian Crossroads: A History of Xinjiang* (New York: Columbia University Press, 2006); on Tibet, see Hsiao-ting Lin, *Tibet and Nationalist China's Frontier: Intrigues and Ethnopolitics, 1928–49* (Vancouver, 2006).

4. Andres Rodriguez, "Building the Nation, Serving the Frontier: Mobilizing and Reconstructing China's Borderlands during the War of Resistance (1937–1945)," *Modern Asian Studies* 45:2 (March 2011).

5. Theodore White and Annalee Jacoby, *Thunder out of China* (New York, 1946), 13.

6. Southwestern Normal University Chongqing Bombing Research Centre et al., ed., *Chongqing da hongzha* [*The Great Chongqing Bombings*] (Chongqing, 2002) [hereafter CQDH], 92–93.

7. Zhou Yong, *Chongqing tongshi* [*Comprehensive History of Chongqing*] (Chongqing, 2002), vol. 2, 876.

8. Sichuan Provincial Archives, *Kang-ri zhanzheng shiqi Sichuan sheng ge lei qingkuang tongji* [*Statistics on Various Situations in Wartime Sichuan Province*] (Chengdu, 2005), 29.

9. QDHF, 394.

10. Ibid., 408.

11. Chang Jui-te, "Bombs Don't Discriminate? Class, Gender, and Ethnicity in the Air-Raid-Shelter Experience of the Wartime Chongqing Population," in James Flath and Norman Smith, *Beyond Suffering: Recounting War in Modern China*

(Vancouver, 2011); Edna Tow, "The Great Bombing of Chongqing and the Anti-Japanese War, 1937–1945," in Mark Peattie, Edward Drea, and Hans van de Ven, *The Battle for China: Essays on the Military History of the Sino-Japanese Wa*r (Stanford, CA, 2011).

12. QDHF, 411–412.
13. Ibid., 416.
14. "War in China: Heavenly Dog," *Time* (May 15, 1939).
15. QDHF, 410–411.
16. Tow, "The Great Bombing of Chongqing," 265. Jay Taylor, *The Generalissimo: Chiang Kai-shek and the Making of Modern China* (Cambridge, MA, 2009), 179.
17. MacKinnon, *Wuhan 1938*, 55–59.
18. Rana Mitter, "Classifying Citizens in Nationalist China during World War II," *Modern Asian Studies* 45:2 (March 2011), 258–259. Sichuan Provincial Archives, *Min* [Republican-era files] 38, folder 2/614 (June 1940).
19. Chongqing Municipal Archives [hereafter CQA], 0067-1-1150 (May 1939).
20. CQA, 0053-12-91 (May 1939).
21. Ibid.
22. CQA, 0053-12-91 (June 1939). Lu Liu, "A Whole Nation Walking," 202–10.
23. Mitter, "Classifying Citizens," 262.
24. Ibid., 265–267.
25. Hans J. van de Ven, *War and Nationalism in China, 1925–1945* (London, 2003), 255–258.
26. Mitter, "Classifying Citizens," 272–273. See also Helen Schneider, "Mobilising Women: The Women's Advisory Council, Resistance, and Reconstruction during China's War with Japan," *European Journal of East Asian Studies* 11:2 (2012).
27. Van de Ven, *War and Nationalism in China*, 260–262.
28. William C. Kirby, "The Chinese War Economy," in Hsiung and Levine, *China's Bitter Victory*, 191; Felix Boecking, "Unmaking the Chinese Nationalist State: Administrative Reform among Fiscal Collapse, 1937–1945," *Modern Asian Studies* 45:2 (March 2011), 283.
29. Ibid., 190–191.
30. Ibid., 196.
31. Ibid., 192–193.
32. KH, "Diary," May 2, 1938.
33. Timothy Brook, *Collaboration: Japanese Agents and Local Elites in Wartime China* (Cambridge, MA, 2005), especially chapters 2 and 3.
34. Yale Divinity Library, M. M. Rue papers: Y. L. Vane, "One Month among the Bandits."
35. Timothy Brook, "The Great Way Government of Shanghai," in Christian Henriot and Wen-hsin Yeh, eds., *In the Shadow of the Rising Sun: Shanghai under Japanese Occupation* (Cambridge, 2004), 161.
36. Timothy Brook, "Collaborationist Nationalism in Wartime China," in Timothy

Brook and Andre Schmid, *Nation Work: Asian Elites and National Identities* (Ann Arbor, MI, 2000), 170ff.

37. Shanghai Municipal Archives [hereafter SMA]: Q113–2–12. Q165–1–64.

38. Yale Divinity Library, M. M. Rue papers: Mrs. C. M. Lee, "Impressions of Camp No. 100."

39. SMA (U1–16–1039).

40. Ibid., 2.

41. See, for instance, "Who Ran the Treaty Ports? A Study of the Shanghai Municipal Council," in Robert Bickers and Isabella Jackson (eds.), *Treaty Ports in Modern China: Law, Land, and Power* (London, 2013).

42. SMA (U1–16–1039), 101.

43. Ibid., 121.

44. KH, "Diary," February 12, 1939.

45. Zhu Hongzhao, *Yan'an richang shenghuo zhong de lishi* [*The History of Everyday Life in Yan'an*] (Guilin, 2007), 11.

46. Zhu, *Yan'an*, 11–29.

47. Lyman P. Van Slyke, "The Chinese Communist Movement during the Sino-Japanese War, 1937–1945," in Lloyd E. Eastman et al., *The Nationalist Era in China, 1927–1949* (Cambridge, 1991), 183–187.

48. Van Slyke, "Chinese Communist Movement," 181, 189.

49. "Interview with Nym Wales on Negotiations with the Guomindang and the War with Japan," MZD, vol. VI, 16–17.

50. Mark Selden, *The Yenan Way in Revolutionary China* (Cambridge, MA, 1971).

51. For instance, "On Protracted War" (May 26, 1938), MZD, vol. VI, 319–389.

52. Van Slyke, "Chinese Communist Movement," 203.

53. Ibid., 200.

54. Zhu, *Yan'an*, 12.

55. Ibid., 8.

56. Ibid., 34.

57. See Joshua H. Howard, *Workers at War: Labor in China's Arsenals, 1937–1953* (Stanford, CA, 2004), on Chongqing workers, particularly chapters 3, 4, and 5.

58. Zhu, *Yan'an*, 6.

59. Ibid., (citing 1992 memoir).

60. Ibid., 238, 243, 245–250.

61. Ibid., 351.

62. Ibid., 319–321. Wang Guangrong, "Rijun feiji hongzha Yan'an jishi" ["A Record of the Bombing of Yan'an by Japanese Aircraft"], *Dangshi bolan* 2 (2003), 46–47.

63. Zhu, *Yan'an*, 319–321. Wang Guangrong, "Rijun," 46–47.

64. Van Slyke, "Chinese Communist Movement," 200–02.

65. Selden, *Yenan Way*, 161–171; Lyman van Slyke, *Enemies and Friends: The United Front in Chinese Communist History* (Stanford, CA, 1967), 142–153.

66. Van Slyke, "Chinese Communist Movement," 185–187.

67. On Pingxingguan, see Satoshi and Drea, "Japanese Operations," in Peattie, Drea, and Van de Ven, *The Battle for China*, 164–167. On Communist base areas and resistance outside Yan'an see, for instance, Gregor Benton, *Mountain Fires: The Red Army's Three-Year War in South China, 1934–1938* (Berkeley, CA, 1992), and on the New Fourth Army, Gregor Benton, *New Fourth Army: Communist Resistance Along the Yangtze and the Huai, 1938–1941* (Berkeley, CA, 1999); David Goodman, *Social and Political Change in Revolutionary China: The Taihang Base Area in the War of Resistance to Japan, 1937–1945* (Lanham, MD, 2000); Pauline Keating, David Goodman, and Feng Chongyi, eds., *North China at War: The Social Ecology of Revolution* (New York: M. E. Sharpe, 1999); Pauline B. Keating, *Two Revolutions: Village Reconstruction and the Cooperative Movement in Northern Shaanxi, 1934–1945* (Stanford, CA, 1997); and Dagfinn Gatu, *Village China at War: The Impact of Resistance to Japan, 1937–1945* (Vancouver, 2008).

68. Van Slyke, "Chinese Communist Movement," 188–189.

69. Taylor, *Generalissimo*, 171.

70. Van de Ven, *War and Nationalism*, 220.

11. FLIGHT INTO THE UNKNOWN

1. ZFHR, November 26–December 1, 1938.

2. Gao Zongwu, *Gao Zongwu huiyilu* [*The Memoirs of Gao Zongwu*] (Beijing, 2009) [hereafter GZW], 30.

3. GZW, 30–32.

4. ZFHR, December 1 and 3, 1938.

5. Ibid., December 5, 1938.

6. Jbid., December 5, 7, and 8, 1938.

7. Ibid., December 9, 12, and 17, 1938.

8. "Wei guojun tuichu Wuhan gao quanguo guomin shu" ["A Message to the Whole Nation about the Withdrawal from Wuhan"] (October 31, 1938), ZT, vol. 30, 305.

9. "Wei guojun tuichu," 301–302.

10. Drea and Van de Ven, "Overview," in Mark Peattie, Edward Drea, and Hans van de Ven, *The Battle for China: Essays on the Military History of the Sino-Japanese War of 1937–1945* (Stanford, CA, 2011), 35.

11. "Di yi ci Nanyue junshi huiyi kaihui xunci" ["Opening Speech to the First Nanyue Military Conference"], ZT (November 25, 1938), 486–487.

12. "Di yi ci Nanyue junshi huiyi," 486–510.

13. "Di yi ci Nanyue junshi huiyi xunci (4)," ZT, 545, 546.

14. Hans J. van de Ven, *War and Nationalism in China, 1925–1945* (London, 2003), 232.

15. "Di yi ci Nanyue junshi huiyi," 486–510.

16. GZW, 26.

17. However, the volume for 1939 is missing.

18. John Hunter Boyle, *China and Japan at War, 1937–1945: The Politics of Collaboration* (Stanford, CA, 1972), 168–169.

19. Ibid., 168.

20. ZHFR, August 21, 1937.

21. Ibid., August 16 and 17, 1937; GZW, 30.

22. Boyle, *China and Japan at War*, 168.

23. ZFHR, August 30 and 31, 1937, September 1 and 3, 1937, and September 11, 1937.

24. Boyle, *China and Japan at War*, 141.

25. Ibid., 179–187.

26. Ibid., 187.

27. Huang Meizhen and Yang Hanqing, "Nationalist China's Negotiating Position during the Stalemate, 1938–1945," in David P. Barrett and Larry N. Shyu, *Chinese Collaboration with Japan, 1932–1945: The Limits of Accommodation* (Stanford, CA, 2001), 57.

28. ZHFR, October 30, 1938, November 15 and 23, 1938.

29. Ibid., October 30, 1938.

30. Boyle, *China and Japan at War*, 195–199.

31. ZFHR, December 19, 1938.

32. GZW, 29–30.

33. Ibid., 30.

34. ZFHR, December 20, 1938.

35. ZFHR, December 21 and 26, 1938.

36. Boyle, *China and Japan at War*, 212–213.

37. CKSD (Box 40, Folder 2), December 21, 1938.

38. Boyle, *China and Japan at War*, 213.

39. Pei-kai Cheng and Michael Lestz with Jonathan D. Spence, "Generalissimo Chiang Assails Prince Konoye's Statement," in *The Search for Modern China: A Documentary Collection* (New York, 1999), 321.

40. Boyle, *China and Japan at War*, 223–224.

41. ZFHR, December 27, 29, and 31, 1938.

12. THE ROAD TO PEARL HARBOR

1. Ye Chao, "Wannan shibian jingguo de huigu" ["Looking back on my Experiences during the Wannan Incident"], *Anhui wenshi ziliao*, vol. 6 (telegram from 26 December 1940), 5.

2. Hans J. van de Ven, *War and Nationalism in China, 1925–1945* (London, 2003), 237–239.

3. Ibid., 240–246.

4. Christopher Thorne, *Allies of a Kind: The United States, Britain, and the War against Japan, 1941–1945* (Oxford, 1978), 52.

5. John Garver, "China's Wartime Diplomacy," in James C. Hsiung and Steven I. Levine, eds., *China's Bitter Victory: The War with Japan, 1937–1945* (Armonk, NY, 1992), 10–11.

6. Ibid., 13.

7. For the most comprehensive account of this campaign, see the monumental book by Alvin D. Coox, *Nomonhan: Japan against Russia, 1939* (Stanford, CA, 1985).

8. Garver, "China's Wartime Diplomacy," 16.

9. John Hunter Boyle, *China and Japan at War, 1937–1945: The Politics of Collaboration* (Stanford, CA, 1972), 243–246.

10. Ibid., 246.

11. Ibid., chapter 13.

12. GZW, 74–75.

13. Boyle, *China and Japan at War,* 279.

14. ZFHR, January 13, 1940, 230.

15. Ibid., January 26, 1940, 237.

16. Boyle, *China and Japan at War,* 282–285.

17. The newspaper *Zhonghua ribao* [hereafter ZHRB], March 30, 1940.

18. ZFHR, March 30, 1940, March 31, 1940, 272–273.

19. Boyle, *China and Japan at War,* 304.

20. FRUS, 1940, vol. IV (February 17, 1940), 287.

21. Garver, "China's Wartime Diplomacy," 8–9.

22. Boyle, *China and Japan at War,* 303.

23. ZFHR, May 13, 1940, 280.

24. Huang Meizhen and Yang Hanqing, "Nationalist China's Negotiating Position during the Stalemate, 1938–1945," in David P. Barrett and Larry N. Shyu, *Chinese Collaboration with Japan, 1932–1945: The Limits of Accommodation* (Stanford, CA, 2001), 65.

25. FRUS, 1940, vol. IV (January 15, 1940), 263.

26. Huang and Yang, "Nationalist China's Negotiating Position," 61.

27. Boyle, *China and Japan at War,* 303–305; Jay Taylor, *The Generalissimo: Chiang Kai-shek and the Making of Modern China* (Cambridge, MA, 2009), 174–175.

28. "Persist in Long-term Cooperation between the Guomindang and the Communist Party," MZD, vol. VI, 153.

29. Taylor, *Generalissimo,* 166–167.

30. Lloyd E. Eastman, "Nationalist China during the Sino-Japanese War, 1937–1945," in Lloyd E. Eastman et al., *The Nationalist Era in China, 1927–1949* (Cambridge, 1991), 152–160.

31. Lyman P. Van Slyke, "The Chinese Communist Movement during the Sino-Japanese War, 1937–1945," in Eastman et al., *The Nationalist Era in China, 1927–1949,* 253.

32. Ibid., 254–255.

33. Ibid., 244–245.

34. Wang Jianguo, "Gu Zhutong yu Wannan shibian" ["Gu Zhutong and the Wannan Incident"], *KangRi zhanzheng yanjiu* 3 (1993), 197. Gregor Benton, *New Fourth Army: Communist Resistance Along the Yangtze and the Huai, 1938–1941* (Berkeley, CA, 1999), 515–516.

35. For instance, "It is best that the forces south of the river move to southern Jiangsu in groups" (December 30, 1940), and "Smash the Guomindang's offensive and bring about a change for the better in the situation" (December 31, 1940), MZD, vol. 6, 610, 611. Benton, *New Fourth Army*, 513.

36. "Mao Zedong and Zhu De to Zhou Enlai and Ye Jianying concerning the negotiations with Chiang Kai-shek on the New Fourth Army's route for moving northward" (December 25, 1940), MZD, vol. 6, 593. Benton, *New Fourth Army*, 530.

37. Benton, *New Fourth Army*, 530.

38. Dong Nancai, "Wannan shibian tuwei ji" ["A Record of Breaking out of Encirclement during the Wannan Incident"], *Yuhuan wenshi ziliao*, vol. 3 (January 5, 1941), 79.

39. Dong Nancai, "Wannan shibian," 81.

40. Benton, *New Fourth Army*, 572.

41. Zhang Guangyu and Li Zhongyuan, "Xinsijun zai Wannan shibian zhong junshi shiwu yu jiaoxun zai shentao" ["An Investigation into the Mistakes and Lessons of the Wannan Incident"], *Wuhan daxue xuebao* 6 (1992), 72.

42. Taylor, *Generalissimo*, 176–177.

43. "To Zhou Enlai and Ye Jianying concerning political and military preparations for an overall counterattack" (January 15, 1941), MZD, vol. 6, 637.

44. "Chiang and the Communists," *Time*, February 3, 1941.

45. Benton, *New Fourth Army*, 597.

46. FRUS, 1940, vol. IV, January 3, 1941, 477.

47. Ibid., 479.

48. "On New Democracy" (January 15, 1940), MZD, vol. VII, 340, 351, and 355.

49. Federica Ferlanti, "The New Life Movement in Jiangxi Province, 1934–1938," *Modern Asian Studies* 5:44 (2010).

50. SMA: Q130–1–1; R18–1–321; R48–1–801.

51. See Mitter, *Manchurian Myth*, chapters 3 and 4.

52. Wang Jianguo, "Qingxiang yundong yu Li Shiqun zhi si" ["The 'qingxiang' Campaign and the Death of Li Shiqun"], in *Anhui shixue* 6 (2004), 56–57.

53. Hu Jucheng, "Jiang Weiqing yu Sunan fan 'qingxiang'" ["Jiang Weiqing and Opposing 'qingxiang' in Sunan"], in *Tiejun* 11 (2011), 9.

54. Hu Jucheng, "Jiang Weiqing," 9–10.

55. Xie Shilian, ed., *Chuanyu da hongzha (The Great Bombing of Sichuan and Chongqing)*, (Chengdu, Xinan jiaotong daxue chubanshe, 2005), 76–89.

56. FRUS, 1940, vol. IV, January 3, 1941, 484.

57. Taylor, *Generalissimo*, 181–183.

58. On Stalin's refusal to accept German hostility, see Constantine Pleshakov, *Stalin's Folly: The Tragic First Ten Days of WWII on the Eastern Front* (Boston, MA, 2005).

59. "Decision Regarding the International United Front against Fascism," MZD, vol. VII (June 23, 1941), 764.

60. ZFHR, June 22, 1941, 481.

61. Ibid., June 29, 1941, 484.
62. Mikiso Hane, *Modern Japan: A Historical Survey* (Boulder, CO, 1992), 298–308.
63. David A. Titus, "Introduction," in James W. Morley, ed., *The Final Confrontation: Japan's Negotiations with the United States, 1941* (New York, 1994), xxiii.
64. Taylor, *Generalissimo*, 179.
65. Charles F. Romanus and Riley Sunderland, *Stilwell's Mission to China* (Washington DC, 1953), 30–31.
66. Yu Maochun, *OSS in China: Prelude to Cold War* (New Haven, CT, 1997), 25.
67. Gerhard Weinberg, *A World at Arms: A Global History of World War II*, 2nd ed. (Cambridge, 2005), 252–264.
68. Taylor, *Generalissimo*, 188.
69. ZFHR, December 8, 1941, 548.

13. DESTINATION BURMA

1. Yale Divinity Library (RG08, Box 31), Velva V. Brown, MD [hereafter VVB], letter of October 4, 1937.
2. VVB, letter of November 17, 1941, from the American Baptist Foreign Mission Society to "Friends and relatives of East and South China missionaries."
3. Robert J. C. Butow, *Tojo and the Coming of the War* (Stanford, CA, 1969), 402.
4. VVB, letter of December 7, 1941, from the American Baptist Foreign Mission Society to "Friends and relatives of all missionaries in the Far East."
5. VVB, letter of September 1, 1942, from VVB to "friends and family."
6. Ibid.
7. Ibid.
8. "Zhonghua minguo 31 nian yuadan gao quanguo junmin tongbao shu" ("Letter to the Soldiers and People of the Whole Country on New Year's Day, 1942"), at http://www.chungcheng.org.tw/thought/class07/0016/0001.htm, 275–282.
9. CKSD (December 1941 monthly reflection).
10. CKSD, December 27, 1941, cited in Wang Jianlang, "Xinren de liushi: cong Jiang Jieshi riji kan kangRi zhanhou qi de ZhongMei guanxi" ["The Erosion of Trust: Sino-American Relations for the Postwar Period as Seen through Chiang Kai-shek's Diary"], *Jindaishi yanjiu* 3 (2009), 50.
11. CKSD (Box 41, folder 18), December 15, 1941.
12. CKSD, December 17, 1941.
13. Ibid., December 20, 1941.
14. Christopher Thorne, *Allies of a Kind: The United States, Britain, and the War against Japan, 1941–1945* (Oxford, 1978), 189.
15. FRUS, 1942: China (January 7, 1942), 193. Thorne, *Allies of a Kind*, 181.
16. Thorne, *Allies of a Kind*, 183.
17. Hans J. van de Ven, *War and Nationalism in China, 1925–1945* (London, 2003), 25.
18. Theodore White and Annalee Jacoby, *Thunder out of China* (New York, 1946), 146.

19. Barbara W. Tuchman, *Stilwell and the American Experience in China, 1911–1945* (New York, 1971), 251.

20. Lloyd E. Eastman, "Nationalist China during the Sino-Japanese War, 1937–1945," in Eastman et al., *The Nationalist Era in China, 1927–1949* (Cambridge, 1991), 145.

21. Barbara D. Metcalf and Thomas R. Metcalf, *A Concise History of India* (Cambridge, 2002), 200.

22. Jay Taylor, *The Generalissimo: Chiang Kai-shek and the Making of Modern China* (Cambridge, MA, 2009), 194.

23. Metcalf and Metcalf, *A Concise History of India*, 201–202.

24. Guido Samarani, "Shaping the Future of Asia: Chiang Kai-shek, Nehru, and China-India Relations during the Second World War Period," LSE working paper, http://www.ace.lu.se/images/Syd_och_sydostasienstudier/working_papers/ Samarani.pdf.

25. CKSD (Box 47, folder 7), February 27, 1942.

26. CKSD, February 15, 1942.

27. Ibid., February 19, 1942.

28. B. K. Mishra, *The Cripps Mission: An Appraisal* (Delhi, 1982), 48.

29. "Gao Indu guomin shu" ["To the Indian People"], ZT, 289–292.

30. CKSD, February 21, 1942.

31. "Fangwen Indu de ganxiang yu duiyu Taipingyang zhanju de guancha" ["Feelings on Visiting India and Viewpoint on the Pacific War Situation"] (March 9, 1942), in *Zongtong Jiang gong sixiang yanlun zongji* [*Collection of the Thought and Speeches of President Chiang Kai-shek*], at www.chungcheng.org.tw/thought/ class06/0019/0008.htm, 56.

32. Joseph W. Stilwell, ed. Theodore H. White, *The Stilwell Papers* (Beijing, 2003) [originally New York, 1948] [hereafter SP], 14 January 1942, 14.

33. Tuchman, *Stilwell*, 172.

34. Taylor, *Generalissimo*, 191.

35. NARA (National Archives and Records Administration, Washington, DC) RG 493 (171 [3]).

36. Xu Wancheng, *Chongqing Huaxu* [*Chongqing Gossip*] (Shanghai, 1946) [hereafter CQHX], 7.

37. Graham Peck, *Two Kinds of Time* (Seattle, 2008) [originally published Boston, 1950], 384.

38. Taylor, *Generalissimo*, 194.

39. Charles F. Romanus and Riley Sunderland, *China-Burma-India Theater: Time Runs Out in CBI* (Washington, DC, 1959), 19.

40. Van de Ven, *War and Nationalism*, 23.

41. Ibid., 29.

42. SP, January 24, 1942, 26.

43. See Xu Guoqi, *China and the Great War: China's Pursuit of a New National Identity*

and Internationalization (Cambridge, 2005). Thorne, *Allies of a Kind,* 187, 189 (regarding the British fear of Chinese nationalism).

44. Christopher Bayly and Tim Harper, *Forgotten Armies: Britain's Asian Empire and the War with Japan* (London, 2004), 156–166; Van de Ven, *War and Nationalism,* 30.

45. SP, March 6, 1942, 43.

46. Ibid., March 9, 1942, 44. Taylor, *Generalissimo,* 197. Van de Ven, *War and Nationalism,* 31.

47. Van de Ven, *War and Nationalism,* 26.

48. SP, March 14, 1942, 53.

49. Ibid., March 12, 1942, 51.

50. Ibid., March 19, 1942, 55.

51. Ibid., March 23, 1942, 59.

52. Ibid., March 24, 1942, 59–60.

53. Ibid., March 25–26, 1942, 60–61. Bayly and Harper, *Forgotten Armies,* 180, notes the long-lasting and devastating effects that this would have on the Burmese economy.

54. CKSD, March 29, 1942, cited in Yang Tianshi, *Kangzhan yu Zhanhou Zhongguo* [*China during the War of Resistance and the Postwar*] (Beijing, 2007), 386.

55. SP, April 1, 1942, 65–67.

56. White and Jacoby, *Thunder,* 147.

57. CKSD, April 8, 1942, cited in Yang Tianshi, *Kangzhan yu Zhanhou Zhongguo* [*China during the War of Resistance and the Postwar*] (Beijing, 2007), 387.

58. SP, April 1, 1942, 68.

59. Ibid., April 2, 1942, 68.

60. Taylor, *Generalissimo,* 202; Van de Ven, *War and Nationalism,* 32.

61. SP, April 20, 1942, 76.

62. Ibid., April 30, 1942, 80.

63. Taylor, *Generalissimo,* 204.

64. Ibid., 204–205.

65. CKSD, May 6, 1942, cited in Yang, *Kangzhan,* 387.

66. SP, May 14, 1942. Tuchman, *Stilwell,* 298.

67. SP, May 26, 1942, 89.

68. Taylor, *Generalissimo,* 203–204.

69. CKSD, May 1942, cited in Wang, "Xinren de liushi," 52.

70. Luo Gu, *Zhanzheng zhi MianYin* [*India and Burma in War*] (Shanghai, 1945), June 4–August 4, 1942, 35–75.

71. Taylor, *Generalissimo,* 206–207.

72. Ibid., 207–208.

73. Van de Ven, *War and Nationalism,* 35.

74. Wang, "Xinren de liushi," 52.

75. Taylor, *Generalissimo,* 209. Van de Ven, *War and Nationalism,* 34–35.

76. NARA, RG 493 (616/178).

14. HUNGER IN HENAN

1. Li Shu, "Zaiqu xilie tongxun yu Yuzai jianying" ["A Series of Communications from the Disaster Area and the Outline of the Henan Disaster"], in Song Zhixin, ed., *1942: Henan da jihuang* [*1942: The Great Henan Famine*], 66.

2. Ibid., 79.

3. Graham Peck, *Two Kinds of Time* (Seattle, 2008) [originally published Boston, 1950], 386.

4. Zhang Rixin, ed., *Jiang Jingguo riji (1925–1949)* [*Chiang Ching-kuo's Diary*] (Beijing, 2010) (June 26, 1940), 55–56.

5. Zhang Rixin, ed., *Jiang Jingguo riji* (September 14, 1942), 107.

6. Arthur N. Young, *China's Wartime Finance and Inflation, 1937–1945* (Cambridge, MA, 1965), 23.

7. Hans J. van de Ven, *War and Nationalism in China, 1925–1945* (London, 2003), 277.

8. Brian G. Martin, "Shield of Collaboration: The Wang Jingwei Regime's Security Service, 1939–1945," *Intelligence and National Security* 16:4 (2001), 117.

9. Van de Ven, *War and Nationalism*, 269.

10. Ibid., 276.

11. Ibid., 263.

12. Van de Ven, *War and Nationalism*. Zhang Zonglu, "1942 nian Henan dahuang de huiyi" ["Memories of the Great 1942 Henan Famine"], in Song Zhixin, *1942: Henan*, 144.

13. Zhang, "1942 nian Henan," 144.

14. Ibid., 145.

15. Ibid., 150.

16. Ibid., 151.

17. Liu Zhenyun, *Mangu 1942* [*Looking Back on 1942*] (Beijing, 2009).

18. Zhang, "1942 nian Henan," 151. Li Shu, "Zaiqu xilie," 107.

19. "Quequ canshi jilu" ["Records of Horrors in the Flood Zones"], *Weishi Wenshi ziliao*, no. 5, 70.

20. Li Shu, "Zaiqu xilie," 111.

21. Theodore White and Annalee Jacoby, *Thunder out of China* (New York, 1946), 166.

22. "Until the Harvest Is Reaped," *Time*, March 22, 1943.

23. White and Jacoby, *Thunder*, 177.

24. Zhang, "1942 nian Henan," 148.

25. CKSD, April 5, 1943, April 11, 1943.

26. Ibid., April 18, 1943, April 20, 1943.

27. R. Keith Schoppa, *In a Sea of Bitterness: Refugees during the Sino-Japanese War* (Cambridge, MA, 2011).

28. Christopher Bayly and Tim Harper, *Forgotten Armies: Britain's Asian Empire and the War with Japan* (London, 2004), 285–286. For a comparative analysis of wartime famine, see Sugata Bose, "Starvation amidst Plenty: The Making of

Famine in Bengal, Honan and Tonkin, 1942–1945," *Modern Asian Studies* 24:4 (October 1990).

29. On rural involution, see Prasenjit Duara, *Culture, Power, and the State: Rural North China, 1900–1942* (Stanford, CA, 1988).

30. Young, *China's Wartime Finance,* 23.

31. Frank Dikötter, *Mao's Great Famine: The History of China's Most Devastating Catastrophe, 1958–1962* (London, 2010).

32. Young, *China's Wartime Finance,* 25–26.

33. Ibid., 299.

34. Ibid., 302.

35. Ibid., 319.

36. CQHX, 29.

37. Ibid., 30.

38. Peck, *Two Kinds of Time,* 385, 386.

39. CQHX, 5.

40. Young, *China's Wartime Finance,* 320.

41. Ibid., 321.

42. Ibid., 323.

43. QDHF, 400–401.

44. Van de Ven, *War and Nationalism,* 270.

45. Peck, *Two Kinds of Time,* 478.

46. Lyman P. Van Slyke, "The Chinese Communist Movement during the Sino-Japanese War, 1937–1945," in Lloyd E. Eastman et al., *The Nationalist Era in China, 1927–1949* (Cambridge, 1991), 252–253.

47. "Economic and Financial Problems in the Anti-Japanese War" (December 1942), in Mao Zedong, *Selected Works,* vol. III (Beijing, 1967) [hereafter MSW], 111.

48. Van Slyke, "The Communist Movement," 253–254.

49. "Economic and Financial Problems in the Anti-Japanese War," 111, 114.

50. Van Slyke, "The Communist Movement," 254–255.

51. Chen Yung-fa, "The Blooming Poppy under the Red Sun: The Yan'an Way and the Opium Trade," in Tony Saich and Hans van de Ven, *New Perspectives on the Chinese Communist Revolution* (Armonk, NY, 1995).

52. QDHF, 400.

15. STATES OF TERROR

1. "Rectify the Party's Style of Work" (February 1, 1942), Mao Zedong, *Selected Works,* vol. III (Beijing, 1967) [hereafter MSW], 35, 39, 44.

2. Peter Vladimirov, *The Vladimirov Diaries: Yenan, 1942–1945* (New York, 1975) [hereafter PVD], May 22 and 29, 1942. Vladimirov's real name was Piotr Parfenovich Vlasov. The authenticity of the Vladimirov diaries was questioned when they were first published in the West. After the Russian materials from which they were translated were made available after the Cold War, it became

clear that while the Soviet authorities had manipulated the order of the material and deleted some of it to serve their purpose of worsening Mao's reputation, the contents were in line with what Vladimirov had written.

3. Frederic Wakeman Jr., *Spymaster: Dai Li and the Chinese Secret Service* (Berkeley, CA, 2003), 388–389, fn 40, 39. On the role of Keswick, SOE, and the British in China, see Richard Aldrich, *Intelligence and the War against Japan: Britain, America, and the Politics of Secret Service* (Cambridge, 2000), chapter 15.

4. Wakeman, *Spymaster*, 333–334, 337.

5. Yu Maochun, *OSS in China: Prelude to Cold War* (New Haven, CT, 1997), 43–44. On Yan Baohang's career as an activist for the northeastern cause, see Rana Mitter, "Complicity, Repression, and Regionalism: Yan Baohang and Centripetal Nationalism, 1931–1949," *Modern China* 25:1 (January 1999).

6. John Israel, *Lianda: A Chinese University in War and Revolution* (Stanford, CA, 1998).

7. Wakeman, *Spymaster*, 282–283.

8. On the Stilwell-Chennault conflict, see Hans J. van de Ven, *War and Nationalism in China, 1925–1945* (London, 2003), 36–37.

9. Yu, *OSS in China*, 25; Aldrich, *Intelligence and the War against Japan*, 267. See also Michael Schaller, *The American Crusade in China, 1938–1945* (New York, 1979).

10. Wakeman, *Spymaster*, 316–317.

11. Yu, *OSS in China*, 97.

12. Aldrich, *Intelligence and the War against Japan*, 287, 296.

13. On intelligence issues, see the essays in Hans van de Ven, ed., "Lifting the Veil of Secrecy: Secret Services in China during World War II," *Intelligence and National Security* 16:4 (Winter 2001).

14. Wakeman, *Spymaster*, 291–292.

15. Ibid., 310.

16. Ibid., 294, 299.

17. Brian G. Martin, "Shield of Collaboration: The Wang Jingwei Regime's Security Service, 1939–1945," *Intelligence and National Security* 16:4 (2001), 95.

18. Martin, "Shield of Collaboration," 99.

19. Ibid., 101.

20. John Hunter Boyle, *China and Japan at War, 1937–1945: The Politics of Collaboration* (Stanford, CA, 1972), 281–285.

21. ZFHR, January 6, 1943, 690.

22. Brian G. Martin, "Collaboration within Collaboration: Zhou Fohai's Relations with the Chongqing Government, 1942–1945," *Twentieth-Century China* 34:2 (April 2008), 59, 60.

23. ZFHR, December 1942.

24. Martin, "Collaboration within Collaboration," 66–67.

25. Martin, "Shield of Collaboration," 133; 131ff.

26. Boyle, *China and Japan at War*, 285.

27. Lyman P. Van Slyke, "The Chinese Communist Movement during the Sino-Japanese War, 1937–1945," in Lloyd E. Eastman et al., *The Nationalist Era in China, 1927–1949* (Cambridge, 1991), 247–249.

28. See, for instance, Feng Chongyi and David Goodman, eds., *North China at War: The Social Ecology of Revolution, 1937–1945* (Lanham, MD, 2000).

29. David E. Apter, "Discourse as Power: Yan'an and the Chinese Revolution," in Tony Saich and Hans van de Ven, eds., *New Perspectives on the Chinese Communist Revolution* (Armonk, NY, 1995).

30. John Byron, *The Claws of the Dragon: Kang Sheng* (New York, 1992), 125.

31. "When I Was in Xia Village," in Ding Ling, *Miss Sophie's Diary and Other Stories*, trans. W. J. F. Jenner (Beijing, 1983).

32. Jonathan D. Spence, *The Gate of Heavenly Peace: The Chinese and Their Revolution, 1895–1980* (London, 1981), 330.

33. Spence, *Gate*, 332.

34. Bonnie S. Macdougall, *Mao Zedong's Talks at the Yan'an Conference on Literature and Art: A Translation of the 1943 Text with Commentary* (Ann Arbor, MI, 1980).

35. "Talks at the Yenan Forum on Literature and Art" (May 1942), MSW, 71–72.

36. Ibid.

37. Lyman P. Van Slyke, "The Chinese Communist Movement during the Sino-Japanese War, 1937–1945," in Lloyd E. Eastman et al., *The Nationalist Era in China, 1927–1949* (Cambridge, 1991), 251–252.

38. Byron, *Claws*, 172–179.

39. Ibid., 179–180.

40. Zhu Hongzhao, *Yan'an richang shenghuo zhong de lishi* [*The History of Everyday Life in Yan'an*] (Guilin, 2007), 132–133.

41. Ibid.

42. Spence, *Gate*, 334–335.

16. CONFERENCE AT CAIRO

1. Hannah Pakula, *The Last Empress: Madame Chiang Kai-shek and the Birth of Modern China* (New York, 2009), 419.

2. Graham Peck, *Two Kinds of Time* (Seattle, 2008) [originally published Boston, 1950], 477.

3. CKSD, monthly reflection, February 1943, cited in Wang Jianlang, "Xinren de liushi: cong Jiang Jieshi riji kan kangRi zhanhou qi de ZhongMei guanxi" ["The Erosion of Trust: Sino-American Relations for the Postwar Period as Seen through Chiang Kai-shek's Diary"], *Jindaishi yanjiu* (2009:3), 51.

4. ZFHR, January 26, 1943, 699; January 29, 1943, 701.

5. Ibid., February 2, 1943, 703.

6. CKSD, February 28, 1943.

7. Ibid., February 13, 1943, 707; February 21, 1943, 710; March 4, 1943, 714.

8. Ibid., April 16, 1943.

9. Ibid., June 30, 1943, August 19, 1943.
10. Christopher Thorne, *Allies of a Kind: The United States, Britain, and the War against Japan, 1941–1945* (Oxford, 1978), 306.
11. Ibid., 311.
12. Ibid., 319.
13. Ibid., 187–188.
14. John Hunter Boyle, *China and Japan at War, 1937–1945: The Politics of Collaboration* (Stanford, CA, 1972), 308.
15. CKSD, June 29, 1943.
16. Ibid., February 7, 1943.
17. SP, January 19, 1943, 161.
18. Jay Taylor, *The Generalissimo: Chiang Kai-shek and the Struggle for Modern China* (Cambridge, MA, 2007), 219–220.
19. NARA RG 493 (616/174).
20. Stilwell note from May 1943 conference, SP, May, 172. Hans J. van de Ven, *War and Nationalism in China, 1925–1945* (London, 2003), 36–37.
21. SP, May, 173.
22. Van de Ven, *War and Nationalism*, 37.
23. Ibid., 39–40.
24. Thorne, *Allies of a Kind*, 299.
25. SP, September 4, 1943, 186.
26. Ramon H. Myers, "Casting New Light on Modern Chinese History: An Introduction," in Wu Jingping and Tai-chun Kuo, eds., *Song Ziwen ZhuMei shiqi dianbaoxuan* [*Select Telegrams between Chiang Kai-shek and T. V. Soong*] (Shanghai, 2008), 256.
27. SP, September 25, 1943, 193.
28. Van de Ven, *War and Nationalism*, 39.
29. SP, October 16, 1943, 196.
30. CKSD, September 18, 1943.
31. SP, September 17, 1943, 187–188.
32. CKSD (Box 43, folder 9), October 18, 1943.
33. ZFHR, October 5, 1943, 803.
34. R. B. Smith, *Changing Visions of East Asia, 1943–1993: Transformations and Continuities* (London, 2010), 18.
35. Smith, *Changing Visions*, 19.
36. Ba Maw cited in Boyle, *China and Japan at War*, 323.
37. Gerhard Weinberg, *A World at Arms: A Global History of World War II*, 2nd ed. (Cambridge, 2005), 624–629.
38. Thorne, *Allies of a Kind*, 294.
39. CKSD (Box 43, folder 10), November 12, 1943.
40. CKSD, November 17, 1943.
41. Pakula, *Last Empress*, 471.

42. Ibid., 470.
43. Thorne, *Allies of a Kind,* 319.
44. CKSD, November 21, 1943, November 22, 1943.
45. Ibid., November 21, 1943.
46. Van de Ven, *War and Nationalism,* 42.
47. CKSD, November 21, 1943.
48. Ibid., November 23, 1943.
49. Thorne, *Allies of a Kind,* 333.
50. Van de Ven, *War and Nationalism,* 43. CKSD, November 23, 1943. Weinberg, *A World at Arms,* 628.
51. CKSD, November 23, 1943.
52. Ibid.
53. CKSD, November 25, 1943, November 26, 1943.
54. Thorne, *Allies of a Kind,* 275–279.
55. Ibid., 291, 292, 288.
56. CKSD, week's reflections after November 26, 1943.
57. Ibid., monthly reflections, November 1943.
58. Van de Ven, *War and Nationalism,* 45.
59. CKSD, October 1, 1943.
60. Ibid., October 3, 1943.
61. Van de Ven, *War and Nationalism,* 46.
62. CKSD, November 30, 1943.
63. FRUS, 1943: China (November 30, 1943), 167–176.
64. CKSD, April 20, 1943.
65. Van de Ven, *War and Nationalism,* 62, argues this point forcefully.
66. *FRUS,* 1943: China (December 9, 1943), 180.

17. ONE WAR, TWO FRONTS

1. Huang Yaowu, *Wode zhanzheng, 1944–1948* [*My War, 1944–1948*] (Shenyang, 2010), 24.
2. Document dated January 1, 1944 (PRO), in Hans J. van de Ven, *War and Nationalism in China, 1925–1945* (London, 2003), 46.
3. "Di si ci Nanyue junshi huiyi kaihui xunci" ["Speech to the Fourth Nanyue Military Conference"] (10 February 1944), ZT, 324.
4. FRUS, 1944: China (March 23, 1944), 43.
5. "Battle of Asia: A Difference of Opinion," *Time,* February 15, 1944.
6. Van de Ven, *War and Nationalism,* 49.
7. Ibid., 54.
8. Huang, *Wode zhanzheng,* 28–29.
9. Ibid., 60.
10. Gerhard Weinberg, *A World at Arms: A Global History of World War II,* 2nd ed. (Cambridge, 2005), 647.

11. Hara Takeshi, "The Ichigô Offensive," in Mark Peattie, Edward Drea, and Hans van de Ven, eds., *The Battle for China: Essays on the Military History of the Sino-Japanese War of 1937–1945* (Stanford, CA, 2011), 392–398.
12. Christopher Bayly and Tim Harper, *Forgotten Armies: Britain's Asian Empire and the War with Japan* (London, 2004), 370.
13. Van de Ven, *War and Nationalism*, 47.
14. Wang Qisheng, "The Battle of Hunan and the Chinese Military's Response to Operation Ichigô," in Peattie, Drea, and Van de Ven, *Battle for China*, 406.
15. Van de Ven, *War and Nationalism*, 271–273.
16. Jiang Dingwen, "Jiang Dingwen guanyu Zhongyuan huizhan kuibai yuanyin zi jiantao baogao" ["Jiang Dingwen's Report on the Investigation into the Reasons for the Defeat in the Central China Battle"] (June 1944), *Zhonghua minguo shi dang'an shiliao huibian*, 97.
17. Ibid., 98.
18. Ibid.
19. "Guo Zhonghuai deng yaoqiu yancheng Tang Enbo deng ti an ji Guomin Canzheng jueyi" ["Resolution from Guo Zhonghuai and Others Demanding the Serious Punishment of Tang Enbo and Others"] (1945), in No. 2 National Archives, ed., *Zhonghua minguoshi dang'an shiliao huibian* [*Selected Archival Materials on Republican Chinese History*] (5:2 — Military: 4) (Nanjing, 1991), 115.
20. Ibid., 114.
21. Ibid., 114–115.
22. Jiang Dingwen, "Jiang Dingwen," 98.
23. FRUS, 1944: China (May 20, 1944), 77.
24. Theodore White and Annalee Jacoby, *Thunder out of China* (New York, 1946), 178.
25. Wang Qisheng, "Battle of Hunan," 409.
26. White and Jacoby, *Thunder*, 183.
27. Jay Taylor, *The Generalissimo: Chiang Kai-shek and the Struggle for Modern China* (Cambridge, MA, 2007), 272.
28. "Zhuzhong kexue zhuzhi de fangfa" ("Emphasizing Methods of Scientific Organization"), June 25, 1944, ZT, vol. 20, 430–432.
29. ZT, CKS speech, July 21, 1944, 445.
30. Peter Vladimirov, *The Vladimirov Diaries: Yenan, 1942–1945* (New York, 1975) [hereafter PVD].
31. Barbara Tuchman, *Stilwell and the American Experience in China, 1911–1945* (New York, 1971), 473. Tuchman gives a sympathetic interpretation of Stilwell's words, arguing that he had given considerable assistance to Chennault and Chiang, and that the request to relieve Xue Yue was merely an attempt to cover up the former's incompetence without acknowledging that Stilwell's judgment had been correct.
32. Taylor, *Generalissimo*, 282. Wang Qisheng, "Battle of Hunan," 407–413.
33. Van de Ven, *War and Nationalism*, 55; Taylor, *Generalissimo*, 277.
34. CKSD, April 15, 1944, May 15, 1944, and August 1, 1944, cited in Wang Jianlang,

"Cong Jiang Jieshi riji kan kangRi zhanhou qi de ZhongYingMei guanxi" ["Chinese-British-American Relations in Wartime and After, Seen through Chiang Kai-shek's Diary"], *Minguo dang'an* 4 (2008), 107.57.

35. FRUS, 1944: China [Wallace Visit, June 1944] (July 10, 1944), 242.
36. FRUS, 1944: China (June 12, 1944), 98–99.
37. Ibid. (January 15, 1944), 308.
38. Ibid., 306–307.
39. SP, n.d., 1944, 268.
40. CKSD, March 24, 1944, cited in Wang, "Cong Jiang Jieshi," 56.
41. FRUS, 1944: China (Wallace Visit), July 10, 1944, 241.
42. CKSD, July 26, 1944, cited in Wang, "Cong Jiang Jieshi," 56.
43. PVD, July 15, 1944, 229–230.
44. Ibid., July 22, 1944, 233.
45. Ibid., September 10, 1944, 253.
46. FRUS, 1944: China (July 28, 1944), 518.
47. On Communist adaptations of traditional folk art forms, see Chang-tai Hung, *War and Popular Culture: Resistance in Modern China, 1937–1945* (Berkeley, CA, 1994).
48. FRUS, 1944: China (July 28, 1944), 517–520.
49. Ibid. (September 4, 1944), 553.
50. PVD, August 16, 1944, 240.
51. FRUS, 1944: China (July 27, 1944), 523.
52. SP, "reek of corruption."
53. Michael Sheng, *Battling Western Imperialism: Mao, Stalin, and the United States* (Princeton, NJ, 1997), 74, 90.
54. FRUS, 1944: China (September 1, 1944), 534.
55. PVD, September 7, 1944, 252.
56. Huang, *Wode zhanzheng*, 61–62.
57. Van de Ven, *War and Nationalism*, 51.
58. SP, Letter (probably June 15, 1944), JWS to Mrs. JWS, 256.
59. Ibid. (probably July 2, 1944), JWS to Mrs. JWS, 258.
60. Bayly and Harper, *Forgotten Armies*, 390.
61. Ibid.
62. FRUS, 1944: China (June 15, 1944), 100.
63. Taylor, *Generalissimo*, 309.
64. Huang, *Wode zhanzheng*, 76–77.

18. SHOWDOWN WITH STILWELL

1. SP, 19 September 1944, 281.
2. Jay Taylor, *The Generalissimo: Chiang Kai-shek and the Struggle for Modern China* (Cambridge, MA, 2007), 288.
3. CKSD, August 17–28, 1944, and September 2, 1944, in Wang Jianlang, "Xinren de

liushi: cong Jiang Jieshi riji kan kangRi zhanhou qi de ZhongMei guanxi" ["The Erosion of Trust: Sino-American Relations for the Postwar Period as Seen through Chiang Kai-shek's Diary"], *Jindaishi yanjiu* 3 (2009), 56.

4. Charles F. Romanus and Riley Sunderland, *China-Burma-India Theater: Time Runs Out in CBI* (Washington, DC, 1959), 19.

5. CKSD, August 29, 1944, in Wang, "Xinren de liushi," 60.

6. Ibid., August 31, 1944, in Wang, "Xinren de liushi," 60.

7. FRUS, 1944: China 1944 (September 4, 1944), 546.

8. CKSD, August 6, 1944, in Wang, "Xinren de liushi," 56.

9. SP, September 9, 1944, 276.

10. Ibid., September 15, 1944, 279. Taylor, *Generalissimo,* 285.

11. CKSD (September 15, 1944), in Wang, "Xinren de liushi," 59.

12. Taylor, *Generalissimo,* 286.

13. FRUS, 1944: China (September 16, 1944), 157.

14. Taylor, *Generalissimo,* 288. Barbara Tuchman, *Stilwell and the American Experience in China, 1911–1945* (New York, 1971), 494.

15. Taylor, *Generalissimo,* 289–290.

16. SP, September 21, 1944 (letter to Mrs. Stilwell), 282.

17. FRUS, 1944: China (October 2, 1944), 163.

18. Ibid., 164.

19. Long Yun to He Yingqin, telegram of January 22, 1944, cited in Zhang Zhenli, "Cong minguo dang'an kan 1944 nian zhu Zhen meijun roulei gongying fengbo" ["The 1944 Crisis over Beef Supply for the American Army"], *Yunnan dang'an* (December 2011), 21.

20. Chiang to Long Yun, telegram September 11, 1944; Long Yun to Chiang, September 18, 1944, cited in Zhang, "Cong minguo . . . fengbo," 20.

21. Lloyd E. Eastman, "Nationalist China during the Sino-Japanese War, 1937–1945," in Lloyd E. Eastman et al., *The Nationalist Era in China, 1927–1949* (Cambridge, 1991), 157.

22. CKSD, September 1944, monthly reflections, cited in Wang, "Xinren de liushi," 60.

23. Tuchman, *Stilwell,* 495; Taylor, *Generalissimo,* 291.

24. Taylor, *Generalissimo,* 292.

25. FRUS, 1944: China (October 5, 1944), 165.

26. SP (n.d.), October 1944, October 1, 1944, 287–288.

27. SP, October 7, 1944, 289.

28. FRUS, 1944: China (October 9, 1944 [note]), 169.

29. SP, October 20, 1944, 293.

30. Ibid., October 24, 1944, 293.

31. Hans J. van de Ven, *War and Nationalism in China, 1925–1945* (London, 2003), articulates this argument with great clarity; see especially chapter 1.

32. Graham Peck, *Two Kinds of Time* (Seattle, 2008) [originally published Boston, 1950], 582.

19. UNEXPECTED VICTORY

1. Barbara Tuchman, *Stilwell and the American Experience in China, 1911–1945* (New York, 1971), 505–506.
2. Tohmatsu Haruo, "The Strategic Correlation between the Sino-Japanese and Pacific Wars," in Mark Peattie, Edward Drea, and Hans van de Ven, *The Battle for China: Essays on the Military History of the Sino-Japanese War* (Stanford, CA, 2011), 443–444.
3. Hara Takeshi, "The Ichigō Offensive," in Peattie, Drea, and Van de Ven, *The Battle for China*, 394.
4. Ibid., 401.
5. CKSD, January 5–7, 1945, in Wang Jianlang, "Xinren de liushi: cong Jiang Jieshi riji kan kangRi zhanhou qi de ZhongMei guanxi" ["The Erosion of Trust: Sino-American Relations for the Postwar Period as Seen through Chiang Kai-shek's Diary"], *Jindaishi yanjiu* 3 (2009), 61.
6. Albert C. Wedemeyer, *Wedemeyer Reports!* (New York, 1958), 294.
7. CKSD, January 14, 1945, cited in Wang, "Xinren de liushi," 61.
8. CKSD, December 22, 1944, cited in Wang, "Xinren de liushi," 61.
9. Chen Jian, *Mao's China and the Cold War* (Chapel Hill, NC, 2001), 22.
10. Lyman P. Van Slyke, "The Chinese Communist Movement during the Sino-Japanese War, 1937–1945," in Lloyd E. Eastman et al., *The Nationalist Era in China, 1927–1949* (Cambridge, 1991), 279.
11. PVD, November 8, 44, 287.
12. Chen Jian, *Mao's China*, 24.
13. "The Hurley-Chiang Duet Is a Flop" (July 10, 1945), MSW, 281.
14. Herbert Feis, *The China Tangle: The American Effort in China from Pearl Harbor to the Marshall Mission* (Princeton, NJ, 1953), 266–267.
15. Ibid., 271.
16. NARA, RG 493 (614/170 [8]).
17. FRUS, 1945: The Far East, China (March 13, 1945), 277, 279.
18. ZFHR, August 10, 1944, 909.
19. Ibid., November 11, 1944, 948.
20. Charles F. Romanus and Riley Sunderland, *China-Burma-India Theater: Time Runs Out in CBI* (Washington, DC, 1959), 258.
21. Brian G. Martin, "Collaboration within Collaboration: Zhou Fohai's Relations with the Chongqing Government, 1942–1945," *Twentieth-Century China* 34:2 (April 2008), 77.
22. John Hunter Boyle, *China and Japan at War, 1937–1945: The Politics of Collaboration* (Stanford, CA, 1972), 318.
23. On this period, see Julian Jackson, *France: The Dark Years, 1940–1944* (Oxford, 2003).
24. ZHFR, August 21, 1944, August 26, 1944.

25. Joseph K. S. Yick, "Communist-Puppet Collaboration in Japanese-Occupied China: Pan Hannian and Li Shiqun, 1939–1943," *Intelligence and National Security* 16:4 (2001), 76–78.

26. Jay Taylor, *The Generalissimo: Chiang Kai-shek and the Struggle for Modern China* (Cambridge, MA, 2007), 300–301; Weinberg, *A World at Arms,* 806–807.

27. CKSD, February 10, 1945 (weekly reflection), February 17, 1945 (monthly reflection), cited in Wang, "Xinren de liushi," 61–62.

28. Taylor, *Generalissimo,* 302–303. Chen Jian, *Mao's China,* 24.

29. Feis, *China Tangle,* 273.

30. "Hurley-Chiang Duet," 282.

31. "On the Danger of the Hurley Policy" (July 12, 1945), MSW, 285.

32. Chen Jian, *Mao's China,* 25.

33. CKSD, July 28, 1945, cited in Wang, "Xinren de liushi," 62.

34. UNA (United Nations Organization Archives, New York): S-0528–0032 (Correspondence — Chungking to Washington, 1944–1946).

35. UNA S-0528–0053 (China Weekly Reports, 1941–945).

36. UNA S-0528–0032 (Correspondence, Chungking to Washington).

37. Tehyun Ma, "A Chinese Beveridge Plan? The Discourse of Social Security and the Postwar Reconstruction of China," *European Journal of East Asian Studies* 11:2 (2012).

38. See Janet Chen, *Guilty of Indigence: The Urban Poor in China, 1900–1953* (Princeton, NJ, 2012); and Ruth Rogaski, *Hygienic Modernity: Meanings of Health and Disease in Treaty-Port China* (Berkeley, CA, 2004).

39. Rogaski, *Hygienic Modernity.*

40. United Nations Archive (UNA) S-0528–0053 (China Weekly Reports, 1944–1945) (document not dated: July ?, 1945).

41. Ibid.

42. Sichuan Provincial Archives, 113–116.

43. See *European Journal of East Asian Studies,* 11:2 (2012).

44. Lloyd E. Eastman, "Nationalist China during the Sino-Japanese War, 1937–1945," in Lloyd E. Eastman et al., *The Nationalist Era in China, 1927–1949* (Cambridge, 1991), 145.

45. UNA S-0528–0053 (China Weekly Reports, 1944–1945).

46. UNA S-0528–0060 (Hunan, 1944–1949).

47. Taylor, *Generalissimo,* 305.

48. "The Foolish Old Man Who Moved the Mountains" (June 11, 1945), MSW, 272.

49. NARA, RG 493 (614 / 170 [8]).

50. On the Potsdam Declaration, see Weinberg, *A World at Arms,* 837–841.

51. Taylor, *Generalissimo,* 311.

52. Robert J. C. Butow, *Tojo and the Coming of the War* (Stanford, CA, 1969), 151.

53. Ibid., 154.

54. Ibid., 183–186.

55. CKSD, August 15, 1945, cited in Ye Yonglie, "Zai Meiguo kan Jiang Jieshi riji" ["Reading Chiang Kai-shek's Diary in America"], *Tongzhou gongjin* 2 (2008), 47.

56. "Kangzhan shengli gao quanguo junmin ji quan shijie renshi shu" ("Announcement to the Soldiers and People of the Whole Country and to the World on the Victory in the War of Resistance"), August 15, 1945, ZT, vol. 32, 121.

57. CKSD, August 15, 1945, in Ye Yonglie, "Zai Meiguo," 47.

58. Taylor, *Generalissimo,* 314.

59. CKSD, August 15, 1945, in Ye Yonglie, "Zai Meiguo," 47.

EPILOGUE: THE ENDURING WAR

1. Chen Jian, *Mao's China and the Cold War* (Chapel Hill, NC, 2001), 26.

2. CKSD, August 15, 1945, in Ye Yonglie, "Zai Meiguo kan Jiang Jieshi riji" ["Reading Chiang Kai-shek's Diary in America"], *Tongzhou gongjin* 2 (2008), 47.

3. Jay Taylor, *The Generalissimo: Chiang Kai-shek and the Struggle for Modern China* (Cambridge, MA, 2007), 318; Chen Jian, *Mao's China,* 27.

4. Chen Jian, *Mao's China,* 32.

5. Taylor, *Generalissimo,* 327.

6. Chen Jian, *Mao's China,* 33.

7. Taylor, *Generalissimo,* 364.

8. Odd Arne Westad, *Decisive Encounters: The Chinese Civil War, 1946–1950* (Stanford, CA, 2003), 89.

9. John Hunter Boyle, *China and Japan at War, 1937–1945: The Politics of Collaboration* (Stanford, CA, 1972), 362. Charles Musgrove, "Cheering the Traitor: The Postwar Trial of Chen Bijun, April 1946," *Twentieth-Century China* 30:2 (April 2005).

10. Neil Boister and Robert Cryer, eds., *The Tokyo International Military Tribunal: A Reappraisal* (Oxford, 2008).

11. Xu Wancheng, *Chongqing Huaxu* [*Chongqing Gossip*] (Shanghai, 1946) [hereafter CQHX].

12. CQHX (appendix), 5.

13. Ibid., 6, 8.

14. Taylor, *Generalissimo,* 378, 392.

15. Ibid., 385. Westad, *Decisive Encounters,* chapter 6.

16. Theodore White and Annalee Jacoby, *Thunder out of China* (New York, 1946), 310.

17. Graham Peck, *Two Kinds of Time* (Seattle, 2008) [originally published Boston, 1950], 690.

18. John Earl Haynes and Harvey Klehr, *Venona: Decoding Soviet Espionage in America* (New Haven, CT, 2000).

19. Chalmers Johnson, *Peasant Nationalism and Communist Power: The Emergence of Revolutionary China, 1937–1945* (Stanford, CA, 1962).

20. Barbara Tuchman, *Stilwell and the American Experience in China, 1911–1945* (New York, 1971).

21. Roderick MacFarquhar and Michael Schoenhals, *Mao's Last Revolution* (Cambridge, MA, 2006), 217.

22. Rana Mitter, "Old Ghosts, New Memories: Changing China's War History in the Era of Post-Mao Politics," in *Journal of Contemporary History* (January 2003).

23. Details of the committee's composition and procedures can be found at http://www.mofa.go.jp/region/asia-paci/china/meet0612.html.

24. Ian Buruma, *The Wages of Guilt: Memories of War in Germany and Japan* (New York, 1994); Franziska Seraphim, *War Memory and Social Politics in Japan, 1945–2005* (Cambridge, MA: Harvard University Asia Center Press, 2006).

25. Ruan Jiaxin, "Kangzhan shiqi zhuHua Meijun bushu ji zuozhan gaikuang" ["The Situation of the Deployment and Warmaking of US Troops Stationed in China during the War of Resistance"], *KangRi zhanzheng yanjiu* 3 (2007), 27. Zhao Rukun, "Erzhan jieshu qianhou Meiguo duiHua zhengce wenti zai shentao" ["A Reexamination of American Policy toward China before and after the Conclusion of World War II"], *Guangxi shifan daxue uebao: zhexue shehui kexue ban* 43:6 (December 2007), 104.

26. Hongping Annie Nie, "Gaming, Nationalism, and Patriotic Education: Chinese Online Games Based on the Resistance War against Japan (1937–1945)," *Journal of Contemporary China* 22:18 (May 2013).

27. Rana Mitter, "China's 'Good War': Voices, Locations, and Generations in the Interpretation of the War of Resistance to Japan," in Sheila Jager and Rana Mitter, eds., *Ruptured Histories: War, Memory, and the Post–Cold War in Asia* (Cambridge, MA, 2007).

28. "Cui Yongyuan tan Wode Kangzhan" ["Cui Yongyuan Talks about 'My War of Resistance'"], *Nanfang Zhoumo*, October 7, 2010.

29. Hollington K. Tong, *China after Seven Years of War* (London, 1945).

FURTHER READING

Although China's war with Japan has generated far less scholarship in English than the European and Pacific fronts of the Second World War, there is still a substantial body of work for those who wish to go further. This short guide to further reading is not intended to be comprehensive. Rather, it provides pointers to useful books and articles in the English-language scholarship that in turn could stimulate further reading and research.

OVERALL HISTORY OF THE WAR

This book has taken a new approach by examining China's war with Japan as one continuous narrative combining the viewpoints of the Nationalists, the Communists, and the collaborators. However, there have of course been previous very important accounts that bring together various of these elements, usually through combining edited essays by different authors. The volume by Lloyd Eastman et al., *The Nationalist Era in China, 1927–1949* (Cambridge, 1991), has two excellent overview essays, by Lloyd Eastman on the Nationalists and Lyman van Slyke on the Communists, that cover the wartime period. (These essays are also to be found in volume 13 of *The Cambridge History of China.*) James Hsiung and Steven Levine's volume *China's Bitter Victory: The War with Japan, 1937–1945* (Armonk, NY, 1992), contains superb essays by leading scholars on topics including China's wartime diplomacy, its economy, and changes in its political system. Chinese politics in the period leading up to the war is dealt with in Parks M. Coble Jr., *Facing Japan: Chinese Politics and Japanese Imperialism, 1931–1937* (Cambridge, MA, 1991). On the fate of Hong Kong, see Philip Snow, *The Fall of Hong Kong: Britain, China, and the Japanese Occupation* (New Haven, 2004); for a daring episode within that story, Tim Luard, *Escape from Hong Kong: Admiral Chan Chak's Christmas Day Dash, 1941* (Hong Kong, 2012). There is a wealth of literature on the Japanese side of the war in China and in the Pacific more broadly. Akira Iriye, *The Origins of the Second World War in Asia and the Pacific* (London, 1987), is a compelling analysis of the key factors that led to Japan's decision for war, as well as giving a detailed account of the scholarly debates underlying this issue.

BIOGRAPHIES

For many years there were few biographies of Chiang Kai-shek. Access to new sources, in particular the Chiang Kai-shek diaries at the Hoover Institution, has enriched the fine biography by Jay Taylor, *The Generalissimo: Chiang Kai-shek and the Struggle for Modern China* (Cambridge, MA, 2007), which gives comprehensive coverage of Chiang's whole life, including his period on Taiwan. An earlier biography by Jonathan Fenby, *Generalissimo: Chiang Kai-shek and the China He Lost* (London, 2003), broke new ground in reassessing Chiang outside the existing Cold War templates.

Mao Zedong has been reassessed in several major biographies in recent years. All are marked by a great deal of assiduous research, but take different views on this most controversial of figures. Jung Chang and Jon Halliday's *Mao: The Unknown Story* (London, 2006) provides a great deal of new detail, and assesses Mao in ultimately negative terms. Philip Short, *Mao: A Life* (London, 2001), and Alexander Pantsov and Steven Levine, *Mao: The Real Story* (New York, 2012), suggest that Mao both made important contributions to the revolution and committed terrible crimes. A fine guide to the controversies over Mao is Timothy Cheek, ed., *A Critical Introduction to Mao* (Cambridge, 2010).

It is still difficult, though no longer impossible, to discuss Wang Jingwei in China without his being dismissed as a mere traitor and therefore of no further interest. One of the earliest biographies is still among the very best and most nuanced works on Wang: John Hunter Boyle's *China and Japan at War, 1937–1945: The Politics of Collaboration* (Stanford, CA, 1972). There are also useful insights in Gerald Bunker, *The Peace Conspiracy: Wang Ching-wei and the China War, 1937–1941* (Cambridge, MA, 1972).

THE NATIONALISTS: THE POLITICAL, SOCIAL, AND MILITARY HISTORY OF WARTIME

Perhaps the most significant military history of the war in recent years is Hans J. van de Ven, *War and Nationalism in China, 1925–1945* (London, 2003), which draws important revisionist conclusions on a whole variety of topics from the relationship between Stilwell and Chiang to military and food security during the war, embedded in an argument that revises the view that the Nationalist war effort was unimportant and ill-managed. For details of individual campaigns, Mark Peattie, Edward Drea, and Hans van de Ven, eds., *The Battle for China: Essays on the Military History of the Sino-Japanese War of 1937–1945* (Stanford, CA, 2011), is essential. These works are in some sense a response to the classic works of an earlier generation: Lloyd Eastman's *Seeds of Destruction: Nationalist China in War and Revolution, 1937–1949* (Stanford, CA, 1984), is condemnatory of a regime that he characterizes as already flawed and doomed to collapse, and Hsi-sheng Chi, *Nationalist China at War: Military Defeats and Political Collapse, 1937–1945* (Ann Arbor, MI, 1982), details the way that military disaster fueled the disintegration of the government. Aaron William Moore, *Writing War: Soldiers Record the Japanese Empire* (Cambridge, MA, 2013), has powerful new material from Nationalist soldiers. John Garver's *Chinese-Soviet Relations, 1937–1945: The Diplomacy of Chinese Nationalism* (Oxford, 1988) deals ably with the diplomacy of the period between China and the USSR.

Morris Bian, *The Making of the State Enterprise System in Modern China: The Dynamics of Institutional Change* (Cambridge, MA, 2005), and Mark W. Frazier, *The Making of the Chinese Industrial Workplace: State, Revolution, and Labor Management* (Cambridge, 2002), are examples of revisionist work that attributes significant social formations in the post-1949 era to wartime changes under the Nationalists.

THE RELATIONSHIP BETWEEN THE WEST AND CHINA

Revisionist views of the alliance between the Western powers and China during the Second World War are covered in Van de Ven, *War and Nationalism,* and Taylor, *Generalissimo.* The more long-standing view that Chiang's regime was an unworthy ally for the West is detailed in Barbara Tuchman's *Stilwell and the American Experience in China, 1911–1945* (New York, 1971). Older works, including Herbert Feis, *The China Tangle: The American Effort in China from Pearl Harbor to the Marshall Mission* (Princeton, NJ, 1953), also expose how raw the wounds of the experience in China were in American public life during the early Cold War. Tom Buchanan, *East Wind: China and the British Left, 1925–1976* (Oxford, 2012), charts the mobilization of British leftist opinion in favor of the Chinese war effort; and Christopher Thorne, *Allies of a Kind: The United States, Britain, and the War against Japan, 1941–1945* (Oxford, 1978), shows how fraught relations between the US and Britain often left China caught in the middle. The Burma campaign is dealt with in brilliant, horrific detail in Christopher Bayly and Tim Harper, *Forgotten Armies: Britain's Asian Empire and the War with Japan* (London, 2004). Frank McLynn, *The Burma Campaign: Disaster into Triumph, 1942–1945* (New Haven, CT, 2011), gives compelling portraits of the Western commanders. There is a very thoughtful essay on China's wartime relations with the wider world in chapter 7 of Odd Arne Westad's *Restless Empire: China and the World since 1750* (London, 2012).

WAR ATROCITIES

On the Nanjing Massacre, rigorous studies have emerged in recent years that give a clear account of what the historically valid parameters of debate on these and related questions are. Among them are Bob Tadashi Wakabayashi, *The Nanking Atrocity, 1937–1938: Complicating the Picture* (Oxford, 2007); Joshua Fogel, ed., *The Nanjing Massacre in History and Historiography* (Berkeley, CA, 2000); Takashi Yoshida, *The Making of the 'Rape of Nanking': History and Memory in Japan, China, and the United States* (New York, 2006); and Daqing Yang, "Convergence or Divergence? Recent Historical Writings on the Rape of Nanjing," *American Historical Review* 104:3 (1999). Although some of this work takes issue with it, a significant proportion of the Anglophone debate in the 2000s was stimulated by the publication of Iris Chang's *The Rape of Nanking* (New York, 1997). Accounts of other war atrocities are to be found in Diana Lary and Stephen R. MacKinnon, eds., *The Scars of War: The Impact of Warfare on Modern China*, and James Flath and Norman Smith, eds., *Beyond Suffering: Recounting War in Modern China* (Vancouver, 2011).

THE COMMUNISTS AND THEIR REVOLUTION

The origins of the Communist peasant revolution in wartime China have been a central theme in the study of modern Chinese political and social history for some decades. The debate was started by Chalmers Johnson's classic *Peasant Nationalism and Communist Power: The Emergence of Revolutionary China, 1937–1945* (Stanford, CA, 1962), which argued for the CCP's ability to stimulate anti-Japanese nationalism as the key factor in the rise of the Communists. This was answered by Mark Selden in *The Yenan Way in Revolutionary China* (Cambridge, MA, 1971), which argued instead for social revolution and a more self-sufficient economic model as the reasons for Mao's success. A variety of important studies then added nuance to the debate in the following years, for example Kathleen Hartford and Steven M. Goldstein, eds., *Single Sparks: China's Rural Revolutions* (Armonk, NY, 1989). The debate on the origins of the rural revolution is synthesized very effectively in Suzanne Pepper, "The Political Odyssey of an Intellectual Construct: Peasant Nationalism and the Study of China's Revolutionary History: A Review Essay," *Journal of Asian Studies* 63:1 (2004).

The concentration on Mao is understandable, but runs the danger of ignoring important Communist activity outside Yan'an. On Communist base areas and resistance outside Yan'an see, for instance, Gregor Benton's monumental *Mountain Fires: The Red Army's Three-Year War in South China, 1934–1938* (Berkeley, CA, 1992), and *New Fourth Army: Communist Resistance Along the Yangtze and the Huai, 1938–1941* (Berkeley, CA, 1999); David Goodman, *Social and Political Change in Revolutionary China: The Taihang Base Area in the War of Resistance to Japan, 1937–1945* (Lanham, MD, 2000); Pauline Keating, David Goodman, and Feng Chongyi, eds., *North China at War: The Social Ecology of Revolution* (Armonk, NY, 1999); Pauline Keating, *Two Revolutions: Village Reconstruction and the Cooperative Movement in Northwest China, 1934–1945* (Stanford, CA, 1997); Dagfinn Gatu, *Village China at War: The Impact of Resistance to Japan, 1937–1945* (Vancouver, 2008); Chen Yung-fa, *Making Revolution: The Communist Movement in Eastern and Central China, 1937–1945* (Berkeley, CA, 1986); Odoric Wou, *Mobilizing the Masses: Building Revolution in Henan* (Stanford, CA, 1994); and Sherman Xiaogang Lai, *A Springboard to Victory: Shandong Province and Chinese Communist Military and Financial Strength, 1937–1945* (Leiden, 2011).

The opening of new sources in Russia and China has revived a debate about how far Mao's revolution drew on Stalin and how far it was indigenous. Although it is clear that neither explanation is sufficient in itself, a necessary and useful corrective to any idea that Mao's revolution was entirely separate from that of Stalin's is Michael Sheng, *Battling Western Imperialism: Mao, Stalin, and the United States* (Princeton, NJ, 1997).

INTELLIGENCE

Wartime China was the scene of a variety of murky intelligence operations, many of which remain mysterious to this day. The China sections of Richard Aldrich, *Intelligence and the War against Japan: Britain, America, and the Politics of Secret Service* (Cambridge, 2000), are very useful for understanding the position from the Western point of view, as is Yu Maochun, *OSS in China: Prelude to Cold War* (New Haven, CT, 1997). Chinese intelligence efforts are detailed in essays in the special edition of *Intelligence and National Security* 16:4 (2001), ed. Hans van de Ven. Dai Li's role is analyzed in Frederic Wakeman Jr., *Spymaster: Dai Li and the Chinese Secret Service* (Berkeley, CA, 2003).

COLLABORATION WITH THE JAPANESE

This remains a touchy subject, and for political reasons it has mostly not yet developed the nuance that has marked studies of European wartime collaboration. A path-breaking work is Timothy Brook, *Collaboration: Japanese Agents and Chinese Elites in Wartime China* (Cambridge, MA, 2005), which discusses the messy reality of local compromise in the Yangtze delta in the years after the invasion. A very useful edited volume is David Barrett and Larry Shyu, *Chinese Collaboration with Japan, 1932–1945: The Limits of Accommodation* (Stanford, CA, 2001). Christian Henriot and Wen-hsin Yeh, eds., *In the Shadow of the Rising Sun: Shanghai under Japanese Occupation* (Cambridge, 2004), gives vivid details of the fate of Shanghai after 1937. For the occupation and subsequent collaboration that set the stage for the invasion of China, see Rana Mitter, *The Manchurian Myth: Nationalism, Resistance, and Collaboration in Modern China* (Berkeley, CA, 2000). A compelling insight into the mind-set that led to "collaborationist nationalism" is Margherita Zanasi, *Saving the Nation: Economic Modernity in Republican China* (Chicago, IL, 2006). Brian G. Martin, "Shield of Collaboration: The Wang Jingwei Regime's Security Service, 1939–1945," *Intelligence and National Security* 16:4 (2001), and "Collaboration within Collaboration: Zhou Fohai's Relations with the Chongqing Government, 1942–1945," *Twentieth-Century China* 34:2 (April 2008), provide a comprehensive view of the use of intelligence and security by Wang Jingwei's government to try to solidify its position.

ARTS AND CULTURE

The war saw the transformation of the cultural and artistic world in China. So far there has been more work on the Communist contributions to cultural change during that period than on the Nationalists. Chang-tai Hung, *War and Popular Culture: Resistance in Modern China, 1937–1945* (Berkeley, CA, 1994), analyzes a variety of wartime cultural forms including the press, cartoons, and performance art. The dilemmas of literary figures in occupied Shanghai are considered in Edward M. Gunn Jr., *Unwelcome Muse: Chinese Literature in Shanghai and Peking, 1937–1945* (New York, 1980), and Poshek Fu, *Passivity, Resistance, and Collaboration: Intellectual Choices in Occupied Shanghai* (Stanford, CA, 1993). Jonathan Spence's *The Gate of Heavenly Peace: The Chinese and Their Revolution, 1895–1980* (New York, 1981) brings to life the journeys of artistic figures who spent time in Yan'an during the war. John Israel's *Lianda: A Chinese University in War and Revolution* (Stanford, CA, 1998) focuses on the difficult lives of intellectuals who made the journey to the Nationalist areas of China.

SOCIAL HISTORY

The social history of wartime China is developing strongly as new sources open up. Aside from work on the Communist areas (discussed above), there is stimulating new work on social change in the Nationalist zones. A pioneering work on labor history in wartime Chongqing is Joshua H. Howard, *Workers at War: Labor in China's Arsenals, 1937–1953* (Stanford, CA, 2004). Gender issues are addressed in Danke Li, *Echoes of Chongqing: Women in Wartime China* (Chicago, 2009) and Nicole Huang, *Women, War, Domesticity: Shanghai Literature and Popular Culture of the 1940s* (Leiden, 2005). Essays in the following two special journal issues also deal with aspects of China's wartime social and economic history: *Modern Asian Studies* 45:1 (March 2011), special edition "China in World War II, 1937–1945," ed. Rana Mitter and Aaron William Moore; and *European Journal of East Asian Studies* 11:2 (December 2012) special edition "Welfare, Relief, and Rehabilitation in Wartime China," ed. Rana Mitter and Helen Schneider.

One important subfield of wartime social history is the new history of refugee flight in China. Important work includes Stephen R. MacKinnon, *Wuhan 1938: War, Refugees, and the Making of Modern China* (Berkeley, CA, 2008), and R. Keith Schoppa, *In a Sea of Bitterness: Refugees during the Sino-Japanese War* (Cambridge, MA, 2011). A powerful social history of wartime Chinese experience that engages with refugee experience is Diana Lary, *The Chinese People at War: Human Suffering and Social Transformation, 1937–1945* (Cambridge, 2010). A fascinating study of the links between ecological change and refugee flight is Micah S. Muscolino, "Refugees, Land Reclamation, and Militarized Landscapes in Wartime

China: Huanglongshan, Shaanxi, 1937–1945," *Journal of Asian Studies* 69:2 (2010).

LEGACY

The legacy of the conflict between China and Japan has been explored in a variety of studies. James Reilly's *Strong Society, Smart State: The Rise of Public Opinion in China's Japan Policy* (New York, 2011) and Peter Hays Gries's *China's New Nationalism: Pride, Politics, and Diplomacy* (Berkeley, CA, 2004) give insights into the links between memory of wartime and contemporary international relations. Caroline Rose's *Sino-Japanese Relations: Facing the Past, Looking to the Future?* (London, 2004) and *Interpreting History in Sino-Japanese Relations* (London, 1998) give valuable insights into the relevance of the "history debates" between the two sides in the present day. Yinan He's *The Search for Reconciliation: Sino-Japanese and German-Polish Relations since World War II* (Cambridge, 2009) gives a welcome comparative perspective. War and memory in China and in the region more widely is addressed in Sheila Jager and Rana Mitter, eds., *War, Memory, and the Post–Cold War in Asia* (Cambridge, MA, 2007).

ACKNOWLEDGMENTS

I have been privileged to work with not one but several inspiring and rigorous editors. At Houghton Mifflin Harcourt, Amanda Cook took charge of the book through most of its life. Amanda was simultaneously unfailingly supportive and absolutely insistent on making sure the manuscript was revised as many times as it took to make it right. Her contribution to the final version is immeasurable. In the last few months before completion, I benefited from meticulous editing by Ben Hyman and generous and thoughtful input from Bruce Nichols. At Penguin, I had the brilliant input of Simon Winder, who provided the rather terrifying advantage of being an editor who has detailed knowledge of the Second World War in Asia and isn't afraid to deploy it (in the most collegial way possible). Richard Mason and Cecilia Mackay did a wonderful job with copy editing and picture research, respectively, and the process was overseen by Richard Duguid. My agent Susan Rabiner has been a source of endless encouragement and good sense, and I am extremely grateful to her for using her long experience in publishing to place the project so well.

So many colleagues have contributed to this book over the years that I am reluctant to single out too many. But I am extremely grateful to friends who have inspired ideas, read sections, and made suggestions, including Robert Bickers, Karl Gerth, Graham Hutchings, Toby Lincoln, Andres Rodriguez, Patricia Thornton, Steve Smith, and Hans van de Ven. Friends and colleagues in China have also been immensely collegial with aspects of the project over the years, including Wu Jingping, Chen Qianping, Chen Hongmin, and Zhou Yong, and I am very grateful to all of them. It has also been a privilege to write the book while employed in the stimulating circumstances of the Faculty of History and Department of Politics and International Relations at Oxford, as well as enjoying the pleasures of a fellowship at St. Cross College.

I had a wonderful research team in 2007–2012, funded by the Leverhulme Trust, all of whom contributed immensely to this project: Lily Chang, Federica Ferlanti, Sha Hua, Matthew Johnson, Amy King, Sherman Xiaogang Lai, Tehyun Ma, Aaron William Moore, James Reilly, Helen Schneider, Isabella Jackson, Elina Sinkkonen, Akiko Frellesvig, and Christine Boyle. I also want to give thanks in particular to Annie Hongping Nie, whose patient work has been crucial to this project. Our several years of joint document reading were one of the great pleasures of writing this book.

I am also very grateful for the assistance of colleagues and staff at various archives, including the Chongqing Municipal Archive; Shanghai Municipal Archive; No. 2 National Archive in Nanjing (in particular, Ma Zhendu); the United Nations Archive in New York; the Public Record Office (National Archive), London; the Yale Divinity Library; and the National Archives at College Park, Maryland. I am most grateful for permission to cite from the unpublished sections of the Chiang Kai-shek diary held at the Hoover Institution, Stanford University. At the Bodleian Library, David Helliwell has always been a fount of knowledge about sources and always resourceful in helping to fund the purchase of new materials.

The existence of this book is due, in very large part, to the generosity of one external funder: the Leverhulme Trust. In 2004 the Trust awarded me a Philip Leverhulme Prize, which allowed me an extended period of research leave to gather materials and spend time thinking about the shape of this project. In 2007 I was honored to receive a Leverhulme Research Leadership Award, a five-year project grant that allowed me to manage a team of postdoctoral fellows and graduate students, to hold conferences, and to travel to China. All of this activity hugely enriched the book, and I am immensely grateful to Leverhulme for their support; with a combination of financial support and light-touch management, they are the ideal funder. I was also supported at various times by grants including the British Academy-China Academy of Social Sciences exchange scheme, for which I am also most grateful.

No book exists without context, and for me the most joyous part of its voyage to publication has been to share it with my family (who were increasingly unselfish in the face of my ever more urgent need to finish the manuscript): Katharine, Malavika, Pamina, Iskandar, my parents Partha and Swasti, and Gill, Hal, William, Darunee, Miranda, and Charlotte.

Rana Mitter
Oxford, January 2013

PHOTO CREDITS

Garden Bridge, Shanghai, August 18, 1937: © Randall Chase Gould Papers, [Box / album fH], Hoover Institution Archives, Stanford University, CA. *Chiang Kai-shek, 1937:* © IN / Gen / Camera Press, London. *Refugees on Shanghai's Bund, 1937:* © Hulton-Deutsch Collection / Corbis. *Fires set by retreating Chinese, Nanjing, December 1937:* © Hulton-Deutsch Collection / Corbis. *General Matsui Iwane in his headquarters, Shanghai, 1938:* © Keystone / Hulton Archive / Getty Images. *Lieutenant General Dai Li working with special police forces, China, November 1945:* © Jack Wilkes / Time and Life / Getty Images. *Chinese troops on the Suzhou front, Battle of Taierzhuang, April 1938:* © Robert Capa / Magnum Photos. *Japanese troops using a boat during Yellow River floods, July 1938:* © Press Association Images. *Mao Zedong speaks at Lu Xun Arts Institute in Yan'an, May 1938:* © CQ / Camera Press, London. *Canton civilians take flight, June 1938:* © Hulton-Deutsch Collection / Corbis. *Chiang Kai-shek at Supreme War Council meeting in Wuhan, July 1938:* © Robert Capa / Magnum Photos. *Wang Jingwei with Dr. Chu Minyi in Nanjing before inauguration, April 1940:* © Bettman / Corbis. *Homeless people escape Congqing during bombing, May 1939:* © Hulton-Deutsch Collection / Corbis. *Cartoon depicting Wang Jingwei:* © Zhonghua Ribao, March 30, 1940. *General Claire Lee Chennault, 1943:* © Myron Davis / Time and Life / Getty Images. *General Joseph Stilwell:* © Topham Picturepoint / Topfoto. *Chiang Kai-shek and Mahatma Gandhi near Calcutta, 1942:* © Topham Picturepoint / Topfoto. *Mao inspects Eighth Route Army troops stationed in Yan'an:* © J. A. Fox Collection / Magnum Photos. *Wounded Chinese troops, Burma, 1942:* © George Rodger / Magnum Photos. *Refugees fleeing famine-stricken Henan province, 1943:* Harrison Forman / American Geographical Society Library, University of Wisconsin–Milwaukee Libraries. *Female famine victim, Henan, 1943:* Harrison Forman / American Geographical Society Library, University of Wisconsin–Milwaukee Libraries. *A Chinese soldier guards a squadron of Curtiss P-40 Warhawk fighter planes, 1943:* © The Granger Collection / Topfoto. *Colonel David Barrett and diplomat John Service outside their Yan'an billet:* © Courtesy of the Service Family. *Song Meiling on the rostrum of the US House of Representatives, Washington, January 18, 1943:* © Bettmann / Corbis. *Chiang Kai-shek, Franklin D. Roosevelt, Winston Churchill, and Song Meiling at the Cairo Conference, 1943:* © Topham Picturepoint / Topfoto. *Participants in the Greater East Asia Conference: Ba Maw, Zhang Jinghui, Wang Jingwei, Hideki Tojo, Wan Waithayakon, José P. Laurel, Subhas Chandra Bose, Tokyo, November 1943:* © Mainichi Shimbun / Aflo Images. *Refugees on foot, November 1944:* © Press Association Images. *Chinese-manned American tanks enter Burma, January 1945:* © Press Association Images. *General Okamura Yasuji of the Imperial Japanese Army in China during the surrender ceremony, with the Chinese delegation under General He Yingqin, Nanjing, September 9, 1945:* © akg-images. *Zhang Zizhong, Mao Zedong, Patrick Hurley, Zhou Enlai, and Wang Ruofei, en route to Chongqing for negotiations after the Japanese surrender, 1945:* © Wu Yinxian / Magnum Photos. *Chinese paramilitary policemen carrying wreaths of flowers march toward the Nanjing Massacre Memorial Hall in Nanjing, December 13, 2012, to mark the seventy-fifth anniversary:* © CQ / Camera Press, London. *Anti-Japanese demonstration during the Diaoyu Islands dispute, Shenzhen, September 16, 2012:* © Imaginechina / Rex Features.

INDEX

Ai Qing, 188

air power: in Sino-Japanese War, 113, 118, 176–78, 213, 251, 261, 300, 317, 318, 336

Alexander, Harold, 253

All-China Cultural Committee on Resistance to Japan, 151

All-China Writers' Association, 147

Alley, Rewi, 228

Allies: Burma's role in strategy of, 252, 301–2, 307, 308, 311; CCP's relations with, 233; China's role in strategy of, 5, 6, 8, 13, 223, 233, 241–44, 259, 263–64, 266, 298–99, 306, 308, 310, 313, 315–16, 330, 341, 343–44, 350; "Europe First" strategy, 13, 244, 266, 297–98, 301, 314, 315, 319, 345; global wartime strategy of, 297–98; India's role in strategy of, 246, 248–49, 252; Japan declares war on, 239; mutual distrust of Chiang, 10, 13, 242–43, 260–61, 265, 278–79, 296–98, 301, 304, 311; plan invasion of Japan, 352; postwar strategy of, 298–99, 306–7, 309–10, 337, 352–53; Soviet role in strategy of, 244; strategic disagreements among, 244, 306

Alsop, Joseph, 339

American Baptist Foreign Mission Society, 239

American Military Mission to China (AMMISCA), 235

American Volunteer Group (AVG), 251, 260; Chennault recruits and commands, 178, 250, 261

Amery, Leo, 273

anarchist philosophy: in Russia, 39

Anti-Comintern Pact (1936), 72, 214

Arima Yoriyasu, 221

Arita Hachirō, 74

Art of War, The (Sunzi), 201

Asaka (prince), 133

Atkinson, Brooks, 345

atomic bomb: development of, 352; dropped on Japan, 361, 375

Attlee, Clement, 357

Auden, W. H., 108, 145; "Sonnets from China," 9

Axis: formation of, 214; targets India, 245

Azad, Maulana, 246

Ba Maw, 305

Bai Chongxi, 141, 147, 150–51, 155, 339

Baldwin, Stanley, 113

Ballard, J. G.: *Empire of the Sun,* 240

Barrett, David D.: and contact with CCP, 328, 329, 330, 358

Battle of Britain, 222

Battle of Midway (1942), 304

Battle of Nomonhan (1939), 215, 217

Battle of Southern Henan (1941), 266

Battle of Stalingrad (1942–43): as turning point in the war, 297, 298, 304

Battle of Taierzhuang (1938), 151–53, 154–55, 156, 157, 200, 271

Battle of the Hundred Regiments (1940), 225, 289

Beijing: collaborationist government in, 198–99, 216; Japanese capture, 90, 93, 111, 134; Japanese threaten, 81–82

Berle, Adolf A., 310

Bertram, James, 71

Bo Gu, 90

Bogomolov, Dmitri, 104

Borodin, Mikhail, 47, 303–4

Bose, Subhas Chandra, 245–46, 305

Boxer Rebellion (1900), 32, 36, 57, 79, 106

Braun, Otto, 69

Brooke, Alan, 307, 310

214, 228, 240, 242, 243–44, 297–98, 339–40, 345, 347; US denies ground combat forces to, 251–52; US loans to, 244–45; USAAF in, 324, 336, 346; war memorials and museums in, 373–74, 376; warlords hold power in, 32, 40, 50, 51, 58, 62, 72, 83, 88, 129, 248, 354; war's psychological and social effects on, 12–14, 372, 377–79; Wedemeyer as commander-in-chief in, 346–47, 360; and Western imperialism, 28, 29–32, 35, 46–47, 51–52, 164, 240–41, 242–43, 299–300, 305–6, 346, 362; Wilkie visits, 300; in World War I, 41, 253

China, Republic of: Japan pressures, 41; militarist takeover of, 40–41; Sun as president of, 40; warlords hold power in, 41–43; Yuan as president of, 40–41

China Campaign Committee, 10

"China Lobby": in US, 370–71

Chinese air force: Chennault trains, 178

Chinese army. *See* National Revolutionary Army (NRA); Red Army

Chinese Army in India ("X Force"), 312, 337

Chinese Communist Party (CCP): allies with KMT, 44–45, 47–49, 68; analysis of victory over KMT, 371–72, 373; Chiang refuses to compromise with, 336–37, 349–50; Chiang's suppression efforts against, 47–49, 64, 68–69, 70–71, 92, 184–85, 189, 223–24, 282; Civil War victory by, 5, 7, 11, 14, 344, 370, 377; Civil War with KMT, 9, 71, 73, 274, 327, 347, 350, 354, 363, 365–66, 368, 369–70; and civilian welfare programs, 378; competes with KMT, 57, 63, 324; competes with National Government, 173, 180, 347, 358–59; cooperates with National Government, 70–71, 90–91, 92–93, 111, 167, 188–89, 194, 200, 211, 217,

225, 228, 233; Davies on, 326–27; establishes Red Army, 68; factional fighting within, 68–69; and food supply, 278; formed, 42; high morale and discipline in, 329–30; Hurley opposes, 347, 366; Hurley's contact with, 348–49, 350; and inflation, 277–78; intellectuals in, 140, 280, 291–92; Kang Sheng as head of security for, 282, 290, 292–93, 295; land and production reforms by, 68, 71, 224–25, 273, 294, 330; Mao attacks leadership of, 69; Mao heads, 68–70, 227–28, 290, 359–60, 377; minor military role of, 330–31, 348; National Government blockades areas controlled by, 223–25, 277, 320, 326; negotiations with Japanese, 352; "New Fourth Army Incident," 227–28; OSS and, 349; popularity with civilian population, 190–91, 358; possible US support for, 349, 353; postwar consolidation of, 365–66; postwar mythology of, 371–72; progressive taxation by, 278, 294; proposed coalition with National Government, 349–50, 354; Rectification Movement in, 280–81, 290–91, 292–94, 295, 328, 330, 360; relations with Allies, 233; resists Japanese occupation, 5, 7, 64, 123; Service on US contact with, 328–30; Soviet Union supports, 195, 291, 328; Stilwell on, 327; Sun and, 44–45; US contact with, 326–31, 347, 348, 358; US relations with, 360; use of terrorism and torture by, 281, 292–94; Vladimirov on, 324, 327–28, 406–7; war's effect on ideology of, 188–90, 193–96, 281, 291–92, 295, 371; wartime expansion of, 194–95, 290, 347–48, 363; Xu Wancheng on, 368–69;

Zhang Boquan, 95
Zhang Deneng, 324
Zhang Guotao, 189, 193–94
Zhang Qun, 75
Zhang Xiluo, 1–3
Zhang Xueliang, 50, 61, 62, 154; kidnaps
    Chiang, 71–73, 83, 103
Zhang Zhonghui, 91
Zhang Zizhong, 148
Zhang Zonglu: on famine, 267, 268–69
Zhang Zuolin, 54, 62
Zheng Dongguo, 312
Zhengzhou: defense of, 157
Zhou Enlai, 45, 47, 49, 70, 86, 90, 92, 225,
    227, 364; Chiang and, 224; and
    kidnapping of Chiang, 73
Zhou Fohai, 104, 106, 108, 125, 203–4, 282;

death of, 367; defects to Japanese,
    197–200, 206–7, 208–10, 217,
    218, 363; and Marco Polo Bridge
    Incident, 86–87; and Pearl Harbor
    attack, 236; in Reorganized
    Government, 219–20, 221, 233–34,
    304, 305, 350, 363; as secret agent
    for National Government, 288–89,
    297, 304, 351; as "true" Nationalist,
    234; on Wang, 197, 204, 207, 209–10,
    287, 351
Zhou Yang, 293
Zhu De, 225; commands Red Army, 68, 92,
    211
Zhukov, Georgi: defeats Japanese, 215,
    217
Zuo Zongnian, 268